5/04

04

Blood, Bedlam, Bullets, and Badguys

Genreflecting Advisory Series

Diana T. Herald, Series Editor

Blood, Bedlam, Bullets, and Badguys

A Reader's Guide to Adventure/Suspense Fiction

Michael B. Gannon

Genreflecting Advisory Series

Diana T. Herald, Series Editor

LIBRARIES

UNLIMITED

A Member of the Greenwood Publishing Group

Westport, Connecticut • London

Library of Congress Cataloging-in-Publication Data

Gannon, Michael B.
    Blood, bedlam, bullets, and badguys : a reader's guide to adventure/suspense fiction /
    Michael B. Gannon.
        p. cm.
    Includes bibliographical references and index.
    ISBN 1-56308-732-4 (alk. paper)
    1. Adventure stories, American—Bibliography—Handbooks, manuals, etc. 2. Adventure
stories, English—Bibliography—Handbooks, manuals, etc. 3. Suspense
fiction—Bibliography—Handbooks, manuals, etc. 4. Adventure stories, American—Stories,
plots, etc. 5. Adventure stories, English—Stories, plots, etc. 6. Suspense fiction—Stories,
plots, etc. I. Title.
Z1231.A39G36 2004
[PS374.A35]
016.813'087—dc22   2003060527

British Library Cataloguing in Publication Data is available.

Library of Congress Catalog Card Number: 2003060527
ISBN: 1–56308–732–4

First published in 2004

Libraries Unlimited, 88 Post Road West, Westport, CT 06881
A Member of the Greenwood Publishing Group, Inc.
www.lu.com

Printed in the United States of America

The paper used in this book complies with the
Permanent Paper Standard issued by the National
Information Standards Organization (Z39.48–1984).

10   9   8   7   6   5   4   3   2   1

To my mother,
N. Annette Gannon

Thanks Mom!

Contents

Introduction

We all live in suspense, from day to day, from hour to hour;
in other words we are the hero of our own story.

—*Mary McCarthy*

Why?

At this writing, there exists no guide exclusively for the adventure/suspense genre, yet readership is strong and many authors who write in this genre frequently dominate the best-seller lists. Pretty good for a genre that, similar to romance, gets little respect from the literary establishment. Unlike romance, however, there are no awards, no comprehensive Web sites, and few organized writer-fan organizations for adventure and suspense. These books are great ways to involve in reading people who may not fit the mold of the traditional reader, such as men aged twenty-one to forty or teenage reluctant readers. With its high levels of excitement, action, and intrigue, adventure/suspense also provides great material for blockbuster Hollywood movies.

This resource primarily covers books published since 1941 (except for landmark "classics" that are included for their historical significance) and up into 2003. Sixteen subgenres and themes are discussed in terms of definition, appeal, and history followed by a thorough bibliography for each. I have read many of the titles, but I also used reviews and information to create the annotations. The criteria for selection was general availability in public libraries with a more comprehensive coverage of in-print and more recently released titles. More than 3,100 titles are included, with approximately 2,000 of those annotated. The audience for this volume is librarians and readers in public libraries and middle and high school libraries.

How to Use This Book

This book is arranged into two parts: Subgenres and Locales and Themes. Within these two sections are the chapters that cover each of the subgenres and primary locales and themes of the adventure/suspense genre. I define the subgenre, discuss its appeal, and provide a brief history of it. I follow this with a selective bibliography, including titles that are either still in print or that could be found in the collections of most large libraries. I have included only books that were originally published in hardcover, except for titles in a series that began or ended up in hardcover, as well as titles in Chapter 17, which are part of original paperback action series.

These bibliographies are intended to be used to find read-alikes for particular authors or titles; as a resource when building or expanding a collection; to assist in the creation of bookmarks, booklists, or displays; to find a title in a series or the sequence of a series; or simply to find out what a book is about. This work can be used as a professional reference and readers' advisory tool, and also as a source that the reader may browse to discover new reading material.

Entries are alphabetical by author, with titles alphabetized under each author's name. Because most readers prefer reading series titles in order, however, if a book is part of a series, the series' title is listed alphabetically and the individual titles within the series are listed in chronological (series) order. Many series do not have official "series titles." In such cases, a title has been assigned, usually comprising the name of the chief protagonist(s). Icons (described below) are used to denote titles that have been made into movies, that have multicultural main characters, and that I recommend. All titles that have been made into films or television movies are listed in Appendix A. This listing contains the film's year of release, its director, and the major actors and actresses who appeared in it. Multicultural characters are listed in the subject and character index. Appendix B lists authors who can be considered essential for each subgenre as part of a core collection. Finally, there is a glossary that defines unfamiliar words or phrases.

Annotation Icons

⬜ = page-turner/recommended

FILM = also a movie

M = multicultural main character

Definition

Lusty spies, deadly plagues, courtroom intrigue, fanatical terrorists, murderous psychopaths, state-of-the-art weaponry, destructive acts of nature, political conspiracies, evil Nazis, Russian crime kingpins, and international drug cartels are but a few examples of the elements that can be found in the adventure/suspense genre. Oftentimes lumped under the catchall label of "thrillers," it is difficult to define the term "adventure/suspense" precisely because authors often combine situations from other genres such as mystery, horror, science fiction, and even romance.

Although an eclectic mix, all adventure/suspense novels have a few basic commonalties. The characters (and the reader) can always expect the worst—the main characters (the hero or heroine) can, and usually do, have everything thrown at them as they proceed on their quest, search, or mission. The protagonists are often thrown into a dangerous situation and must rely on their physical and mental abilities to survive. Action and excitement are hallmarks of a good adventure/suspense book. The entire read is a roller-coaster ride of chills and thrills with the last stop (and page) not always ending happily. Finally, there must be a villain, for without an adversary or obstacle, there can be no adventure.

The following listing of "rules" for understanding the adventure/suspense genre may also be of some assistance to the reader.

Gannon's Adventure/Suspense Rules

1. Sometimes your friends are deadlier than your enemies.

2. Cynicism is a prerequisite for success in the spy business.

3. Never sit next to anyone on a plane who is sweating profusely, talking to himself, and clutching a large, bulky item.

4. You have a better chance of surviving a disaster if you are evil, insane, or both.

5. If your country doesn't have a secret weapon, you can always steal one!

6. All secret weapons have cool code names.

7. The United States always wins!

8. Just when you think you've forgotten all about a former lover, he or she is accused of murder and becomes your client.

9. It takes a thief to catch a thief!

10. Female serial killers are much more common than in real life.

11. You can always count on maniacs to reappear in a sequel.

12. Serial killers *always* have a method to their madness.

13. There is no such thing as "minor" surgery.

14. Bioengineered viruses always cause those infected to become homicidal maniacs, who eventually explode in a shower of blood.

15. There is never a simple "off" switch.

16. Sometimes it's not paranoia—they really *are* out to get you!

17. Heroes always start out by being in the wrong place at the wrong time.

18. Hitler did not die in his Berlin bunker.

19. Nazis are very long-lived, and loads of them still exist today.

20. Nazis are no match for vampires or werewolves.

21. Anyone can be brainwashed to do anything.

22. Masters of the martial arts can kill with any part of their body—*any* part . . .

23. Old KGB agents never die, they just pop up now and then, nastier than ever!

24. Evil dictators are notoriously difficult to bump off.

Brief History

The adventure/suspense story is probably the oldest of human kind's fiction genres and can be traced back to tales that prehistoric people told around a flickering fire or scratched with charcoal onto cave walls. The archetypal hero who must surmount overwhelming obstacles is not only the basis of much of our earliest literature, he (and now she) is also the foundation of all modern adventure stories. *The Iliad* and *The Odyssey* by Homer, *Beowulf,* the *Song of Roland,* Shakespeare's tragedies are gripping adventure stories as well as classic literature.

Before the twentieth century, all fiction was considered literature, and novels were not labeled according to what we today consider genres—mysteries, science fiction, romance, or adventure, for example. In the early twentieth century librarians became inspired to "elevate the masses" by having them read fine literature; at the same time, common people wanted to read what they considered fun and entertaining. This dichotomy of literature versus genre fiction resulted in the elevation of the adventure-filled works of authors such as Charles Dickens, Victor Hugo, Robert Louis Stevenson, Stephen Crane, James Fennimore Cooper, and Joseph Conrad to the level of classics, while contemporary authors were considered throwaway or trash fiction.

The first decade of the twentieth century saw the publication of two books that are acknowledged to be the first modern suspense novels: Erskine Childers's *The Riddle of the Sands* (1903) and *The Four Just Men* by Edgar Wallace (1906). The year 1915 brought the first modern spy novel, *The Thirty Nine Steps* by John Buchan, which was an antecedent to Helen MacInnes's classic *Above Suspicion* (1941). The end of World War II and the beginning of the Cold War saw a huge growth in the publication of adventure/suspense books with the gradual demarcation into distinct subgenres, the most popular being the espionage novel. *The Hunt for Red October* by Tom Clancy, published in 1984, set the standard for one of the newest subgenres, the technothriller, combining adventure with state-of-the-art weaponry. Another new subgenre, the legal thriller, was born from the ashes of Perry Mason courtroom dramas in 1987 with Scott Turow's *Presumed Innocent*.

Appeal

In adventure/suspense novels readers are able to visit exotic places, be privy to secrets, associate with the powerful, and jump from one narrow escape to another. The ability to experience vicarious thrills by viewing violence and destruction from a safe distance—all without the fear of grievous bodily harm—also has a strong attraction. Story line, plot and pacing, and character (heroic or villainous) are major appeals of the genre, but some fans are especially interested in the settings, whether exotic locales or the familiar home turf.

Additional appeals include the allure of wealth and power, the glamour of evil, the voyeuristic pleasure gained through spying and secret activities, and fascination with the "special effects" of military weapon systems and cutting-edge (or "bleeding-edge") technology. Like the classic fairy tale, there is a clear distinction between good and evil, and sometimes the villain proves more fascinating than the hero (e.g., Thomas Harris's Hannibal Lector). Series are popular in this genre because readers like a hero they can follow through many adventures. Specific subgenres have other appeals, which are discussed in each chapter introduction.

The appeal of adventure/suspense can be likened to the appeal of fast food—it's cheap, easily available, enjoyable, and you always know what you're going to get.

The Reader's Advisory Interview

The two questions you want to ask the reader who is looking for good books are the following: "What was the last book you read that you liked?" and "Why did you like it?" What was it about the book that was pleasurable—the setting, the plot, the characters, the ending? These can all be factors that contribute in an enjoyable read. Because many subgenres are a part of adventure/suspense, question the reader further to help guide him or her to the right title.

Do not make the mistake of immediately offering alternative titles by the same author; many authors write across subgenres. William Diehl, for example, has written about serial killers (*Primal Fear*), Nazis (e.g., *27*), and the Asian drug trade (*Thai Horse*). If the reader enjoys Diehl's writing style, then fine, suggest his other titles; but if the reader is looking for a gripping serial killer novel, then Diehl's *27* is not an appropriate suggestion.

Chapter 1

"Licensed to Kill"

Spies and Secret Agents

Definition: This subgenre includes espionage activities (secret observation to obtain information) involving representatives of countries or autonomous international organizations (or both). Other themes comprising this subgenre are the fate of spying after the Cold War, assassins, everyday people caught up in intelligence operations, spying as a career with related "burnout" and retirement issues, and what happens when the spy is considered expendable or in need of termination by his or her employer.

The Appeal: The ability to let the ends justify the means has a certain allure, and spies certainly are not averse to breaking the rules to carry out their mission. Like these fictional spies, readers are able to visit exotic places, be privy to secrets, jump from one narrow escape to another, and still feel secure that it was all for the good of society. American novels usually are more action-oriented and violent than their more intellectual British counterparts. Exotic locales and dark, mysterious atmospheres are often featured.

Brief History: The earliest espionage novel is considered to be James Fennimore Cooper's *The Spy* published in 1821. The first real modern spy novel, however, is *The Thirty-Nine Steps* by John Buchan, published in Britain in 1915. This novel set the framework for later British authors such as Eric Ambler, Graham Greene, and Ian Fleming to follow during the 1930s through 1950s. Len Deighton and John le Carré tarnished the classic British spy in the 1960s and 1970s by adding cynicism and ambiguous morality to his repertoire. Robert Ludlum contributed the convoluted plots and intense action that have become the hallmarks of the American spy novel. With the end of the Cold War, the Soviet Union and its villainous KGB agents no longer make convenient adversaries, so novelists have turned to terrorists, rogue agents and countries, avaricious international cartels, and double-crossing elements within a spy's own agencies. The traditional spy novel seems to be in decline today, as technology has become a more appealing method to gather intelligence, and thus we see in the ever-increasing popularity of the technothriller.

Advising the Reader: The key elements to remember when advising the reader and suggesting appropriate titles are the following:

- Is the reader interested in classic spy novels, or in novels that are more current?

- Many espionage activities took place during World War II; the reader may be interested in titles dealing with the Nazis.

- What type of setting does the reader prefer—the United States, Great Britain, the Soviet Union/Russia, and so forth?

- What type of antagonist does the reader enjoy? The Soviets, members of evil international cartels, the Chinese, and terrorists are all popular villains in the espionage novel. Many of these can be found as subjects of their own subgenre and are discussed in other chapters.

- Government agencies working at cross purposes are a common theme in this subgenre; suggest political thrillers to readers who enjoy this theme.

- Does the reader enjoy spy movies (such as those featuring James Bond)? Many espionage novels have been made into movies; the reader may enjoy novels with that connection.

- If a reader has enjoyed a book by a particular author, check to see if the author has written more titles—authors often carry over characters into other books.

- The reader my find the spying element found in many historical naval adventures to be of interest.

- Readers who read "everything" may be interested in nonfiction accounts of military and Cold War–era espionage.

- There are many titles (and several series) with female protagonists (such as O'Donnell's Modesty Blaise, Tan's Jane Nichols, Gilman's Mrs. Pollifax, or Weber's Leslie Frost). Does the reader prefer female protagonists?

- Technothrillers often have an element of espionage; guide your readers to this subgenre.

- *You Can Judge a Book by Its Cover:* look for shadowy figures; flags of the United States, Great Britain, or the Soviet Union; dark colors; night scenes; a man or woman running, and so on.

British Spies and Secret Agents

. . . truth is so precious that she should always be attended by a bodyguard of lies.

—*Winston Churchill*

Aaron, David

Crossing by Night. William Morrow, 1993.
American-born Elizabeth Pack was the wife of a British diplomat, but she was actually a spy for the British government during WWII. (This is the fictionalized account of her exploits. She was known to Ian Fleming and is said to be an inspiration for his famous literary spy.)

Allebeury, Ted

The Judas Factor. Mysterious, 1984.
Former British operative Tad Anders is now in the nightclub business, but he's still available for the occasional secret mission. His latest is to track down Vasili Burinski, a top Soviet assassin.

Amis, Kingsley

Colonel Sun. Harper, 1968.
A(nother) James Bond adventure. For more titles featuring Bond, see Raymond Benson, Ian Fleming, and John Gardner.

Anthony, Evelyn

Davina Graham series

The Defector. Coward, 1981.
Davina falls in love with Soviet defector Colonel Ivan Sasanov as she struggles to get him and his family to England.

Avenue of the Dead. Coward, 1982.
Davina Graham follows the trail of the Plumed Serpent, which starts in Russia, continues to the United States, and culminates in a small Mexican village.

Albatross. Putnam, 1983.
Top British intelligence agent Davina Graham must leave the service to track down a high-level mole, code-named *Albatross*.

The Company of Saints. Putnam, 1984.
Davina Graham, the new head of British intelligence, takes a much-needed vacation to Venice, where she stumbles onto an assassination plot.

Armstrong, Campbell

Jig. William Morrow, 1987.
The Irish Republican Army's top assassin is called "Jig" because he is so dexterous at eluding capture. Now he is in the United States to retrieve $10 million that's been stolen from the IRA. Sent to capture him is British counterterrorism operative Frank Pagan, whose wife was killed by IRA terrorists.

White Light. William Morrow, 1988.

Bagley, Desmond

Running Blind. Doubleday, 1971.

Benson, Raymond

James Bond series

For more titles featuring James Bond, see Kingsley Amis, Ian Fleming, and John Gardner.

Zero Minus Ten: The New Bond Adventure. Berkley, 1997.
James Bond is sent to Hong Kong to stop a powerful drug lord from detonating a nuclear bomb on the day the colony reverts to the People's Republic of China.

Tomorrow Never Dies (based on the screenplay by Bruce Feirstein). Boulevard, 1997. **FILM**
Agent 007 must stop a crazed media tycoon from starting a war between Great Britain and China.

The Facts of Death. Putnam, 1998.
Bond goes against a Greek terrorist group that plans to unleash biological and chemical weapons of mass destruction against Turkey.

High Time to Kill. Putnam, 1999.
James Bond must get back the secret formula for Skin 17, a material that will allow a jet to reach Mach 7. The formula was stolen by an international terrorist group known as the Union.

The World Is Not Enough (based on the screenplay by Neil Purvis and Robert Wade). Boulevard, 1999. **FILM**
Bond must protect the beautiful daughter of a murdered oil tycoon from an assassin who is impervious to pain.

Double Shot. Putnam, 2000.
The international terrorist organization, the Union, is back, and this time they have created an assassin that has been surgically altered to look exactly like James Bond.

Never Dream of Dying. Putnam, 2001.
Bond is in France and Monaco as he faces the Union once again.

The Man with the Red Tattoo. Putnam, 2002. **M**
Bond teams up with old pal Tiger Tanaka and beautiful Japanese agent Reiko Tamura as he searches for a terrorist who intends to unleash a deadly disease on an unsuspecting world.

Cape, Tony

The Cambridge Theorem. Doubleday, 1989.
Cambridge University graduate student Simon Bowles is found hanged—a supposed suicide until Detective Sergeant Derek Smailes discovers what Bowles was researching.

Deighton, Len

Bernard Samson trilogy

Berlin Game. Knopf, 1983.
> British intelligence agent Bernard Samson unmasks a traitor at the highest level of his organization.

Mexico Set. Knopf, 1985.
> Bernard Samson, top agent for British intelligence, is given the mission of recruiting a KGB operative to work as a double agent.

London Match. Knopf, 1985.
> In this climax to the trilogy begun in *Berlin Game* and *Mexico Set,* Bernard Samson faces his KGB counterpart in a match to the death.

Faith, Hope, and Charity trilogy

Faith. HarperCollins, 1994.
> It is 1987 and British agent Bernard Samson must fight to save his job, his family, and his life as he embarks on a mission to East Berlin.

Hope. HarperCollins, 1995.
> Bernard Samson's mission leads him from Poland to the heart of British intelligence in search of a traitor.

Charity. HarperCollins, 1996.
> The conclusion to the Bernard Samson trilogy beginning with *Faith* and *Hope.*

The Ipcress File. Simon & Schuster, 1962.
> Why are Britain's top scientists disappearing?

Spy trilogy

Spy Hook. Knopf, 1988.
> British intelligence agent Bernard Samson has fallen out of favor and now gets the assignments no one else wants. This time he must track down financial shenanigans within his own organization.

Spy Line. Knopf, 1989.
> Bernard Samson, set up and labeled a traitor, is now on the run from his own employer, British intelligence.

Spy Sinker. HarperCollins, 1990.
> In this final installment in the trilogy begun in *Spy Hook* and *Spy Line,* readers discover why British operative Bernard Samson's wife Fiona disappeared in East Berlin.

Eddy, Paul

Grace Flint series

Flint. Putnam, 2000.
> Undercover agent Grace Flint goes after the people who almost killed her in a bungled sting operation and finds herself in the middle of an international conspiracy.

Flint's Law. Putnam, 2002.

Now married and living in the United States, Grace Flint discovers that her husband is not at all who she thought he was. Now he has disappeared, and she's determined to track him down and find the answers to her questions.

Egleton, Clive

A Different Drummer. Scarborough, 1985.

A spy thriller with a Christmas theme.

A Double Deception. St. Martin's, 1992.

Andrew Korwin supposedly disappeared in 1939 when Warsaw fell to the Nazis, but in the 1960s, his niece arrives in London claiming to authorities that he is alive and living under the name Arthur Kershaw.

Hostile Intent. St. Martin's, 1993.

It is the dawn of the Cold War, and British agent Harry Freeland must fight the suspicions of his superiors that he is "in the red"—a double agent for the Soviets.

Peter Ashton series

A Killing in Moscow. St. Martin's, 1994.

British agent Peter Ashton is sent to Moscow to uncover a spy who is stealing industrial secrets. When he finds her, he soon discovers that a professional killer trained by the KGB is using her.

Death Throes. St. Martin's, 1995.

Peter Ashton of British intelligence heads to Moscow on the trail of "Valentin," a former high-ranking KGB officer who has secrets to sell.

A Lethal Involvement. St. Martin's, 1996.

British agent Peter Ashton goes on a seemingly routine mission to investigate an AWOL Royal Army captain, but he soon runs into Eastern European assassins.

Warning Shot. St. Martin's, 1996.

British SIS agent Peter Ashton's newest mission is to investigate a bombing in Berlin, which leads him on an international chase for terrorists that ends at the terrorists' main target in the United States.

Blood Money. St. Martin's, 1997.

British intelligence operative Peter Ashton's newest assignment is to discover why three agents at a Yorkshire safe house were savagely murdered—and whether his wife is next on the hit list.

Dead Reckoning. St. Martin's, 1999.

Three women are brutally murdered in a London psychotherapist's office, —one of them is identified as the wife of British intelligence agent Peter Ashton. But the dead woman is not really Harriet Ashton.

Honey Trap. St. Martin's, 2000.

British SIS agent Peter Ashton is assigned to discover why the courier in a routine delivery to Costa Rica was tortured and murdered. To complicate matters, the death of a London housewife is linked to the courier's murder.

Cry Havoc. St. Martin's, 2002.
> Peter Ashton, now the head of the Eastern European section, must deal with an Islamic terrorists group and a cache of dangerous chemicals.

Fleming, Ian

James Bond series

For more titles featuring James Bond, see Kingsley Amis, Raymond Benson, and John Gardner.

Casino Royale. MJF Books, 1981 (original publication date: 1953). **FILM**
> The first of the James Bond adventures introduces a character very different from the one portrayed in the movies—he's a much more ruthless secret agent with none of the charm and panache of the screen legend. (Fleming was a former intelligence operative.)

Live and Let Die. MJF Books, 1982 (original publication date: 1954). **FILM**
> Bond's second adventure finds him up against bad guys in the Harlem section of New York City.

Moonraker. MJF Books, 1983 (original publication date: 1955). **FILM**
> Agent 007 must stop the Moonraker missile from destroying London.

Diamonds Are Forever. MJF Books, 1984 (original publication date: 1956). **FILM**
> Bond, aided by beautiful agent Tiffany Case, must stop American mobsters who are running an international diamond-smuggling business.

From Russia with Love. MJF Books, 1985 (original publication date: 1957). **FILM**
> Bond is working with a beautiful Soviet embassy clerk to steal an encryption device, but suspects she may be a double agent.

Doctor No. MJF Books, 1986 (original publication date: 1958). **FILM**
> Bond tangles with the sadistic Dr. No in the Caribbean.

Goldfinger. MJF Books, 1987 (original publication date: 1959). **FILM**
> British secret agent James Bond must stop the evil financier Auric Goldfinger and his deadly assistant Pussy Galore from controlling the world's gold supply.

For Your Eyes Only. MJF Books, 1988 (original publication date: 1960). **FILM**
> Collection of short stories: *From a View to a Kill* (film), *For Your Eyes Only* (film), *Quantum of Solace, Risico,* and *The Hildebrand Reality.*

Thunderball. MJF Books, 1989 (original publication date: 1961). **FILM**
> A NATO bomber armed with two nuclear bomb vanishes, and Bond follows the trail to the Bahamas, where he teams up with CIA agent Felix Leiter.

The Spy Who Loved Me. MJF Books, 1990 (original publication date: 1962). **FILM**
> The story is told through from the perspective of Vivienne Michel, whom 007 saves.

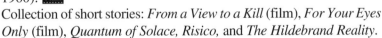

On Her Majesty's Secret Service. MJF Books, 1991 (original publication date: 1963). **FILM**

Bond battles the evil forces of SPECTRE and falls in love.

You Only Live Twice. MJF Books, 1992 (original publication date: 1964). 2x

On a vacation in Japan, Bond meets up with the diabolical Dr. Shatterhand and dallies with the beautiful Kissy Suzuki.

The Man with the Golden Gun. MJF Books 1993 (original publication date: 1965). **FILM**

Bond goes after Paco Scaramanga, an international assassin who kills with his trademark golden gun.

Octopussy: The Last Great Adventures of James Bond 007. Signet, 1993 (original publication date: 1966). **FILM**

Collection of short stories: *Octopussy* (film), *The Living Daylights* (film), and *Portrait of a Lady*.

Forsyth, Frederick

The Deceiver. Bantam, 1991.

British agent Sam McCready is up before a hearing to justify his continued employment and tells of his past exploits, which are set out as four novellas.

Freemantle, Brian

Charlie Muffin series

Charlie M. Doubleday, 1977 **FILM**

Introduces the character of Charlie Muffin, a working-class James Bond. Charlie is an agent for the Britain's spy agency, MI-6. (Film is titled *Charlie Muffin.*)

Here Comes Charlie M. Doubleday, 1978.

Charlie Muffin's newest adventure lands him in Switzerland.

The Inscrutable Charlie Muffin. Doubleday, 1979.

Charlie is sent to Asia to investigate the destruction of an ocean liner that was being used as a university devoted to peace.

Charlie Muffin U.S.A. Doubleday, 1980.

Charlie Muffin tangles with both the FBI and the American Mafia.

Madrigal for Charlie Muffin. 1981.

Charlie Muffin on a mission in Rome.

The Blind Run. Bantam, 1986.

Muffin is imprisoned for a crime he did not commit. He escapes to Moscow with his cellmate, Russian spy Edwin Sampson, in an attempt to exonerate himself.

See Charlie Run. Bantam, 1987.

Charlie Muffin gets involved in a triple cross.

The Run Around. Bantam, 1989.

Muffin must stop a Soviet assassin at a conference of international leaders.

Comrade Charlie. St. Martin's, 1989.

> The Soviet Union attempts to steal the secrets of the U.S. Star Wars defense system, and British agent Charlie Muffin is called on to stop them before the KGB can assassinate him.

Charlie's Apprentice. St. Martin's, 1994.

> Charlie Muffin, now training new agents, must rescue one of his students, who is caught in a bad situation on a mission in China.

Bomb Grade. St. Martin's, 1996.

> British secret agent Charlie Muffin must go undercover as a member of the Russian mafia to expose a nuclear weapons smuggling plot.

Dead Men Living. St. Martin's, 2000.

> Muffin uncovers a conspiracy that has been kept secret for more than fifty years.

Kings of Many Castles. St. Martin's, 2002.

> Charlie Muffin investigates assassination attempts on the Russian and U.S. presidents.

Gardner, John

James Bond series

For more titles featuring James Bond, see Kingsley Amis, Raymond Benson, and Ian Fleming.

License Renewed. Marek, 1981.

> The Bond franchise is given an update with this first installment of a new series. Bond battles maniac nuclear physicist Anton Murik, laird of Murcaldy.

For Special Services. Coward, 1982.

> Bond teams up with old pal Felix Leiter's daughter, Cedar, and tangles once again with SPECTRE.

Icebreaker. Putnam, 1983.

> Bond teams up with an international crew of fellow agents from the CIA, KGB, and Mossad to fight neo-Nazis.

Role of Honor. Putnam, 1984.

> Agent 007 once again goes up against the evil forces of SPECTRE.

Nobody Lives Forever. Putnam, 1986.

> Agents of SPECTRE hunt down Bond in a an international chase.

No Deals, Mr. Bond. Putnam, 1987.

> General Chernov, the former head of SMERSH, is out to get Bond.

Scorpius. Putnam, 1987.

> Bond must stop a cult of bomb-wearing assassins headed by the evil Vladimir Scorpius.

Win, Lose or Die. Putnam, 1989.

> Bond must protect the leaders of Great Britain, Russia, and the United States from the Brotherhood of Anarchy and Secret Terror (BAST).

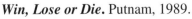

License to Kill (based on the screenplay by Richard Maibaum and Michael G. Wilson) Putnam, 1989. **FILM**

This time it's personal for 007—his old pal CIA agent Felix Leiter and Felix's wife are murdered.

Brokenclaw. Putnam, 1990. **M**

Bond is up against villain Brokenclaw Lee, who is half Chinese, half Native American.

The Man from Barbarossa. Putnam, 1991.

James Bond is on loan to the KGB.

Death Is Forever. Putnam, 1992.

James Bond versus "The Poison Dwarf," an East German spy and assassin who has been orchestrating the assassination of other spies.

Never Send Flowers. Putnam. 1993.

Bond teams up with a Swiss agent and goes after a serial killer and a terrorist for hire.

Seafire. Putnam, 1994.

Bond now has a steady girlfriend, Flicka von Grusse, a former agent for Swiss intelligence (introduced in *Never Send Flowers*). He's headed up the Double-Oh section, which deals with breaches in international law.

Goldeneye (based on the screenplay by Michael France and Jeffrey Caine). Boulevard, 1995. **FILM**

Bond must recover Goldeneye, secret technology that could endanger the financial markets of the West, from a Russian organization.

Cold Fall. Putnam, 1996.

Bond is sent to Washington, D.C., to investigate the destruction of a passenger jet.

Greene, Graham

The Confidential Agent. Heinemann, 1939. **FILM**

Former lecturer in medieval French, D is now a confidential agent sent to England to buy coal, but he is implicated in a murder and forced to flee.

Our Man in Havana. Viking, 1958. **FILM**

What happens when a divorced vacuum cleaner salesman becomes a spy in Cuba?

Hall, Adam

Quiller series

The Quiller Memorandum. Simon & Schuster, 1965. **FILM**

He is code-named Quiller; his real name is unknown. He works for the Bureau, the British super-secret spy agency. He works alone, without a gun. He gets the missions that are too sensitive or too hazardous for Britain's "regular" spies. In this first of the series, Quiller is in West Berlin fifteen years after WWII. (Hall is the pseudonym of Elleston Trevor.)

The 9th Directive. Simon & Schuster, 1966.
> Quiller must stop an assassin who has targeted an important representative of the queen, who has come to Thailand on a diplomatic mission.

The Striker Portfolio. Simon & Schuster, 1969.
> Quiller investigates mysterious plane crashes.

The Warsaw Document. Doubleday, 1971.
> Quiller travels to Poland to ensure the success of détente.

The Tango Briefing. Doubleday, 1973.
> Quiller is sent on an undercover mission to the Sahara, where he must find and destroy a crashed aircraft before anyone learns of its existence.

The Mandarin Cypher. Doubleday, 1975.
> For this mission, Quiller is in Hong Kong.

The Kobra Manifesto. Doubleday, 1976.
> Quiller is in hot pursuit of a terrorist group known as Kobra.

The Sinkiang Executive. Doubleday, 1978.
> Quiller is sent to investigate a secret Soviet missile base.

The Scorpion Signal. Doubleday, 1980.
> Quiller is sent to Moscow to recover a fellow agent and old partner who has escaped from a Soviet prison.

The Peking Target. HarperCollins, 1982.
> Quiller pursues an assassin to Asia.

Quiller. HarperCollins, 1985.
> Quiller must discover if the Soviets were to blame for the destruction of a U.S. submarine.

Quiller's Run. HarperCollins, 1988.
> Now Quiller is up against a beautiful—but deadly—female arms smuggler.

Quiller KGB. HarperCollins, 1989.
> Quiller, assisted by Soviet agents, uncovers a plot to prevent the unification of Germany.

Quiller Barracuda. William Morrow, 1990.
> Quiller heads to Miami and discovers a mind-control conspiracy.

Quiller Bamboo. William Morrow, 1991.
> Quiller is assigned to protect a dissident from assassination by the Chinese government.

Quiller Solitaire. William Morrow, 1992.
> Quiller goes undercover in a German terrorist group.

Quiller Meridian. William Morrow, 1993.
> Quiller travels to the former Soviet Union where he tangles with the military, terrorists, and an ex-KGB agent.

Quiller Salamander. Simon & Schuster, 1994.

    Quiller goes to Cambodia to stop Pol Pot's successor, General Kheng, from returning the Khmer Rouge to power.

Quiller Balalaika. Carroll & Graf, 1996.

    Quiller must infiltrate the Russian *mafiya* and find the British criminal who heads its most powerful "family"—a man who is determined to bring back the old Soviet Union. (This was completed shortly before Hall's death in 1995.)

Harrison, Payne

Black Cipher. Crown, 1994.

    Nestled in a quiet village in England is the Government Communications Headquarters—a secret spy agency devoted to code breaking. Famed cryptanalyst Faisal Shaikh is given the assignment of deciphering an unusual code and soon finds his life in danger.

Higgins, Jack

Exocet. Stein, 1983.

    A masked intruder sneaks into Queen Elizabeth's bedroom—and what he does there is only the first of many surprises.

The Savage Day. Holt, 1972.

    Simon Vaughn infiltrates the IRA in the guise of a gun runner as part of a deal to get out of prison.

Sean Dillon series

Eye of the Storm. Putnam, 1992.

    During the Persian Gulf War, Saddam Hussein hires master terrorist Sean Dillon to assassinate Margaret Thatcher and her war cabinet at 10 Downing Street.

Thunder Point. Putnam, 1993.

    A German U-boat wreck has been found off Thunder Point in the Virgin Islands. Inside rests Martin Bormann's briefcase, which holds papers that name prominent Britons who were Nazi sympathizers as well as the Windsor Protocol—a document signed by the duke of Windsor in which he undertook to ascend to the throne after the successful invasion of Britain by German forces. What other secrets are hidden in the briefcase?

On Dangerous Ground. Putnam, 1994.

    British spies, the American Mafia, and the Chinese are all searching for a document known as the Chungking Covenant—a document signed in 1944 extending the Hong Kong Treaty by one hundred years.

Angel of Death. Putnam, 1995.

    Brigadier Charles Ferguson of the British Group 4 and former IRA enforcer Sean Dillon are assigned to hunt down the terrorist group January 30—a group whose targets seem to be everyone and anyone.

Drink with the Devil. Putnam, 1996.

    Former IRA terrorist and now British intelligence operative Sean Dillon is assigned the task of recovering sunken gold before it can be used to finance an Irish civil war.

The President's Daughter. Putnam, 1997.

> Security officer and former IRA terrorist Sean Dillon and FBI special agent Blake Johnson team up to rescue the U.S. president's kidnapped daughter.

The White House Connection. Putnam, 1999.

> Sean Dillon and Blake Johnson are teamed up again as they must track down a female assassin before she brings down two governments.

Day of Reckoning. Putnam, 2000.

> Former FBI agent Blake Johnson is now the head of a secret White House operation called the Basement and, along with former IRA terrorist Sean Dillon, is on the hunt for the international crime boss who had his journalist wife, Katherine, murdered.

Edge of Danger. Putnam, 2001.

> Blake Johnson, head of the secret U.S. agency known only as the Basement teams up with former IRA terrorist Sean Dillon to stop a powerful and wealthy Arab family from attacking the American president.

Midnight Runner. Putnam, 2002.

> British agent Sean Dillon must stop Kate Rashid, of the murderous Arab-English Rashid family. Kate has sworn vengeance on those who killed her brothers, who themselves were trying to assassinate the U.S. president.

Bad Company. Putnam, 2003.

> Evil Baron Max von Berger has inherited the mighty riches (and the dastardly plans) of the Rashid family (the Rashids were taken down by Sean Dillon in *Midnight Runner*), and he attempts to avenge their deaths.

A Season in Hell. Simon & Schuster, 1989.

> Young widow Sarah Talbot is single-minded in her quest to discover why her son, a student at Cambridge, was murdered after asking a question in a Paris café.

Solo. Stein, 1980.

> John Mikali is not only an internationally renowned concert pianist, but an international assassin as well.

James, Bill

Split. Do-Not, 2001. **M**

> Black and an Oxford graduate, Simon Abelard is also a spy for British intelligence. His latest assignment is to "recover: a former colleague who is now an international criminal.

le Carré, John

George Smiley series

Call for the Dead. Bantam, 1961. **FILM**

The first appearance of George Smiley, a spy for Britain's military intelligence (MI-6), also known as the Circus. The first chapter gives a short biography of the character. (The author's real name is David John Moore Cornwall, and he was a member of the British Foreign Service.) (Film was titled *The Deadly Affair*.)

A Murder of Quality. Walker, 1962.

Smiley gets involved in a murder mystery at the behest of an old friend.

The Spy Who Came in from the Cold. Coward, 1963. **FILM**

Alec Leamas is coordinating double agents in Berlin, but when the East Germans start killing them, he is called back to London (out of the "cold") for new orders. He is then sent back out into the cold to find out who is channeling information to the East Germans.

The Looking Glass War. Coward, 1965. **FILM**

The British government draws Fred Leiser out of retirement on a mission to uncover Soviet missiles in East German.

Tinker, Tailor, Soldier, Spy. Knopf, 1974. **FILM**

British spy George Smiley is trying to uncover a Soviet mole in the British Secret Service.

The Honourable Schoolboy. Knopf, 1977.

British spy George Smiley is now the head of the British Secret Service (aka the Circus) and redoubles his efforts to find a Soviet double agent.

Smiley's People. Knopf, 1979. **FILM**

Smiley attempts to trap his Soviet counterpart Karla and settle some old scores.

The Secret Pilgrim. Knopf, 1991.

Ned has been a member of the Circus—British intelligence—for thirty years, and his mentor is George Smiley. Ned tells the story of his career—his secret pilgrimage.

The Night Manager. Knopf, 1993.

Jonathan Pine, night manager at a Cairo hotel, finds himself inadvertently involved in international espionage when he assists a beautiful women in some photocopying.

Our Game. Knopf, 1995.

Retired Cold War agent Tim Cranmer thinks he has found the perfect life with his vineyard and Emma, his beautiful young mistress. Then Emma disappears, and Cranmer finds himself running for his life as his old employers try to kill him.

Tailor of Panama. Knopf, 1996. **FILM**

Harry Pendel runs the finest tailoring business in Panama. He's also a spy for British intelligence. A humorous satire.

Lyall, Gavin

Spy's Honour. St. Martin's, 1993.
> A light-hearted romp through the origins of the British Secret Service Bureau.

McEwan, Ian

The Innocent. Doubleday, 1989.
> It is 1955, and in postwar Berlin a lowly young British post office technician, Leonard Marnham, finds himself caught up in dangerous intrigues.

McNab, Andy

Nick Stone series

Remote Control. Ballantine, 1997.
> British intelligence agent Nick Stone goes to visit an old friend in Washington, D.C., and finds his friend's entire family slaughtered—except for a seven-year-old girl. With the girl in tow, Stone soon finds that anonymous assassins are hunting them.

Crisis Four. Ballantine, 1999.
> British intelligence agent Nick Stone is ordered to kill a fellow agent and his former lover, Sarah Greenwood, but ends up saving her life and preventing the destruction of the world by Muslim extremists.

Firewall. Pocket Books, 2001.
> Nick Stone's last mission left his best friend's family murdered, and he has been furloughed from the Firm. He takes on a freelance assignment that gets him involved in the Russian *mafiya*.

Last Light. Atria, 2002.
> Government assassin Nick Stone just bungled his last hit, and now he must finish it—or someone very dear to him will die instead.

Liberation Day. Atria, 2003.
> Stone is now working for a U.S. antiterrorism team, and his mission is to keep money from getting to al-Qaida.

O'Donnell, Peter

Modesty Blaise series

Modesty Blaise. Doubleday, 1965. **FILM**
> The first adventure of Modesty Blaise, the former head of an international crime syndicate who is now helping British intelligence when there is a need to operate outside the law. The beautiful Ms. Blaise is ably assisted by her (platonic) partner Willie Garvin.

Sabre-Tooth. Doubleday, 1966.
> Modesty goes up against the evil Karz and his henchmen, the Twins, deadly conjoined twins.

I, Lucifer. Doubleday, 1967.
> The bad guys use a psychic who can predict death and thinks he's Satan.

A Taste for Death. Doubleday, 1969.
> Modesty hunts for buried treasure.

The Impossible Virgin. Doubleday, 1971.
> Modesty must discover the secret of the Impossible Virgin—a secret that could be the key to unsurpassed riches.

Pieces of Modesty. Doubleday, 1972.
> A collection of short stories featuring Modesty Blaise.

Silver Mistress. Mysterious, 1973.
> Modesty and partner Willie try to recover a captured British agent from the clutches of a strange crew of villains.

Last Day in Limbo. Mysterious, 1976.
> Modesty has been abducted and must use all her wits to gain her freedom.

Dragon's Claw. Mysterious, 1978.
> Modesty and Willie take to the sea to wrangle with a gang of art thieves.

Xanadu Talisman. Mysterious, 1981.
> Modesty's adventures span the globe in this series installment as she battles the evil minions of El Mico.

Night of the Morningstar. Mysterious, 1982.
> Modesty faces off against a terrorist group known as the Watchmen. In the process, she even saves the Golden Gate Bridge from destruction.

Dead Man's Handle. Mysterious, 1985.
> Willie is captured by the bad guys, and Modesty has to save him from torture and death.

Cobra Trap. Souvenir, 2001.
> A collection of five short stories that span the entire career of Modesty Blaise and sidekick Willie Garvin with the final, title story featuring a fifty-two-year-old Modesty called out of retirement for one more adventure.

Porter, Henry

A Spy's Life. Simon & Schuster, 2001.
> Former British spy Robert Harland is the lone survivor of a mysterious United Nations plane crash outside La Guardia Airport. He must discover if he was the target and why.

Sebastian, Tim

The Memory Church. William Morrow, 1993.
> James Martin, a British agent who has been stationed in East German for many years, finds he has new enemies after the Berlin Wall falls.

Seymour, Gerald

A Song in the Morning. Norton, 1986.

Former British intelligence agent "Jeez" Carew has been accused of terrorism and sentenced to hang in South Africa. Deserted by everyone but his son, whom he has not seen in twenty years, Jeez must fight for his survival.

Spicer, Michael

Lady Jane Hildreth series

Cotswold Manners. St. Martin's, 1989.

British agent Lady Jane Hildreth becomes tangled up in a series of murders at her ex-husband's Cotswold manor.

Cotswold Murders. St. Martin's, 1990.

British agent Lady Jane Hildreth's investigation into a strange murder linked to the IRA leads her to Hong Kong, where she teams up with an old boyfriend, Major Simon Carey.

Cotswold Mistress. St. Martin's, 1992.

British secret agent Lady Jane Hildreth is assigned to look into the recent death's of Britain's leading scientists.

Cotswold Moles. St. Martin's, 1993.

Intelligence agent Lady Jane Hildreth, along with her semiretired partner Patricia Huntington, is off to Australia to investigate nefarious goings-on.

Tan, Maureen

Jane Nichols series

AKA Jane. Mysterious, 1997.

Former British MI-5 agent Jane Nichols now writes private-eye novels, but she finds that she cannot escape her past when an old enemy comes calling.

Run Jane Run. Mysterious, 1999.

Returning to her life as an agent for MI-5, Jane Nichols newest mission is to rescue the kidnapped nephew of an important government official. But the mission soon goes awry when she discovers a connection between the nephew and her parents' murder.

Thomas, Craig

Sir Kenneth Aubrey series

Lion's Run. Doubleday, 1985.

Sir Kenneth Aubrey must defend himself against charges of treason.

Wildcat. Putnam, 1989.

Sir Kenneth Aubrey's mission is to oversee the defection of a high-ranking East German official.

The Last Raven. HarperCollins, 1990.

Sir Kenneth Aubrey's top agent, Patrick Hyde, is caught in a web of lies and deceit as he investigates the wreck of military transport plane inside the Russian border with Afghanistan.

A Hooded Crow. HarperCollins, 1992.
> British spymaster Sir Kenneth Aubrey must stop the illegal flow of high technology to the Soviets.

Playing with Cobras. HarperCollins, 1993.
> British agent Philip Cass has information that the next prime minister of India has family ties to drug smuggling, and this information has him targeted for termination.

Espionage American Style (with a Little Help from Other Countries)

Spying is the world's second oldest profession.

—Anonymous

Aline, Countess of the Romanones
The Well-Mannered Assassin. Putnam, 1993.
> Another fictionalized account of a real female secret agent, Aline Romanones, "American beauty, Spanish socialite, devoted mother, and spy." Here she "tackles" the infamous terrorist Carlos the Jackal.

Allebeury, Ted
Show Me a Hero. Mysterious, 1992.
> Andrei Aarons is a double agent: the Soviets have planted him undercover in the United States to be a spy, but he is really reporting to the Americans.

Andrew, Joseph J.
The Disciples. Simon & Schuster, 1993.
> T. C. Boyle, former National Security Agency information analyst, is called out of retirement to track down a former colleague, Rebecca Townsend, who along with her organization, the Disciples, is planning to reveal every country's most closely held secrets.

Bickham, Jack
Tiebreaker. Forge, 1989.
> On the side, former tennis champion Brad Smith helps the CIA, and this time his mission is to go to Yugoslavia to help a female tennis player defect.

Buckley, William F., Jr.
Blackford Oakes series

Saving the Queen. Doubleday, 1976.
> In 1952, CIA agent Blackford Oakes is a Yale graduate and former fighter pilot. In this first installment of the series, Oakes travels to England to protect the queen from the Soviets.

Stained Glass. Doubleday, 1978.
> German aristocrat Count Axel Wintergrin is planning to reunite the divided Germanys, and Oakes's mission is to deal with the ramifications.

High Jinx. Doubleday, 1986.
> In 1954, Oakes is assigned to avenge the murders of thirty-one CIA agents on a botched mission in Albania.

Who's on First. Doubleday, 1980.
> In 1956, Oakes must kidnap two Soviet missile scientists to help the United States win the race to space.

Marco Polo, If You Can. Doubleday, 1981.
> It's 1958, and Oakes's U-2 spy plane crashes over the Soviet Union.

The Story of Henri Tod. Doubleday, 1984.
> During the time leading up to the construction of the Berlin Wall, Oakes mission is to infiltrate a band of German freedom fighters.

See You Later Alligator. Doubleday, 1985.
> In Operation Alligator, Oakes is sent to Cuba to negotiate a trade agreement with Che Guevara, but he is actually a pawn in a Soviet plot.

Mongoose, R.I.P. Doubleday, 1987.
> It is 1962, and the CIA has presented President Kennedy with three separate plans to assassinate Castro. Oakes has been sent to Cuba to coordinate the revolution that will follow his death; things do not turn out as planned, however.

Tucker's Last Stand. Random House, 1991.
> In 1964, Blackie Oakes and army special projects major Tucker Montana hatch a plan to stall troops and supplies from traveling down the Ho Chi Minh Trail in Vietnam.

A Very Private Plot. William Morrow, 1994.
> It is 1995, and a retired Blackford Oakes refuses a subpoena to testify before Congress on Reagan-era spying.

Spytime. Harcourt, 2000.
> The fictionalized account of the espionage career of James Jesus Angleton, founder of U.S. counterintelligence.

Carroll, James
Family Trade. Little, Brown, 1982.

Correa, Arnaldo
Spy's Fate. Akashic, 2002.
> Explores the history of Castro's Cuban espionage efforts.

Day, DeForest
Fatal Recall. Carroll & Graf, 1991.
> Former naval intelligence officer Chase Defoe teams up with his childhood sweetheart to discover why her grandfather, a retired general, burned the notes for his memoirs and then shot himself.

DeMille, Nelson

Cathedral. Delacorte, 1981.
> IRA terrorists seize St. Patrick's Cathedral in New York City on St. Patrick's Day.

Edouard, Dianne, and Sandra Ware

Sacred Lies. Doubleday, 1993.
> Beautiful spy Romany Chase is torn between the Israeli operative she wants and the priest she is ordered to seduce.

Forsyth, Frederick

The Day of the Jackal. Viking, 1971. **FILM**
> An assassin, code-named the Jackal, is hired to kill France's Charles de Gaulle. The only one who can stop him is the best detective in France: Deputy Commissaire Claude Label.

No Comebacks. Viking, 1982.
> Collected short stories.

The Veteran. St. Martin's, 2001.
> Collected short stories.

Freemantle, Brian

Little Grey Mice. St. Martin's, 1991.
> Elke Meyer is one of the "little gray mice," smart but lonely women who work for the many West German government ministries located in Bonn. She has been targeted for her knowledge, and a foreign agent has been sent not to kill her, but to seduce her.

The Watchmen. St. Martin's, 2002.
> FBI agent William Cowley and Russian crime expert Dimitri Danilov team up to track down a U.S. terrorist group that has allied itself with the Russian mob.

> *Gannon's Adventure/Suspense Rule Number 1: Sometimes your friends are deadlier than your enemies.*

Frey, James N.

Winter of the Wolves. Holt, 1992.
> Tom Croft was an operative for the Exchange, but one too many dirty ops caused him to retire to a small town in the Adirondacks. Now the Exchange wants him back for one more job—either he must kill again or be killed.

Friedman, Philip

Termination Order. Dial, 1979.
> Gregory Moore is about to face every spy's biggest nightmare: being terminated (permanently) by his own agency.

Gilman, Dorothy

Mrs. Pollifax series

The Unexpected Mrs. Pollifax. Doubleday, 1966. **FILM**
The first of the zany adventures of Emily Pollifax: a grandmotherly New Jersey widow and member of the Garden Club who waltzes into CIA HQ and volunteers to be a spy. A supposedly quick courier trip to Mexico City for the CIA ends up getting her kidnapped and taken to Albania.

The Amazing Mrs. Pollifax. Doubleday, 1970.
Mrs. Pollifax is sent to Turkey to help a female Russian spy defect, but things do not turn out as planned.

The Elusive Mrs. Pollifax. Doubleday, 1971.
Mrs. Pollifax smuggles forged passports into Bulgaria.

A Palm for Mrs. Pollifax. Doubleday, 1973.
Mrs. Pollifax heads to Switzerland to track down a missing package of plutonium.

Mrs. Pollifax on Safari. Doubleday, 1976.
Mrs. Pollifax's new assignment is to locate the assassin who has targeted the president of Zambia, but then she is kidnapped by Rhodesian terrorists.

Mrs. Pollifax on the China Station. Doubleday, 1983. **M**
Mrs. Pollifax poses as a tourist in China and once again risks her life as she attempts to recover a treasure for the CIA.

Mrs. Pollifax and the Hong Kong Buddha. Doubleday, 1985. **M**
Mrs. Pollifax is off to Hong Kong to save agent Sheng Ti, whom she smuggled out of China in *Mrs. Pollifax on the China Station,* from getting involved with a deadly double agent.

Mrs. Pollifax and the Golden Triangle. Doubleday, 1988.
On assignment in Bangkok, Mrs. Pollifax must set out to rescue her new husband, Cyrus, when he is kidnapped.

Mrs. Pollifax and the Whirling Dervish. Doubleday, 1990.
Mrs. Pollifax is sent undercover to Morocco to pose as another agent's aunt, but her "nephew" is really an imposter and tries to kill her.

Mrs. Pollifax and the Second Thief. Doubleday, 1993.
Mrs. Pollifax is called to Sicily to help a former colleague who is now a safecracker.

Mrs. Pollifax Pursued. Fawcett, 1995.
Mrs. Pollifax goes into hiding at a country circus to escape two men who keep following her.

Mrs. Pollifax and the Lion Killer. Fawcett, 1996.
Mrs. Pollifax travels to the African nation of Ubangiba to help out the person, now her friend, who she found hiding in her closet in *Mrs. Pollifax Pursued.*

Mrs. Pollifax, Innocent Tourist. Fawcett, 1997.

> Mrs. Pollifax is neither innocent nor a tourist as she travels to the Middle East on a secret mission to smuggle an important manuscript out of Jordan. Mrs. Pollifax's "souvenir" gets her in more trouble than she could have imagined as she attempts to flee the country.

Mrs. Pollifax Unveiled. Ballantine, 2000.

> Grandmother, member of the garden club, and part-time CIA spy Mrs. Pollifax snoops around Syria in this adventure.

Goddard, Ken

Harry Lightstone series

Prey. Forge, 1992.

> U.S. Fish and Wildlife Service undercover agent Harry Lightstone must stop a secret alliance of international industrialists and professional assassins from destroying the environmental movement.

Wildfire. Forge, 1994.

> Harry Lightstone, U.S. Fish and Wildlife Service agent, must face villains left over from *Prey* as well as Wildfire, a group of environmental extremists.

Double Blind. Forge, 1997.

> The ICER Committee from the two previous novels returns once again to fight dirty with Harry Lightstone, agent for the U.S. Fish and Wildlife Service.

Grady, James

River of Darkness. Warner, 1991.

> Jud Stuart was one of the CIA's top spies until the end of the Cold War, and then someone decided he knew too many secrets.

Six Days of the Condor. Norton, 1974. **FILM**

> A renegade organization is working within the CIA and murdering its agents. (Filmed as *Three Days of the Condor*.)

Thunder. Warner, 1994.

> Former CIA operative John Lang is now the agency's liaison with the U.S. Senate, but then a "stray" bullet kills his partner, and Lang must find out what secrets within his own government caused the death.

Granger, Bill

November Man series

The November Man. Ballantine, 1979.

> The adventures of Devereaux, code-named November, the jaded operative of the ultra-secret R Section, a group set up in 1961 by President Kennedy to "watch the watchers."

Schism. Random House, 1981.

> After twenty years, a man has stumbled out of the Cambodian jungle with a secret of staggering importance.

The Shattered Eye. Crown, 1982.

> Devereaux uncovers a Soviet plot against NATO.

The British Cross. Random House, 1983.
The November Man faces betrayal in Finland.

The Zurich Numbers. Random House, 1984.
November uncovers an international conspiracy to smuggle illegal immigrants into the United States and tracks the mastermind behind it to Switzerland.

Hemingway's Notebook. Random House, 1986.
The CIA wants a notebook that proves they committed a debacle in the Bay of Pigs invasion, but R Section wants it, too.

There Are No Spies. Warner, 1987.
November comes out of retirement when his former boss, Hanley, is shipped off to a mental institution by his superiors. He must battle a deadly female Soviet spy and find a mole hidden deep within the U.S. intelligence network.

The Infant of Prague. Warner, 1987.
A semiretired Devereaux is involved with a Czech defector and goes up against his old enemy, Colonel Ready.

Henry McGee Is Not Dead. Warner, 1988.
Now head of R Section, Devereaux is in pursuit of Soviet scientist Henry McGee who defected to the West but has now disappeared from a research base in Alaska.

The Man Who Heard Too Much. Warner, 1989,
The November Man must protect a translator who is carrying a tape that contains highly classified information from both the KGB and the CIA.

League of Terror. Warner, 1990.
Devereaux is up against his evil adversary Henry McGee and his deadly female accomplices.

The Last Good German. Warner, 1991.
Devereaux confronts Double Eagle, the East German agent who nearly killed him years earlier.

Burning the Apostle. Warner, 1993.
The November Man must stop a plot to create a nuclear disaster that will bring down the nuclear power industry.

Hallahan, William H.

The Trade. William Morrow, 1981.
Colin Thomas, an international arms trader, must find the Doomsday Book before its deadly plan causes World War III.

Harrington, Kent

A Brother to Dragons. Fine, 1993.
The Mafia and the Irish Republican Army agree to an unholy alliance and out to stop them is Frank DiGenero, FBI agent and grandson of a Mafia kingpin.

Harrington, Kent

Endgame in Berlin. Fine, 1991.

The Cold War is over, and what's the classic spy to do? Industrial espionage.

Heffernan, William

Corsican Honor. Dutton, 1992.

The lives of two generations of American spies are entangled in the deadly scheming of the Mafia.

Hood, William

The Sunday Spy. Norton, 1996.

Alan Trosper of the CIA faces a post–Cold War espionage arena where information goes to the highest bidder.

Hunter, Jack D.

The Potsdam Bluff. Forge, 1991.

Sweeney's Run. Forge, 1992.

Tom Sweeney, a retired Department of Defense intelligence agent, must discover why an old friend and CIA agent scrawled a cryptic message in his own blood on Sweeney's bathroom floor just before dying.

Hunter, Stephen

Bob Lee Swagger series

Point of Impact. Bantam, 1993.

Former Vietnam ace sniper Bob Lee Swagger is now living in a backwoods Arkansas trailer and wants nothing more than to be left alone. Then one day, a shady organization with ties to the CIA, RamDyne Security, recruits him for a mission doomed to fail . . . they think.

Black Light. Doubleday, 1996.

Vietnam vet and master sniper Bob Lee Swagger is back and trying to discover the real reason behind his father's death forty years ago.

Time to Hunt. Doubleday, 1998.

Bob Lee Swagger is back, this time facing his deadly nemesis from Vietnam in a battle for the lives of his wife and daughter.

The Second Saladin. William Morrow, 1982.

Ignatius, David

A Firing Offense. Random House, 1997.

Eric Truell, a young journalist with a promising career with the *New York Mirror,* discovers that an undercover spy is also working at the paper. He decides to risk his career—and even his life—to find out the truth.

Ing, Dean

Spooker. Forge, 1995.

When Gary Landis, a Drug Enforcement Administration agent deep under cover, has his cover blown, he's left for dead. Unfortunately for the would-be assassins, Landis survives and comes looking for revenge.

Jacobson, Alan

The Hunted. Pocket, 2001.

> Psychologist Dr. Lauren Chambers, herself an agoraphobic, teams up with private investigator Nick Bradley to find her husband, Michael, who has disappeared.

Lehrer, Jim

Blue Hearts. Random House, 1993.

> Charles Avenue Henderson learns that one can never really retire from the CIA when his Washington, D.C., hotel room blows up one morning. (The author is a professional print and television journalist.)

Liddy, G. Gordon

Out of Control. St. Martin's, 1979.

> When former CIA agent Richard Rand finds that his old employers are out to get him, he turns to his friends in organized crime to help him.

Lira, Gonzalo

Acrobat. St. Martin's, 2002.

> Generation X joins the CIA: a group of young CIA agents (code-named Acrobat) are targeted for assassination by their own agency.

Littell, Robert

The Company. Overlook, 2002.

> A fictionalized history spans the fifty-year existence of the CIA.

The Defection of A.J. Lewinter. Overlook, 1973.

> American scientist A.J. Lewinter contacts the KGB and wants to defect, but is his request genuine?

The Sisters. Bantam, 1986.

> *Gannon's Adventure/Suspense Rule Number 2: Cynicism is a prerequisite for success in the spy business.*

Walking Back the Cat. Overlook, 1996.

> An assassin has been living deep undercover in a small New Mexico town—he is Parsifal, a KGB agent from the Soviet era. He has now been reactivated, and the only one who can stop him is a cynical Gulf War vet by the name of Finn.

Ludlum, Robert

Covert-One series

Robert Ludlum's The Hades Factor. St. Martin's, 2000.

> Lieutenant Colonel Jonathan Smith assembles a team of crack operatives to find out the truth behind a deadly new virus that has already claimed the life of his fiancée. The first in a new series called Covert-One. (Written with Gayle Lynds.)

Robert Ludlum's The Cassandra Compact. St. Martin's, 2001.

> Unknown agents are attempting to steal Russia's stores of the smallpox virus and unleash it on an unsuspecting and unprotected world—only Jon Smith and the other operatives of Covert-One can stop them. (Written with Philip Shelby.)

Robert Ludlum's The Paris Option. St. Martin's, 2002.

> Covert-One agent Jon Smith goes to Paris to discover the reason for an explosion at one of the laboratories at the world-renowned Pasteur Institute, along with the theft of the world's first DNA-based computer.

Robert Ludlum's The Altman Code. St. Martin's, 2003.

> The gang at Covert-One gets called in by the president when a Chinese cargo ship headed for Iraq is suspected to be full of chemicals that could be used to make biological weapons.

The Cry of the Halidon. Bantam, 1974.

The Janson Directive. St. Martin's, 2002.

> Former intelligence agent Paul Janson is recruited to retrieve international financier Peter Novak from the deadly clutches of the Caliph, a brutal international terrorist.

Jason Bourne series

The Bourne Identity. Merek, 1980 📄 🎞️**FILM**

> A bullet-ridden man is pulled out of the water in Greece with no memory of who he is or who shot him. He eventually learns that he is Jason Bourne, a spy assigned to track down Carlos, an international assassin.

The Bourne Supremacy. Random House, 1986.

> David Webb must resurrect his assassin alter ego, Jason Bourne, when his wife is kidnapped and his own life is threatened.

The Bourne Ultimatum. Random House, 1990.

> The world's deadliest terrorist, Carlos the Jackal, is back and wants a final confrontation with his nemesis, Jason Bourne.

The Prometheus Deception. St. Martin's, 2000.

> Nicholas Bryson spent many years as an undercover agent for the Directorate, but he learns that the agency was not working for but against the United States. He must now find out who is really running the Directorate and what their ultimate plans are.

The Scorpio Illusion. Bantam, 1993.

> The beautiful assassin known as the Scorpio has vowed vengeance on the world's leaders and only former operative Tyrell Hawthorne can stop her.

Lynds, Gayle

Masquerade. Doubleday, 1996.

> Liz Sansborough wakes up one morning not knowing who or what she is— deadly government agent or innocent victim.

MacInnes, Helen

Cloak of Darkness. Harcourt, 1982.
> Counterterrorist operative Bob Renwick uncovers an international terrorist training network.

The Decision at Delphi. Harcourt, 1960.
> While in Greece, an American architect is caught up in international intrigue.

The Hidden Target. Harcourt, 1980.
> A naïve young girl becomes caught up in a terrorist conspiracy.

North from Rome. Harcourt, 1958.

Pray for a Brave Heart. Harcourt, 1955.

Ride a Pale Horse. Harcourt, 1984.
> Journalist Karen Cornell is in Prague to cover an international peace conference but soon finds herself involved in an assassination conspiracy.

The Venetian Affair. Harcourt, 1963.

Mathews, Francine

The Secret Agent. Bantam, 2002.
> International fund agent Stefani Fogg is recruited to be a secret agent by Max Roderick, who wants her to discover why his infamous father disappeared into the Vietnam jungle forty years earlier.

Maxim, John R.

Paul Bannerman series

Bannerman Solution. Avon, 1999.
> Paul and his gang of ex-secret agents have settled into retirement in a small Connecticut town, but they cannot escape from their evil nemesis, Palmer Reid.

Bannerman Effect. Avon, 2000.
> Bannerman and his crew once again come out of retirement to tussle with drug dealers and terrorists.

Bannerman's Law. Avon, 2000.
> Bannerman's crew of ex-assassins and secret agents uncover a deadly conspiracy when Carla's sister is murdered in a Hollywood mental institution.

Bannerman's Promise. Avon, 2001.
> Paul Bannerman leaves his suburban retirement in Connecticut for a trip to Moscow, where he tangles with ex-KGB agents and vicious Russian mobsters.

Whistler's Angel. William Morrow, 2001.
> Adam Whistler is a government assassin who wants out of the business, a possibility he finds much harder to achieve than he had thought. Complicating things is the fact that his lover, Claudia Gellar, thinks she's his guardian angel—literally.

Bannerman's Ghosts. William Morrow, 2003.

Psychotic billionaire Artemus Bourne gets more than he bargained for when he finds himself on the wrong side of some "retired" government operatives.

Morrell, David

Assumed Identity. Warner, 1993.

A master of disguise, undercover operative Brendan Buchanan goes by two hundred other names, but when he has to operate on a mission as his true self, he runs into difficulty.

Brotherhood of the Rose. Ballantine, 1984.

Two orphaned boys, raised as brothers and trained to be assassins, find themselves on opposite sides.

Burnt Sienna. Warner, 2000.

Artist Chase Malone is persuaded by the CIA to spy on Sienna Bellasar, wife of an international arms dealer, under the pretense of painting her portrait. Malone is convinced that Sienna is in deadly danger and must protect her from powerful husband who is preparing to test a lethal new weapon.

Desperate Measures. Warner, 1994.

Just as he is preparing to commit suicide, Journalist Matt Pittman is stopped and given an assignment to write an obituary for a man not yet dead. His assignment leads him into mortal danger as he uncovers a secret kept since the birth of the Cold War.

Extreme Denial. Warner, 1996.

Former antiterrorist operative Steve Decker has retired to New Mexico after a botched mission that resulted in the deaths of twenty-three people. He meets a woman, Beth Dwyer, who helps him grow out of his pain and guilt—and then disappears. Decker must discover why.

The Fifth Profession. Warner, 1990.

Savage is a bodyguard, or an executive protector, whose job it is to protect the wealthiest and most powerful people in the world—and if necessary, to avenge them.

Moss, Robert

Carnival of Spies. Villard, 1987.

North, Oliver, with Joe Musser

Mission Compromised. Broadman, 2002.

U.S. Marine Major Peter Newman is appointed as the head of the White House Special Projects Office with the mandate to track down and eradicate terrorists planning massive destruction in the United States. He soon finds himself on a mission so sensitive it threatens everything he holds dear. (The author was a counterterrorism coordinator for the U.S. government from 1983 through 1986).

Reed, John R.

Thirteen Mountain. St. Martin's, 1995.

At thirty-two, CIA analyst Jim Gadsden is cynical and burned out. He is given one more chance to redeem himself: find a deadly weapon created before the end of the Cold War and then supposedly destroyed.

Seymour, Gerald

 Dead Ground. Simon & Schuster, 1998.

  Years ago Tracy Barnes saw her lover murdered by the Stasi, the East German secret police. Now, after the end of the Cold War, she finds the killer and plans to make him pay. She soon finds herself a pawn in international politics.

Silva, Daniel

 Gabriel Allon series

  The Kill Artist. Random House, 2000.

   Former Mossad agent Gabriel Allon is called out of retirement to assassinate a Palestinian terrorist before he can kill Yasir Arafat.

  The English Assassin. Putnam, 2002.

   Former Israeli spy Gabriel Allon, now an art restorer, discovers his new client, a Swiss millionaire banker, murdered and finds himself drawn back into the activities of his past profession.

  The Confessor. Putnam, 2003.

   Gabriel Allon finds himself drawn into a mystery as he uncovers evidence that the Vatican may have turned a blind eye on the Holocaust.

  A Death in Viena. Putnam, 2004.

   While on an assignment in Viena to verify that a painting is not a forgery, Gabriel Allon searches for the man who assaulted his mother at the end of World War II.

  The Mark of the Assassin. Villard, 1998.

   CIA operative Michael Osbourne is investigating a terrorist bombing when he uncovers clues that appear to lead to an international assassin—the same person who killed his lover years before.

Thomas, Ross

 The Mordida Man. Simon & Schuster, 1981.

  Chubb Dunjee accepts an assignment from the president of the United States when an international terrorist is kidnapped and the terrorist's associates kidnap the president's brother in retaliation.

Trevanian

 Jonathan Hemlock series

  The Eiger Sanction. Crown, 1972. 🗋 **FILM**

   Jonathan Hemlock is both an art professor and a government assassin. (The author's real name is Rodney Whitaker.)

  The Loo Sanction. Crown, 1973. 🗋

   Hemlock is blackmailed into performing a high-level political assassination or "sanction."

Weber, Janice

Leslie Frost series

Frost the Fiddler. St. Martin's, 1992.
> Leslie Frost, code-named Smith, is a member of a secret network of female spies. Her cover is that of an internationally renowned concert violinist—a great cover for her spying activities.

Hot Ticket. Warner, 1998.
> Leslie Frost is a beautiful concert violinist and an American spy. In the first few pages of this book, she goes from performing at a formal White House concert to dangling off the ninth-floor balcony of the Watergate while a murder is taking place inside.

West, Cameron

The Medici Dagger. Pocket, 2001.
> Movie stuntman Reb Barnett finds himself a pawn in a game played by a shadowy spy organization when he sets off to find the fabled Medici Dagger, a weapon invented by Leonardo da Vinci and made of an indestructible alloy.

Wise, David

Spectrum. Viking, 1981.
> Based on a true incident that occurred in 1965 when weapons-grade uranium disappeared from a Pennsylvania processing plant. Sixteen years later all the CIA agents involved in the investigation have either died or disappeared.

Wynne, Marcus

No Other Option. Forge, 2001.
> A rogue agent, commando Jonny Maxwell, has become a dangerous rapist. His fellow agents must capture him before the police do because he knows too many government secrets.

Short Stories

Smith, Martin Cruz, editor

Death by Espionage: Intriguing Stories of Betrayal and Deception. Cumberland, 1999.
> Authors include Michael Collins, Brian Garfield, Edward D. Hoch, Stuart M. Kaminsky, John Jakes, and John Lutz.

Furst, Alan, editor

The Book of Spies: An Anthology of Literary Espionage. Modern Library, 2003.
> Authors include Eric Ambler, John le Carré, John Steinbeck, and Rebecca West.

Chapter 2

What Else Can Go Wrong?

Disasters

Definition: In this subgenre, the titles have as their basic premise a disaster situation and the events occurring before, during, and after it. These disasters could be natural (an earthquake, volcano, plague) or manmade (nuclear explosion, aircraft crash, nerve gas leak). The plot revolves around the characters' adventures that result from the various disasters. The disaster event(s) may have already happened or may happen early in the story, or it may be predicted to happen and the characters must work to stop it. The result can be either success or destruction.

The Appeal: The appeal of this subgenre can be likened to automobile drivers who slow down to observe a car accident—it's the vicarious thrill of destruction. "It's scary, it's horrendous, it's exciting . . . and it's not happening to me." Many people are fascinated by disasters and the events surrounding them. They like to posit, "What if that had happened to me? How would I react in that situation? Would I survive?" These books generally have a high level of action, heroism, and a cynical or bleak outlook.

Brief History: The modern disaster novel first appeared in the late 1950s with the fear of nuclear Armageddon brought about by the Cold War. Such books as *Alas, Babylon* and *On the Beach* portrayed a bleak, pessimistic view of the diplomatic process, leading to an inevitable nuclear war—a war with no victor. The 1970s saw the growth of the disaster novel along with star-studded disaster movies. The popularity of the destruction and chaos portrayed in Irwin Allen epics such as *Earthquake* and *Towering Inferno* contributed to the success of their written counterparts. The fear of nuclear disaster became popular again in the 1980s and 1990s as the world saw the growth of terrorism and easier access to dangerous nuclear materials. The fear of bioengineered viruses and diseases also influenced the disaster novel, and we are seeing more novels written with this as the central theme.

Advising the Reader: The key elements to remember when advising the reader and suggesting appropriate titles are the following:

- What type of disaster does the reader prefer, natural or manmade?

- If natural disasters, what type—earthquake, hurricane, volcano?

- Does the reader also like disaster movies? Many disaster novels have been made into movies, and the reader may enjoy novels with that connection.

- Readers who like horror fiction about werewolves or other supernatural monsters might be interested in the "Animals Run Amok" subgenre.

- The reader may prefer the apocalyptic aspects of the disaster genre. If so, life following a nuclear war or a deadly plague would be more suitable than an earthquake or plane crash.

- The apocalyptic subgenre is also seen in science fiction, and readers who ordinarily only read in that genre could be guided to the titles found in the sections "Disasters from Out of This World," "Nuclear Disasters," or "Biological Disasters."

- Readers who enjoy reading about biological disasters may also be interested in the biothriller titles found in "Science Gone Awry."

- Does the reader like the global setting or a smaller area of destruction? Some readers prefer an arena only where a few people are trapped but horrible things are happening, such as an airline disaster, a shipwreck, or an island full of dangerous animals.

Ill-luck, you know, seldom comes alone.

—Miguel de Cervantes

"Fasten your seatbelts, it's gonna be a bumpy ride!": Planes, Trains, and Other Moving Disasters

This section includes titles that feature transportation disasters, with airborne catastrophes being the most popular. Oftentimes the actual disaster (crash or sinking) is secondary to the other horrible things happening to the passengers, such as the presence of fellow passengers who are homicidal maniacs or dangerous bumbling cowards.

Block, Thomas H.

Orbit. Coward, 1982.

> Similar plotline as in Block's *Mayday*, but the action takes place aboard the hypersonic rocket-powered passenger liner, *Silver Streak*.

Block, Thomas H., and Nelson DeMille

Mayday. Marek, 1979.

> A passenger jet containing three hundred passengers is on a routine flight from San Francisco to Tokyo when a missile fired from a U.S. Navy fighter inadvertently hits it. The jet is damaged and looses all cabin pressure, leaving most of the

crew and passengers (all but five) dead, in a coma, or brain-damaged, homicidal maniacs. (In this edition, Block thanked Nelson DeMille for his "editorial assistance," but in the 1998 edition DeMille was cited as a "collaborator" and his name appeared first on the cover.)

Crichton, Michael

Airframe. Knopf, 1996.
A jet airliner en route to Denver from Hong Kong is hit with disaster— the main cabin is almost destroyed, three passengers are killed and fifty-six injured; but the pilot manages to bring the plane down for a landing. For those investigating the accident, the disaster has just begun . . .

Gallico, Paul

The Poseidon Adventure. Coward, 1969.
One of the classic disaster novels. An ocean liner full of diverse passengers gets hit by a huge wave, created by an undersea earthquake, which turns the craft upside down. Who will survive?

Hailey, Arthur

Airport. Doubleday, 1968. **FILM**
A classic disaster tale: an interesting, diverse group of people on an airliner that's about to crash. What more can be said?

Koontz, Dean R.

Sole Survivor. Knopf, 1997.
Although more of a political thriller than a disaster story, this novel has one of the most horrifying plane crash scenes ever written.

> *Gannon's Adventure/Suspense Rule Number 3: Never sit next to anyone on a plane who is sweating profusely, talking to himself, and clutching a large, bulky item.*

Nance, John J.

Final Approach. Crown, 1990.

Fire Flight. Simon & Schuster, 2003.
The plot revolves around "smoke jumpers," or airborne firefighters, but does have two types of disaster: wildfires and a plane crash.

Katherine Bronsky series

The Last Hostage. Doubleday, 1998.
Unless law enforcement officials find and arrest the murderer of an eleven-year-old girl within eight hours, Airbridge Flight 90, carrying 130 passengers, will be blown up. As the only hostage negotiator available, psychologist and rookie FBI agent Katherine Bronsky must deal with the increasingly unstable hijacker. She soon learns that one of the passengers is the nominee to be the new U.S. attorney

general, and that the Justice Department has no intention of meeting the hi-jacker's demands.

Blackout. Putnam, 2000.

FBI agent Katherine Bronsky is back, this time teaming up with journalist Robert MacCabe and investigating a horrific airplane crash. A terrorist group is behind the disaster, and its members are preparing for their next target, a Boeing 747.

Medusa's Child. Doubleday, 1997. `FILM`

Captain Scott McKay discovers to his horror that there is a bomb aboard his Boeing 727—a bomb that could destroy every computer chip in North America. One wrong move could detonate it.

Pandora's Clock. Doubleday, 1995. `[icon]` `FILM`

A scientist unknowingly contracts a deadly new virus while working in a secret European lab, gets on board a plane bound for New York, and suddenly falls ill. The extremely contagious virus causes its victims to become homicidal before it kills them. Captain James Holland, the pilot of the flight, is in big trouble: no country will let his plane land for fear of causing an epidemic, his passengers are quickly deteriorating into a murderous rabble, and he's running out of jet fuel. (Nance is a former U.S. Air Force pilot, an attorney, and an airline captain for a major U.S. carrier.)

Turbulence. Putnam, 2002.

The passengers on Meridian Flight Six have had it! They are tired of the incompetent and mean employees and are not going to take it anymore. When Captain Phil Knight makes an emergency landing in a war zone, the passengers mutiny.

Thayer, James Stewart

Terminal Event. Simon & Schuster, 1999.

Wager, Walter

58 Minutes. MacMillan, 1987. `FILM`

Planes are trying to land in a blinding blizzard, and terrorists have destroyed the entire air traffic control system. In fifty-eight minutes the first plane will run out fuel and crash into New York City. (The basis for the movie *Die Hard II*.)

Willis, Maralys

Scatterpath. Lyford, 1993.

"Help, I'm trapped and I can't get out!"

In this section are titles that feature a cast of eclectic characters (one or more of whom is usually a homicidal maniac) who are trapped somewhere (underground, on an island, in a secret laboratory, or in the jungle) and to whom horrible things are happening, ultimately culminating in most of them being killed.

Aldrin, Buzz, and John Barnes

The Return. Forge, 2000.

India and Pakistan declare war against each other. The war soon involves nuclear weapons, and the world's space vehicles are all grounded because of the radiation storm created by a nuclear blast in the upper atmosphere. This is bad news for residents of the orbiting International Space Station, who only have a few weeks before they all die of radiation poisoning. (Aldrin was one of the astronauts from the *Apollo 11* mission.)

Brown, Jim

24/7. Ballantine, 2001.

Contestants on a television reality show, *True Life,* are stranded on a Caribbean island with a madman. They must endure daily trials; the winners receive an antidote to the deadly virus with which they've been infected . . . and the losers die.

Crichton, Michael

Congo. Knopf, 1980. **FILM**

Scientist Karen Ross and primatologist Peter Elliott (along with Amy, a gorilla proficient in sign language) lead an expedition deep into the jungles of the Congo to seek the Lost City of Zinj. They follow a previous expedition where all members were brutally murdered by unknown forces.

Prey. HarperCollins, 2002.

Scientists in a remote desert research facility are trapped by the intelligent microscopic robots they have created.

Timeline. Knopf, 1999.

Through new advances in quantum technology, any moment in the past is open to exploration. A team of historians goes back in time to see firsthand the sights of fourteenth-century France . . . but then can't get back.

Dietrich, William

Dark Winter. Warner, 2001.

In this twist on Agatha Christie's *And Then There Were None,* a small band of scientists are trapped at a remote Antarctic research station with no communications or transportation and soon find themselves being killed, one by one.

Getting Back. Warner, 2000.

In the near future, huge corporations rule a world where there are no untamed places except for one: Australia—depopulated by a biological accident. A secret organization, Outback Adventure, will send the adventurous on a trip to this last remote region for the price of a year's salary. Outback's newest customer, Daniel Dyson, doesn't realize that this package deal comes with only a one-way ticket.

Gray, Robert Steele

Survivor. St. Martin's, 1998.

Mark Lewellyn is your typical middle-aged American couch potato until one evening he is caught outside in a thunderstorm and hit by lightning. He finds himself transported back to the Stone Age where he must deal wild animals and savage cavemen.

Hall, James W.

Buzz Cut. Delacorte, 1996.

The rich and famous are held captive aboard the luxurious cruise ship M.S. *Eclipse,* and a lunatic is murdering them one by one.

Hurwitz, Gregg Andrew

Minutes to Burn. HarperCollins, 2001.

Scientists along with their SEAL escorts are stranded without weapons on an island where a virus has created nine-foot-tall monsters.

Kerr, Philip

The Grid. Warner, 1995.

The new Yu Corporation Building, located in downtown Los Angeles, is totally computer controlled. When a "shoot 'em up" computer game is accidentally installed into its memory, the master computer for the building thinks it's playing the game. And for it to win, it has to kill everyone in the building. The computer as serial killer.

Long, Jeff

The Descent. Crown, 1997.

Vast tunnels are discovered beneath the surface of the earth—tunnels that have been inhabited for thousands of years by cruel creatures resembling legendary demons and gargoyles. A scientific expedition is sent underground on a seemingly one-way mission to discover the secrets of Hell.

MacLean, Alistair

Bear Island. Doubleday, 1971.

One by one a small band of researchers at a remote Arctic base are being killed.

Pearson, Ridley

The Seizing of Yankee Green Mall. St. Martin's, 1987.

Preston, Douglas, and Lincoln Child

Natural History series

Relic. Forge, 1995.

Something nasty has come back from an archeological dig in the Amazon Basin, and now it's loose in the dark halls and corridors of the New York Museum of Natural History. Don't stay late—it gets hungry at night.

Reliquary. Forge, 1997.

Last seen stalking the shadows in the dark recesses of the New York Museum of Natural History and thought to be dead, it's back—this time prowling for prey in the bowels of the New York subway system.

Riptide. Warner, 1998.

In the seventeenth century, the ruthless pirate Edward Ockham kidnapped the renowned architect Sir William MaCallan and forced him to design a structure in which to hide and protect "Red Ned's" legendary treasure—the Money Pit. Now more than three hundred years later, the Pit is still keeping its deadly secret, still killing everyone who tries to decipher the mystery of its inner workings. Dr. Malin Hatch, owner of Ragged Island, which is not only where the Money Pit is located but where his brother died twenty-five years earlier, is approached by Captain Gerard Neidelman to allow a new treasure-hunting expedition using the latest in underwater technology. Will the Money Pit yield its riches so easily, or will it once again claim the ultimate sacrifice from those who would trespass?

Rollins, James

Amazonia. William Morrow, 2002.

Nathan Rand leads a team of scientists and U.S. Army Rangers on a mission deep into the rainforest of the Amazon where they face terrifying perils and deadly traps.

Scortia, Thomas N.

Blowout. Watts, 1987.

A new transit tunnel between Chicago and New York collapses.

Scortia, Thomas N., and Frank M. Robinson

Glass Inferno. Doubleday, 1974. **FILM**

The movie *Towering Inferno* was based both on this book and Richard Martin Stern's *Tower* (see next entry).

Stern, Richard Martin

Tower. McKay, 1973. **FILM**

The movie *Towering Inferno* was based both on this book and Thomas N. Scortia's *Glass Inferno* (see previous entry).

Sullivan, Mark T.

Labyrinth. Atria, 2002.

Cave researcher and marine biologist Whitney Burke has had an overwhelming fear of caves since her assistant died in a tragic accident. But to save her husband and daughter, whom terrorists have taken hostage and held in Labyrinth Cave, she must now overcome her fear.

Wager, Walter

Tunnel. Forge, 2000.

Criminal mastermind Gunther is planning the biggest heist of his life, but he needs a major diversion so he will be free to pull it off. He blocks off the Lincoln Tunnel at both ends, trapping thousands of people.

Glowing in the Dark: Nuclear Disasters

In this section are titles with plots that concern life after a nuclear war or holocaust or the use of nuclear weapons that have in some way had a negative impact on the environment. Many of these have a science fiction slant and may appeal to readers of that genre.

Bagley, Michael
The Plutonium Factor. Allison, 1982.

Barnes, John
Mother of Storms. Forge, 1994.
A nuclear accident at the Arctic icecap in 2028 results in massive global warming and the creation of a gigantic hurricane in the middle of the Pacific Ocean. The hurricane is thousands of miles in diameter, with supersonic winds, a destructive path that cannot be predicted, and a potential death toll in the tens of millions.

Bell, Madison Smartt
Waiting for the End of the World. Ticknor, 1985.

Block, Thomas H.
Airship Nine. Putnam, 1984.
A U.S. space station accidentally launches forty-eight nuclear missiles at the Soviet Union; the Russians (justifiably) retaliate with nuclear strike of their own. Surviving the attack are *Airship Nine,* a state-of-the-art American dirigible flying over the Antarctic; and the Soviet ship *Primorye,* anchored in an Antarctic harbor. In an irradiated world, two sworn enemies must learn to survive together or die.

Brin, David
The Postman. Bantam, 1985.
After a limited nuclear war, the earth is enshrouded in a nuclear winter, and an itinerant storyteller, wearing the coat and carrying the bag of a dead postman, brings hope to a devastated United States. Do not judge this book by the movie!

Davis, Robert Charles
The Plutonium Murders. Horizon, 1997.
Internist Dr. Alex Seacourt bumps into a man on a New York street and unwittingly becomes poisoned. He then races around the world for the antidote and to stop a conspiracy that threatens the world with plutonium poisoning. The climactic final scene occurs on top of Hoover Dam.

Du Brul, Jack B.
Vulcan's Forge. Forge, 1998.
Planning a vacation getaway to Hawaii? You might want to put it off for a while—at least until that manmade volcano in the Pacific Ocean has finished erupting. Aloha. But wait—racing to the rescue is Philip Mercer: geologist, adventurer, former commando, and all-around hero. (More titles featuring Philip Mercer can be found in Chapter 4.)

Frank, Pat

Alas, Babylon. Lippincott, 1959.

A classic novel of apocalyptic disaster. The residents of Fort Repose, Florida, struggle to survive after nuclear holocaust has devastated the earth.

Gannett, Lewis

Magazine Beach. HarperPrism, 1996.

Ready for a vacation in Hell? Grace and Brian Trefethen, wins who put the "D" in dysfunctional, will be your tour guides. Nuclear bombs will soon detonate under the Antarctic icecap, so the only way to visit the Statue of Liberty will be by submarine . . .

MacLean, Alistair

Goodbye California. Doubleday, 1978.

A mysterious terrorist known only as Morro has gotten his crazed hands on some nuclear devices—devices powerful enough to create an earthquake that will submerge off California into the Pacific Ocean. Only the investigative skills of Detective Sergeant John Ryder, whose wife Susan has been taken hostage by Morro's gang, can stop the disaster that's about to happen.

Powlik, James

Meltdown. Delacorte, 2000.

Biologist Carol Harmon and her ex-husband oceanographer Brock Garner are faced with a mysterious and deadly radioactive plague that is having a terrifying effect on all life in the Arctic.

Reeves-Stevens, Judith, and Garfield Reeves-Stevens

Icefire. Pocket, 1998.

The Ross Ice Shelf in Antarctica: more than 3,000 feet thick and the size of France. Eight nuclear warheads buried in the ice detonate, sending the shelf into the Pacific Ocean and creating a tidal wave 1,400 feet tall. Soon Nevada will be ocean-front property.

Scortia, Thomas N., and Frank M. Robinson

Prometheus Crisis. Doubleday, 1975.

Shute, Nevil

On the Beach. William Morrow, 1957. FILM

A classic look at nuclear holocaust, fifties-style: "duck and cover" . . .

Short Stories

Franklin, H. Bruce, editor

Countdown to Midnight: Twelve Great Stories about Nuclear War. Daw, 1984.

"Is there a doctor in the house?": Biological Disasters

In this section are titles that feature biological disasters on a broad, worldwide scale. Although similar to the bio-thrillers in Chapter 8, these novels are on a much more epic scale with the death toll from disease in the millions and the end of civilization imminent. The disease can be either a natural one, one that has mutated, or one created by scientists through genetic engineering. The diseases always have horrific side effects and usually end in a messy death.

Anderson Kevin J., and Doug Beason

Ill Wind. Forge, 1995.

> A supertanker capsizes off the coast of California, producing the largest oil spill in history. Trying to avert an ecological disaster, the oil company involved uses an untried virus designed to digest petroleum on the spill. It works, but it doesn't die out as planned and is carried across the country on the wind, destroying all petroleum products. Not only are oil and gasoline obliterated, but so is the very fabric of our modern civilization: plastic.

Beller, Isi

Sacred Fire. Arcade, 1990.

> Spermatic fever, a mutant strain of HIV, attaches itself to DNA molecules in sperm cells, which threatens to destroy the population of the United States. The only solution? Outlaw male sexuality. Men have devices implanted in their brains to shut down their sex drive, babies are born in artificial wombs, the FBI is transformed into the FBBS (Federal Bureau of Biological Supervision), and terrorist groups such as RUT (aka Women for a Return to the Uterus) stalk the land.

Bosse, Malcolm J.

Mister Touch. Ticknor, 1991.

Canning, Victor

The Doomsday Carrier. William Morrow, 1977.

Freemantle, Brian

Ice Age. Severn, 2002.

> It starts at a remote Antarctic research base where all the personnel have been killed, victims of a mysterious disease that causes rapid aging. Now the end of civilization could be imminent.

Herbert, Frank

White Plague. Putnam, 1982.

> A scientist whose wife is killed by terrorists decides to get revenge by creating a plague that kills only women.

Herzog, Arthur

IQ 83. Simon & Schuster, 1978.

Hogan, Chuck

The Blood Artists. William Morrow, 1998.

"Everything that begins, begins with blood . . ." And blood is the operative word in this tense thriller: a super-virus born in the jungles of the Congo and mutated from exposure to uranium ore causes death by turning the internal organs into slush. Infectious disease experts Drs. Stephen Pearse and Peter Maryk, once close friends and now deadly enemies, must work together to stop the deadly virus, which has spread to the United States—a virus that has a disturbingly familiar face.

Knight, Harry Adam

The Fungus. Franklin, 1989.

A grotesque plague created by a genetically engineered microbe is sweeping England. People are filling the emergency wards covered in mold, fungus, and toadstools. Not only are their bodies affected, but their minds as well, mutating them into evil, murderous monsters.

Lerner, Richard, M.D., and Max Gunther

Epidemic 9. William Morrow, 1980.

Nourse, Alan E.

The Fourth Horseman. Harper, 1983.

Ouellette, Pierre

The Third Pandemic. Pocket, 1996.

The end of the world starts out with a common cold, which soon leads to death. A super-bacteria, highly contagious and supposedly with no known cure, kills 60 percent of the world's population within one year. But one woman, epidemiologist Elaine Wilkes, has a cure—and she is fleeing for her life from a madman.

Slaughter, Frank G.

Plague Ship. Doubleday, 1976.

A hospital ship full of quarantined victims of an ancient plague is set adrift, only to face a hurricane, sharks, and mutiny.

Standiford, Les

Spill. Atlantic, 1991.

The U.S. government, in its infinite wisdom, has sent a tanker truck carrying an extremely virulent strain of hemorrhagic fever through Yellowstone National Park (don't ask why). The truck crashes, of course, into a creek and spills its deadly cargo into the water, infecting everything that comes into contact with it. Before the infected explode into a shower of blood, they want to kill everyone and everything with which they come into contact. Not only people are affected, but also bears, deer, bunnies, chipmunks. . . .

"Nice doggie . . .": Animals Running Amok

In this section are titles that feature ravenous creatures (usually much larger than normal size) that go berserk (usually through some fault of humans) and embark on a feeding frenzy, their favorite food being humans. No creatures are spared—everything from insects to fish to reptiles to mammals can become killing machines.

Alten, Steve

Megalodon series

Meg. Doubleday, 1997.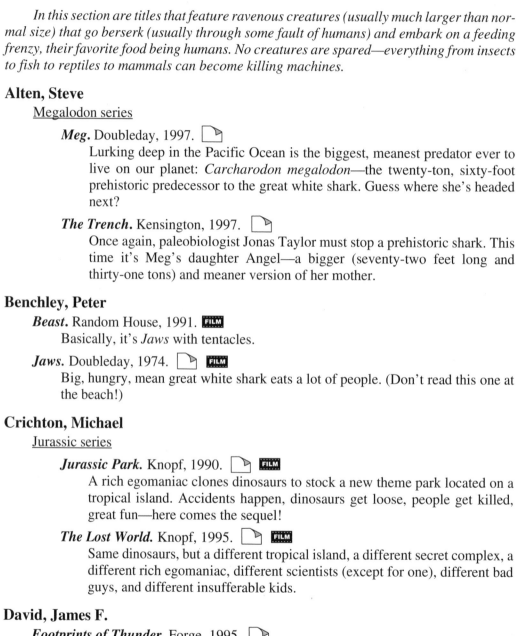

Lurking deep in the Pacific Ocean is the biggest, meanest predator ever to live on our planet: *Carcharodon megalodon*—the twenty-ton, sixty-foot prehistoric predecessor to the great white shark. Guess where she's headed next?

The Trench. Kensington, 1997.

Once again, paleobiologist Jonas Taylor must stop a prehistoric shark. This time it's Meg's daughter Angel—a bigger (seventy-two feet long and thirty-one tons) and meaner version of her mother.

Benchley, Peter

Beast. Random House, 1991. **FILM**

Basically, it's *Jaws* with tentacles.

Jaws. Doubleday, 1974. **FILM**

Big, hungry, mean great white shark eats a lot of people. (Don't read this one at the beach!)

Crichton, Michael

Jurassic series

Jurassic Park. Knopf, 1990. **FILM**

A rich egomaniac clones dinosaurs to stock a new theme park located on a tropical island. Accidents happen, dinosaurs get loose, people get killed, great fun—here comes the sequel!

The Lost World. Knopf, 1995. **FILM**

Same dinosaurs, but a different tropical island, a different secret complex, a different rich egomaniac, different scientists (except for one), different bad guys, and different insufferable kids.

David, James F.

Footprints of Thunder. Forge, 1995.

Suddenly, the boundary between the past and the present can be easily crossed: Portland, Oregon, becomes a tropical jungle where *Tyrannosaurus rex* reigns supreme, a family is shipwrecked onto the back of a brontosaurus that is being attacked by killer whales, pterodactyls swoop down and carry small children back to their nests, and looters fight dinosaurs in the Bronx.

Dvorkin, David

Ursus. Watts, 1989.

    No friendly Smokey the Bear here . . .

Elze, Winifred

Here, Kitty, Kitty. St. Martin's, 1996.

    Saber-toothed tigers and other prehistoric animals terrorize a small community.

Eulo, Ken, and Joe Mauck

Claw. Simon & Schuster, 1994.

    Rajah, a seven-hundred-pound, four-foot-tall Siberian tiger, escapes from the Los Angeles Zoo and embarks on a killing spree. Young and beautiful veterinarian Dr. Meg Foster tries to stop the bloodthirsty animal before he can kill again.

Garrison, Paul

Sea Hunter. William Morrow, 2003.

    The villainous Bill Tree has created giant killer dolphins and plans to unleash them on an unsuspecting world.

Godey, John

Snake. Putnam, 1978.

Herzog, Arthur

The Swarm. Simon & Schuster, 1974.

Levy, Edward

Came a Spider. Arbor, 1978.

Maryk, Michael

Deathbite. McNeel, 1979. **FILM**

    A giant snake is discovered on a remote island and brought to the United States for research, but it soon escapes and starts killing people.

Pellegrino, Charles

Dust. Avon, 1998.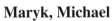

    What if the events that caused the dinosaurs' extinction happened again, this time affecting us? Slowly, silently, the earth's ecology starts to change and soon begins to have a deadly effect on humanity. Usually shy vampire bats attack villages, normally harmless mites strip to the bone cities full of people, bees and other insects destroy everything in sight—is this our final destiny? (Pellegrino's theory of dinosaur cloning [using blood from ancient mosquitoes preserved in amber], published in a 1985 *Omni* article, was used as the scientific foundation for Michael Crichton's *Jurassic Park*.)

Rovin, Jeff

Fatalis. St. Martin's, 2000.

    Defrosted saber-toothed tigers from the last ice age roam California eating whomever gets in their way.

Vespers. St. Martin's, 1998.

> Detective Robert Gentry of the NYPD Accident Investigation Squad and Bronx Zoo bat expert Dr. Nancy Joyce are called in to investigate a strange bat attack during a Little League game. The attacks quickly escalate as a young woman is found gutted in Grand Central Station, and several homeless people are killed in the subway. Soon New York is a city under siege. As the body count skyrockets, Dr. Joyce and Detective Gentry frantically attempt to discover the shocking secret behind the attacks. This exciting "Giant Bats Take Manhattan" yarn culminates in a gruesome midnight bloodfest at the Statue of Liberty. (Rovin is reportedly the ghostwriter for Tom Clancy's Op-Center paperback novels.)

Smith, Martin Cruz

Nightwing. Hill, 1977. **FILM**

> These vicious killers come by night and leave no tracks. Thousand of vampire bats carrying a deadly plague fly out of the deserts of the American Southwest to hunt for human blood.

"It came from outer space!": Disasters from Out of This World

This section features titles in which the disaster if caused by something that has come from space—asteroids, meteors, comets, or supernovas. Many of these have a science fiction slant and may appeal to readers of that genre.

Baxter, John

The Hermes Fall. Simon & Schuster, 1978.

> An asteroid is about to collide into the Western Hemisphere. NASA has only eighty-two hours to come up with a plan to avert disaster.

Baxter, Stephan

Moonseed. HarperPrism, 1998.

> It started the night the planet Venus exploded, bombarding the earth with radiation. The protective ozone layer was destroyed, crops and ocean life died, survivors must wear protective suits to venture outside. But then something worse happens . . .

Florman, Samuel C.

The Aftermath: A Novel of Survival. St. Martin's, 2001.

> In 2009, a comet crashes into the earth on Christmas Day, obliterating most of the population. A cruise ship full of scientists and 25,000 South African survivors must start civilization anew.

McDevitt, Jack

Moonfall. HarperCollins, 1998.

> It is the year 2024. The United States is preparing for the grand opening of its exciting new moonbase with Vice President Charlie Haskell officiating.

Unfortunately, the festivities are short-lived as astronomers discover Comet Tomiko heading straight for the moon. With just five days to evacuate the base, Vice President Haskell, in an ill-conceived public relations ploy, vows that he "will lock the door and turn off the lights." But evacuation is only the beginning of Haskell's worries—the destruction of the moon will cause killer storms, earthquakes, and tidal waves on the earth. How can one brave, but not very experienced, hero stop an event that could cause the extinction of mankind?

Niven, Larry, and Jerry Pournelle

Lucifer's Hammer. Fawcett, 1977.

A gigantic comet, Lucifer's Hammer, slams into the earth, creating a new ice age.

Preston, Douglas, and Lincoln Child

The Ice Limit. Warner, 2000.

A mysterious meteorite is discovered on a desolate island off the coast of Chile, near the frigid waters of Antarctica. Billionaire collector Palmer Lloyd decides he must have it for his new museum and is willing to pay anything to possess it. He finances a secret expedition to retrieve the massive rock—an expedition that soon leads to disaster.

Robertson, Pat

The End of the Age. Word, 1995.

A giant meteor crashes into the Pacific Ocean near Southern California. A Christian apocalyptic novel from the host of the *700 Club*.

Sheffield, Charles

Supernova series

Aftermath. Bantam, 1998.

It is 2026, and a supernova in the Alpha Centauri system has wreaked vast destruction on the earth, causing devastating weather fluctuations and killing millions with disease and famine. Adding to the horrors, gamma rays from the nova fry all the computers across the world, sending civilization back hundreds of years. Standing in the midst of this devastation is one man, U.S. president Saul Steinmetz, who must make a decision so climactic that it will determine the fate of humanity.

Starfire. Bantam, 1999.

The sequel to *Aftermath*. Added to the disaster this time is a serial killer and aliens who do not "come in peace."

"If the earth's a-rockin', don't come 'a-knockin'!": Earthquakes

This section includes titles that feature earthquakes, the most popular of the natural disasters in this subgenre. The earthquakes are always horrendously devastating, leveling huge portions of the United States, killing tens of thousands, and leaving the survivors without food or shelter.

Clarke, Arthur C., and Mike McQuay.

Richter 10. Bantam, 1996.

> Thirty-seven-year-old seismologist Lewis Crane has devised a radical new theory to predict earthquakes—he knows where a Richter 10 quake will hit and even when. Only no one will believe him.

Follett, Ken

The Hammer of Eden. Crown, 1998.

> The frightening terrorist group Hammer of Eden gains control of a method to create earthquakes at will and intends to use it on San Francisco. FBI agent Judy Maddox and seismologist Michael Quercus must stop them before the Golden Gate Bridge is history.

Graham, Winston

Tremor. St. Martin's, 1995.

> The Hotel Saada is an elegant resort hotel on the coast of Morocco with a guest list that includes everyone from a thief to a glamorous movie star. Hotel Saada is also soon to be the epicenter of a devastating earthquake. Think of it as *Grand Hotel . . .* shaken to pieces.

Hernon, Peter

8.4. Putnam, 1997.

> Not as well known as the San Andreas Fault, the New Madrid Fault runs along an area that covers a third of the United States. When an earthquake registering 8.4 on the Richter scale hits the fault, the damage is so great that the Mississippi River actually runs backward. Forensic seismologist Elizabeth Holleran and John Atkins, a geologist with the U.S. Geological Survey, team up to stop more quakes from occurring by creating their own earthquake!

Herzog, Arthur

Earthsound. Simon & Schuster, 1975.

> *Gannon's Adventure/Suspense Rule Number 4: You have a better chance of surviving a disaster if you are evil, insane, or both.*

Laymon, Richard

The Quake. St. Martin's, 1995.

> It finally happens, just as the experts have been predicting: the "big one" hits Los Angeles, and total chaos is the result. The survivors find their thin veneer of

civilization ripped away as they fight each other tooth and nail for the basics of survival.

Scarborough, Chuck

Aftershock. Crown, 1991.

> A massive earthquake hits New York City. A cast of characters including a famous author, a television actress, a Mafia boss, and an ER doctor struggle to cope during the five days after the quake.

Williams, Walter J.

The Rift. HarperPrism, 1997.

> It's 8.9 on the Richter scale—the largest earthquake since 1755 rocks America's heartland. The little town of New Madrid, Missouri, is at the epicenter of a disaster. Dams burst, bridges collapse, cities crumble, thousands die. But the worst is yet to come as those remaining desperately attempt to survive.

Mother Nature's Revenge: Miscellaneous Natural Disasters

In this section are titles that center the action around other types of natural disasters (blizzards, global warming, flooding, radiation). These events are on a grand scale, sometimes worldwide, and always cause massive amounts of death and destruction.

Althof, T. H.

Three Days in November. St. Martin's, 1978.

> A massive blizzard during the Thanksgiving holiday.

Brynner, Rock

The Doomsday Report. William Morrow, 1998.

> Renowned NASA scientist Roger Belacqua predicts that forty years of global warming will result in mass extinction of the human race and that nothing can prevent the irreversible ecological damage. How will humankind react when it finds out it has no future? (The author is the son of late actor Yul Brynner.)

Herzog, Arthur

Heat. Simon & Schuster, 1977.

MacDonald, John D.

Condominium. Lippincott, 1977.

> Hurricane threatens sleazy people in a poorly constructed building.

Moran, Richard

Cold Sea Rising. Arbor, 1986.

> Oceans rise twenty feet and threaten coastal cities.

The Empire of Ice. Forge, 1994.

An undersea volcano near the coast of Ireland erupts, blocking the flow of the North Atlantic Current that brings warmth to the European coast. Soon the English Channel is full of icebergs, and the Irish Sea is frozen solid. Crops fail, heating fuel supplies dwindle, and once-calm citizens panic as the temperature drops and Europe enters a new ice age.

Preuss, Paul

Core. William Morrow, 1993.

Our planet's magnetic field starts to collapse, leaving the earth vulnerable to solar flares and cosmic rays. If the field collapses completely, cancer, birth defects, and eventual sterility will become the fate of the entire population. Two scientific geniuses, the father-and-son team of Cyrus and Leiden Hudder, must bore through to the earth's core to save humankind.

Stern, Richard Martin

Flood. Doubleday, 1979.

Snowbound Six. Doubleday, 1977.

Tsunami! Norton, 1988.

It starts out as wave about a foot high, but it soon reaches a height of several hundred feet, traveling at four hundred miles an hour and destroying everything in its path.

Wildfire. Norton, 1985.

Stone, George

Blizzard. Grosset, 1977.

The snow begins on December 21. Soon the entire northeastern United States is blanketed. What happens if it never stops?

Chapter 3

War Is Hell

Modern Military Fiction

Definition: This subgenre covers military fiction since World War II up through the Vietnam War. Earlier wars are considered historical fiction and are not included here; likewise, military conflicts after the Vietnam War are incorporated in the chapter on technothrillers. The titles included here have military conflict as their theme: the home front, family life, and politics have little or no direct impact on the plot.

The Appeal: The action of these titles always seems to center on the grunt down in the trenches where the reader is able to experience vicariously the "blood, sweat, and tears" of the characters. Although the main allure of this subgenre has to do with its battle sequences and the character of the hero—a common man thrown into uncommon circumstances—setting can also play an important role. Older readers may experience a kind of nostalgia for times gone by, whereas for younger readers these are historical works delineating a time period for which they may have a particular interest.

Brief History: All modern wars have been the subject of fiction, written both during and after the events; some have even become classics, such as Beach's *Run Silent, Run Deep*, MacLean's *The Guns of Navarone,* and Webb's *Fields of Fire*. The huge popularity of the technothriller as well as the prolific output of W. E. B. Griffin (and his many pseudonyms) have helped to raise interest in previous wars, creating a growth in this subgenre.

Advising the Reader: The key elements to remember when advising the reader and suggesting appropriate titles are the following:

- Does the reader have a particular preference concerning the time period or theater of action?

- "I've read all the W. E. B. Griffin books": suggest Alistair MacLean or Mark Berent because their descriptive styles are similar.

- Does the reader prefer land, air, or sea battles? Some readers have a clear preference.

- Technothrillers deal with imaginary or future military conflicts; suggest these to the reader who has read "everything."

- A growing science fiction subgenre is that of military fiction. Suggest this subgenre to readers who may be looking for alternative titles.

- Guide readers to sea adventures. Although these encompass more historical wars, the marine conflicts and military exploits may be of interest.

- Readers who have read "everything" may be interested in nonfiction accounts of battles and military campaigns.

- *You Can Judge a Book by Its Cover:* Soldiers, battleships, and vintage planes figure prominently on the covers of most military fiction.

"War is hell."

—General William Tecumseh Sherman

World War II, 1939–1945

Allington, Maynard
The Fox in the Field. Brassey's, 1994.

Bassett, James
Commander Prince, USN. Simon & Schuster, 1971.
> Eponymous hero takes command of a rust-bucket destroyer stationed off the Philippines.

Beach, Edward L.
Dust on the Beach. Henry Holt, 1972.
> Toward the end of WWII, the USS *Eel* engages the enemy in Japan's Inner Sea.

Run Silent, Run Deep. Henry Holt, 1955. **FILM**
> The classic novel of the men who crewed the submarines in the Pacific.

Boulle, Pierre
The Bridge over the River Kwai. Vanguard, 1954. **FILM**
> Allied prisoners are forced to build a bridge for the Japanese in Burma—and then destroy it.

Boyne, Walter J.
Eagles trilogy

> *Trophy for Eagles.* Crown, 1989.
>> The growth of aviation after the First World War and up to the first rumblings of WWII.

> *Eagles at War.* Crown, 1991.
>> The story of how the United States finally took command of the air during WWII.

Air Force Eagles. Crown, 1992.
> After WWII and during the Korean War, aviation giants Frank Bandfield and Hadley Roget team up with former Tuskegee fighter ace John Marshall to build U.S. air superiority.

Brady, James

Warning of War. Dunne, 2002.
> A detachment of U.S. Marines, stationed in North China at the outbreak of World War II, must march through hostile territory and meet up with their comrades.

Brinkley, William

The Ninety and Nine. Doubleday, 1966.

Buchheim, Lothar Geunther (Translated from German by Lindley Denver)

The Boat. Knopf, 1975. **FILM**
> A novel of submarine warfare told from the German perspective. (The movie version retained the German title: *Das Boot.*)

Callison, Brian

The Judas Ship. Dutton, 1978.

Clagett, John

Papa Tango. Crown, 1982.
> Charles Noble, former commander of the PT 97 sunk by a Japanese destroyer during the Guadalcanal campaign, recounts via flashbacks the war experiences that left him scarred and mutilated. (The author is a graduate of the U.S. Naval Academy and served in WWII aboard a PT boat until he was wounded and retired.)

Collenette, Eric J.

Ninety Feet to the Sun. Walker, 1984.

Deighton, Len

Goodbye Mickey Mouse. Knopf, 1982.

Denny, Robert

Aces. Fine, 1990.
> The heroic tale of the men who flew the U.S. Army Air Corps B-17 bombers from 1942 to 1945 deep into German territory. They battle to survive as the Luftwaffe uses everything in its arsenal against them, including the revolutionary Messerschmidt-262, the world's first operational jet fighter. (The author was a bomber pilot during WWII.)

Night Run. Fine, 1992.
> Forced to bail out of his mortally wounded aircraft behind Russian lines, American pilot Lieutenant Mike Gavin winds up as a volunteer with the Soviet Air Force flying against the Germans.

Dibner, Martin
The Admiral. Cassell, 1967.

Dodson, Kenneth
Away All Boats. Little, Brown, 1954.

Fleming, Thomas
Time and Tide. Simon & Schuster,1987.
> The cruiser USS *Jefferson City* is a beleaguered survivor of the worst naval defeat in American history, the Battle of Savo Island. Now it has a new skipper, Captain Arthur McKay, who must take a dishonored ship and crew and make them whole again.

Forester, C. S.
The Good Shepherd. Little, Brown, 1955.
> Allied destroyers escort a convoy across the North Atlantic.

The Last Nine Days of the Bismarck. Little, Brown, 1958. **FILM**
> Fictionalized account of the destruction of Germany's greatest battleship. (Later reissued as *Sink the Bismarck!* to coincide with the movie.)

Griffin, W. E. B.
Brotherhood of War series

The Lieutenants. Jove, 1982.
> Tank commander Major Robert Bellmon is captured by the Germans in 1943 Tunisia. (The author's name is a pseudonym for William E. Butterworth III.) The next titles in this series can be found in the Korean and Vietnam War sections.

The Corps series

Semper Fi. Jove, 1986.
> Follow the pre-WWII members of the U.S. Marine Corps from the 1930s to 1941.

Call to Arms. Jove, 1987.
> The U.S. Marine Raiders in the South Pacific.

Counterattack. Putnam, 1990.
> From Pearl Harbor to the first counterstrike against the Japanese at Guadalcanal.

Battleground. Putnam, 1991.
> The story of one of the bloodiest battles of the Pacific: Guadalcanal.

Line of Fire. Putnam, 1992.
> Two Marines are trapped on a Pacific island and must wait for rescue as a special team is prepared.

Close Combat. Putnam, 1993.
> A captain and a correspondent are involved in one of the most ferocious air battles of the Pacific theater.

Behind the Lines. Putnam, 1995.
A motley band of marines goes behind enemy lines to check on a self-styled "general" who has set himself up as a guerilla leader to harass the Japanese.

In Danger's Path. Putnam, 1998.
A band of American soldiers and their dependents are on the run from the Japanese in the Gobi Desert of China. The next title in this series can be found in the Korean War section.

Hardy, William M.

USS **Mudskipper.** Dodd, 1967.

Homewood, Harry

Final Harbor. McGraw-Hill, 1980
The adventures of the submarine USS *Mako* and her crew, who fought the Japanese in the Pacific theatre.

O God of Battles. William Morrow, 1983.
Michael O'Connor, the U.S. Navy's most decorated submarine captain, and his younger brother, ace fighter pilot Andrew O'Connor, battle the Japanese above and below the Pacific.

Silent Sea. McGraw-Hill, 1981.

Jones, James

The Thin Red Line. Doubleday, 1962.
The shattering story of Charlie Company as they discover the "thin red line" that separates the living from the dead on Guadalcanal.

Katzenbach, John

Hart's War. Ballantine, 1999.

Mack, William P.

Checkfire! Nautical, 1992.
The USS *Truxton* is an old destroyer converted into an amphibious transport for the Pacific campaign and can barely keep up with the newer, more advanced destroyers, but the resourceful crew keep her and themselves afloat. (The author is a retired vice admiral who served aboard destroyers during WWII.)

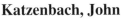

Normandy. Nautical, 1995.
June 1944: Commander Pete Fannon and his crew aboard the destroyer USS *Lawrence* are in the English Channel preparing to support the Allied invasion of France.

Straits of Messina. Nautical, 1994.
It is 1943, and the crew of the destroyer USS *Lawrence* must traverse the Axis-controlled Straits of Messina to land troops.

USS O'Leary series

> ***South to Java.*** Nautical, 1987.
>> The adventures of the rundown destroyer USS *O'Leary,* along with her sui-
>> cidal captain and rowdy crew, come up against the might of the Imperial
>> Japanese Navy.

> ***Pursuit of the Seawolf.*** Nautical, 1991.
>> Fresh from fighting the Japanese, an aging destroyer, the USS *O'Leary,* has
>> been fitted out with new weaponry and assigned to convoy duty in the North
>> Atlantic. Skippered by Captain Jack Meredith, the ship faces an implacable
>> enemy in the German U-boat *Seawolf,* the first of a new class of German
>> submarines.

MacLean, Alistair

Navarone series

> ***The Guns of Navarone.*** Doubleday, 1956. **FILM**
>> The guns of Navarone controlled the approaches to the Mediterranean island
>> of Kheros where twelve hundred British soldiers waited to be evacuated—
>> so the guns had to be silenced.

> ***Force Ten from Navarone.*** Doubleday, 1956. **FILM**
>> The survivors from ***The Guns of Navarone*** are sent to Yugoslavia to rescue
>> partisans.

> ***Partisans.*** Doubleday, 1983.
>> Major Peter Peterson leads a commando raid to free partisans in Yugoslavia.

> ***San Andreas.*** Doubleday, 1985.
>> A Red Cross medical ship, the *San Andreas,* undergoes a mysterious power fail-
>> ure, which cuts the power to the lights identifying her as a medical transport ship.
>> She is then attacked and seriously crippled by German fighters and U-boats. With
>> most of the officers injured, it is up to the boson, Archie McKinnon, to take com-
>> mand and to find the saboteur aboard.

> ***Where Eagles Dare.*** Eagle, 1967. **FILM**
>> An Allied general with top-secret information must be freed from Schloss Adler,
>> high in the German Alps and the headquarters of the Gestapo, before his secrets
>> are tortured out of him.

McCutchan, Philip

Cameron series

> Featuring Donald Cameron of the Royal Navy and his rising career during World
> War II.

> ***Cameron Comes Through.*** St. Martin's, 1980.

> ***Lieutenant Cameron RNVR.*** St. Martin's, 1981.

> ***Cameron's Convoy.*** St. Martin's, 1982.

> ***Cameron in the Gap.*** St. Martin's, 1982.

> ***Orders for Cameron.*** St. Martin's, 1983.

Cameron in Command. St. Martin's, 1983.

Cameron and the Kaiserhof. St. Martin's, 1984.

Cameron's Raid. St. Martin's, 1984.

Cameron's Chase. St. Martin's, 1986.

Cameron's Troop Lift. St. Martin's, 1987.

Cameron's Commitment. St. Martin's, 1989.

Cameron's Crossing. St. Martin's, 1993.

Kemp series

Featuring John Mason Kemp, drafted from his job as a steamship captain to command convoys.

The Convoy Commodore. St. Martin's, 1986.

Convoy North. St. Martin's, 1988.

Convoy South. St. Martin's, 1988.

Convoy East. St. Martin's, 1989.

Convoy of Fear. St. Martin's, 1990.

Convoy Homeward. St. Martin's, 1992.

Mailer, Norman

The Naked and the Dead. Henry Holt, 1948. **FILM**

Monsarrat, Nicholas

The Cruel Sea. Knopf, 1951.

The trials and tribulations of the British corvette *Compass Rose* in the Battle of the North Atlantic.

Nathanson, E. M.

Capt. John Reisman series

The Dirty Dozen. Random House House, 1965. **FILM**

OSS Captain John Reisman recruits military criminal misfits for a secret mission into Germany.

A Dirty Distant War. Viking, 1987.

Reisman is back with some of his misfits—this time on a mission into Southeast Asia against Japan.

Oxford, James

The Night of the Falcon. St. Martin's, 1981.

Pollack, J. C.

Mission M.I.A. Crown, 1982.

Betty Detimore turns to former Green Beret Jack Callahan to free her husband, Frank, and six other prisoners.

Reeman, Douglas

His Majesty's U-Boat. Putnam, 1973.

Lieutenant Commander Steven Marshall of the British Royal Navy is given command of a captured German U-boat used to confuse and torment the enemy in the Mediterranean theatre.

The Iron Pirate. Putnam, 1986.

In the waning days of the war, the German heavy cruiser *Prinz Luitpold,* renowned for her luck in combat, is ordered into the Atlantic. Her captain, Dieter Hechler, must count on that luck to keep them afloat.

A Prayer for the Ship. Putnam, 1958.

The Light Coastal Forces was a branch of the British Royal Navy that consisted of small gunboats manned by amateur sailors who patrolled the Narrow Seas. This is the story of Clive Royce, who rose to leadership among these ships even though he doubted his own abilities.

A Ship Must Die. William Morrow, 1979.

Before the British light cruiser *Andromeda* can be handed over to the Royal Australian Navy, word comes that a powerful German cruiser is raiding shipping in the Indian Ocean and Captain Richard Blake is sent to destroy the German ship.

Strike from the Sea. William Morrow, 1978.

In 1941, Commander Robert Ainslie arrives in Singapore to find and seize control of the largest submarine in the world, the French *Sourfière,* which is now under Nazi control.

To Risks Unknown. Putnam, 1969.

Captain John Crespin, commanding officer of the corvette HMS *Thistle,* is assigned to carry the war deep into the enemy territory of the Adriatic.

Torpedo Run. William Morrow, 1981.

The story of five British torpedo boats, built of fragile plywood and under the command of Lieutenant-Commander John Devane, as they fight against German light naval forces in the Black Sea.

The Volunteers. William Morrow, 1985.

The story of the brave men and women of the Royal Navy's special operations forces and their hazardous assignments against the Nazis.

Rosenbaum, Ray

Wings of War series

Falcons. Lyford, 1993.

Follows the careers of two U.S. Army Air Corps pilots, enemies Ross Colyer and Broderick Templeton III, from Pearl Harbor to the European and Pacific theatres.

Hawks. Lyford, 1994.
> Bomber pilot Ross Colyer is retrained to flying fighters and sent to China to fly a P-51B against the Japanese.

Condors. Lyford, 1995.
> At the end of the war, highly decorated combat pilot Ross Colyer finds that he has a powerful enemy in the U.S. Senate, who has blocked him from getting a regular commission. He then joins an air freight company that is contracted out to the Jewish Relief Foundation and soon finds himself embroiled in the Jewish fight for a homeland.

Shaw, Irwin
The Young Lions. Random House, 1948. **FILM**

Taylor, Theodore
To Kill the Leopard. Harcourt, 1993.
> Merchant marine Sully Jordan squares off against Horst Kammerer, captain of the U-boat that is torpedoing U.S. tankers.

Tillman, Barrett
WWII Flyers series

Dauntless. Bantam, 1992.
> Features what was considered the workhorse of the Pacific War, the ABD-3 Dauntless, a single-engine, two-person dive-bomber.

Hellcats. Brassey's, 1996.

Trew, Antony
Kleber's Convoy. St. Martin's, 1973.
> U-boats against an Allied convoy of thirty-five ships headed for Russia.

Westheimer, David
Von Ryan series

Von Ryan's Express. Doubleday, 1964. **FILM**
> U.S. Army Air Corps colonel Joseph Ryan is shot down and brought to a prison camp in southern Italy where, as the senior officer, he quickly brings military discipline to the unruly bunch, earning the moniker of "Von" Ryan. He then plans an audacious mass escape by train.

Von Ryan's Return. Coward, 1980.
> Colonel Joseph "Von" Ryan returns, this time teaming up with a seductive contessa, to expose a Nazi plot to break the Allied effort in Italy.

Willard, Tom
Wings of Honor. Forge, 1999. **M**
> After the bombing of Pearl Harbor, third-generation military Adrian Samuel Sharp trains to become a Tuskegee airman and joins the all-black 99th Pursuit Squadron—the "Red-Tail Squadron."

Wouk, Herman

The Caine Mutiny. Little, Brown, 1951. **FILM**
> The classic tale of Captain P. F. Queeg and the mutiny aboard the USS *Caine.* Winner of the Pulitzer Prize in 1952.

Korean War, 1950–1953

Brady, James

The Marines of Autumn. St. Martin's, 2000.
> Marine captain Thomas Verity is first assigned to Korea in an advisory role but is soon a part of the disastrous Chosin Reservoir campaign.

Crawford, C. S.

The Four Deuces. Presidio, 1989.
> Based on Crawford's own experiences as a young Marine during the war.

Frank, Pat

Hold Back the Night. Lippincott, 1951.
> The remnants of Dog Company rally against the North Koreans in below freezing temperatures.

Griffin, W. E. B.

Brotherhood of War series
> The saga continues from World War II (see annotation in previous section) and then continues to the Vietnam War (featured in the following section).

The Captains. Jove, 1982.
> A tough crew of U.S. Army officers confront the life- and career-threatening dangers of the Korean War.

The Corps series
> The saga continues from World War II (see annotations in previous sections).

Retreat, Hell. Putnam, 2004.
> In 1950, the marines have had a success in Inchon but then must face the might of the Chinese.

Hickey, James Richard

Chrysanthemum in the Snow. Crown, 1990.
> The account of a rifle company's tour of duty as they fight for survival in Korea.

Michener, James

The Bridges of Toko-Ri. Random House, 1953. **FILM**
> The story of the men if a naval task force assigned to keep the heavily guarded bridges of Toko-Ri out of commission to stop supplies from reaching communist front lines.

Simmons, Edwin Howard

Dog Company Six. Naval Institute, 2000.

> Captain George Bayard, a reserve officer called back to active duty, is the commanding officer of the marine rifle Company D. He must lead his men ashore at Inchon and then through the battles of Seoul and the Chosin Reservoir. (The author is a retired brigadier general who served during the Korean War.)

Vietnam War, 1961–1975

Berent, Mark

Air Force saga

Rolling Thunder. Putnam, 1989.

> The lives and fates of three men, USAF captain Court Bannister, special forces colonel Wolf Lochert, and USAF first lieutenant Toby Parker, as they fight in and above the jungles of Vietnam.

Steel Tiger. Putnam, 1990.

> It is five months after the end of *Rolling Thunder,* and the characters introduced in that novel are now starting their second tour of duty.

Phantom Leader. Putnam, 1991.

> It is January 1968, and the Tet Offensive is imminent—Berent's memorable characters face the Viet Cong everywhere.

Eagle Station. Putnam, 1992.

> USAF major Court Bannister and special forces colonel Wolf Lochert, assigned the defense of Eagle Station, find themselves facing treachery.

Storm Flight. Putnam, 1993.

> Familiar characters from Berent's previous novels are back as they attempt an audacious raid to free prisoners from the Son Tay camp.

Carroll, Gerry

Boyle and Santy series

North SAR. Pocket, 1991.

> The adventures of the U.S. Navy's attack bomber pilot Lt. Mike Santy and his buddy, helicopter pilot Lt. Tim Boyle, flying combat search and rescue missions.

No Place to Hide. Pocket, 1995.

> It is April 1975, and helicopter pilot Lieutenant Tim Boyle, along with A-7 Corsair pilot Mike Santy, is working to evacuate the last American personnel from Saigon when things go awry.

Ghostrider One. Pocket 1993.
Commander Jim "Hog" Hogan is assigned to the aircraft carrier USS *Shiloh* to be in charge of a demoralized A-4 Skyhawk attack squadron. He must gain their confidence before they embark on a dangerous mission.

Coonts, Stephen
Intruder series

Flight of the Intruder. Naval Institute, 1986. FILM
Naval pilots flying A-6 intruders in the skies over Vietnam. The author flew A-6 Intruders in the Vietnam War and later served as a flight instructor.

The Intruders. Pocket, 1994.
The United States has withdrawn from Vietnam, but Lieutenant Jake Grafton finds no rest—he is assigned to teach Marines how to fly carrier jets aboard the USS *Columbia*.

Del Vecchio, John M.
The 13th Valley. Bantam, 1982.
Travails of an infantry unit in 1970.

Deutermann, P. T.
The Edge of Honor. St. Martin's, 1994.
Lt. Brian Holcomb is given a new assignment as the weapons officer aboard the USS *John Bell* and soon finds that the ship has problems that make it vulnerable to attack, but the inscrutable captain of the ship decides not to deal with them. Should Holcomb also ignore the problems and risk his life, or push for changes and damage his career?

Griffin, W. E. B.
Brotherhood of War series
The series continues from the World War II and the Korean Wars (see annotations in the previous sections).

The Majors. Jove, 1983.
A group of American soldiers assists the French in fighting Ho Chi Minh's guerrilla forces.

The Colonels. Jove, 1983.
Paul T. Hanrahan returns from Vietnam, is made a colonel, and is assigned to command the U.S. Army Special Warfare School.

The Berets. Jove, 1985.
An elite group of American soldiers are sent to fight in Vietnam.

The Generals. Jove, 1986.
Army officers prepare their soldiers for a new kind of war in Vietnam.

The New Breed. Putnam, 1987.
This does not take place in the Vietnam theatre, but continues the series as the U.S. military becomes involved in the Congo Rebellion of 1964.

The Aviators. Putnam, 1988.
> In 1964, there are problems associated with creation of the new Air Assault Division in Vietnam.

Special Ops. Putnam, 2001.
> This does not take place in the Vietnam theatre, but continues the series as the Green Berets stop Che Guevara from inciting revolution in the Congo and Bolivia in 1964.

Harrison, Marshall

The Delta. Lyford, 1992.

Heath, Layne

Blue Deep. William Morrow, 1993.

CW2. William Morrow, 1990.
> Helicopter pilot Billy Roark, whose every flight mission tempted disaster, was about to fly a mission that would transform him into a hardened soldier. (The author served two tours in Vietnam as a helicopter pilot.)

Kross, Walt

Splash One. Brassey's, 1991.
> Fictionalized account of Operation Bolo told from the point of view of U.S. Air Force Colonel Clint Adams, commander of the 8th Tactical Fighter Wing. (The author flew more than one hundred fighter missions over North Vietnam.)

Leib, Franklin Allen

William Stuart series

The Fire Dream. Presidio, 1989.
> An epic novel with a cast that includes navy lieutenant William Stuart and two marines, the crazed Billy Hunter from Arkansas and the angry Bobby Coles.

Valley of the Shadow. Presidio, 1991.
> Lieutenant William Stuart and SEAL commander Philip Hooper free a comrade from a horrific prisoner-of-war camp in Laos.

Moore, Robin

The Green Berets. Crown, 1965. FILM

Scott, Leonard B.

The Expendables. Ballantine, 1991.
> The story of the 1st Air Cavalry and the gory battle of Ia Drang.

The Hill. Ballantine, 1989.

Stella, Charles

Blue Lightning. Warner, 1990. **M**

> In the air over North Vietnam, two crack pilots clash: Lieutenant Jim Campbell and Major Quac To Quang, known to the Americans as the Gray Ghost.

Webb, James H., Jr.

Army Blue. Crown, 1989.

> Lieutenant Matthew Nelson is being held in a held in a military prison in Saigon awaiting a court-martial for cowardice and desertion. Only his father, a colonel, and his grandfather, a general and WWII hero, can save him from the trumped-up charges and discover the scandal that Matthew's superiors are trying to cover up.

Fields of Fire. Naval Institute, 1978.

> The story of a platoon of young marines fighting in the tropical jungles of Vietnam. The author is a former marine captain and former secretary of the U.S. Navy.

Weber, Joe

Brad Austin series

> *Rules of Engagement*. Lyford, 1991.
>
> > Brad Austin and the naval aviators based on the aircraft carriers of the Seventh Fleet.
>
> *Targets of Opportunity*. Putnam, 1993.
>
> > Brad Austin's secret mission is to fly a captured jet into Vietnamese airspace and shoot down North Vietnamese fighters.

Willard, Tom

The Stone Ponies. Forge, 2000. **M**

> Son of a brigadier general, African American Franklin LeBaron Sharps is a young paratrooper sent to Vietnam in 1965 as a member of the Screaming Eagles, the 101st Airborne Division. He's looking for revenge against the Viet Cong for the death of his brother.

Short Stories

Anderson, David "Doc," editor

Adventures in Hell: Vietnam War Stories by Vietnam Vets. Ritz, 1990.

Coonts, Stephen, editor

Victory. Forge, 2003.

> Contains ten novellas about World War II from such authors as James Cobb, Harold Coyle, David Hagberg, Dean Ing, and Barrett Tillman.

Faulks, Sebastian, and Jorg Hensgen, editors

The Vintage Book of War Fiction. Vintage, 1999.

> Contributing authors include Pat Barker, Ernest Hemingway, Joseph Heller, Alistair MacLean, and Tim O'Brien.

Fenton, Charles A., editor
Best Short Stories of World War II: An American Anthology. Viking, 1957.

Underwood, Lamar, editor
The Greatest War Stories Ever Told. Lyons, 2001.

Contributing authors include Stephen Ambrose, Bruce Catton, Ernie Pyle, and Irwin Shaw.

Chapter 4

Man, Woman, and Machine

Technothrillers

Definition: In a technothriller (technology + thriller), the plot revolves around a military weapons system such as a plane, submarine, naval surface ship, or nuclear bomb. Traditional military fiction is combined here with facets of the science fiction and espionage genres. Technology, action, and pacing take precedence over the characters, who are usually military personnel. The action is of a high and sustained level, and authors often make heavy use of military terms, jargon, and acronyms. Most technothrillers take place in a time period that ranges from just after the Vietnam War until a few years into the future. The ideology is usually of a decidedly conservative bent, with a militarily superior United States always the victor. In a world where the United States is the only remaining superpower, might makes right.

The Appeal: The hero, almost always a man, is a throwback to the heroes of earlier years—he fights for "truth, justice, and the American way" and doesn't have any quirky hang-ups. As in a classic fairy tale, the reader knows there will be a happy ending, with the hero coming out on top. The hero is noble and good, the villain evil and dastardly.

Because the United States has not been involved in a real, prolonged war since Vietnam (as of this writing), the technothriller allows the reader to experience war in a contemporary setting and allows an opportunity to explore the effects of new technologies and their potential. Some readers may prefer certain technologies over others. For example, the submarine offers a particularly dramatic setting, where military personnel are more or less trapped in a pod underwater.

With these books the reader also feels as if he or she is an insider to military secrets because many of the authors do extensive research. *Kirkus Reviews* (September 15, 1993) commented that Clancy has an "almost erotic admiration for technology." As the United States comes under increasing criticism by other countries and international groups, the technothiller gives the American reader a chance to revel in patriotic fervor. The terrorist attacks of September 11, 2001, and the resultant uncertainty about national security have also created a renewed interest in these novels.

Brief History: Tom Clancy can be said to be the "Father of the Technothriller." His novel *The Hunt for Red October* (1984) is considered the first true example of the subgenre. British author Craig Thomas's earlier work, *Firefox* (1977), features the U.S. theft of a Soviet fighter jet controlled by its pilot's mental commands. The main character, Mitchell Gant, is such an emotional and mental wreck (except as a pilot), however, that he hardly exudes the classic heroic spirit of Clancy's protagonists. Larry Bond, who collaborated with Clancy on *Red Storm Rising,* has become a prolific author in the technothriller pantheon, along with Dale Brown, Stephen Coonts, and Harold Coyle. Because the Iron Curtain has disintegrated and the Soviet Union is no longer a military threat, authors have found new enemies to fight, including South American drug lords, Middle Eastern terrorists, an increasingly militant Communist China, and assorted Eastern European rogue states.

Advising the Reader: The key elements to remember when advising the reader and suggesting appropriate titles are the following:

- "I've read all the Tom Clancy books!" Direct the reader to the various paperback series Clancy has created (e.g., Op-Center, Net Force, or Power Plays).

- Does the reader prefer a particular weapons system? Some readers prefer naval adventure as opposed to action that takes place in the skies.

- If a reader has enjoyed a book by a particular author, check to see if the author has written more titles. Many prolific technothriller authors often carry over characters into other books.

- What type of antagonist does the reader enjoy? The old Soviet Union, terrorists, and China are all popular villains in the technothriller. Many of these can be found as subjects of their own subgenre and are discussed in other chapters.

- Does the reader enjoy military fiction? Many technothrillers use the premise of an imaginary war to unleash the full potential of the weapons. Conversely, think of suggesting general military fiction to the technothriller fan who has read "everything."

- The reader may like the spy element of this subgenre and be interested in other espionage books.

- Science fiction readers who enjoy the battles and advanced weaponry of the "space opera" might be a good audience for technothrillers, especially those that take place in the near future.

- *You Can Judge a Book by Its Cover:* Many technothrillers have weapons prominently displayed on the jacket cover, such as a fighter jet, a submarine, a tank, or an aircraft carrier.

  ⬦ = submarine(s)

  ✈ = plane(s)

You can't say that civilizations don't advance . . .
in every war they kill you in a new way.

—Will Rogers

Alten, Steve

Goliath. Forge, 2002.

In 1998, a Department of Defense secret project, code-named *Goliath,* is sabotaged—and the research stolen. Its aim was to build a nuclear powered submarine with a biochemical brain. Ten years later, a lone manta ray–shaped sub attacks the U.S. Navy's most powerful aircraft carrier, the USS *Ronald Reagan,* sending the supercarrier and all her escort ships to the bottom of the Atlantic Ocean. It's the *Goliath,* armed with nuclear weapons and under the control of a DNA-based computer named Sorceress that is determined to destroy humanity and recreate it in her own image.

Anderson, Kevin J., and Doug Beason

Ignition. Forge, 1997.

Terrorists are in control of Space Shuttle Launch Control at Cape Canaveral and are threatening to blow up the shuttle *Atlantis* unless their demands are met. The only one who can stop them is Colonel "Iceberg" Friese—only he knows the *real* danger . . .

Antal, John

Proud Legions: A Novel of America's Next War. Presidio, 1999.

North Korea invades South Korea intent on a quick victory before major problems occur on the home front. The action concentrates on ground combat. (The author, a lieutenant colonel, formerly commanded the U.S. Army's major armored units in Korea.)

Ballard, Robert, and Tony Chiu

Bright Shark. Delacorte, 1992.

A submarine that vanished twenty years ago is discovered two and a half miles beneath the surface of the Mediterranean. It disappeared with a top-secret cargo that could change the balance of power in the Middle East. It falls to navy lieutenant Edna J. Haddix and government troubleshooter Wendell Trent to retrieve the cargo before it falls into enemy hands.

Bond, Larry

Cauldron. Warner, 1993.

Europe once again becomes a battlefield, this time with new high-tech weapons, as France and Germany square off against the U.S. and Britain.

Red Phoenix. Warner, 1989.

A second Korean War erupts. The United States must intervene before it spreads to the entire Pacific Rim, but the Communist bloc also becomes involved.

Vortex. Warner, 1991.

South Africa is seized by right-wing militants. Soon their imperialistic designs are put into practice, and Africa is plunged into a war that sees the use of both chemical and tactical nuclear weapons.

Brown, Dale

Chains of Command. Putnam, 1993.

This novel features an incompetent Democratic U.S. president from the South and his ruthless, domineering wife (the Steel Magnolia) in a global situation in which Russia and the Ukraine are at war.

Ian Hardcastle series

Hammerheads. Fine, 1990. ✈ ⬜

Using tilt-rotor V-22C Sea Lions based on large offshore platforms, the United States fights powerful South American drug lords.

Storming Heaven. Putnam, 1994. ⬜

Terrorist Henri Cazaux is buying old airliners, modifying them to carry bombs, and then bombing airports across the United States. Working to stop him before he reaches his ultimate target of Washington, D.C., is Rear Admiral Ian Hardcastle.

Patrick McClanahan series

Flight of the Old Dog. Fine, 1987. ✈ ⬜

The Soviet Union has perfected a super-laser that can reach targets around the world. The only chance to destroy it is with *Old Dog Zero One,* a veteran aircraft that has had its antiquated weapons removed and replaced with experimental armaments and stealth hardware. (Brown is a former U.S. Air Force captain.)

Day of the Cheetah. Fine, 1989. ✈

The U.S. Air Force begins the operational testing phase of its newest fighter, code-named *Dreamstar,* a craft that responds directly to the pilot's thought commands. Then it's hijacked by a KGB mole.

Sky Masters. Putnam, 1991.

Lt. Colonel McClanahan is given one more chance to redeem himself. B-52s, B-1s, and B-2 stealth bombers versus the imperialistic actions of the Communist Chinese.

Night of the Hawk. Putnam, 1992. ⬜

The United States intervenes in a war between Belarus and Lithuania, using the super-helicopters of *Hammerheads.* The gang from *Flight of the Old Dog* has to rescue a compatriot who has been brainwashed into believing he's a Soviet engineer so that he will design a Stealth bomber for them.

Shadows of Steel. Putnam, 1996. ⬜

To deal with a newly nuclear and saber-rattling Iran, the United States deploys a CIA group code-named Future Flight and a B-2 Spirit stealth bomber to find and destroy Iran's key military and industrial centers.

The Tin Man. Bantam, 1998. ⬜

Patrick McLanahan, aerial combat expert and hero, returns as a vigilante in this flag-waving, testosterone-packed technothriller. McLanahan's brother Paul, a rookie Sacramento cop, is seriously wounded his first day on the job by paramilitary crooks. Led by the savagely suave Gregory Townsend, international terrorist turned drug lord, the criminals are collecting a fortune through various nefarious means to finance an ingenious and dia-bolical act of terrorism. Unable to stand idly by while the blunder-ing police force and the blustering politicos do nothing to stop Townsend, McLanahan takes charge. Wearing a carbon-filament suit of body armor that is impervious to bullets and gives him super-human strength, the *Tin Man* starts taking names and kicking criminal butt.

Battle Born. Bantam, 1999.
McClanahan must stop the world's newest nuclear power, United Korea, from starting a war with China.

Warrior Class. Putnam, 2001.
Patrick McLanahan is back, and, against the wishes of the U.S. pres-ident, he intends to stop the Russians from building an oil pipeline through the Balkans and creating a new empire.

Wings of Fire. Putnam, 2002.
Air force general Patrick McClanahan and his team come to the as-sistance of the widow of the assassinated Egyptian president, Susan Salaam. She vows vengeance on the new Libyan president who was behind the murder and wants to destabilize the Egyptian govern-ment.

Air Battle Force. William Morrow, 2003.
Major General McClanahan commands the First Air Battle Force, a top-secret experimental U.S. Air Force unit that must stop a high Russian government official from starting a war between the United States and Russia.

Silver Tower. Fine, 1988.
A weapons platform in space.

Brown, Dan

Deception Point. Pocket, 2001.
NASA discovers a huge meteor imbedded in the Arctic ice and sends a team to investigate—a team targeted by a secret death squad.

Buff, Joe

Jeffrey Fuller/USS *Challenger* series

Deep Sound Channel. Bantam, 2000.
In 2011, Germany and South Africa have formed an alliance and built a bioweapons lab to create deadly new pathogens. The United States sends the submarine USS *Challenger* on a mission to destroy the lab.

Thunder in the Deep. Bantam, 2001.
A new alliance between Germany and South Africa has created a nuclear submarine fleet and blockaded England. The United States joins in the fray by sending its newest ceramic-hulled submarine, the USS *Challenger,* with Lieutenant Commander Jeffrey Fuller at the helm.

Crush Depth. William Morrow, 2002.

South Africa and Germany have joined forces to attack U.S. and European shipping lanes using a state-of-the-art submarine, *Voortrekker,* that commands more firepower than the submarines of any other nation. The only boat that can match the *Voortrekker* is the USS *Challenger,* but she is in drydock for repairs. Captain Jeffrey Fuller has forty-eight hours to get her seaworthy and ready to confront the *Voortrekker.*

Tidal Rip. William Morrow, 2003.

It's 2012 and the Berlin-Boer Axis is up to its dirty tricks again as Commander Fuller and the crew of the USS *Challenger* must stop the Axis' newest submarine, the SMS *Admiral von Scheer,* from destroying a convoy sailing toward Africa with much-needed supplies.

Butler, Jimmie H.

Red Lightning Black Thunder. Dutton, 1991.

A superpower showdown in space. The United States launches *Defender 1,* an armed defensive satellite, and the Soviet Union responds with its own space weapons.

Carpenter, Scott

Steel Albatross series

The Steel Albatross. Pocket, 1991.

The Soviet Union has created an underwater base, code-named *Operation Oblivion,* that can destroy every computer system in the United States. The *Steel Albatross* is a prototype navy sub; it works like a glider and is undetectable to enemy sonar. Although just barely in the testing stage, it is the United States' best chance to destroy the base. (Author and former astronaut Scott Carpenter flew the second manned orbital mission aboard in 1962.)

Deep Flight. Pocket, 1994.

The crew members of the Steel Albatross are involved in a search for a legendary sword that pits them against a group of right-wing Japanese nationalists.

Carroll, Ward

Punk's War. Naval Institute, 2001.

The exciting story of fighter pilots in the high-tech world of today's U.S. Navy. (The author is a graduate of the U.S. Naval Academy and flew F-14 Tomcats for fifteen years.)

Cassutt, Michael

Missing Man. Forge, 1998.

U.S. astronauts go into orbit to join Russia's Mir space station, only to find danger.

Clancy, Tom

Jack Ryan series

Patriot Games. Putnam, 1987. **FILM**

Years before the incidents in *Hunt for Red October*, Jack Ryan saves the prince and princess of Wales and their infant son from a terrorist attack.

Red Rabbit. Putnam, 2002.

In the early 1980s, on Jack Ryan's first day on the job as a CIA analyst, he is given a copy of an ultimatum from the new pope, John Paul II, to the Polish government: if it did not stop the repression of the nation's populace, he would resign the papacy and return to Poland. The head of the KGB, Yuri Andropov, has also seen the document and vows to silence the pope forever.

Hunt for Red October. Naval Institute, 1984.

The Soviet Union's most powerful submarine, the *Red October,* is planning to defect to the United States, and CIA analyst Jack Ryan must find her and take her to safety before the Soviets destroy the craft.

Cardinal of the Kremlin. Putnam, 1988.

With the help of former U.S. Navy SEAL "Mr." Clark, CIA analyst Jack Ryan must rescue the top U.S. agent in the Kremlin, codenamed the Cardinal, before the agent is betrayed to the KGB.

Clear and Present Danger. Putnam, 1989. **FILM**

John Kelly, aka Mr. Clark, leads aerial raids against drug lords, while Jack Ryan must confront the U.S. president over what he knows is the right course of action.

The Sum of All Fears. Putnam, 1991. **FILM**

Jack Ryan saves the world from nuclear terrorism.

Debt of Honor. Putnam, 1994.

Jack Ryan is the national security advisor and later becomes vice president.

Executive Orders. Putnam, 1996.

Jack Ryan is now president of the United States.

The Bear and the Dragon. Putnam, 2000.

It's problems galore for U.S. president Jack Ryan in this over-the-top plot that involves Russian hoodlums, Internet-addicted CIA agents, evil Chinese officials, and loads of technology.

The Teeth of the Tiger. Putnam, 2003.

Jack Ryan Jr. jumps into the fray as his dad, President Ryan, is getting a bit long in the tooth for the fieldwork. In Jack Jr.'s first outing, he tangles with the dangerous alliance between Islamic terrorists and Columbian drug lords.

John Kelly/Mr. Clark series

Without Remorse. Putnam, 1993.

John Kelly is tapped by the Pentagon to rescue an important group of prisoners from a North Vietnamese POW camp, but Kelly has a mission of his own to complete. Gives some background information and character development on Kelly, who has appeared in some Jack Ryan novels.

Rainbow Six. Putnam, 1998.
Ex-navy SEAL John Kelly (aka Mr. Clark) is the head of an international antiterrorist task force.

Clancy, Tom, and Larry Bond

Red Storm Rising. Putnam, 1986.
The Soviet Union plans to seize the oil in the Persian Gulf, code-named *Red Storm,* and ends up in a shooting match with NATO.

Cobb, James H.

Amanda Lee Garrett series

Choosers of the Slain. Putnam, 1996.
Commander Amanda Lee Garrett and her ship, the untested, stealth-guided missile destroyer USS *Cunningham,* must stop an armed takeover of the Antarctic Peninsula by Argentina. A strong female main character and great military action.

Sea Strike. Putnam, 1997.
Commander Garrett and the USS *Cunningham* are back, this time in the Pacific where they must stop a nuclear confrontation between the People's Republic of China and Taiwan.

Sea Fighter. Putnam, 2000.
In the third in the series featuring Commander Amanda Lee Garrett, she is in command of a United Nations taskforce ordered to stop an African civil war. The new technology at her command includes stealth hovercraft and a huge ocean-faring fortress.

Target Lock. Putnam, 2002.
Commander Amanda Lee Garrett is given the command of a U.S. Navy taskforce with the mission of finding and stopping a modern-day pirate. This villain is a match for her formidable talents: he's incredibly wealthy, is skilled in all types of high-tech skullduggery, and even commands his own powerful private navy.

Coonts, Stephen

Fortunes of War. St. Martin's, 1998.
Using a high-tech stealth jet, Japan invades Russia to get to the rich oil fields of Siberia. The United States sends air force colonel Bob Cassidy and a squadron of fighter jets to try and stop them.

Jake Grafton series

Flight of the Intruder. Naval Institute, 1986.
Starring Lieutenant Jake "Cool Hand" Grafton—naval pilots at war in the skies over Vietnam. (Coonts flew A-6 Intruders in the Vietnam War and later served as a flight instructor.)

Final Flight. Doubleday, 1988.
Lieutenant Jake Grafton is back, now the commander of an air wing on the aircraft carrier USS *United States.* He must thwart a plan by international terrorist Colonel Qazi to steal six nuclear weapons from the carrier.

The Minotaur. Doubleday, 1989.

Jake Grafton is now assigned to the Pentagon, where he is in charge of developing the navy's new top-secret stealth attack jet, the A-12. He soon finds himself in a deadly hunt to find the Minotaur, a Russian agent in the Pentagon.

Under Siege. Pocket, 1990.

Captain Jake Grafton versus Colombian drug lords.

The Red Horseman. Pocket, 1993.

As the Soviet Union crumbles, twenty thousand tactical nuclear weapons are available to the highest bidder. Rear Admiral Jake Grafton's mission is to head to Moscow and ensure that those weapons don't end up in terrorist hands.

The Intruders. Pocket, 1994.

The Vietnam War is over. U.S. Navy lieutenant Jake Grafton is now assigned to the aircraft carrier *Columbia,* where he is teaching marines the finer points of carrier aviation.

Cuba. St. Martin's, 1999.

Jake Grafton, now a rear admiral on an aircraft carrier off the coast of Cuba, can prevent the United States from a disaster that would far surpass that of the Bay of Pigs.

America. St. Martin's, 2001.

The newest state-of-the-art U.S. submarine, USS *America,* has been hijacked and is launching missiles at U.S. cities. Admiral Jake Grafton to the rescue.

Liberty. St. Martin's, 2003.

Grafton must stop a radical Islamic terrorist group from detonating four nuclear warheads in the United States.

Couch, Dick

Silent Descent. Putnam, 1993.

Russia is covertly selling its nuclear weapons to Third World countries in exchange for grain, while also contaminating the Arctic Ocean with radiation. It falls to five navy SEALs to find the evidence.

Coyle, Harold

Against All Enemies. Forge, 2002.

A rebel band of domestic terrorists based in Idaho and known as the Patriots demands freedom from government control and vows to cause death and destruction until their demands are met.

Bright Star. Simon & Schuster, 1990.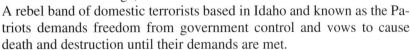

Code of Honor. Simon & Schuster, 1994.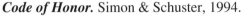

U.S. troops versus drug lords in Colombia, South America. A strong female protagonist in Captain Nancy Kozak.

Dead Hand. Forge, 2001.

An asteroid strikes the Siberian wasteland and activates Dead Hand, a Soviet-era doomsday device. A NATO special operations unit parachutes into Siberia to prevent a global holocaust.

God's Children. Simon & Schuster, 2000.

The 3rd Platoon of C Company, 2nd Battalion, is part of a NATO peacekeeping force in a near future war-torn Slovakia.

Sword Point. Simon & Schuster, 1988.

The Soviet Union invades Iran to stop the spread of Islamic fundamentalism across its borders and to secure the country's rich oilfields.

Team Yankee. Presidio, 1987.

World War III: NATO forces against the Warsaw Pact countries; seen through the eyes of the armored tank forces.

The Ten Thousand. Simon & Schuster, 1993.

When the Ukraine refuses to hand over its stock of nuclear weapons to Russia, the United States sends in troops to enforce compliance. The U.S. troops soon find themselves trying to keep the weapons from falling into the hands of a new right-wing nationalistic Germany.

DeFelice, Jim

Coyote Bird. St. Martin's, 1992. ✈

The *Coyote,* a secret U.S. plane so advanced that nothing can harm it, meets its match in its Japanese twin.

War Breaker. St. Martin's, 1993.

Deutermann, P. T.

Scorpion in the Sea. George Mason, 1992.

The U.S. Navy is denying that something deadly is hunting along Florida's coast.

DiMercurio, Michael

Barracuda: Final Bearing. Fine, 1991. 🖿 **M**

A militant Japan, armed with a massive submarine fleet and fighter jets, must be stopped before it invades the Chinese mainland. (DiMercurio is a former navy lieutenant and served as the chief propulsion officer aboard the USS *Hammerhead.*)

Michael "Patch" Pacino series

Voyage of the Devilfish. Fine, 1992.

Cat and mouse games under the Polar Icecap between advanced American and Russian submarines.

Attack of the Seawolf. Fine, 1993.

The crew of the submarine USS *Tampa* is caught spying on the Chinese and taken prisoner, and it's up to the Captain "Patch" Pacino and the crew of the USS *Seawolf* to rescue them.

Phoenix Sub Zero. Fine, 1994.
The United States faces the United Islamic Front, and the USS *Seawolf* ends up damaged on the bottom of the ocean in a tense rescue situation.

Barracuda: Final Bearing. Fine, 1996.
Admiral Michael Pacino leads a mission to destroy the powerful submarine fleet of a belligerent Japan.

> *Gannon's Adventure/Suspense Rule Number 5: If your country doesn't have any secret weapons, you can always steal one!*

Piranha Firing Point. Dutton, 1999.
Red China has stolen six Japanese submarines to attack the new Free China. The U.S. Navy uses its most advanced submarine, the *SSNX,* in a bid to avert a disastrous war.

Threat Vector. Onyx, 2000.
An international criminal organization has created a super-sub, the *Vepr*, designed to prey on international trade.

Terminal Run. Onyx, 2002.
Former navy admiral Michael Pacino must act to save his son, Anthony, who is trapped in a damaged submarine.

Dinallo, Greg

Purpose of Evasion. St. Martin's, 1990.
The director of the CIA authorizes a secret deal with Libyan dictator Qaddafi to trade two F-111 bombers for seven American hostages. To do this, however, the two F-111 pilots must die. One of them, Major Walter Shepherd, escapes, and to keep him from exposing the shady plot, a team of assassins is dispatched to hunt him down.

Rockets' Red Glare. St. Martin's, 1988.
October 28, 1962: the end of the Cuban Missile Crisis—until 25 years later.

Du Brul, Jack B.

Philip Mercer series

Vulcan's Forge. Forge, 1998.
Planning a vacation getaway to Hawaii? You might want to put it off for awhile, at least until that manmade volcano in the Pacific Ocean has finished erupting. Aloha. But wait—racing to the rescue is Philip Mercer: geologist, adventurer, former commando, and all-around hero.

Charon's Landing. Forge, 1999.
In cahoots with an ex-KGB agent, a renegade Arab oil minister plans to overthrow his own government and make himself head of OPEC. That is until he collides with geologist and action hero Philip Mercer.

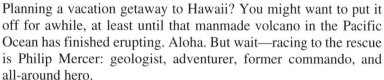

The Medusa Stone. Onyx, 2000.

A group of Middle Eastern terrorists kidnaps Philip Mercer's old friend Harry White in an attempt to force Mercer to find a legendary diamond in the middle of the very dangerous North Eritea.

Pandora's Curse. Onyx, 2001.

This time Mercer's in the Arctic to stop a mercenary's plot to sell a deadly radioactive weapon to the highest bidder.

River of Ruin. Onyx, 2002.

Mercer must stop the Chinese with bombing the Panama Canal with nuclear weapons.

Durham, Guy

Michael Pretorius series

Stealth. Putnam, 1989.

Defense Intelligence Agency officer Michael Pretorius is betrayed by his own people and left to the not-so-tender mercies of the KGB. His mission was to spread misinformation about the next-generation stealth bomber, a flying weapon that will make the current B-2 obsolete, but he is now fighting for his life against multiple opponents.

Extreme Prejudice. Putnam, 1991.

Michael Pretorius on a mission featuring a spy satellite code-named LACROSSE.

Flannery, Sean

Winner Take All. Forge, 1994. 🢀

During a joint Russian-U.S. training exercise off the coast of Brazil, hardline generals who want the return of the Soviet Union use rogue submarines and saboteurs to provoke a nuclear war.

Garrison, Paul

Red Sky at Morning. Avon, 2000. 🢀

A fleet of Chinese submarines attacks Manhattan!

Grant, Pete

Destination 2020 White House. Newmark, 1999. ✈

Kelli Fitzgerald is a U.S. Naval Academy pilot who heads her squadron of strike fighters and eventually becomes a senator, and then a candidate for the presidency.

Hagbert, David

By Dawn's Early Light. Forge, 2003.

Commander Frank Dillon Jr., captain of the *Seawolf*, is assigned the mission of retrieving a captured CIA team—one commanded by the president's own brother, former navy SEAL Scott Hanson.

Harrison, Payne

Black Cipher. Crown, 1994.

Storming Intrepid. Crown, 1989.
> The space shuttle *Intrepid,* carrying top-secret military equipment in its cargo bay, suddenly looses communication with ground control. It has been hijacked by the Soviet Union and must be rescued before its secrets are lost.

Thunder of Erebus. Crown, 1991.
> The United States and the "Soviet Confederation" go head to head in the Antarctic. At stake is a new technology that will give its owner the ultimate weapon.

Harry, Eric L.

Arc Light. Simon & Schuster, 1994.
> Russia plans to launch a nuclear attack on China . . . the U.S. president warns China of the impending attack . . . China launches nuclear missiles at Russia . . . in retaliation, Russia launches nuclear intercontinental ballistic missiles at the United States . . . the U.S. counterattacks . . .

Hawksley, Humphrey, and Simon Holberton

Dragon Strike. St. Martin's, 1997. **M**
> The Chinese military invades the South China Sea to claim its oil deposits and then clashes with Vietnamese and Taiwanese forces. The United States and Great Britain send task forces in an attempt to alleviate the fighting but are quickly drawn into the mounting conflagration. Not even a week into the fighting, U.S. satellites detect Chinese nuclear missiles being readied for launch. (Both authors are members of the media assigned to China.)

Henrick, Richard P.

Attack on the Queen. Avon, 1997. **M**
> The leader of the People's Republic of China will join the U.S. president for a historic meeting in the mid-Atlantic aboard the *Queen Elizabeth II.* A group of ultra-nationalist Chinese terrorists have hijacked a Han-class nuclear submarine and are set to intercept the ocean liner in the North Atlantic. At the same time, more of the terrorists have gotten aboard the *Queen Elizabeth II* and stolen the codes to China's nuclear weapons.

Herman, Richard, Jr.

Firebreak. William Morrow, 1991.
> Iraq develops a deadly nerve gas and the means to deliver it into the heart of Israel. Faced with this threat, the Israeli prime minister's only recourse is the nuclear destruction of Iraq. Desperate to avoid such a scenario, the United States sends in a squadron of F-15 Eagle fighter-bombers.

Iron Gate. Simon & Schuster, 1996.
> AWB, the Afrikaner Resistance Movement, discovers the secret of controlled nuclear fusion and plots to sell it for arms and power. To prevent a

war over gaining the secret information, the United States sends in an air wing of A-10 Warthogs, C-130 Hercules Transports, and CH-53 helicopters.

The Last Phoenix. William Morrow, 2002.

Maddy Turner is the first American woman to become president, and she's about to be tested during war as radical Islamic states ally with China to control the rich oil fields of the Middle East. She turns to Brigiadier General Matt Pontowski, a brilliant military tactician, to command a secret mission that might mean success for the United States.

The Trojan Sea. William Morrow, 2001.

The United States attempts to seize a massive oil lake, bigger than Saudi Arabia, that lies inside the territorial waters of Cuba.

Hewson, David

Solstice. Warner, 1999.

An evil villainess has discovered the secret of harnessing the rays of the sun and creating the ultimate weapon.

Hickam, Homer H., Jr.

Back to the Moon. Delacorte, 1999.

Wealthy engineer and former NASA hotshot Jack Medaris hijacks the space shuttle *Columbia* and forces the crew to take an unscheduled trip to the moon, where dark and deadly secrets from his past lie dormant. (Hickam is a retired NASA engineer whose memoirs, *October Sky,* was made into the movie *Rocket Boys.*)

Hogan, James P.

Endgame Enigma. Bantam, 1987.

The Soviet Union has launched a massive space station, the *Valentina Tereshkova,* into orbit, and it's capable of housing 12,000 people. Suspecting that super-weapons have been placed on the station, the United States sends computer scientist Paula Bryce and government agent Lew McCain on an undercover mission to the *Valentina Tereshkova.*

Huston, James W.

Fallout. William Morrow, 2001.

Terrorists plan on inciting a nuclear war between India and Pakistan after first creating a devastating attack on American soil.

Flash Point. William Morrow, 2000.

After the woman he loves and his best friend are brutally attacked by a terrorist who claims to be part of a nine-hundred-year-old secret society, naval F-14 pilot Sean Woods joins forces with a group of Israeli Air Force pilots to exact revenge.

Jim Dillon series

Balance of Power. William Morrow, 1998.

A cowardly U.S. president submits to terrorists, so Congress employs a loophole in the Constitution to conduct a limited, private war without presidential approval.

The Price of Power. William Morrow, 1999.
> Another little-known Constitutional power, the Rules of Capture, is the springboard to action.

Kent "Rat" Rathman series

Shadows of Power. William Morrow, 2002.
> Kent "Rat" Rathman is a member of the navy's secret counterterrorism team who has been assigned to investigate the death of a famous Blue Angels pilot by terrorists.

Secret Justice. William Morrow, 2003.
> "Rat" Rathman leads his Special Forces team on a daring mission to capture notorious arms dealer Wahamed Duar, who is planning to use radioactive material from abandoned Russian nuclear plants as fuel for a bomb.

Gannon's Adventure/Suspense Rule Number 6: All secret weapons must have cool code names.

Joseph, Mark

To Kill the Potemkin. Fine, 1986.
> In this *Hunt for Red October* read-alike, American subs hunt for the Soviet Union's top-secret submarine with a super-strong hull that allows it to dive deeper than any other.

Typhoon. Simon & Schuster, 1991.
> Submarines under the Arctic ice.

Ing, Dean

Butcher Bird. Forge, 1993.
> The Butcher Bird is a nuclear-powered death machine. It can't be seen or heard, but it will find you . . . and then kill you. (Ing has been both a U.S. Air Force interceptor crew chief and an aerospace designer.)

The Nemesis Mission. Forge, 1991.
> The story of the *Nemesis,* a solar-powered craft that can stay aloft for weeks and fly at any altitude undetected.

The Ransom of Black Stealth One. St. Martin's, 1989.
> It can only go 150 miles per hour, but it is the most dangerous aircraft ever designed—and it's missing.

Kent, Gordon

Alan Craik series

Peacemaker. Putnam, 2001.
> U.S. Navy intelligence officer Alan Craik must save his best friend, a CIA agent who has been kidnapped in Africa, as well as prevent the nation's newest weapon, *Peacemaker,* from falling into enemy hands.

Top Hook. Delacorte, 2002.

> Alan Craik, now commanding an airborne unit about the USS *Thomas Jefferson,* finds his wife, astronaut-in-training Rose Siciliano, under investigation for leaking confidential government secrets.

Hostile Contact. Delacorte, 2003.

> Alan Craik has two jobs: he is a counter-espionage expert who must deal with a Chinese double agent and also the commander of an S-3B submarine hunter off the coast of the Pacific Northwest.

LaManna, Ross

Acid Test. Ballantine, 2001.

> A ruthless military genius who calls himself Batu Khan is creating a modern-day Mongol Empire in Asia, and he has plans for further conquest. Counterintelligence operative and former fighter pilot Matt Wilder discovers Khan's secret plans and must stop him before the whole world is at war.

Marcinko, Richard, and John Weisman

Rogue Warrior® series

Rogue Warrior®: Red Cell. Pocket, 1994.

> The government calls on Marcinko, the author as well as protagonist, to head a counterterrorist unit of SEALs called Red Cell to stop the smuggling of nuclear materials to North Korea.

Rogue Warrior®: Green Team. Pocket, 1995.

> The Rogue Warrior takes on Islamic extremists who plan to use a secret weapon to bring down the West.

Rogue Warrior®: Task Force Blue. Pocket, 1996.

> The Rogue Warrior and his SEAL group must stop terrorists—terrorists who are also fellow American citizens.

Rogue Warrior®: Destination Gold. Pocket, 1997.

> This time the Rogue Warrior is up against the Russian mafia and the corrupt Russian politicians they control.

Rogue Warrior®: SEAL Force Alpha. Pocket, 1998.

> Marcincko and SEAL Force Alpha must stop traitors in the U.S. government from smuggling state-of-the-art weaponry to the Chinese.

Rogue Warrior®: Option Delta. Pocket, 1999.

> The Rogue Warrior and his SEAL team must stop a billionaire defense contractor from using nuclear weapons to bring about Germany's Fourth Reich.

Rogue Warrior®: Echo Platoon. Pocket, 2000.

> It's up to the Rogue Warrior to stop the machinations of the Russians and Iranians who are trying to gain control of the world's oil supply.

Rogue Warrior®: Detachment Bravo. Pocket, 2001.

> The Rogue Warrior and his SEAL unit team up with the British to stop a high-tech army of terrorists financed by the Irish Republican Army.

Rogue Warrior®: Violence of Action. Atria, 2002.
> The Rogue Warrior and an entirely new team of operatives must stop terrorists from using a nuclear bomb hidden in a suitcase to destroy Portland, Oregon. (Long-time collaborator John Weisman is not longer listed as a coauthor in this series installment.)

Mayer, Bob

Dave Riley series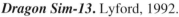

Eyes of the Hammer. Lyford, 1991.
> U.S. Special Forces A-Team is sent to Colombia, South America, to destroy cocaine-processing laboratories.

Dragon Sim-13. Lyford, 1992.
> Dave Riley and his Green Beret A-Team are sent on a secret mission into the heart of Communist China—a mission organized by a rogue computer programmer that could get them all killed.

Synbat. Lyford, 1994.
> SYNBATs (synthetic battle forms), mutated baboons designed to be lethal soldiers, escape from the secret Tennessee laboratory and create deadly havoc, ultimately reaching Chicago. Riley and his A-Team are called in for clean up.

Cut-Out. Lyford, 1995.
> Riley assists a friend who has entered the Witness Protection Program to escape vengeance from former organized crime associates.

Z. Lyford, 1997.
> Retired Green Beret Dave Riley is the only person able to penetrate a South American diamond cartel's heavily guarded headquarters, where the antidote for an Ebola-like plague, code named "Z" is hidden.

Merek, Jack

General Scott Cartwright series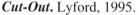

Target Stealth. Warner, 1989.
> Iranian agents have stolen everything but the keys to an STB-1 stealth bomber armed with eight B-83 nuclear bombs ready for flight in a secret California hanger. The only ones stopping them are former astronaut General Scott Cartwright and aviation ace Major Adam Glassman.

Blackbird. Contemporary, 1990.
> General Scott Cartwright sits in the cockpit of an SR-71 Blackbird reconnaissance plane prepared for a dangerous mission from which neither he nor the plane is expected to return.

Mooney, Chris

World without End. Pocket, 2001.

CIA operative Stephen Conway must protect a new secret weapon (a stealth suit) from members of the Russian mafia intent on getting their hands on it at all costs.

Morgan, Douglas

Tiger Cruise. Forge, 2000.

Captain Andrew Warner's ship, the USS *Cushing,* is a destroyer mounting state-of-the-art weaponry, but at the moment it is being used to ferry the crew's family members to Japan. Unfortunately, they are about to tangle with a group of highly organized—and highly dangerous—pirates who plan on capturing a U.S. destroyer.

Mullane, Mike

Red Sky. Northwest, 1993.

A Soviet insider plots to blackmail the West with a secret space-based weapon—Red Sky. The U.S. sends astronauts aboard the space shuttle to destroy the device before it becomes fully operational. (Colonel Mike Mullane is a former NASA space shuttle astronaut.)

O'Brien, Frank J.

Stealth Strike. Tab, 1990. ✈

The Soviets have developed a laser system able to destroy U.S. defense satellites. This weapon must be destroyed—the Soviets are holding the world hostage to their outrageous demands.

Peel, Colin D.

Dark Armada. St. Martin's, 1995.

Peters, Ralph

Red Army. Pocket, 1989.

The Soviet army and its Warsaw Pact allies invade Europe—NATO armies make their last, desperate stand.

The War in 2020. Pocket, 1991.

The United States and a crumbling Soviet Union allied against Japan and South Africa.

Pineiro, R. J.

Firewall. Forge, 2002.

Former CIA agent Bruce Tucker must find the code known as the Ultimate Encryption, which is capable of launching enough nuclear missiles to obliterate humankind, before it falls into the wrong hands.

Siege of Lightning. Berkley, 1993.

The new space shuttle *Lightning* has been sabotaged. Racing against time, the crew members desperately try to land her, but an unseen enemy is determined that her maiden flight will be her last.

Poyer, David

<u>Tales of the Modern Navy series</u>

The Med. St. Martin's, 1988.

Terrorists take a hundred hostages captive from the American Embassy in Cyprus and fly them to a heavily fortified location in Syria. The U.S. 6th Fleet, under fire from hostile aircraft and tracked by Soviet spy ships, mobilizes off the coast of Syria for a rescue mission.

The Gulf. St. Martin's, 1990.

An Iranian missile destroys a U.S. destroyer and the stage is set for conflict in the Persian Gulf.

The Circle. St. Martin's, 1992.

An old WWII-era destroyer, the USS *Ryan,* is sent to the Arctic Circle to test top-secret sonar equipment. The new sonar system picks up a rogue Soviet submarine carrying nuclear weapons.

The Passage. St. Martin's, 1995.

A U.S. attack submarine has been lost on a secret mission off the coast of Siberia. Assigned to the technologically innovative USS *Barrett,* Lieutenant Dan Lenson must find the sub.

Tomahawk. St. Martin's, 1998.

Lieutenant-Commander Dan Lenson is given a top-secret assignment: design and test deadly Tomahawk missiles armed with nuclear warheads. Leaks indicate that there is a spy on the project, and Lenson comes under suspicion—he must find the spy before he is further implicated.

China Sea. St. Martin's, 2000.

Dan Lenson, last seen in *Tomahawk,* has finally been given command of his own ship—unfortunately it is an obsolete frigate soon to be handed over to Pakistan. Lenson finds himself battling Chinese-backed pirates, a mutiny, and a serial killer.

Black Storm. St. Martin's, 2002.

Saddam Hussein issues an ultimatum to the United States: invade Iraq and Israel will become a "crematorium." It's up to marine gunnery sergeant Marcus Gault and his team to enter Iraq, along with Lieutenant-Commander Dan Lenson and biological warfare expert Major Maureen Maddox, find the Iraqi dictator's doomsday weapon, and target it for destruction by U.S. cruise missiles. They have four days to implement Operation Signal Mirror before the ground war begins.

Reeves-Stevens, Judith, and Garfield Reeves-Stevens

Quicksilver. Pocket, 1999.

A team of commandos take control of the Pentagon, and their hostages include not only top military officials of twenty nations, but also the vice president, the first lady, and the joint chiefs of staff. They have also taken control of the nation's most powerful secret weapon: a powerful satellite weapon code-named QUICKSILVER.

Reilly, Matthew J.

Shane "Scarecrow" Schofield series

Ice Station. St. Martin's, 1999. ✈ 🗋

A group of U.S. scientists have made a shocking discovery at a remote base in Antarctica. A team of marines led by Lieutenant Shane "Scarecrow" Schofield is sent to secure the find; however, the team members soon learn that in the new world order, our supposed French and British allies are no longer our friends.

Area 7. St. Martin's, 2001.

A rogue U.S. Air Force general has taken control of the country's most secret military outpost, Area 7, and has also taken the U.S. president hostage. It's up to marine captain Shane M. "Scarecrow" Schofield to save the president and stop the general before he destroys major U.S. cities.

Temple. St. Martin's, 1999. 🗋 FILM

William Race, a professor of linguistics, is recruited by the U.S. Army to decipher an ancient manuscript that could lead to the construction of an awesome new weapon. Unfortunately others want the secret of the manuscript as well, including neo-Nazis, survivalists, and other governments.

Rizzi, Timothy

Duke James series

Nightstalker. Fine, 1992. ✈

1984: the B-2 stealth bomber *Nightstalker* is fully operational and is launched against a secret Soviet radar complex that could be used to prevent any satellite surveillance.

Strike of the Cobra. Fine, 1993.

The Space Shuttle *Atlantis,* carrying a Cold War–era Russian satellite armed with nuclear weapons, is hijacked by Palestinian terrorists. Cobra Team, an elite special operations team of the U.S. Air Force, is called in to rescue the shuttle and its crew.

The Phalanx Dragon. Fine, 1994.

Iran salvages an intact U.S. cruise missile that had gone off course during the Gulf War and uses the advanced technology to upgrade their own weapons. Duke James is sent in to destroy their secret munitions factory before the Iranians stop the flow of oil from the Persian Gulf.

Eagles of Fire. Fine, 1996. ✈

Recurring character Duke James is back, as combat takes to the skies over North and South Korea.

Robinson, Patrick

H.M.S. **Unseen.** HarperCollins, 1999.
> The H.M.S. *Unseen* is the deadliest and quietest submarine ever constructed, and it has just disappeared. One year later, the Concorde, on a routine transatlantic flight, and *Air Force Three,* carrying the U.S. vice president, are shot down—all evidence points to the *Unseen.*

Kilo Class. HarperCollins, 1998.
> Russia is having a sale on its most dangerous underwater weapon, the 240-foot-long Kilo Class submarine. And its willing to sell it to anyone—including terrorists, Third World dictators, and Communist China.

Nimitz Class. HarperCollins, 1997.
> The *Thomas Jefferson* is a Nimitz-class nuclear aircraft carrier—the most powerful and most sophisticated weapons system ever created—and it has just been vaporized in a nuclear explosion. What will be the next target?

The Shark Mutiny. HarperCollins, 2001.
> After years of building a modernized navy, the Chinese decide to make use of it. In a conflict with Iran, they have mined the Strait of Hormuz to cut off the flow of oil. The United States retaliates in a massive display of force—only to find that the mining was merely a diversion.

USS **Seawolf.** HarperCollins, 2000.
> The USS *Seawolf* falls into the hands of the People's Republic of China when it is damaged on a secret reconnaissance mission. Admiral Zhang Yushu imprisons and tortures the crew in an attempt to gain the secrets of the U.S. submarine, and a SEAL team is sent to rescue them.

Baracuda 945. HarperCollins, 2000.
> Major Ray Kerman is a traitor who plans on attacking the United States with a state-of-the-art Russian stealth submarine capable of staying submerged indefinitely where it can fire its nuclear missiles at targets across the globe.

Ruggero, Ed

Mark Isen series

38 North Yankee. Pocket, 1990.
> U.S. Army Captain Mark Isen and Charlie Company fight against the odds as they are deployed in the earliest days of the Second Korean War.

The Common Defense. Pocket, 1992.
> Captain Mark Isen teams up with the U.S. Army's elite counterterrorist unit Delta Force to stop a mastermind German terrorist from using deadly nerve gas against the United States.

Firefall. Pocket, 1994.
> In a coup, the Nazi-like German People's Union takes over Germany and attacks U.S. forces, including Major Mark Isen who is stationed there.

Breaking Ranks. Pocket, 1995.
Isen pursues an investigation into an apparent suicide of a young officer, an investigation that threatens to ruin his career.

Smith, Michael A.
Jeremiah series

Jeremiah: Terrorist Prophet. Forge, 1998.
Jeremiah's agenda is the total collapse of the United States, and he'll use anything he can to reach that goal: television, the Internet, and two nuclear bombs he's smuggled into the country.

New America. Forge, 1999.
Terrorist Jeremiah is back, and lashing out from his separatist state of New America and armed with B1 bombers, nuclear weapons, and a trained army of zealots.

Stewart, Chris

The Kill. Box. Evans, 1998.
Returning from Kuwait, *Air Force One* crashes. The vice president and former president are dead, along with everyone else on board—not from the crash but from a deadly virus. Air force captain Charlie McKay must lead a mission to destroy a biological weapons lab hidden beneath the Iraqi desert before its deadly germs can be dropped on Washington, D.C.

Shattered Bone. Evans, 1997.
According to the Air Force Code Manual 13-12, *shattered bone* means "the theft, hijacking, or unauthorized flight of a B-1B bomber loaded with nuclear weapons . . ."

The Third Consequence. Evans, 2000. ✈
U.S. Air Force pilot Ryan C. Callan is part of a fighter taskforce assigned to protect American oil tankers in the Persian Gulf. He discovers that the people that want to shoot him down are not the Iranians, but fellow Americans.

Thomas, Craig
Mitchell Gant series

Firefox. Henry Holt, 1977. ✈ 🗋 🎞FILM
Mitchell Gant must infiltrate a secret Soviet airbase and steal the *Firefox,* an advanced jet fighter that can be controlled by its pilot's thoughts.

Firefox Down! Bantam, 1983. ✈
The Soviet Union's deadly Mig-31, *Firefox,* has sunk beneath the waters of a frozen lake. The CIA and British Intelligence race to salvage the plane before the Soviets can find it.

Winterhawk. William Morrow, 1987.
Mitchell Gant must rescue a defecting Soviet scientist who has information about a laser satellite that the USSR is about to launch, but to get the scientist out of the Soviet Union, Gant must fly a captured Soviet helicopter out of the country.

Van Tine, Stuart M.

A Fine and Private War. Force, 2002.

The world's most dangerous terrorist, Jinnah, threatens a group of wealthy Westerners to extort enough money from them to buy nuclear weapons on the global black market. He also intends to steal their super state-of-the-art yacht, *Seafire,* to aid him in his schemes. His victims have their own plan, however: enlist the aid of George Holbrook, a test pilot with a military background, and turn the *Seafire* into a modern-day Trojan horse.

Weber, Joe

Dance with the Dragon. Presidio, 2002.

Former CIA operatives and fighter pilots Scott Dalton and Jackie Sullivan are put in charge of an investigation to discover why navy fighter jets are mysteriously blowing up in midflight. They uncover a plot by the Chinese for domination of the Pacific.

DEFCON One. Presidio, 1989.

Defense Readiness Condition: DEFCON

DEFCON FIVE: normal peacetime activities

DEFCON FOUR: increase intelligence watch and increase security

DEFCON THREE: forces on standby, awaiting further orders

DEFCON TWO: forces ready for combat

DEFCON ONE: forces deployed for combat

Shadow Flight. Presidio, 1990.

A B-2 stealth bomber has been hijacked during a special training exercise. All clues lead to Cuba as the destination of the bomber, and CIA agent Steve Wickham is sent to the island to find the B-2 before the president orders an invasion.

West, Owen

Sharkman Six. Simon & Schuster, 2001.

U.S. Marines against armed warlords in Somalia.

White, Robin A.

Angle of Attack. Crown, 1992.

Iraq's Saddam Hussein on the warpath—this time with something far more dangerous than a Scud missile.

The Flight from Winter's Shadow. Crown, 1990.

Project Aurora, a hypersonic, stealth fighter, bomber, and reconnaissance aircraft that is the fastest and deadliest weapon ever created, is caught in a deadly tug-of-war between renegade elements of the U.S. military and a desperate group of Soviet hard-liners. The result could be nuclear disaster.

Sword of Orion. Crown, 1993.

Afghan religious extremists steal a nuclear bomb from Russia and promise to detonate it unless their demands are met. A U.S. Navy nuclear detection crew flying a sophisticated P-3 Orion must find the weapon before it can be activated.

Typhoon. Putnam, 2003.

A cat-and-mouse game under the surface of the Arctic Ocean between the USS *Portland* and the Russian *Typhoon,* the largest submarine ever built.

Woods, Stuart

Deep Lie. Norton, 1986.

CIA analyst Katherine Rule discovers the invasion plans of a renegade Soviet commander of a secret submarine base in the Baltic Sea, but no one will believe her warning.

Short Stories

Coonts, Stephen, editor

Combat. Forge, 2001.

A collection of short stories by Larry Bond, Dale Brown, James Cobb, Stephen Coonts, Harold W. Coyle, David Hagberg, Dean Ing, Ralph Peters, R. J. Pineiro, and Barrett Tillman.

> *Gannon's Adventure/Suspense Rule Number 7: The United States always wins!*

Chapter 5

Order in the Court!

Legal Thrillers

Definition: A suspense novel where the main character is an attorney, a judge, a paralegal, or another member of the legal community. What separates the legal thriller from the legal mystery or courtroom drama is that there is much more action going on beyond simply trying to solve a mystery. Some of the exploits do take place in the courtroom and require brainy courtroom maneuvers, but the protagonist is also fighting against external machinations that could prove deadly for both the attorney and the client. In the legal mystery, the lawyer is solving a case, but the fact that he or she is actually a lawyer has little real bearing on the story—the individual could easily be a private detective or journalist. In the legal thriller, the law (and usually its corruption) is an integral part of the plot.

The Appeal: The public is fascinated with the maneuverings of the legal system, as can be witnessed by all the media attention given to high-profile lawsuits and criminal trials. The fact that many of these thrillers are written by actual lawyers also adds an element of authenticity to them. Mega best-selling novelist and attorney John Grisham has hit the jackpot by tapping into the public's attraction to the prurient underbelly of the judicial process. In series legal thrillers, character can become a secondary appeal because the character and style of the protagonist draws loyal readers.

Brief History: The archetype for the legal mystery can be traced back to the 1896 publication that was the inspiration for Earle Stanley Gardner's Perry Mason series—*The Strange Schemes of Randolph Mason* by Melville D. Post. Perry Mason would become the most famous of all courtroom detectives after he made his debut in 1933 in *The Case of the Velvet Claws*. But the birth of the true legal thriller can be traced to Scott Turow's 1987 seminal work: *Presumed Innocent*. In this novel, the protagonist is not only performing courtroom gymnastics and finding the perpetrator of the crime but is simultaneously undergoing growth as a character while being immersed in action-packed situations.

Advising the Reader: The key elements to remember when advising the reader and suggesting appropriate titles are the following:

- If a reader has enjoyed a book by a particular author, check to see if the author has written more titles. Authors sometimes carry over characters into other books.

- Many actual attorneys write in this subgenre. Does this level of realism and a professional background appeal to the reader?

- The legal elements that are primary to this subgenre can also be found in many of the political thrillers.

- There are nearly as many female protagonists as male in this subgenre. Does the reader have a preference?

- Readers who have exhausted this subgenre may be guided to financial thrillers, which offer similar "real-life" premises, as well as authors who write from their own experiences.

- If the reader has exhausted this subgenre, guide the reader to nonfiction titles about famous trials and lawyers.

- Readers looking for new titles can be introduced to legal mystery series written by such authors as Linda Fairstein, Joe L. Hensley, Michael Kahn, Michael Nava, or Barbara Parker.

- *You Can Judge a Book by Its Cover:* Look for judge's gavels, the columned entrance to a courthouse, running men or women carrying a portfolio or attaché case, the "scales or justice," or a blindfolded statue of "Justice."

There are times when even justice brings harm with it.

—Sophocles

Amiel, Joseph

A Question of Proof. Crown, 1993.

Philadelphia trial attorney Dan Lazar must defend the woman he loves after she is accused of murdering her husband.

Bernhardt, William

Ben Kincaid series

Primary Justice. Ballantine, 1992.

Fresh from the district attorney's office, Ben Kincaid is hired by the prestigious Oklahoma legal firm of Raven, Tucker & Tubb but soon finds his ethics challenged when his desire to do the right thing conflicts with his client's interests. (The author is a defense attorney with a large Tulsa law firm.)

Blind Justice. Ballantine, 1992.

Former corporate lawyer Ben Kincaid has set up his own private practice in the seamier side of town, and it seems like all he defends are reprobates and scoundrels—until a friend is accused of murder.

Deadly Justice. Ballantine, 1993.
> Needing the money, Ben Kincaid takes a job as the counsel for the disreputable Apollo Consortium. He soon finds himself framed for murder and has only one week to clear his name.

Perfect Justice. Ballantine, 1994.
> While vacationing in the Arkansas mountains, Ben Kincaid is caught up in a hate-crime murder that soon leads to even deadlier events.

Cruel Justice. Ballantine, 1996.
> Oklahoma lawyer Ben Kincaid must find the link between a boy abducted by a child molester and a man who has been caught in the legal system for ten years.

Naked Justice. Ballantine, 1997.
> The first black mayor of Tulsa is accused of murdering his wife and two young daughters—the case seems airtight against him as the bloodstained politician was seen leaving the murder site and was on national television as he tried to flee from the police. It's another seeming impossible case for defense lawyer Ben Kincaid.

Extreme Justice. Ballantine, 1998.
> Burned-out criminal attorney Ben Kincaid decides to leave his law career and become a jazz musician—until a corpse comes crashing through the ceiling at a high-society gala where Kincaid is playing.

Dark Justice. Ballantine, 1999.
> Looking for a much needed vacation, lawyer Ben Kincaid heads for the Pacific Northwest where he becomes involved in a deadly battle between the local logging industry and conservationists.

Silent Justice. Ballantine, 2000.
> Ben Kincaid finds himself facing off against his former employer, Raven, Tucker & Tubb, as he takes a case against an industry giant accused of dumping toxic chemicals into a small community's drinking water. Kincaid is not the only person fighting against the company—a killer is targeting its employees for death.

Murder One. Ballantine, 2001.
> Criminal lawyer Ben Kincaid takes the case of Keri Delcanton, a nineteen-year-old former stripper, who has been accused of brutally murdering her married lover. He gets her off on a technicality, but when the bloody murder weapon is found in his office he soon finds himself accused of conspiracy and murder.

Criminal Intent. Ballantine, 2002.
> Tulsa attorney Ben Kincaid must once again help out his old friend Father Daniel Beale, who is the prime suspect in the brutal murder of female member of his parish. Proving Father Beale innocent is an increasingly tough job as the prosecution presents more and more evidence of his guilt.

Death Row. Ballantine, 2003.

Ben Kincaid races to clear his client Ray Goldman of the mass murder charges that put him on death row. The only witness to the torture and murder of her family has recanted the testimony that convicted Goldman, but she then commits suicide, leaving Kincaid the only witness to her confession.

Hate Crime. Ballantine, 2003.

Kincaid's newest case involves a brutal extremist who stabs a gay man and leaves him to die.

Double Jeopardy. Ballantine, 1995.

Former Dallas policeman Travis Byrne has made a midlife career change and become a lawyer. Now he must defend a man he despises, and he soon finds himself accused of committing murder—and with a contract out on his own life.

Blum, Bill

Prejudicial Error. Dutton, 1995. **M**

Juan Thomas, a black gang leader, is accused of shooting an LAPD vice cop, and his court-appointed attorney is John Phillip Solomon, a burned-out cynic who was once the star of the Los Angeles district attorney's office. This is his one chance for a comeback, but all the cards are stacked against him. (The author is an administrative law judge.)

Brandon, Jay

Loose among the Lambs. Pocket, 1993.

Rules of Evidence. Pocket, 1992. **M**

With only a gut instinct as to the man's innocence, African American criminal lawyer Raymond Boudro accepts as his client San Antonio Police detective Mike Stennent who is accused of beating a black homeless man to death.

Buffa, D. W.

Joseph Antonelli series

The Defense. Holt, 1997.

Seemingly unbeatable defense attorney Joseph Antonelli has no problem defending a man he knows is guilty . . . until a seemingly easy case ends in murder. (The author is a former defense attorney.)

The Prosecution. Holt, 1999.

It started out as a favor to an old friend, but when Joseph Antonelli agrees to serve as a special prosecutor against the man who is accused of having his former wife murdered, events don't turn out as expected.

The Judgement. Warner, 2001.

Unscrupulous Judge Calvin Jeffries is found murdered in a courthouse parking lot, but his killer is quickly apprehended, confesses, and then commits suicide in his jail cell. Then another judge is murdered, and attorney Joseph Antonelli agrees to defend the accused. Is it just a copycat murder, or is there more?

The Legacy. Warner, 2002.

> Joseph Antonelli heads for San Francisco to defend young Jamaal Washington, who is accused of murdering Senator Jeremy Fullerton, a man with many powerful enemies. Unfortunately, Washington, a premed honor student, cannot explain why he was found with the murder weapon.

Death Row. Ballantine, 2003.

Star Witness. Putnam, 2003.

> Joseph Antonelli takes the case of one of Hollywood's successful moviemakers, who is on trial for the murder of a young woman.

Busch, Frederick

Closing Arguments. Ticknor, 1991.

> Vietnam veteran and trial lawyer Mark Brennan is asked to do pro bono work defending a woman accused of murdering her lover, but he soon finds himself becoming obsessed with her.

Connors, Rose

Martha "Marty" Nickerson series

Absolute Certainty. Scribner, 2002.

> Martha "Marty" Nickerson, an assistant district attorney for Barnstable County, Massachusetts, is instrumental in the conviction and imprisonment of a man accused of brutally murdering a college student. But when another victim is killed in a shockingly similar fashion, she wonders if she put the wrong man behind bars.

Temporary Sanity. Scribner, 2003.

> Martha "Marty" Nickerson, now a Cape Cod defense attorney, takes the case of Buck Hammond, a man who kills the pedophile who raped and murdered his seven-year-old son.

Cose, Ellis

The Best Defense. HarperCollins, 1998.

> Hotshot defense lawyer Felecia Fontaine has agreed to represent a man accused of killing his coworker over a question of affirmative action policies. Unfortunately for her, the prosecutor in this controversial case is her former lover, the now-married Mario Santiago, who is desperate to get revenge on Felicia by winning the case.

Coughlin, William J.

Charley Sloan series

Shadow of a Doubt. St. Martin's, 1991.

> Former big city trial lawyer and recovering alcoholic Charley Sloan is now struggling to make a living in a small Michigan city. He is confronted by his past, however, when a former lover asks him to defend her stepdaughter, who is accused of killing her millionaire father. (The author is a former federal judge.)

Death Penalty. HarperCollins, 1992.

Detroit criminal attorney Charley Sloan is a recovering alcoholic who was nearly disbarred because of his drinking. He agrees to take on a personal injury case for a friend, a case that soon explodes into a corrupt doings that could destroy him and his client.

The Judgement. St. Martin's, 1997.

Charley Sloan defends Detroit's police chief Mark Conroy against the charges that he embezzled millions from his department's slush fund for paying informants while he also searches for a serial child murderer.

Proof of Intent. St. Martin's, 2002.

Charley Sloan's newest case is the defense of famous novelist Miles Dane, who is accused of murdering his wife. Unfortunately for Charley, Dane's account of events keeps changing, and the police have uncovered evidence linking him to the murder scene. (Actually written by Walter Sorrells.)

The Heart of Justice. St. Martin's, 1995.

Federal judge Paul Murray is trapped between his wife and his dedication to the law—he must make a decision that could cost him everything.

Her Honor. NAL, 1987.

Neophyte circuit court judge Kathleen Talbot is handed her first important case: a controversial "mercy" killing.

In the Presence of Enemies. St. Martin's, 1993.

Jake Martin, a partner in a prestigious Detroit law firm, finds his own life in danger as the struggle over a dead billionaire's will turns deadly. (This is the author's last work before his death in 1992, but other manuscripts that he allegedly wrote keep "turning up.")

Cray, David

Bad Lawyer. Carroll, 2001.

Criminal lawyer Sid Kaplan once had it all, but liquor and cocaine took it away. Looking for some publicity to shore up his career, Kaplan takes on a murder case that is all over the media and finds that his life is in danger—along with what's left of his career.

Daley, Robert

Tainted Evidence. Little, Brown, 1993.

Karen Henning, head of the trial division of the Manhattan district attorney's office, is assigned a high-profile and highly political case that will probably ruin her career. What at first appeared to be a simple, open-and-shut murder case has now become a civil rights battle that could stop her career in its tracks. (The author is a former New York City deputy police commissioner.)

Darden, Christopher, and Dick Lochte

The Last Defense. NAL, 2002.

Mercer Early, an up-and-coming hotshot lawyer at the most prestigious African American legal firm on the West Coast, seems to have everything going for him until his recently acquitted client ends up dead.

Nicolette Hill series

> ***The Trials of Nikki Hill.*** Warner, 1999. M
>
> > Nicolette Hill, an ambitious black prosecutor in the Los Angeles district attorney's office, is handed a supposedly airtight case against a young man accused of killed a popular television personality. But the case soon becomes less than tight, and Nikki must search for the real killer.
>
> ***L.A. Justice.*** Warner, 2000. M
>
> > Black prosecutor Nicolette Hill finds herself dealing with dirty cops, organized crime, and a murderous psychopath. (Darden was a prosecutor in the much-publicized O. J. Simpson trial.)

Denker, Henry

> ***Labyrinth.*** William Morrow, 1994.
>
> > An account that strangely parallels the O. J. Simpson case but was written a year before it occurred.

Dershowitz, Alan M.

> ***The Advocate's Devil.*** Warner, 1994.
>
> > Abe Ringel is a prominent attorney in Cambridge, Massachusetts, who is hired to defend a professional basketball player against the charge of rape. All the evidence points to the accused being guilty—evidence that even Ringel admits is overwhelming.

Devane, Terry

> ***Uncommon Justice.*** Putnam, 2001.
>
> > Disenchanted corporate lawyer Mairead O'Clare quits her high-powered Boston firm and decides to practice criminal law, even though she doesn't have any experience in that arena. Her first case is defending one homeless man accused of killing another.

Eberhardt, Michael C.

> ***Against the Law.*** Dutton, 1995. M
>
> > Hawaii's governor and a prostitute are murdered in a hotel suite, and all the evidence points to wealthy landowner Peter Maikai. The prosecuting attorney is Dan Carrier, who finds the case deeply personal—as a child, Maikai had been his mentor. To prove Maikai innocent, Carrier and Maikai's daughter initiate an unofficial investigation that uncovers a series of scandalous schemes.

> ***Body of a Crime.*** Dutton, 1994.
>
> > Defense attorney Sean Barrett takes the case of an former professional athlete accused of murdering his high school girlfriend. The evidence against him is devastating except for one thing: the woman's body cannot be found.

Freedman, J. F.

Against the Wind. Viking, 1991.

Santa Fe defense attorney Will Alexander's newest clients are four members of the Scorpions motorcycle gang who have been accused of a gruesome murder. Even though the evidence is against them, they insist on their innocence, and, against his better judgment, Alexander believes them.

Friedman, Philip

Grand Jury. Fine, 1996.

Two grand jurors, David Clark and Susan Linwood, are caught up in a deadly conspiracy that stretches from the skyscrapers of Hong Kong to the streets of New York's Chinatown.

Inadmissible Evidence. Fine, 1992.

Manhattan prosecutor Joe Estrada is assigned to try a case in which a millionaire is accused of the vicious rape and murder of his mistress. At first the case appears airtight, but when important evidence is declared inadmissible, Estrada must search for something new—a search that could end both his career and his life.

Gannon's Adventure/Suspense Rule Number 8: Just when you think you've forgotten all about a former lover, he or she is accused of murder and becomes your client.

Reasonable Doubt. Fine, 1990.

Attorney Michael Ryan's son, Ned, has been found murdered, bludgeoned to death in private room during a Manhattan art reception. Ned's former wife is the prime suspect. She insists on hiring Michael to defend her, and, after much soul searching, he finally agrees.

Genberg, Ira

Reckless Homicide. St. Martin's, 1998.

Golub, Aaron Richard

The Big Cut. St. Martin's, 2000.

Johnny Ocean is a Manhattan lawyer who takes on cases that others consider too hot to handle—like the one he accepts for his mysterious employer Pandora Markham, which quickly drags him into the sinister dominion of the Chinese underworld.

Green, George Dawes

The Juror. Warner, 1995. `FILM`

Annie Laird has been called as a juror in the trial of a member of the Mafia. She's told that all she has to do is say "not guilty"—to ensure the safety of her family and friends.

Green, Tim

The Letter of the Law. Warner, 2000.
> Publicity-seeking lawyer Casey Jordan has been retained to represent her former law professor Eric Lipton; he has been accused of murdering one of his students—caught with the victim's blood-stained underwear in his possession. Jordan finds herself torn between her ethics and her loyalty as more bodies turn up.

Grippando, James

The Pardon. HarperCollins, 1994.
> Jack Swyteck, a Miami defense lawyer, and his father Harry, the governor of Florida, have been estranged ever since Harry refused to grant a death sentence pardon for one of Jack's clients. But now someone has a vendetta against them both: Jack is being tried for a murder he didn't commit, and Harry may see his political career ruined.

Grisham, John

The Brethren. Doubleday, 2000.
> The Brethren are three former judges who are incarcerated in a federal minimum security prison and are getting rich on the criminal rewards of a complicated mail scam. Unfortunately their next victim is a dangerous man to mess with.

The Chamber. Doubleday, 1994. **FILM**
> Young Chicago lawyer Adam Hall asks to be assigned to the case of a man who has been sentenced to the gas chamber for the 1967 murder of two children. The man is his grandfather.

The Client. Doubleday, 1993. **FILM**
> Mark Sway is an eleven-year-old boy who finds himself caught between the FBI and the Mafia when he hears something he shouldn't have. His only hope is feisty female attorney Reggie Love.

The Firm. Doubleday, 1991. 📄 **FILM**
> Ambitious young Harvard Law graduate Mitchell Y. McDeere is recruited by a very rich, very secretive tax law firm. He soon himself a victim of the adage "be careful what you wish for . . . you may get it."

The King of Torts. Doubleday, 2003.
> Washington, D.C., public defender Clay Carter takes the case of a young man accused of murder, but as he researches the case, he finds evidence of a vast conspiracy that centers on a huge international pharmaceutical company.

The Partner. Doubleday, 1997.
> Four years ago, Brazilian resident Danilo Silva was Patrick Lanigan, a young partner in a Mississippi law firm who died tragically in a car crash. Six weeks after his "death," a fortune was stolen from the law firm's bank account. Now the members of the firm have come to Brazil and want Silva to give it back.

The Pelican Brief. Doubleday, 1992. [icon] **FILM**
Two Supreme Court justices are murdered within hours of each other, and there are thought to be no clues. But law student Darby Shaw has found some and is now marked for murder because of that knowledge.

The Rainmaker. Doubleday, 1995. **FILM**
Rudy Baylor is barely out of law school when he takes on a powerful and ruthless company that is making billions in a massive insurance fraud. Unfortunately for Rudy, he hasn't even passed the bar yet and is about to go up against some of the finest lawyers that money can buy.

The Runaway Jury. Doubleday, 1996. **FILM**
A high-stakes trial in Biloxi, Mississippi, begins routinely, but then things begin to go awry when the jury starts acting strangely and must be sequestered. What's going on with the jury? Are they being influenced? If so, by whom and why?

The Street Lawyer. Doubleday, 1998.
Michael Brock is a young lawyer on the rise up the ladder at the prestigious Washington, D.C., law firm of Drake & Sweeney until a violent encounter with a homeless man leaves him with a lot of questions—questions that concern his employer.

The Summons. Doubleday, 2002.
Judge Atlee summons his two sons, law professor Ray Atlee and his profligate younger brother Forrest, home to Mississippi to discuss the details of his estate. But before Ray can arrive in his hometown, his father dies—leaving an astounding secret behind.

The Testament. Doubleday, 1999.
Nate O'Riley, a hot-shot Washington, D.C., lawyer; Troy Phelan, a dying billionaire; and a missionary in the jungle of Brazil by the name of Rachel Lane—what secret will bring them together and change their lives forever?

A Time to Kill. Wynwood, 1989. **FILM** **M**
Young defense attorney Jake Brigance defends a black Vietnam War hero who has killed his daughter's white rapists in the small town of Clanton, Mississippi.

Gruenfeld, Lee

The Expert. Dutton, 1998.
Criminal attorney Rebecca Verona has been retained to defend her ex-lover, computer whiz James Perrein, who has been accused of selling top-secret technology to China. To make matters worse, David Zuckerman is the prosecuting attorney—he's also a former lover.

The Halls of Justice. Dutton, 1996.
When a brutal rapist is set free in a travesty of justice, two of his victims take the law into their hands.

Handberg, Ron

Savage Justice. Carol, 1992.
Emmett Steele is up for confirmation as chief justice for the Minnesota state Supreme Court. He's powerful, respected—and a vicious pedophile. Television anchorman Alex Collier must find the elusive evidence and bring this predator to justice.

Harrington, William

Town on Trial. Fine, 1994.

New York society queen Marietta Rheinlander is accused of murdering her lover, Congressman Charles R. Bailey, in his West Virginia love nest, and an entire nation is riveted to the trial taking place in the small town.

Hoag, Tami

Guilty as Sin. Bantam, 1996.

Ellen North, an assistant county attorney in rural Minnesota, has been assigned a kidnapping case that has attracted the attention of a best-selling true-crime author who intends to shadow her every move. To make matters worse, her ex-lover is the defense lawyer, and North is receiving threatening phone calls.

Irving, Clifford

Final Argument. Simon &Schuster, 1993.

Twelve years ago, Ted Jaffe was the prosecuting attorney who won the case that condemned a man to death, but now Jaffe's back to prove that same convicted murderer is innocent and to save him from being executed.

Trial. Summitt, 1990.

Warren Blackburn is a Texas defense lawyer whose personal and private lives are in shreds—the only cases he can get are appointed to him by the courts. But two of his cases, one involving an illegal alien and the other the owner of a topless nightclub, may somehow be connected—and may just finish off what's let of his career.

Jacobson, Alan

False Accusations. Pocket, 1999.

Junkin, Tim

Good Counsel. Algonquin, 2001.

Jack Stanton was an idealistic Washington, D.C., public defender with a knack for getting his clients an innocent verdict, but then he decides to go for the money and enters a private practice specializing in medical malpractice. In his quest for wealth, Stanton goes too far and lies under oath. (The author is a former Washington, D.C., public defender.)

Keech, Thomas

The Crawlspace Conspiracy. Baskerville, 1995.

Sport Norris, an idealistic attorney for Legal Aid, takes a client who has inherited a row home that is in the way of a multimillion-dollar luxury condo project. Charles Gage wants to live in the tiny house, and the developers want to tear it down. But Norris is also in the middle of a massive class-action suit that is exposing government welfare fraud—Sport Norris versus corrupt politicians and businesspeople.

Kennedy, William P.

Guard of Honor. St. Martin's, 1993.

There is a brutal killer at work in the Green Beret training camp at Fort Francis Marion, a rogue cadet who is practicing on his instructors the torture techniques he learned at the camp. Captain Gordon, the base legal officer, is assigned to the investigation and resulting trial, a trial that forces the Green Berets to face an alarming moral dilemma.

Kerr, Baine

Harmful Intent. Scribner, 1999.

Malpractice lawyer Peter Moss takes the case of Terry Winter, who is suing Moss's former client Dr. Wallace Bondurant for the misdiagnosis and neglect of Terry's breast cancer. (The author is a lawyer who specializes in medical malpractice.)

Wrongful Death. Scribner, 2002.

Attorney Elliot Stone's life has been one tragedy after another, culminating in the death of his wife Kathleen. Now two years after her death, Stone is drawn to another woman, June, who ends up brutally beaten and dies in the hospital after a five-month coma. Now Stone must discover why she was attacked and why she died, as well as the truth about recent suspicious deaths at the hospital.

Klavan, Andrew

True Crime. Crown, 1995.

Journalist Steve Everett has eighteen hours to stop the execution of a convicted murderer—the execution of a man he believes was the victim of flawed justice.

Korelitz, Jean Hanff

A Jury of Her Peers. Crown, 1996.

Legal Aid attorney Sybylla Muldoon is assigned the defense of a man named Trent—a man who viciously stabbed and mutilated a little girl as she waited for her school bus. Her client may be guilty, but everything about the case triggers Muldoon's suspicions.

The Sabbathday River. Farrar, Straus & Giroux, 1999.

In a small New England town, a young single mother with a promiscuous reputation is accused of killing her newborn baby girl, and lawyer Judith Friedman is retained to defend her.

Lashner, William

Victor Carl series

Hostile Witness. HarperCollins, 1995.

Cynical young attorney Victor Carl once dreamed of Philadelphia high-society legal grandeur but is now reduced to collecting debts for his relatives. Handing him his breakout chance is the prestigious William Prescott, who hires Carl to help with his legal firm's defense of a high-profile client. Carl soon finds that he is a pawn, that both his life and his client's are in danger.

Veritas. HarperCollins, 1997.

Hapless young Philadelphia lawyer Victor Carl is back, this time ending up in Belize as he tries to prove that the supposed suicide of a socialite was really a murder.

Fatal Flaw. William Morrow, 2003.

Late one night, Victor Carl receives a frantic call from an old law school classmate—Guy Forrest has just found his beautiful fianceé, Hailey Prouix, murdered. Even though Victor is convinced that Forrest killed her, he takes the case. (The author has served as a trial attorney in the Criminal Division of the U.S. Department of Justice.)

Latt, Mimi Lavenda

Powers of Attorney. Simon & Schuster, 1993.

The story of three glamorous female lawyers—best friends as well as ruthless rivals—as they struggle for the top spot in the murder case of a Los Angeles billionaire. (The author is an attorney in California.)

Lescroart, John T.

Dismas Hardy series

Dead Irish. Fine, 1990.

Currently a bartender, San Francisco ex-cop Dismas "Diz" Hardy investigates the apparent suicide of his friend Eddie.

The Vig. Fine, 1991.

The "vig" is the interest that loan sharks charge on their "loans." Dismas Hardy investigates the murder of his lawyer friend Rusty Ingraham, who may have been murdered because of the vig.

Hard Evidence. Fine, 1993.

The partial body of a California billionaire, shot to death, washes up on a beach; his severed hand is later found in the belly of a shark. The accused is a high-class Japanese call girl. The bizarre case is handed to assistant DA Dismas Hardy—and taken away when Hardy is fired. Then a man, also accused of killing the billionaire, hires Hardy to be his defense lawyer. *Clear as mud?*

The 13th Juror. Fine, 1994.

Dismas Hardy, a San Francisco defense lawyer, undertakes the defense of a woman who is accused of murdering her husband and eight-year-old son—as well as her first husband, who died nine years earlier of a supposed drug overdose. The thirteenth juror referred to in the title is the judge.

A Certain Justice. Fine, 1995.

Kevin Shea's brush with the law causes him to be hunted and nearly killed, all for a crime he never committed. Joining him in flight from "justice" is Melanie Sinclair—together the two become a modern-day (but innocent) Bonnie and Clyde.

Guilt. Delacorte, 1997.
>   A brutal crime leads to a high-profile trial with ramifications (good or bad) for everyone involved.

The Mercy Rule. Delacorte, 1998.
>   San Francisco defense attorney Dismas Hardy finds his life in danger as he takes the case of a former baseball player turned lawyer who is accused of killing his terminally ill father with an overdose of morphine.

Nothing but the Truth. Delacorte, 1999.
>   To get his wife out of jail, Dismas Hardy must clear her friend of murder—if he can find him.

The Hearing. Dutton, 2001.
>   Dismas Hardy takes the case of a homeless heroin addict accused of murdering a prominent female lawyer, but his defendant has already been tried and convicted before the first day of the trial.

The Oath. Dutton, 2002.
>   Dr. Eric Kensing comes to Dismas Hardy for legal help after he is accused of murdering the head of San Francisco's biggest health maintenance organization, who was being treated in his hospital for a hit-and-run accident. Soon Hardy learns that many other patients are dying, victims of murder, in the very same hospital.

The First Law. Dutton, 2003.
>   When the best friend of Abe Glitsky's father is murdered, the prime suspect is John Holiday, owner of a local bar and friend of Dismas Hardy. The police seem to have an excellent case against Holiday, especially when he turns fugitive.

Levine, Paul

9 Scorpions. Pocket, 1998.
>   Young lawyer Lisa Fremont is a new law clerk for Supreme Court Justice Samuel Truitt, and she has a dark secret—a secret that is about to destroy her career unless she is willing to compromise her ethics. (The author is a former trial lawyer.)

Levitsky, Ronald

The Love That Kills. Scribner, 1991.
>   Washington, D.C., civil rights lawyer Nate Rosen is called in to defend Edison Basehart, the head of a Virginia hate group, who is accused of murdering a young Vietnamese woman.

Levy, Harry

Chain of Custody. Random House, 1998.
>   Dr. Michael Malone used to practice medicine, but now practices law—he is also the prime suspect in his estranged wife's murder.

MacDougal, Bonnie

Angle of Impact. Ballantine, 1998.

> Philadelphia lawyer Dana Svenssen takes on a case that involves a midair collision between a light plane and a helicopter. (The author is also a Philadelphia lawyer.)

Out of Order. Ballantine, 1999.

Margolin, Phillip

Amanda Jaffe series

Wild Justice. HarperCollins, 2000.

> Novice lawyer Amanda Jaffe assists her father in defending Portland surgeon Vincent Cardoni against charges that he murdered several people to harvest their organs and sell them to finance his cocaine addiction.

Ties That Bind. HarperCollins, 2003.

> Portland lawyer Amanda Jaffe takes the case of Jon Dupre, a man accused of murdering a U.S. senator. Dupre, who runs a high-class escort service, claims that murder is the initiation into a secret club of powerful political movers and shakers.

After Dark. Doubleday, 1995.

> Abigail Griffen hires Matthew Reynolds, an attorney who specializes in death-penalty defenses, after she is accused of killing her estranged husband, who is an Oregon Supreme Court justice, and his law clerk.

The Associate. HarperCollins, 2001.

> Up and coming young attorney Daniel Ames is an associate at a prestigious Portland, Oregon, law firm. He is persuaded to participate in some unethical dealings by an attractive colleague and eventually finds himself accused of murder.

The Burning Man. Doubleday, 1996.

> Once a rising-star attorney, Peter Hale is now a public defender in a small Oregon town. He takes on the death penalty case of mentally retarded man who is accused of killing a college student with a hatchet. Hale soon realizes that his inexperience and egotism may send his client to his execution.

The Last Innocent Man. Little, Brown, 1981.

> Unflappable defense attorney David Nash is called the Ice Man by the press—he wins most of his cases even though most of his clients are guilty. Finally, Nash has a chance to redeem himself for all the rapists and murders he has helped go free . . . or does he?

The Undertaker's Widow. Doubleday, 1998.

> Judge Richard Quinn is such an advocate of the law that he would risk his own life in defense of it—and Judge Quinn may soon have to do just that.

Martel, John

The Alternate. Dutton, 1999.

Although on opposite sides of a controversial San Francisco murder trial, Grace Harris and Barrett Dickson find themselves powerfully attracted to each other. The prosecution has only circumstantial evidence, while the defense is relying on a paper-thin alibi.

Billy Strobe. Dutton, 2001.

Three-quarters of the way through law school when he is convicted of insider trading and jailed, Bill Strobe finishes his degree via correspondence school and works to free a fellow inmate who was wrongfully convicted of murder.

Conflicts of Interest. Pocket, 1995.

A prestigious San Francisco legal firm hires small-town lawyer Seth "Cowboy" Cameron, who soon finds himself caught up in a power struggle between the firm's senior and junior partners.

Partners. Bantam, 1988.

Martini, Steve

Paul Madriani series

Compelling Evidence. Putnam, 1992.

The mentor of defense attorney Paul Madriani is found shot to death just before he is to be nominated to the U.S. Supreme Court. His wife, and Madriani's former lover, is the prime suspect, and she turns to Paul to defend her against mounting evidence.

Prime Witness. Putnam, 1993.

Criminal defense attorney Paul Madriani locks horns in a small California college town with defense attorney Adrian Chambers, who has secrets and a terrible grudge against him.

Undue Influence. Putnam, 1994.

Just before her death, Paul Madriani's wife Nikki asks him to watch over her younger sister, Laurel Vega, who is battling her politically powerful ex-husband for custody of their children. True to his vow, Paul must defend Laurel when she is arrested for the murder of ex-husband's new wife.

The Judge. Putnam, 1995.

Against his better judgment, attorney Paul Madriani agrees to defend an old adversary, Judge Armando "the Coconut" Acosta who has been arrested for soliciting prostitution. The case heats up as the only person who can give evidence against the judge is murdered.

The Attorney. Putnam, 2000.

Attorney Paul Madriani has moved to San Diego to be closer to the woman he loves and takes on the case of Jonah Hale. Jonah has been raising his eight-year-old granddaughter, who was abandoned by her drug addict mother, but after he wins a multimillion-dollar lottery, his daughter comes back wanting her child . . . unless Jonah pays her off.

The Jury. Putnam, 2001.

Paul Madriani takes on the case of a gifted researcher accused of brutally murdering a female colleague who had filed sexual harassment charges against him.

The Arraignment. Putnam, 2003.

After a lawyer colleague and his client are gunned down outside the San Diego federal courthouse, Paul Madriani takes on a client who he thinks might somehow have been involved in the double murder.

Meltzer, Brad

Dead Even. William Morrow, 1998.

Defense attorney Jared Tate and his wife Sara, a New York assistant DA, are pitted against one another in the courtroom. Jared has been told that if he loses the case, Sara will be killed, and Sara is told that if she loses, Jared will die.

The Tenth Justice. William Morrow, 1997.

O'Shaughnessy, Perri

Nina Reilly series

Motion to Suppress. Delacorte, 1995.

After her divorce, attorney Nina Reilly moves from San Francisco to Lake Tahoe and sets up her one-woman office. (Pseudonym for two sisters: Pamela and Mary O'Shaughnessy.)

Invasion of Privacy. Delacorte, 1996.

Attorney Nina Reilly takes on the case of a filmmaker who is accused of invasion of privacy because of the subject of her new documentary. Her client appears to know quite a bit about Nina, secrets that Nina would like to keep in the past.

Obstruction of Justice. Delacorte, 1997.

Ray de Beers was struck by lightning and died, and attorney Nina Reilly was a witness. So why does his father want the body exhumed to rule out foul play?

Breach of Promise. Delacorte, 1998.

Lake Tahoe attorney Nina Reilly takes on a high-profile palimony case that could either turn her into a millionaire or leave her bankrupt.

Acts of Malice. Delacorte, 1999.

Nina Reilly defends Jim Strong, a member of one of Lake Tahoe's most prominent families, who is accused of murdering his brother.

Move to Strike. Delacorte, 2000.

Nina Reilly's new client is Nicole Zack, the sixteen-year-old friend of her teenage son Bob. Nicole is accused of murdering her uncle with an ancient samurai sword.

Writ of Execution. Delacorte, 2001.

Nina Reilly's new client goes by the name of Jessie Potter, but because she won't divulge her real name, she cannot collect her slot machine jackpot win. Jessie needs the money, but why won't she reveal her identity?

Unfit to Practice. Delacorte, 2002.
Nina Reilly must discover why her truck containing three private case files was stolen and by whom—information from the files is being used to destroy her legal reputation.

Presumption of Death. Delacorte, 2003. **M**
Nina Reilly must help the twenty-one-year-old son of her ex-secretary, Native American Sandy Whitefeather, who has been implicated in a murder and arson investigation.

Parker, Barbara

Blood Relations. Dutton, 1996.
Sam Hagan is the chief of the major crimes section for Dade County, Florida, and is aiming to become the next state's attorney, but his latest case threatens to ruin his career. (The author is a former Florida prosecutor.)

Criminal Justice. Dutton, 1997.
Washed-up Miami lawyer Dan Galindo is drawn into a case that can kill what's left of his career—and him.

Patterson, Richard North

Christopher Paget series

Degree of Guilt. Knopf, 1993.
Attorney Christopher Paget takes the case of his former lover, television reporter Mary Carelli, who is accused of killing a famous author. She claims it was self-defense because he was trying to rape her.

Eyes of the Child. Knopf, 1994.
Defense attorney Caroline Masters's client, Christopher Paget, is himself a famous San Francisco defense attorney, accused of killing his girlfriend's husband and making it look like a suicide.

The Final Judgement. Knopf, 1995.
Attorney Caroline Masters travels to New Hampshire to defend her college student niece, Brett Allen, against charges that she brutally murdered her boyfriend.

Dark Lady. Knopf, 1999.
Defense lawyers know Assistant county prosecutor Stella Marz as the Dark Lady for her unyielding and merciless style in the courtroom. She has only lost one case, and then only because the defendant committed suicide. She has decided to run for the position prosecutor of Erie County, but then her ex-lover is viciously murdered.

The Outside Man. Little, Brown, 1981.

Private Screening. Villard, 1985.

Silent Witness. Knopf, 1996.
San Francisco lawyer Tony Lord defends childhood friend Sam Robb, now a high school vice principal, who is accused of murdering one of his female students. Complicating matters is that Sam is now married to Lord's high school sweetheart.

Picoult, Jodi

Plain Truth. Pocket, 2000.
> Philadelphia defense attorney Ellie Hathaway's aunt asks her to defend a young unmarried Amish woman accused of murdering her newborn child.

Reed, Barry

Dan Sheridan series

The Indictment. Crown, 1994.
> Boston defense attorney Dan Sheridan has a crisis of ethics when he takes the case of Harvard surgeon Christopher Dillard, who is accused of murdering a beautiful young woman. Although Dillard has no alibi, Sheridan senses that he has been set up and must discover the reason.

The Deception. Crown, 1997.
> Attorney Dan Sheridan takes on a medical malpractice case that will test his professional ethics.

Frank Galvin series

The Verdict. Simon & Schuster, 1980. **FILM**
> Lawyer Frank Galvin goes up against the Boston medical establishment and the Catholic Church as he fights for justice in a medical malpractice case.

The Choice. Crown, 1991.
> Frank Galvin is asked to defend a huge pharmaceutical corporation accused of manufacturing a drug with dangerous side effects.

Reuland, Rob

Hollowpoint. Random House, 2001.
> Brooklyn assistant DA Andrew Giobberti is assigned the case of a fourteen-year-old mother who has been shot to death in her bedroom, and eventually finds himself a suspect. (The author is also a Brooklyn assistant DA.)

Rosenberg, Nancy Taylor

Abuse of Power. Dutton, 1997.
Conflict of Interest. Hyperion, 2002.
> Assistant district attorney Joanne Kuhlman is used to showing no mercy to those she thinks are guilty, but she finds herself believing in the innocence of a young man accused of armed robbery. She also finds herself attracted to his handsome defense attorney.

First Offense. Dutton, 1994.
> Probation officer Ann Carlisle is a woman with many secrets. After she is shot one day while leaving work, those secrets threaten to overwhelm her.

Interest of Justice. Dutton, 1993.
Judge Lara Sanderstone is torn between her judicial career and her hunt for the murderer of her younger sister.

Lilly Forrester series

Mitigating Circumstances. Dutton, 1993.
Assistant district attorney and newly appointed chief of the sex crimes division, Lily Forrester makes a choice that takes her outside of the law—with no one to rely on but herself.

Buried Evidence. Hyperion, 2000.
Six years ago, district attorney Lily Forrester committed a crime. Now her ex-husband is threatening to expose her if she doesn't defend him against grave criminal charges.

Trial by Fire. Dutton, 1996.
The assistant district attorney in the city of Dallas, Stella Cataloni has an astonishing 100-percent conviction record. In bizarre set of circumstances, Stella finds herself on trial for murder and must find the true killer before it's too late.

Scottoline, Lisa

Benedetta Rosato series

Legal Tender. HarperCollins, 1996.
Benedetta "Bennie" Rosato is a successful attorney who specializes in police misconduct cases, but she finds the tables turned when all the evidence in a brutal murder points to her as the killer. Now the police she once prosecuted are out to get her—and put her away for good.

Mistaken Identity. HarperCollins, 1999.
Benedetta "Bennie" Rosato is asked to take a client named Alice Connolly, who is accused of savagely murdering her police-detective lover. The fact that Alice looks surprisingly like Bennie and seems to know so much about her life forces Bennie to take her case.

Courting Trouble. HarperCollins, 2002.
Fledgling lawyer Anne Murphy—very much alive—must find out who is trying to kill her after she hears reports of her own murder.

Dead Ringer. HarperCollins, 2003.
Someone is impersonating Philadelphia lawyer Bennie Rosato and, in the process, destroying her life. Could it be Bennie's long-lost identical twin, Alice?

Mary DiNunzio series

Everywhere That Mary Went. HarperCollins, 1993.
Mary DiNunzio has been working day and night for the past eight years trying to become a partner in her prominent Philadelphia law firm—in fact, she's been too busy to worry about the strange phone calls she's been receiving until things become increasingly menacing.

Final Appeal. HarperCollins, 1994.
> After her divorce, Philadelphia lawyer Mary DiNunzio gets a part-time job with the federal appeals court and soon finds herself surreptitiously investigating a case of judicial corruption.

Rough Justice. HarperCollins, 1997.
> Criminal lawyer Marta Richter finds that the man she is defending on a murder charge is actually guilty and has been lying to her from the start. She hires two young lawyers, Mary DiNunzio and Judy Carrier, to find the evidence to prove her client's guilt.

Moment of Truth. HarperCollins, 2000.
> Attorney Jack Newlin frames himself for his wife's murder and then hires the most inexperienced lawyer he can find to defend him in court. Mary DiNunzio may be inexperienced, but she's not stupid. So she begins to investigate why her client is an innocent man claiming to be guilty.

Judy Carrier series

Rough Justice. HarperCollins, 1997.
> Criminal lawyer Marta Richter finds that the man she is defending on a murder charge is actually guilty and has been lying to her from the start. She hires two young lawyers, Mary DiNunzio and Judy Carrier, to find the evidence to prove her client's guilt.

The Vendetta Defense. HarperCollins, 2001.
> Philadelphia lawyer Judy Carrier takes the case of an elderly man who has killed another old man in revenge for something that happened fifty years ago. Now the dead man's family wants revenge, and both Judy and her client are in danger.

Running from the Law. HarperCollins, 1995.
> Philadelphia lawyer Rita Morrone defends a federal judge accused of sexual harassment who is the prime suspect in a murder case.

Siegel, Barry

Lines of Defense. Ballantine, 2002.
> Doug Bard is a detective in the La Graciosa, California, sheriff's office. Defying his boss, district attorney Angela Stark, he struggles to find evidence to clear an innocent man of murder charges and a possible death sentence.

Siegel, Sheldon

Mike Daley series

Special Circumstances. Bantam, 2000.
> Mike Daley is a man of many "ex's": he's an ex-priest, an ex-husband, an ex-public defender, and now an ex-partner of one of San Francisco's most prestigious legal firms. Setting himself up in private practice, his first case is his best friend, who has been charged with a savage double homicide.

Incriminating Evidence. Bantam, 2001.
> Ex-priest Mike Daley takes the case of Prentice Marshall "Skipper" Gates III, the San Francisco DA, when he is accused of murder after being found in a hotel room handcuffed to a dead male prostitute.

Criminal Intent. Putnam, 2002.
> Ex-priest and ex-corporate lawyer Mike Daley runs a San Francisco criminal defense firm, along with his ex-wife, Rosie Fernandez. Their newest case is the defense of Rosie's niece Angelina, who is accused of murdering a movie director.

Final Verdict. Putnam, 2003.
> Mike defends a homeless man (and former client) Leon Walker, who is accused of stabbing a wealthy venture capitalist and leaving his body in a dumpster behind a liquor store.

Sloan, Susan R.

Act of God. Warner, 2002.
> Dana McAuliffe, a partner in a prominent Seattle legal firm, is assigned to defend Corey Dean Lantham, a young naval officer, accused of bombing an abortion clinic and killing more than a hundred people.

Guilt by Association. Warner, 1995.
> Thirty years after being raped by a wealthy Harvard law student, Karen Kern attempts to bring her attacker, who is now running for president of the United States, to justice.

Tanenbaum, Robert K.

Butch Karp and Marlene Ciampi series

No Lesser Plea. Watts, 1987.
> Introduces Roger "Butch" Karp, Manhattan assistant DA in this series set in the 1970s. Karp must stop a sadistic murderer, Mandeville Louis, from faking an insanity plea to avoid prosecution.

Depraved Indifference. NAL, 1989.
> Manhattan assistant DA Butch Karp is caught up in politics, at both the local and national level, when he is involved in the prosecution of a terrorist responsible for killing a policeman.

Immoral Certainty. Dutton, 1991.
> Butch Karp and Marlene Ciampi investigate three brutal murders that may have ties to Satanism.

Reversible Error. Dutton, 1992.
> Butch Karp and his pregnant fiancé, Marlene Ciampi, go after a brutal serial rapist.

Material Witness. Dutton, 1993.
> The husband and wife lawyer team of Butch Karp and Marlene Ciampi investigate the murder of a professional basketball player and find themselves in mortal danger.

Justice Denied. Dutton, 1994.

Bureau chief for the New York DA, Butch Karp finds himself involved in a supposedly open-and-shut murder case. But he suspects a coverup, and, along with his wife assistant DA Marlene Ciampi, he investigates.

Corruption of Blood. Dutton, 1995.

Manhattan assistant DA Butch Karp is assigned the case when Congress reopens the investigation into the John F. Kennedy assassination. He soon uncovers striking new evidence and finds himself caught up in a dangerous conspiracy.

Falsely Accused. Dutton, 1996.

Former Manhattan assistant DA Butch Karp is now in private practice and suing the city for which he once worked.

Irresistible Impulse. Dutton, 1997.

Butch Karp is the homicide bureau chief for the New York district attorney's office and finds himself going up against the country's top defense lawyer in a high-profile murder trial.

Reckless Endangerment. Dutton, 1998.

New York Deputy district attorney for special projects Butch Karp is given two cases that he soon suspects are linked: a racially motivated murder and a cop killing.

Act of Revenge. HarperCollins, 1999.

New York chief assistant DA Butch Karp and his wife Marlene Ciampi, a former prosecutor and now a security consultant, have their hands full when they take on two tough New York criminal organizations: the Mafia and the Chinese gangs.

True Justice. Pocket, 2000.

Chief assistant DA for New York County Butch Karp and his wife Marlene Ciampi, who has given up her job as a private investigator to return to working as a lawyer, find themselves on opposite sides of a case.

Enemy Within. Pocket, 2001.

Chief assistant district attorney for New York County, Butch Karp investigates two puzzling cases: a black man is shot in the back by a rising star of the NYPD and a retarded young man is accused of murdering a Jewish diamond merchant. As for his wife, Marlene Ciampi, she's now wealthy because of her dabbling with the Internet.

Absolute Rage. Atria, 2002.

Butch Karp is appointed special prosecutor by the governor of West Virginia to bring justice to the corrupt town of McCullensburg.

Resolved. Atria, 2003.

Manhattan assistant district attorney Butch Karp is up against an old foe: Felix Tighe, a sociopath he sent to prison more than ten years ago. Now Tighe is an assassin for hire, currently under the employ of Islamic terrorists, and looking to get revenge on Karp.

Tolkien, Simon

Final Witness. Random House, 2002.

Lady Anne Robinson, the wife of the British minister of defense, is murdered by two men who break into her isolated mansion one night. Her son Thomas insists the murder was masterminded by his father's beautiful assistant, Greta Grahame, but no one believes him—including his father, who soon marries Greta. (The author is the grandson of J. R. R. Tolkien of Lord of the Rings fame.)

Turow, Scott

Personal Injuries. Farrar, Straus & Giroux, 1999.

Robbie Feaver is a successful personal injury lawyer who has a way of bribing judges to rule in his clients' favor. Finally caught by the FBI, he agrees to go "undercover" in the courtroom in exchange for leniency. (The author is a former assistant U.S. attorney.)

Pleading Guilty. Farrar, Straus & Giroux, 1993.

Ex-cop and now a lawyer, Mack Malloy goes looking for his partner, who has apparently absconded with more than $5 million of his client's money.

Reversible Errors. Farrar, Straus & Giroux, 2002.

Undistinguished corporate lawyer Arthur Raven is a fish out of water when he is appointed by the court to handle the murder conviction appeal of mildly retarded "Squirrel" Gandolph.

Sabich/Stern/Klonsky series

Presumed Innocent. Farrar, Straus & Giroux, 1987. 📄 **FILM**

Rusty Sabich, Kindle County's longtime chief deputy prosecutor, has been asked to investigate the murder of one of his colleagues, Carolyn Polhemus. But what Sabich's superiors don't know is that Rusty and Carolyn were lovers. The investigation seems to be leading nowhere until Rusty himself is put on trial for the murder.

The Burden of Proof. Farrar, Straus & Giroux, 1990.

Midwestern defense attorney Alejandro "Sandy" Stern (last seen in *Presumed Innocent*) comes home one day to find that his wife of thirty years has committed suicide. Devastated by the loss, he finds solace in his practice, where he defends Dixon Hartnell, a shady businessman and his brother-in-law, in a federal grand jury investigation.

The Laws of Our Fathers. Farrar, Straus & Giroux, 1996.

Judge Sonia "Sonny" Klonsky (last seen in *Burden of Proof*) presides over a trial where a probation officer is accused of killing his mother in a drive-by shooting.

Willet, Sabin

The Deal. Random House, 1996.

A missing "0" in a document results in the death of a New York law firm's senior partner, and a young associate is accused of his murder.

Yastrow, Shelby

Undue Influence. Contemporary, 1990.
> Benjamin Stillman, an unassuming Catholic accountant with no family, dies and leaves a shocking bequest: $8 million to the Beth Zion Synagogue! Philip Ogden was the attorney who drew up the will and who must now defend it against a plethora of criminal accusations.

Under Oath. Diamond, 1994.

Short Stories and Serial Novels

Bernhardt, William, editor

Legal Briefs: Stories by Today's Best Legal Thriller Writers. Doubleday, 1998.
> Authors include Philip Friedman, John Grisham, Phillip M. Margolin, Steve Martini, and Richard North Patterson.

Natural Suspect. Ballantine, 2001.
> A serial novel with chapters by authors such as William Berhardt, John Lescroart, Phillip Margolin, and Brad Meltzer.

Hemmingson, Michael, editor

The Mammoth Book of Legal Thrillers. Carroll, 2001.
> Authors include James Grippando, John Grisham, and Scott Turow.

Chapter 6

The Buck Stops Here

Making a Killing in the World of Big Business and High Finance

Definition: In this subgenre, international corporations, ultra-wealthy business tycoons, and political entities attempt to manipulate and influence national economies. Stock markets, bullion reserves, insurance funds, and corporate earnings are all fair game for the greedy and unscrupulous. The prey can be everything from small companies to entire countries, as long as the plot stays focused on the financial aspects. The story usually contains at least one murder, and multiple forms of mayhem are common.

The Appeal: Wealth and power (and their misuse) are always interesting subjects. The glamorous lives of the rich and famous, the exotic locales, the private jets and yachts, attractive and powerful people—these factors contribute to the allure of this subgenre. The parallels to real business scandals also attract readers. People who cannot even balance their own checkbooks can vicariously manipulate the stock market or influence the economy of a small country by reading these books.

Brief History: One could point to Harold Robbins with his larger-than-life business tycoons and their unprincipled financial dealings as a progenitor of this subgenre, but his novels are better classified as soap opera than suspense. The author who can be credited with combining details of the finance world with the format of the traditional thriller is Paul E. Erdman. An international banker, Erdman wrote his first financial thriller, *The Billion Dollar Sure Thing,* while in a Swiss prison. He had been arrested after the United California Bank of Basel, of which he was the CEO, collapsed because of shady speculations in the silver and cocoa futures market. He then went on to write many more thrillers using his insider knowledge of international banking and corporate finance. Other authors with a financial background, such as Michael Thomas, Linda Davies, and Stephen W. Frey, have also written several titles in this subgenre.

Advising the Reader: The key elements to remember when advising the reader and suggesting appropriate titles are the following:

- What type of setting does the reader prefer, the United States or the international arena?

- If the reader likes titles in which the U.S. economy is threatened by other countries and has read all the financial thrillers, suggest espionage novels.

- Several authors in this subgenre—Davies, Erdman, Frey, and Thomas—have each written many titles. Suggest these authors for the neophyte financial reader.

- Readers who have exhausted this subgenre may be guided to legal thrillers, which offer similar "real-life" premises and authors who write from their own experiences.

When money speaks, the truth keeps silent.

—Russian Proverb

Archer, Jeffrey

Kane & Abel. Simon & Schuster, 1979. `FILM`
> The story of two dueling millionaire businessmen, William Lowell Kane and Abel Rosnovski, who are consumed by ambition and a lust for revenge. The sequel is *The Prodigal Daughter* and is merely a rehash of *Kane & Abel* in a soap-opera style.

Total Control. Warner, 1997.
> Jason Archer, an executive with a skyrocketing career at an international technology concern, suddenly disappears, leaving his wife, Sydney, to pick up the pieces. She searches for him, with the assistance of FBI agent Lee Sawyer, and soon discovers that his disappearance is the result of a sinister plot.

The Winner. Warner, 1997.
> Tough but tender LuAnn Tyler is a twenty-year-old single mother struggling to make ends meet in rural Georgia. One day she is approached by a mysterious man by the name of Mr. Jackson, who offers to make her the next winner of the $100 million national lottery. She refuses and a day later is falsely accused of murder. In desperation, LuAnn takes Mr. Jackson up on his offer and unknowingly becomes part of a massive financial conspiracy.

Block, Lawrence

The Specialists. Carroll, 1969.
> A group of Vietnam vets plans to con a criminal bank owner out of his ill-gotten gains.

Browne, Gerald A.

Hot Siberian. Arbor, 1989.
> The System, a ruthless cartel that controls diamond production and distribution worldwide, will stop at nothing to prevent anyone foolish enough to smuggle what the System consider its property.

Bunn, T. Davis
Drummer in the Dark. Doubleday, 2001.
> A secret group of bankers plots to control the U.S. monetary system using financial derivatives.

Coleridge, Nicholas
Street Smart. St. Martin's, 1999.
> When his sister Saskia dies, photojournalist Max Thompson is left in control of *Street Smart,* a glitzy gossip magazine. He soon finds that several unscrupulous and perhaps murderous investors have lined up to take over the magazine.

Cook, Robin
Toxin. Putnam, 1998.
> Cardiac surgeon Dr. Kim Reggis is shocked when his daughter Becky becomes deathly ill from an *E. coli* infection acquired from a burger she ate a fast-food restaurant. Outraged by the abuses he sees in the meatpacking industry and even with government inspectors, Reggis takes on the entire industry.

Crichton, Michael
Disclosure. Knopf, 1993. **FILM**
> Tom Sanders, a high-powered executive with the Seattle-based DigiCom, is accused of sexually harassing his new boss, a woman who was his lover ten years earlier. Struggling to defend himself, he discovers secrets about the company that will shock him.

Davies, Linda
Nest of Vipers. Doubleday, 1995.
> Successful currency trader Sarah Jensen is recruited by the Bank of England to go undercover and investigate corruption in the Inter-Continental Bank. Sarah soon discovers ties to the Mafia—evidence that endangers her life. (The author worked on Wall Street and is a former merchant banker.)

Wilderness of Mirrors. Doubleday, 1996.
> Tough yet glamorous Eva Cunningham must go undercover to trap an international financier who is suspected of smuggling nuclear weapons.

Duncan, Robert L.
Temple Dogs. William Morrow, 1977.
> Corporate suits become warriors as their machinations threaten to create a political conflict in Asia. (Duncan is the pseudonym of James Hall Roberts.)

Erdman, Paul E.
The Billion Dollar Sure Thing. Scribner, 1973.
> Various countries attempt to manipulate the gold market and the value of the dollar to benefit their own interests. (Erdman wrote this novel—a

benchmark in this subgenre—while incarcerated in a Swiss prison for illicit speculation in the futures market.)

The Crash of '79. Simon & Schuster, 1976.

The Palace. Doubleday, 1987.
High finance, money laundering, Las Vegas casinos, and organized crime all meet in this high-stakes thrill ride.

The Panic of '89. Doubleday, 1987.
Every international player but the pope is scheming to upset the U.S. financial markets and profit from the ensuing chaos.

The Set-Up. St. Martin's, 1997.
Retired chairman of the U.S. Federal Reserve Board Charles Black is arrested in Switzerland and accused of committing massive fraud to the tune of $450 million. His wife Sally must discover why he has been framed and how to get him free before he is sentenced to thirty years of hard labor.

The Silver Bears. Scribner, 1974   📄 **FILM**
The ups and downs of the world silver market and the greedy people out to profit from it.

The Swiss Account. Forge, 1992.

> *Gannon's Adventure/Suspense Rule Number 9: It takes a thief to catch a thief.*

Zero Coupon. Forge, 1993.
Financier and convicted criminal Willy Saxon, aided by a beautiful and ruthless socialite, embarks on a swindle that will bring Wall Street to its knees.

Fleming, Ian

Goldfinger. MJF Books, 1987 (original publication date: 1959). **FILM**
British secret agent James Bond must stop the evil financier Auric Goldfinger and his deadly assistant Pussy Galore from controlling the world's gold supply. See other James Bond titles in Chapter 2.

Forsyth, Frederick

The Dogs of War. Viking, 1974. **FILM**
Sir James Manson, head of Manson Consolidated Mining Company, hires mercenaries to invade a tiny African company to get his hands on a mountain full of platinum.

Frey, Stephen W.

The Day Trader. Ballantine, 2002.
Augustus McNight, a former paper salesman, finds that he has an aptitude for on-line investing and soon becomes a member of a Washington, D.C., day-trading firm. His wife, Melanie (an exotic dancer —a fact of which Augustus is blissfully unaware), is murdered, leaving a million-dollar insurance benefit to her husband, who is now considered the number one suspect in her death.

The Inner Sanctum. Dutton, 1997.

Financial wizard David Mitchell and IRS agent Jesse Hayes become reluctant allies in a web of politics and big business. (The author is a former vice president of corporate finance at a major bank.)

The Insider. Ballantine, 1999.

Jay West has a great job on Wall Street and the promise of a million-dollar bonus at the end of the year—if he can live that long.

The Legacy. Dutton, 1998.

Stockbroker Cole Egan receives a bizarre legacy from his dead father: the key to a safe deposit box containing proof that there was a second gunman at John F. Kennedy's assassination. Along with the beautiful Nicki Anderson, Egan searches for the answers to a thirty-year-old mystery before the government can silence him forever.

Silent Partner. Ballantine, 2003.

Bank vice president Angela Day is having a bad time. Her best friend is raped, her rich husband divorces her and by lying gains custody of their son, and then she finds herself entangled in a shadowy billionaire's schemes.

The Takeover. Dutton, 1995.

If Andrew Falcon can pull off the largest hostile takeover in Wall Street history, he will make a fee of $5 million. Violent events soon lead him to the Sevens, a secret organization with such significant wealth and power that its members do as they please. Falcon soon finds that he is no longer a player, but a pawn.

Vulture Fund. Dutton, 1996.

Mace McLain is the co-manager of a multibillion-dollar international fund that begins to experience certain "irregularities." Research assistant Rachel Sommers alerts McLain to these problems and to the fund's strange connections with drug cartels and the CIA. Soon they both find themselves in mortal danger.

Grant, Linda

Blind Trust. Scribner, 1990.

San Francisco private investigator Catherine Saylor specializes in white-collar crime and is now on the trail of a perpetrator who is using computers to rob banks,

Lethal Genes. Scribner, 1996.

Private investigator Catherine Saylor investigates industrial espionage at an agricultural biotechnology research center.

Grippando, James

Found Money. HarperCollins, 1999.

A King's Ransom. HarperCollins, 2001.

> Nick Rey's father Matthew has been kidnapped while on business in Colombia, and the ransom is $3 million. Although Matthew has an insurance policy for just such event, the company is refusing to pay—so it's up to Nick to save his father.

Grisham, John

The Firm. Doubleday, 1991. 🔲 **FILM**

> Ambitious young Harvard Law School graduate Mitchell Y. McDeere is recruited by a very rich, very secretive tax firm and soon finds himself a victim of the adage "be careful what you wish for . . . you may get it."

Gruenfeld, Lee

The Street. Doubleday, 2001.

> Double-dealing and violence amid the tumultuous world of the Internet dot-coms.

Hailey, Arthur

The Moneychangers. Doubleday, 1975. 🔲 **FILM**

> Two vice presidents of the First Mercantile American Bank, one good and one bad, struggle and scheme to see which one will gain the upper hand.

Harland, James

The Month of the Leopard. Simon & Schuster, 2002.

> British banker Tom Bracewell must take on greedy French financier Jean-Pierre Telmont to save not only the Eastern European banking system, but his wife Tatyana as well.

Harrison, Colin

Afterburn. Farrar, Straus & Giroux, 2000.

> Charlie Ravich, a former Vietnam War POW and now a Wall Street executive, suddenly has his world turned upside down when he meets Christina, a seductress with dangerous secrets.

Kennedy, Douglas

The Job. Hyperion, 1998.

> Yuppie Ned Allen is an advertising salesman for a successful computer magazine, but when he is suddenly fired, he finds his world in pieces. Desperate for employment, he accepts a job with an old high school friend and soon finds himself working on a private equity fund—but the new job quickly becomes sinister.

Kiefer, Warren

The Stanton Succession. Fine, 1992.

> Scheming and backstabbing result when the founder and CEO of Stanton Technologies dies without naming a successor.

Kublicki, Nicolas

The Diamond Conspiracy. Sourcebooks, 2002.

> During a minor lawsuit, Department of Justice attorney Patrick Carlton discovers a vast conspiracy that stretches from the White House to the Vatican, from Africa to Siberia—a conspiracy to control the world's supply of diamonds.

le Carré, John

Single & Single. Scribner, 1999.
Known for his espionage novels, here le Carré explores the deceitful world of high finance. This is the story of two families: one Russian dealing in illegal merchandise, the other British and laundering the profits.

Ledwidge, Michael

Bad Connection. Pocket, 2001.
Manhattan telephone repairman Sean Macklin is catapulted into the dangerous world of high finance when he accidentally overhears a telephone conversation outlining an important scheme for a business merger.

Lynch, Patrick

The Policy. Dutton, 1998.
What secrets lurk beneath the seemingly endless profits of ProvLife, a wildly successful life insurance company? Actuary Alex Tynan discovers that the seemingly perfect statistics she deals with daily are just not adding up.

Martin, Larry Jay

Sounding Drum. Kensington, 1999. **M**
Native American businessman Steve Drum prepares to pull off the ultimate business deal: secretly establish a Native American reservation in the middle of Manhattan and create the world's largest casino inside a building that symbolizes the wealth and power that is New York City.

Martini, Steve

The List. Putnam, 1997.
A daring plan to scam the media world backfires on novelist Abby Chandlis and has her running for her life.

McMillan, Edward J.

The Audit. Harwood, 2000.
Pat McGuire, an auditor for the National Tobacco Federation, uncovers a scandal that threatens to topple an industry.

Meltzer, Brad

The Millionaires. Warner, 2002.
Shady brothers Charlie and Oliver Caruso steal $3 million from their failed bank and soon find themselves running for their lives.

Morris, Ken

Man in the Middle. Bancroft, 2002.
Wall Street executive Peter Neil is swept up in the treacherous world of high finance where ruthless men and women of business think nothing of murder as a means to get what they want.

Nance, John J.

Phoenix Rising. Crown, 1994.

Elizabeth Sterling is the new chief financial officer for a startup airline that promises comfort and superior customer service, but she soon finds herself trying to protect the company from a devious plan to destroy it.

Neville, Katherine

A Calculated Risk. Ballantine, 1992.

Verity Banks, head of Electronic Funds Transfer at the prestigious Bank of the World, is offered a challenge by her one-time mentor Dr. Zoltan Tor: steal a billion dollars and use it to make $30 million in three months. Tor spices up the deal by allowing Verity to use a computer, while he will not.

Patterson, James

The Midnight Club. Little, Brown, 1989.

The members of the Midnight Club, international criminals who pose as respectable businessmen, are mysteriously being murdered one by one, and only a former cop in a wheelchair can find a motive behind the assassinations.

Patterson, Richard North

The Lasko Tangent. Ballantine, 1979.

William Lasko is a self-made multimillionaire who intends to use his wealth and powerful contacts, including the president of the United States, to get exactly what he wants.

Reich, Christopher

The First Billion. Delacorte, 2002.

Former fighter pilot John "Jett" Gavalian is the CEO of investment firm Black Jet Securities. He finds himself ensnared in a global conspiracy—and running from both the FBI and international assassins.

Numbered Account. Delacorte, 1998.

Nicholas Neumann, a former U.S. Marine and a graduate of the Harvard Business School, seems to have it all, but he is still obsessed with his father's death, which occurred seventeen years ago. He discovers evidence that suggests the United Swiss Bank played a role in his father's death and goes undercover in the bank's Zurich headquarters to search for clues.

Rhodes, Stephen

The Velocity of Money. William Morrow, 1997.

Attorney Rick Hansen is ecstatic that he has landed a fantastic job with the investment firm of Wolcott, Fulbright & Company . . . until he finds out that his predecessor's supposed suicide was really murder. He soon uncovers a plot to create the biggest stock market crash since October 1929.

Ridpath, Michael

Free to Trade. HarperCollins, 1995.

Bond trader and ex-Olympic runner Paul Murray suddenly finds his world turned upside down when his lover and colleague Debbie Chater is found drowned in the

Thames. He soon finds evidence that Debbie knew about devious investment deals that caused her murder and that he will soon be the next one to be killed. (The author spent eight years working as a fund manager for an international bank in London.)

Trading Reality. HarperCollins, 1996.

Bond trader Mark Fairfax must take over his older brother Richard's high-tech company, FairSystems, when Richard is viciously attacked and murdered in his own workshop. As Mark uses all his financial skills to keep the struggling company afloat, he tries to find the answers behind his brother's death—before the perpetrators come after him.

Roughan, Howard

The Up and Comer. Warner, 2001.

Philip Randall has it all: a successful career, a beautiful (and wealthy) wife, a great New York city home . . . and he's about to lose it all when a man from his past comes looking for revenge.

Sanders, Lawrence

The Tangent Objective. Putnam, 1976.

Peter Tangent is an executive at a U.S. oil company and willing to do anything—anything—to get what he wants, even overthrow the rightful rulers of an African country.

Schofield, David

The Pegasus Forum. Simon & Schuster, 2002.

The students of Oxford economics professor Wallace Bradley plot to cause the collapse of banks around the world.

Simmons, Dan

Darwin's Blade. William Morrow, 2000.

Former Vietnam War sniper Darwin Minor is now a successful accident investigator who must use his old skills when he becomes embroiled in a massive insurance fraud conspiracy and is targeted for death.

$ 6

Sulitzer, Paul-Loup

<u>Franz Cimballi series</u>

Money. Stuart, 1985.

French financial genius Franz Cimballi goes from rags to riches in just four short years. (Author Sulitzer, like his character Cimballi, became rich as a young man through his own financial know-how.)

Cash. Stuart, 1986.

Financier Franz Cimballi faces an unseen foe who strives to bankrupt his empire.

Fortune. Stuart, 1987.

International businessman Franz Cimballi tangles with mobsters when he invests in an Atlantic City casino.

The Green King. Stuart, 1984.

Thomas, Craig

A Different War. Little, Brown, 1997.

Mitchell Gant, aviation disaster specialist (formerly seen in *Firefox* and *Firefox Down!;* see Chapter 3), is called on to investigate two suspicious airline crashes. Evidence points to a British aircraft manufacturer in search of new markets for its newest jet.

Thomas, Michael M.

Baker's Dozen. Farrar, Straus & Giroux, 1996.

Lucy Preston, vice president of a multibillion-dollar corporation, finds that her boss is not only the most admired CEO in the world, but also a deadly player in the world of international finance.

Black Money. Crown, 1994.

Journalist Lee Boynton teams up with computer fraud expert Thurlow Coole to crack a conspiracy that is laundering billions of dollars through a variety of resources—everything from Wall Street businesses to fast-food restaurants.

Green Money. Wyndham, 1980.

Hard Money. Viking, 1985.

GBG is the largest, most powerful entertainment and telecommunications conglomerate in the United States. Its founder, H. H. Monstrance, or "X," as he is known to both his friends and his enemies, intends to gain control of the company from his son and then use his power to influence U.S. policies.

The Ropespinner Conspiracy. Warner, 1987.

Someone Else's Money. Simon & Schuster, 1982.

The richest man in America sets out to buy his wife the social prestige she desperately desires by obtaining the most extensive collection of Renaissance art in existence—at any cost.

Turow, Scott

Pleading Guilty. Farrar, Straus & Giroux, 1993.

McCormack A. "Mack" Mallowy of the legal firm Gage & Griswell is sent to find the company's star attorney, who has apparently absconded with $5.6 million of a class-action suit settlement.

Willet, Sabin

The Betrayal. Villard, 1998.

Louisa Shidler is a mother, a U.S. ambassador, and a convicted traitor. Everyone has betrayed her except her daughter Isabel, who has been kidnapped. Shidler discovers that she and her daughter are pawns in an international bribery scheme of unparalleled treachery and that she is the only one who can save her daughter.

The Deal. Random House, 1996.

The deal: an $840 million leveraged buyout. The price: murder.

Zagel, James

Money to Burn. Putnam, 2002.

The Honorable Paul E. Devine, a Chicago Federal District Court judge, and three of his cronies have a great plan: steal $100 million from the Federal Reserve.

Chapter 7

Stalking the Predators

Maniacs, Murderers, Psychopaths, and Serial Killers

Definition: In this subgenre, the murderer has star billing—he is usually a serial killer or multiple murderer and almost always insane. Unlike a mystery, there is always more than one death, and we usually meet up with the antagonist and his deadly deeds fairly quickly. The villain is either attractive or hideous—there are no in-betweens. He (the killer is usually male) is out for revenge for some perceived wrong, trying to accomplish a mission and killing people who get in his way, or chooses his victims based on some common criterion (e.g., hair color, age, occupation, etc.). There is always the chance that the killer will not be caught in the end and may show up in a sequel.

The Appeal: There is little likelihood that the average person will be immolated in a volcanic eruption, assassinated by a foreign spy, or killed by a mutated clone, but the fear that one could cross paths with some crazed psychopath is a real one—or so the media would have us believe. These books allow readers to glimpse inside the criminal mind and to learn about the procedures used to investigate and apprehend deadly killers. The character of the criminal is certainly one of the draws—whether charming or creepy. Consider the fascination a character such as Hannibal Lector holds. There is also an appeal to the horror reader who will enjoy the dark atmospheric settings, graphic scenes, and frightening villains. Those who would never condescend to read a ghost story can still safely scare themselves silly by reading novels of "true" horror.

Brief History: One of the earliest titles in this subgenre is *The Lodger* (1912), by Marie Belloc Lowndes, in which a mysterious stranger rents a London couple's spare room during Jack the Ripper's bloody reign. In the 1950s, we see some early incarnations of the modern-day psychopath in the monstrous child Rhoda (William March's *The Bad Seed*) and the amoral Tom Ripley (Patricia Highsmith's *The Talented Mr. Ripley*), but not until 1973 with Lawrence Sander's *The First Deadly Sin* do we see the full-fledged serial killer that we have come to know and love. The past ten years have seen an explosion in this subgenre with writers such as John Sandford and James Patterson creating whole series based on serial killers and their bizarre (yet obviously very interesting) ways of murder and mayhem.

Advising the Reader: The key elements to remember when advising the reader and suggesting appropriate titles are the following:

- What level of gore is the reader is willing to tolerate? Some titles written in the past few years have taken bloodshed and torture to new heights of revulsion.

- If a reader has enjoyed a book by a particular author, check to see if the author has written more titles. many prolific authors sometimes carry over their characters into other books.

- If the reader has exhausted this subgenre, suggest medical thrillers. These two subgenres have similar elements, including intelligent maniacs and horrible deaths.

- If the reader has exhausted this subgenre, you might also guide him or her to nonfiction titles about serial killers and multiple murderers.

- Police procedurals featuring pathologists and their graphic autopsies, such as those written by Patricia Cornwell and Kathy Reichs, might be of interest to this type of reader.

- Romantic suspense titles that feature murderous stalkers, such as those by Mary Higgins Clark and Joy Fielding, might also be of interest.

- *You Can Judge a Book by Its Cover:* Look for sharp implements covered in blood, faces of screaming women, vacant buildings at night, one high-heeled shoe, and lots of black and red.

> *The belief in a supernatural source of evil is not necessary;*
> *men alone are quite capable of every wickedness.*
>
> *—Joseph Conrad*

Ablow, Keith

Frank Clevenger series

Denial. Pantheon, 1997.
> Frank Clevenger, a forensic psychiatrist who is tortured by his demons, is asked to judge the sanity of a homeless man accused of a series of brutal murders.

Projection. Pantheon, 1999.
> The not very well-adjusted Dr. Clevenger must deal with a plastic surgeon who has been convicted of four murders and has now taken control of the hospital for the criminally insane where he has been incarcerated.

Compulsion. Pantheon, 2002.
> Forensic psychiatrist Frank Clevenger aids his old friend, the Nantucket chief of police, in a search for a teenage sociopath who is suspected of killing his infant sister.

Psychopath. Pantheon, 2003.
> Dr. Clevenger is recruited by the FBI to help them find a serial killer, known as the Highway Killer, who has murdered people in twelve states.

Abrahams, Peter

The Fan. Warner, 1995. **FILM**
> Bobby Rayburn is a star baseball player, and Gil Renard the ultimate fan. But soon harmless adoration becomes dangerous obsession.

The Tutor. Ballantine, 2002.
> Julian Sawyer has been hired to tutor the Gardners' troubled teenage son Brandon, but Sawyer has other, more dangerous plans for the family. Only eleven-year-old Ruby can save her family from the insidious stranger they have allowed into their home.

Alexie, Sherman

Indian Killer. Atlantic, 1996. **M**
> A serial killer is scalping white men in Seattle, and the press quickly dubs him the Indian Killer. After each new murder, hate crimes against Native Americans increase, and the city is thrown into a paranoid turmoil. (The author is a Spokane/Coeur d'Alene Indian.)

Anthony, Sterling

Cookie Cutter. Ballantine, 1999. **M**
> African American "Bloody Mary" Cunningham, a lieutenant in Detroit's homicide unit, is tracking a serial killer whose victims are those he considers racial sellouts and in whose hands he leaves a single Oreo cookie.

Appel, William

Whisper . . . He Might Hear You. Fine, 1990.
> Psychologist Kate Berman was an expert on serial killers, but an almost lethal knife attack by one of her subjects put an end to her career—until she's called out of retirement to track down a psychopath who has already killed eight women—and has now abducted her niece.

Atkins, Charles

Risk Factor. St. Martin's 1999.
> An evil murderer in the body of a child is on the loose in Boston, and it's up to senior psychiatric resident Dr. Molly Katz to track the killer down. (The author is a practicing psychiatrist and member of the Yale clinical faculty.)

Bayer, William

Pattern Crimes. Villard, 1987.
> A serial killer is loose in Jerusalem, and it's up to David Bar-Lev of the Jerusalem police's Pattern Crimes Unit to track down the perpetrator.

Switch. Linden, 1984.

> *Gannon's Adventure/Suspense Rule Number 10: Female serial killers are much more common in fiction than in real life.*

Wallflower. Villard, 1991.

A dead weed placed at the scene of each murder is the only clue to a string of seemingly random murders. There are two female serial killers at work—one of whom doesn't even know she's a murderess.

Billingham, Mark

Tom Thorne series

Sleepy Head. William Morrow, 2001.

Detective Inspector Tom Thorne is on the trail of a madman who is inducing debilitating strokes in his victims, leaving them aware but unable to move or speak.

Scaredy Cat. William Morrow, 2002.

Detective Inspector Tom Thorne finds himself investigating two serial killers who both use the same techniques to murder their victims.

Bisell, Sallie

A Darker Justice. Bantam, 2001.

The FBI asks assistant DA Mary Crow to protect Irene Hannah, the presumed next victim of a serial killer targeting federal judges.

Black, Ethan

Conrad Voort series

The Broken Hearts Club. Ballantine, 1999.

A banker, a mechanic, a literary agent, and a psychologist meet one night a week in the back room of a ratty bar in New York City. They all have one thing in common: a broken heart. But now they've decided to get revenge on those who did them wrong, and Conrad Voort, the NYPD's richest detective, goes up against them.

Irresistible. Ballantine, 2000.

Nora Clay knows all her victim's secrets. Once she has seduced her prey, leaving him begging for more, she kills him. NYPD sex crimes detective Conrad Voort is assigned to track down Nora, but he soon finds that he has become the hunted instead of the hunter.

All the Dead Were Strangers. Ballantine, 2001.

After the strange disappearance of a boyhood friend, New York police detective Conrad Voort begins to see a pattern in a series of strange, supposedly accidental deaths. His investigation draws the attention of the forces behind the deaths, and Voort finds his own life in danger.

Blake, Sterling

Chiller. Bantam, 1993.

> A serial killer is targeting scientists who are working on cryonics—preserving bodies at ultra-low temperatures to be revived at some time in the future—because he feels it is an affront against God.

Blauner, Peter

The Intruder. Simon & Schuster, 1996.

> How far will Manhattan lawyer Jacob Schiff go to protect his family from a bizarre homeless man who enters their life and refuses to leave?

Bloch, Robert

Norman Bates series

Psycho. TOR, 1959. **FILM**

> Norman Bates and his loving mother are terrorizing guests at the Bates Motel.

Psycho House. Doherty, 1990.

> Norman Bates is up to his old tricks again.

Blunt, Giles

Forty Words for Sorrow. Putnam, 2001.

> Two brutal killers are targeting adolescents in rural Canada, and John Cardinal, along with his new partner Lisa Delorme, are tapped to investigate.

Bonansinga, Jay

Head Case. Simon & Schuster, 1998.

> John Doe is what the doctors call him: he ran out in traffic, got hit by a truck, and can now remember nothing about his past. But his dreams are full of bloody and mutilated bodies. Jessie Bales is a private investigator whom John hires to help him find answers, but what she finds is shocking: a secret police file and a diary in John's handwriting that describes a trail of murder. What could be the real secret behind John Doe?

Burke, Jan

Nine. Simon & Schuster, 2002.

> A group of rich young men have decided to test their intellectual prowess and are killing the felons on the FBI's Ten Most Wanted List. Los Angeles County Sheriff's Homicide Detective Alex Brandon is assigned to track down these popular vigilantes, whom the public has dubbed "The Exterminators."

Campbell, Ramsey

The Count of Eleven. Doherty, 1992.

> Jack Orchard is a loving husband, a devoted father, a good friend, a guy who likes to have a good time . . . and a serial killer.

The One Safe Place. Doherty, 1995.

The Travises have just moved to England from the United States when Don is involved in a minor fender bender with Phil Fancy, who proceeds to beat Don to a pulp. This is only the beginning of the horror for the Travises, as they soon discover that everyone in the Fancy family is a psychopath.

Chamber, Christopher

Sympathy for the Devil. Crown, 2001. **M**

African American FBI agent Angela Bivins matches wits with a black serial killer who is targeting teenage girls.

Child, Lee

Running Blind. Putnam, 2000.

Women are being murdered, and the only link among them is that they once worked in the military—and that they all knew Jack Reacher.

Clark, Leigh

Shock Radio. Doherty, 1996.

Radio DJ Sunset Scott has an on-air personality that grows more offensive as the ratings climb, until one day a man calls and claims to be the Phantom, a serial killer who has been terrorizing the city of Los Angeles. The caller predicts the next killing, and the ratings soar, but Scott finds himself under suspicion as a suspect in the murders and must find the real killer.

Cline, C. Terry

Quarry. NAL, 1987.

The beautiful Colorado mountain resort of Gatlin Pass is the perfect setting for movie making. Unfortunately, the only films being made there are snuff movies. Journalist Gary Colter's investigation into this depraved gang of filmmakers becomes even more serious when his teenage daughter disappears.

Reaper. Fine, 1989.

Elderly women write letters to Palm Beach astrologist Violet Day, telling her they are about to die. And then they are found brutally murdered. Violet teams up with her old friend former policeman Ken Blackburn when the next target is someone in Violet's own family.

Condé, Nicholas

In the Deep Woods. St. Martin's, 1989.

Connelly, Michael

The Poet. Little, Brown, 1996.

Jack McEvoy is the crime reporter for the *Rocky Mountain News,* and his only brother, a homicide detective, has supposedly committed suicide. Investigating his brother's death, he finds that a string of police suicides across the country are the work of a serial killer.

Connolly, John

Every Dead Thing. Simon & Schuster, 1999.
> Charlie "Bird" Parker is a former NYPD detective still recovering from the death of his wife and daughter when his ex-partner asks him to help track down a serial killer. Assisted by forensic psychologist Rachel Wolfe, Parker searches for the Traveling Man, who skins his victims and takes their faces.

Dark Hollow. Simon & Schuster, 2001.
> Charlie Parker, heads back to his hometown of Scarborough, Maine, and sets up practice as a private investigator. His first case seems fairly straightforward as he attempts to collect overdue child support as a favor to an old friend, but then the dead bodies start piling up.

The Killing Kind. Atria, 2001.
> Charlie Parker investigates the murderous religious organization known as the Fellowship.

Cooke, John Peyton

Torsos. Warner, 1983.
> Cleveland, Ohio, in 1935, before the term "serial killer" had even been coined: a vicious murderer chopped up and beheaded more than a dozen victims. This is the fictionalized account of the "Torso Slayer."

Craig, Kit

Gone. Little, Brown, 1992.
> The Hales are a fairly ordinary family living in a fairly ordinary New England town—until one Saturday morning in late spring, when Michael, Teah, and little Tommy wake up to find their mother gone. A maniac from her past has kidnapped her, and only her children can save her. Here's an interesting tidbit: the maniac has movie star good looks—until he takes his clothes off. (The author's real name is Kit Reed.)

Twice Burned. Little, Brown 1993.
> Fourteen-year-old identical twins Jane and Emily Archer are as beautiful as roses—but beware of their thorns.

Crais, Robert

Demolition Angel. Doubleday, 2000.
> Carol Starkey is a detective with the Los Angeles Police Department and a former member of the bomb squad. She is investigating a series of explosions that are designed to kill bomb squad technicians, and she's next on the hit list.

Crider, Bill

Blood Marks. St. Martin's, 1991.
> Told from the perspective of a Houston, Texas, serial killer who prefers to vary his killing methods and chooses his victims by their "blood marks," which only he can see. Casey Buckland will be his next victim.

Curtis, Jack

Glory. Dutton, 1988.

A murderer hypnotizes his victims so that they don't even know he's there when he's killing them. He also has a split personality—his alter ego is an imaginary sister named Elaine.

Point of Impact. Simon & Schuster, 1991.

First it was a woman in a crowd, then a man on a train, then a young couple—all murdered by the same person. But what is the pattern that connects the murders?

Deaver, Jeffery

The Devil's Teardrop. Simon & Schuster, 1999.

It is December 31, 1999, in Washington, D.C., and the Digger, an assassin programmed to kill every four hours, is loose in the city. His accomplice, the only one who knows how to turn him off, is killed in a freak hit-and-run accident. Now who will stop the Digger? (Deaver also writes as William Jeffries.)

Lincoln Rhyme and Amelia Sachs series

The Bone Collector. Viking, 1997. 📄 **FILM**

Former NYPD detective Lincoln Rhyme, paralyzed from the neck down in a freak explosion, and his "arms and legs," Amelia Sachs, hunt down an ingenious killer known as the Bone Collector. If Rhyme and Sachs can decipher the clues the killer leaves at every murder scene, maybe they can stop him before he kills again.

The Coffin Dancer. Simon & Schuster, 1998. 📄

Former NYPD detective Lincoln Rhyme and his resourceful assistant, Amelia Sachs, match wits with a relentless assassin known only as the Coffin Dancer. The pair have only forty-five hours to find the chameleon-like killer before he completes his mission: the elimination of three federal witnesses. The only thing that can identify him is his tattoo—an image of the Grim Reaper waltzing with a woman in front of a casket.

The Empty Chair. Simon & Schuster, 2000. 📄

Amelia Sachs absconds into the swamplands of North Carolina with a fugitive known as the Insect Boy, and Lincoln Rhyme must find them both before it is too late.

The Stone Monkey. Simon & Schuster, 2002.

Lincoln Rhyme and Amelia Sachs are asked to assist the FBI and the Immigration and Naturalization Service in tracking down a cargo ship containing illegal Chinese immigrants headed for New York City. Unfortunately, the plan goes awry when the ship sinks and only two families aboard survive. The Ghost, the homicidal smuggler in charge of the illicit operation, wants no surviving witnesses and sets out to murder the survivors. Rhyme and Sachs need all their investigative skills to track down the Ghost and stop him.

The Vanished Man. Simon & Schuster, 2003.

In the first scene, a murderer escapes from a locked room, and we soon find out that Lincoln Rhyme and his sidekick (and lover) Amelia Sachs are up against a master illusionist who has many a deadly thing up his sleeve.

Speaking in Tongues. Simon & Schuster, 2000.
Crazed psychologist Aaron Matthews has targeted ex-lawyer Tate Collier and his family for revenge. When daughter Megan is kidnapped, Tate and his ex-wife Bett must reunite to find her and stop madman Matthews from killing again.

Denton, Bradley

Blackburn. St. Martin's, 1993.
Jimmy Blackburn has always asked a lot of questions and never been satisfied with the answers. So he becomes a killer—the killer of those who have lied to him.

Devon, Gary

Bad Desire. Random House, 1990.
How far will a man go under the yoke of erotic obsession? For Henry Lee Slater, the mayor of a prosperous California town, murder could well be the answer.

Lost. Knopf, 1986.
The first page: a twelve-year-old boy shoots a gun at his own head (and survives) while his sister watches. We learn right away that we have a junior psychopath. When a lonely woman who already has two other children in tow takes in the sister, the crazed boy and his vicious dog known as "the Chinaman" stalk them.

Wedding Night. Simon & Schuster, 1995.
After a whirlwind romance, actress Callie McKenna marries the enigmatic Malcolm Rhodes. As she begins to find out the secrets from his past, people start dying.

Dibdin, Michael

Dark Specter. Pantheon, 1995.

> *Gannon's Adventure/Suspense Rule Number 11: You can always count on maniacs to reappear in a sequel.*

Diehl, William
Martin Vail series

Primal Fear. Villard, 1993. **FILM**
Chicago attorney Martin Vail's client is Aaron Stampler, who was found hiding in a confessional, covered in blood and clutching a butcher knife with the mutilated and dismembered body of an archbishop nearby. Vail is about to discover that pure evil can lurk behind the face of an angel.

Show of Evil. Ballantine, 1995.
Martin Vail, now Chicago's chief prosecutor, finds himself in a the middle of a nightmare—murders linked to the one committed by the evil Aaron Stampler, locked away for the past ten years, are occurring.

Reign in Hell. Ballantine, 1997.
Martin Vail has been named assistant U.S. attorney general and is assigned to track down a fanatic terrorist known as Brother Transgressor. To make matters worse, his evil nemesis Aaron Stampler returns—seemingly from the dead.

Dobyns, Stephen

The Church of Dead Girls. Metropolitan, 1997.
Three young girls have disappeared in the small town of Aurelius in northern New York state, and everyone is a suspect.

Elliott, James

Cold Cold Heart. Delacorte, 1994.

Ellis, Brett Easton

American Psycho. Vintage, 1991. **FILM**
Patrick Bateman is a handsome, educated, twenty-six-year-old Wall Street wonder boy. He's is also a serial killer. Graphic gore mixed with literary pretension.

Epperson, S. K.

The Neighborhood. Fine, 1995.
Abra Ahrens moves into a small community and soon learns that new neighbors can be more than a pain in the neck.

Fox, Zachary Alan

Cradle and All. Kensington, 1999.

When the Wind Blows. Kensington, 1998.
When Mark Ritter's mother dies, he finds a death certificate among her possessions stating that he had died as an infant more than thirty years ago in the town of Harmony, Colorado—a town he's never heard of. Mark goes to Harmony to find the answers to his questions but soon finds that someone is willing to kill to keep certain secrets.

Freemantle, Brian

The Button Man. St. Martin's, 1992.

French, Nicci

Beneath the Skin. Warner, 2000.
Three very different women discover that a sexual predator wants to love each one of them . . . to death. Schoolteacher Zoe; Jenny, former model and now mother and wife; and Nadia, an entertainer, have all been targeted by a sociopath who could be anyone around them. (The author is a pseudonym for a husband-and-wife writing team.)

Friedman, Hal

A Hunting We Will Go. HarperCollins, 1998.
Arthur Combs, aka Starman, seeks out beautiful, famous women in Hollywood and lets them know he is their biggest fan . . . and then kills them. Six o'clock

news anchor Katlyn Rome is covering the story when she catches Arthur's eye.

Gallagher, Stephen

Red, Red Robin. Ballantine, 1995.
Successful businesswoman Ruth Lasseter is having an affair with her boss, and to hide that fact from his wife she must bring a "boyfriend" to the company dance. Efficient as always, Ruth heads for an escort service, where she picks Tim Hagan, a sweet, polite, boyishly handsome young man, who's also a psychopathic murderer.

Gerard, Philip

Desert Kill. William Morrow, 1994.
Mutilated bodies are being found in the Arizona desert, and the case falls to chief of police Paul Pope to investigate.

Gilstrap, John

Nathan's Run. HarperCollins, 1996.
Twelve-year-old orphan Nathan Bailey is wrongfully accused of killing a policeman and soon becomes the target of a nationwide man (boy) hunt. He has only himself to count on as not only the police close in on him, but also a contract killer.

Girard, James Preston

The Late Man. Atheneum, 1993.

Glass, Leslie

Burning Time. Doubleday, 1993. **M**
New York Police Detective April Woo and psychoanalyst Jason Frank unite to track down a serial killer who leaves his brand burned into his victims' flesh.

Goddard, Ken

Cheater. Doherty, 1996.
Psychopath "John Doe Thirty-Three" has an inventive way of killing: he enters into a house's crawlspace, cuts a hole in the floor, installs hinges, and then slices through the carpeting springing up on his victims through the newly created trapdoor.

Goldman, William

Magic. Delacorte, 1976. **FILM**

Grant, Michael

Retribution. HarperCollins, 1995.
Ex-cop Mike Devlin takes on what he thinks will be a cushy job as the head of security for a forty-story Manhattan office building, but the job is cushy for all of two weeks before corporate executives start dying "accidental" deaths.

Graziunas, Daina, and Jim Starlin

Thinning the Predators. Warner, 1996.
David Vandemark is the ultimate predator: a serial killer who kills other serial killers.

Grippando, James

The Informant. HarperCollins, 1996.
An anonymous informant contacts FBI special agent Victoria Santos and claims he can predict the next attack of a brutal serial killer who has left a string of gruesome murders across the country. The only catch is that the information comes with a price.

Under Cover of Darkness. HarperCollins, 2000.
The "Bookend Killer" is stalking Seattle, killing in pairs—first two men, then two women—and successful lawyer Gus Wheatley's wife appears to be his newest victim . . . or accomplice.

Guild, Nicholas

Angel. Carroll, 1995.
Angel is beautiful, resourceful, captivating . . . and a brutal killer.

Hall, Matthew

The Art of Breaking Glass. Little, Brown, 1997.
Is there such a thing as a "good" maniac killer? Psychiatric nurse Sharon Blautner is about to embark on a crazed journey in search of the answer to that question.

Harper, Andrew

Bad Karma. Kensington, 1997.
The very dangerous Agnes Hatcher is incarcerated in a hospital for the criminally insane, where the staff knows her as the Gorgon. She escapes and pursues psychiatric technician Trey Campbell and his family as they vacation in Southern California.

Harris, Thomas

Dr. Hannibal (the Cannibal) Lector series

Red Dragon. Putnam, 1981. FILM
Francis Dolarhyde has killed two families in two cities, and once the moon is full he intends to kill again. FBI agent Will Graham is searching for Dolarhyde just as Dolarhyde is searching for him. This book marks the first appearance of Dr. Hannibal Lector—in a cameo role. Filmed first as *Manhunter* and then again under the original title.

The Silence of the Lambs. St. Martin's, 1988. FILM
Serial killer Buffalo Bill is killing women for their skin, and neophyte FBI agent Clarice Starling is assigned to interview the infamous and incarcerated Dr. Hannibal (the Cannibal) Lector to get his insight into the case. His enigmatic clues send her on a strange and savage journey.

Hannibal. Delacorte, 1999.

> Seven years after Dr. Hannibal Lector escaped from custody, his sixth victim, Mason Verger, draws him out of "retirement." Verger, paralyzed and with his faced ripped off, wants revenge for what Lector did to him and intends to feed him to ferocious pigs. FBI agent Clarice Starling is also back—but in a way readers may find unappetizing.

Hayder, Mo

Birdman. Doubleday, 1999.

> A serial killer is stalking and ritualistically murdering young women in England, and the only clue is a bird sewn inside each one of their chests.

Heffernan, William

Blood Rose. Dutton, 1991.

> A serial killer is killing young women in a small Vermont town, leaving a withered rose in place of their heart. Ex-NYPD detective Paul Devlin is the town's chief of police, a job he took after he was almost murdered by a serial killer.

Ritual. American, 1988.

Heller, Jean

Handyman. Doherty, 1995.

> The papers call him the Heartbreak Killer because of his penchant for mutilating his victims' hearts, but he calls himself the Handyman after the guy in an old pop song. First he started with prostitutes, but now he's set his sights on classier prey.

Highsmith, Patricia

Strangers on a Train. Harmondsworth, 1950.

> A warning to keep one's mouth shut when talking to a psychopath during a mundane train ride.

Tom Ripley series

The Talented Mr. Ripley. Harmondsworth, 1955.

> Poor Tom Ripley is recruited by wealthy Herbert Greenleaf to bring his son Dickie home from Europe, but once in Italy, Tom decides to become Dickie and kill anyone who is a threat to his new life.

Ripley Underground. Doubleday, 1970.

> Now married and living in the French countryside, Ripley must be constantly observant, as one slip could ruin his cushy life.

Ripley's Game. Knopf, 1974.

> Social-climbing Tom Ripley is slighted at an exclusive gathering and intends to repay the perceived insult in a deadly way.

The Boy Who Followed Ripley. Lippincott, 1980.

> The murderer finds a protégé in a sixteen-year-old teenage runaway.

Ripley under Water. Knopf, 1991.
> The predator now becomes the prey.

Hill, Richard

What Rough Beast? Countryman, 1992. **M**
> Cuban American private investigator Randall Gatsby Sierra is on the trail of a se-rial killer who targets young women in public campgrounds.

Hoag, Tami

Ashes to Ashes. Bantam, 1999.
> The newspapers have named him the Cremator. He has already killed three peo-ple and then burned their bodies, but he doesn't intend to stop at three.

Hoyt, Richard

Tyger! Tyger! Doherty, 1996.
> The services of ex-CIA agent James Burlane are engaged to break up a smuggling ring that specializes in exotic animals, but his job is complicated by an interna-tional serial killer who is enthralled by tigers and leaves his beautiful young vic-tims painted like the cats.

Hunter, Jessie

Blood Music. Turtle, 1987.

One, Two, Buckle My Shoe. Simon & Schuster, 1997.
> A serial killer who has a compulsive ritual of abducting and murdering little boys is thrown for a loop when he mistakenly kidnaps a little girl. Emily Lookinland, terrified but resourceful, must save herself before her captor makes his decision about what to do with her.

Hurwitz, Gregg Andrew

The Tower. Simon & Schuster, 1999.
> Psychopathic murderer Allander Atlasia has escaped from the Tower, a suppos-edly escape-proof maximum security prison, and starts reenacting scenes from his tortuous childhood. The only one smart enough and relentless enough to stop him is ex-FBI agent Jade Marlow, who has his own secrets from the past.

Iles, Greg

Mortal Fear. Dutton, 1997.
> Six women in six cities have been murdered, with six different weapons, but each time the killer has taken the same unusual souvenir.

Sleep No More. Putnam, 2002.
> John Waters is a happy man, satisfied with his lot in life until secrets from a past he thought long forgotten return to haunt him.

24 Hours. Putnam, 2000.
> Will and Karen Jennings are a successful, happy couple with a five-year-old daughter, but they have been targeted by a psychopathic genius who is deter-mined to make their life a living hell—that is until they decide in desperation to turn the tables on him. (Filmed as *Trapped.*)

Jacobs, Claire Rainwater

Mother, May I Sleep with Danger? Fine, 1997.

When Jessica Lewisohn's daughter, Laurel, comes home from college with her new boyfriend Kevin Glade, Jessica feels there's something just not right with the "perfect" young man. She's right—he's a killer.

Jance, J. A.

Kiss of the Bees. Avon, 2000. M

Serial killer Andrew Carlisle is dead, but his protégé lives on. He has kidnapped a young Native American woman who is said to be "kissed by the bees" or destined for greatness. He intends to torture her to death slowly, in honor of his mentor. Can Diana Walker stop this madman as she had stopped Carlisle twenty years earlier?

Jones, Bruce

In Deep. Crown, 1991.

Eustes Tully is a detective with the Santa Barbara Sheriff's Department and is investigating the murder of a young woman who had been abused with a police billy club. After another body turns up in the same location, he is suddenly transferred off the case.

Katzenbach, John

The Analyst. Ballantine, 2001.

New York analyst has fifteen days to discover the author of a cryptic note left in his waiting room, or he must commit suicide to prevent members of his family from being killed.

Day of Reckoning. Putnam, 1989.

Duncan and Megan Richards have escaped their radical past and are now living the American Dream with their successful careers, house in the suburbs, and three wonderful children . . . until their past comes back to haunt them. Tanya, the leader of the '60s radical group known as the Phoenix Brigade, is finally out of prison and hungering for revenge.

The Shadow Man. Ballantine, 1995. M

Someone is killing Holocaust survivors in Miami Beach, and retired homicide detective Simon Winter comes out of retirement after his neighbor is found strangled to death. He is aided by African American detective Walter Robinson and Latino prosecutor Espy Martinez.

State of Mind. Ballantine, 1997.

A serial killer is murdering young girls in a community designed as an enclave of safety in an increasingly unsafe world.

The Traveler. Putnam, 1987.

A serial killer is traveling across the country photographing his murders for his "private collection." Allied against him are a female police detective, whose niece was one of his victims, and the killer's brother, a psychiatrist who specializes in sex crimes.

Kennett, Shirley

Gray Matter. Kensington, 1996.
> Pauley Mac is cooking up a very special meal for himself in his suburban St. Louis home—a human brain! And this special dinner is not his first.

King, Charles

Mama's Boy. Pocket, 1992.

King, Stephen

Misery. Viking, 1987. **FILM**
> Crazy lady Annie Wilkes imprisons best-selling author Paul Sheldon in her home while she "encourages" him to write a novel just for her. Watch out for the ax!

Rose Madder. Viking, 1995.
> Rosie Daniels flees her psychopathic monster of a husband after a hellish four-teen years of marriage, moves to another city, and starts a new life for herself . . . until her husband tracks her down.

Koontz, Dean R.

Dark Rivers of the Heart. Knopf, 1994.
> Spencer Grant, the son of a serial killer, meets up with an enigmatic woman and soon finds himself running from two over-the-top villains that make Bonnie and Clyde look like Ozzie and Harriet.

Intensity. Knopf, 1995. **FILM**
> Chyna Shepherd is about to embark on a horrifying and savage trip with a human monster by the name Edgler Foreman Vess—a trip on which she will have to tap into reserves of courage she never knew she had.

The Mask. Jove, 1981.
> She was a teenager with no past, no family, and no memories—a girl who just ap-peared out of nowhere. Carol and Paul take her in, the daughter they never had. But what exactly have they brought into their hearts and home?

Krich, Rochelle Majer

Fair Game. Warner, 1993.
> Five people have been murdered in Los Angeles in five different neighborhoods, but all died of the same thing: a fatal injection of curare.

Speak No Evil. Warner, 1996.
> The LAPD is finding the bodies of female attorneys with their tongues cut out, and criminal defense lawyer Debra Laslow finds herself both suspect and prey.

Laidlaw, Marc

The Orchid Eater. St. Martin's, 1994.

Laird, Thomas

Cutter. Carroll, 2001.
> Chicago police detective Jimmy Parisi must track down a killer who is raping and killing his victims and then selling their organs on the international black market.

La Plante, Richard

Mantis. Doherty, 1992.

> A murderer who kills his victims using karate is on the loose in Philadelphia, and on his trail is Japanese American forensic pathologist Josef Tanaka, who is himself a master of the martial arts.

Leigh, Robert

The Turner Journals. Walker, 1996.

Levin, Ira

Sliver. Bantam, 1991.

> Successful Kay Norris moves into a luxury apartment on Manhattan's upscale Upper East Side; the building is a skinny high-rise known as a "sliver." She doesn't realize that from the moment she moves in, she is under observation. . .

Lindsay, Paul

Mike Devlin series

> ### Code Name: Gentkill. Villard, 1995.
>
> > There is a serial killer loose in Detroit, and he is targeting FBI agents. Special Agent Mike Devlin, considered a "loose cannon" in the bureau, is brought in to investigate.
>
> ### Freedom to Kill. Villard, 1997.
>
> > FBI agent Mike Devlin is up against the Cataclysmist, a mass murderer who unleashes a deadly virus at Disney World, puts poison in children's medicine, and blows up a 747.

Lindsey, David L.

A Cold Mind. Harper, 1983.

> A serial killer is stalking Houston, killing his victims with rabies and collecting their eyeballs.

Mercy. Doubleday, 1990.

> Houston homicide detective Carmen Palma is on the trail of a serial killer who is targeting upscale lesbians.

Lovett, Sarah

Sylvia Strange series

> ### Acquired Motives. Villard, 1996.
>
> > A vigilante is dispensing his own kind of justice in Santa Fe, killing convicted murderers who escaped prison because of a legal technicality. Why has forensic psychiatrist Dr. Sylvia Strange become the next target of this self-styled avenger?
>
> ### Dangerous Attachments. Villard, 1995.
>
> > Prisoner Lucas Watson has an odd hobby: mutilating his fellow prisoners and keeping their body parts as souvenirs. When he suddenly escapes, he goes looking for his psychiatrist, Dr. Sylvia Strange, whom he blames for all his troubles.

Lutz, John, and David August

Final Seconds. Kensington, 1998

A serial bomber is targeting celebrities and members of their entourage with increasingly destructive displays of violence. Arrayed against the methodical killer are Will Harper, a member of the NYPD bomb squad until most of his right hand was destroyed in an explosion, and former FBI profiler (and ex-drunk) Harold Addleman. Harper races across the country investigating each bombing, while Addleman, holed up in his run-down apartment, uses dusty books and sophisticated computers to track the killer. As an added bonus, the victims are thinly veiled and wickedly portrayed recreations of real-life celebrities.

Mahoney, Dan

Hyde. St. Martin's, 1997.

NYPD Detective Brian McKenna is investigating the growing number of deaths among the homeless and soon discovers something strange: many of the deaths that have been attributed to "natural causes" have been those of homeless men infected with HIV. His only clue: a letter signed "Hyde."

March, William

The Bad Seed. Rinehart, 1954. **FILM**

What happens to an ordinary family when a psychopath is born into its midst? Rhoda is such a creature: beautiful on the outside and hideously evil within.

Margolin, Phillip

Gone, but Not Forgotten. Doubleday, 1993.

The wives of several prominent businessmen have disappeared in Portland, Oregon. Left at each site is a black rose and a note reading "Gone, but Not Forgotten." Ten years ago, the same type of disappearances occurred in New York, but the killer was caught and the case closed—or was it?

Wild Justice. HarperCollins, 2000.

Margolis, Seth

Perfect Angel. Avon, 1997.

Julia Mallet is one of the "Madison Seven," a group of friends who have been together since their college days in the '70s. Unfortunately, one of her six closest friends is a murderer, and Julia is next on the victim list.

Martin, Julia Wallis

The Bird Yard. St. Martin's, 1998.

Matthews, Anne McLean

The Cave. Warner, 1997.

Widowed clinical psychologist Helen Myrer goes for a much-needed vacation to an isolated cabin in the woods but soon finds that she has little chance for relaxation as a killer stalks her. She finds herself in a cave full of horror as she must use her wits and experience as a therapist to save herself.

McCammon, Robert R.

Mine. Pocket, 1990.

Mary Terror is a survivor of the radical '60s Storm Front Brigade who was horribly scarred in a shootout with the FBI. Now insane and thinking that the former leader of the brigade is communicating with her through the personal ads in *Rolling Stone,* she steals the infant child of journalist Laura Clayborne. Laura is the only one who can save her child as Mary Terror cuts a murderous swath through the country, killing everyone who gets in her way.

McGuire, Christine

Until Proven Guilty. Pocket, 1993.

Assistant district attorney Kathryn Mackay is put in charge of an investigation into a serial killer who calls himself the Gingerbread Man. (The author is a prosecutor with the district attorney's office in Northern California and also teaches at the FBI Academy in Quantico, Virginia.)

McKay, Gardner

Toyer. Little, Brown, 1998.

Toyer is not a killer, but he does destroy lives. He does not kill his victims but leaves them trapped in a body that will never again respond to the most basic commands. Trying to stop his diabolical reign of terror are Sara Smith, a young reporter, and Dr. Maude Garance, herself on the edge of a mental breakdown from treating Toyer's victims.

Miller, John Ramsey

The Last Family. Bantam, 1996.

Renegade DEA agent Martin Fletcher has declared revenge on all his old colleagues and is targeting their families for murder. The only family left belongs to Paul Masterson, who suffered a disabling injury six years earlier and has been estranged from his family ever since. Masterson must use his family as bait to lure the insane Fletcher into his trap.

Monninger, Joseph

Incident at Potter's Bridge. Fine, 1991.

7

Montanari, Richard

Deviant Way. Simon & Schuster, 1995.

Seduction that leads to murder is part of the scene in Cleveland's singles bars. In the past six months, three twenty-something women have been found dead, and their flower tattoos removed.

Kiss of Evil. William Morrow, 2001.

Each murder is different, but for the obscure symbol carved into the victims' flesh. Cleveland homicide detective John Salvatore Paris must find the killer before he succumbs to his own demons.

The Violet Hour. Avon, 1998.

Because of a tragic event that occurred twenty years ago, all the participants will be murdered unless reporter Nick Stella can stop a poetic psychopath.

Morgenroth, Kate

Kill Me First. HarperCollins, 1999.

Merec is a terrorist and a butcher who kills for pleasure. His latest act of destruction is the slaughter of all but one of the residents of the Willowridge Rest Home. He has had the carnage videotaped and released to the media. Sarah Shepherd is in Willowridge recuperating from an automobile accident that killed her husband. Despondent, she offers her life in exchange for that of another. She so intrigues Merec that he kidnaps her and takes her on a twisted journey of terror across the country.

Morrell, David

Long Lost. Warner, 2002.

If Brad Dennings' brother Petey died years ago at the age of nine, then who is this man who has shown up claiming to be Petey, insinuating himself into Brad's life? When he absconds with Brad's family, Brad must hunt them down.

Munson, Ronald

Fan Mail. Dutton, 1993.

An insane admirer is stalking TV news anchor Joan Carpenter. This entire novel is told through e-mail, memos, letters, and faxes.

Murphy, Gloria

Bloodties. Fine, 1987.

The worst time of Chris Matthews's life was when her three-year-old son Kevin was kidnapped and the body found sixteen months later. Now, thirteen years later, a mysterious stranger is a boarder in her house—a stranger who is frighteningly similar to the person Kevin might have become.

Nightshade. Fine, 1986.

Jen Sawyer was raped twelve years ago by a maniac, and from that savage union was born fraternal twins, twins who have now been abducted by their father. Unless Jen agrees to join him and live as his wife, she will never see her children again.

The Playroom. Fine 1987.

Hauntingly beautiful Victoria Louise has come back to Bradley, Massachusetts, for revenge. When she was in high school, and before the plastic surgery, she was the brunt of her classmates' cruel jokes. Now she wants to bring them to her "playroom" for her own kind of fun.

Nasaw, Jonathan

The Girls He Adored. Pocket, 2001.

Over the last ten years a serial killer with multiple personalities has killed a dozen women—all with strawberry-blonde hair. Finally captured by FBI special agent E. L. Pender, the suspect escapes from custody, taking his court-appointed psychiatrist Irene Cogan with him. Holed up with the killer in a remote house in Oregon, Irene must attempt to communicate with all the personalities, male and female, that reside within the murder's mind.

Nykanen, Mark

Hush. St. Martin's, 1998.

Celia Griswold is an art therapist at a school for emotionally disturbed children in a small, remote Oregon town. She has a big old house in the country, a loveable dog, and a philandering husband—in short, a perfectly ordinary life. Until one day, seven-year-old Davy Boyce, who refuses to speak, is enrolled in her school by his mysterious and off-putting stepfather, Chet. Her attempts to unlock the mystery of Davy's mutism soon embroil her in a frightening race against time to save the boy and herself from a deadly psychopath.

Oates, Joyce Carol

Zombie. Dutton, 1995.

Told in first-person narrative is the literary tale of Quentin P., manipulating sociopath, sexual deviant, and killer.

O'Connell, Carol

The Judas Child. Putnam, 1998.

"A child comes out to meet a friend, the friend is the bait—the Judas Child—and is merely used to get to the real target." It is three days before Christmas and two young girls have disappeared. Investigating the crime is police detective Rouge Kendall. Fifteen years earlier, his twin sister was murdered under the same circumstances . . . supposedly the killer was found. Assisting in the investigation is Rouge's former classmate, forensic psychologist Ali Cray, who is hiding a horrendous secret—she was once a Judas Child. Although each is burdened with years of guilt and sorrow, they must work together to prevent another senseless tragedy.

Parsons, Julie

The Courtship Gift. Simon & Schuster, 1999.

Entomologist Anna Neale comes home to find her husband dead of a bee sting. She is immediately suspicious because her husband had known all his life that he was allergic to bee venom. Soon Anna finds that a handsome and kindly man who calls himself Matthew Makepiece wants to gain her interest—an interest that could have deadly consequences.

Patterson, James

Alex Cross series

Along Came a Spider. Little, Brown, 1993.

Mild-mannered Gary Soneji is a popular math teacher at an exclusive school in Washington, D.C. He's is also a psychopathic murderer. When he kidnaps the daughter of a famous movie star and the son of the secretary of the treasury, African American clinical psychologist and homicide detective Alex Cross is assigned to the case.

Kiss the Girls. Little, Brown, 1995. **FILM** **M**
> Two killers are hunting for victims—maybe even cooperating in their deadly endeavors. "Casanova" is abducting female college students from campuses across the country, while the "Gentleman Caller" is horrifying Los Angeles with a series of shocking murders. Detective Alex Cross decides to investigate when his niece Naomi, a law student, is kidnapped.

Jack & Jill. Little, Brown, 1996. **M**
> No one in Washington, D.C.—not even the president of the United States—is safe from a pair of killers who call themselves Jack and Jill.

Cat & Mouse. Little, Brown, 1997. **M**
> Gary Soneji (last seen in *Along Came a Spider*) is back, and he has sworn that before he takes his last breath, he will kill Alex Cross. Meanwhile in Europe, another maniac, Mr. Smith, is cutting a swath of destruction across the continent.

Pop Goes the Weasel. Little, Brown, 1999. **M**
> Detective Alex Cross is engaged to be married, but his happiness quickly fades as Washington, D.C., is terrorized by a series of murders—murders that cast suspicion on a British diplomat who is a very slippery fellow to catch.

Roses Are Red. Little, Brown, 2000. **M**
> Detective Alex Cross is in hot pursuit of a mysterious madman who calls himself the Mastermind. He is behind a recent spate of bank robberies that have hit Washington, D.C., where the robbers are giving precise demands and then killing the employees and their families if those instructions are not followed exactly.

Violets Are Blue. Little, Brown, 2001. **M**
> Detective Alex Cross matches wits with two separate serial killers: the Mastermind (last seen in *Roses Are Red*) and twin-brother "vampires" William and Michael Alexander.

Four Blind Mice. Little, Brown, 2002.
> Detective Alex Cross has decided to resign from the Washington, D.C., police force when his partner, John Sampson, asks for his help to clear one of his oldest friends from a murder charge. Their investigation leads them to three ruthless killers who are being controlled by someone even more deadly.

Big Bad Wolf. Little, Brown, 2003.
> Alex Cross has joined the FBI and is being personally mentored by its director. Cross is assigned to track down a former KGB operative who is kidnapping wealthy women all over the country and supplying them as participants in the perverse "fantasies" of others.

Hide & Seek. Little, Brown, 1996.
Popular singer Maggie Bradford is on trial for murder. She is accused not only of murdering her first husband, but her second as well. Second husband Will Shepherd was a movie star with deadly secrets.

Women's Murder Club series

1st to Die. Little, Brown, 2001.

Four female friends form the Women's Murder Club to find a killer who has been targeting San Francisco newlyweds. They are SFPD homicide detective Lindsay Boxer; Cindy Thomas, a neophyte crime reporter for the *San Francisco Chronicle;* medical examiner Claire Washburn; and Jill Bernhardt, an assistant district attorney.

2nd Chance. Little, Brown, 2002.

The Women's Murder Club investigates a series of brutal murders occurring in San Francisco, which appear to have no common elements. But each had a close relative in a particular occupation—an occupation that could target one of the members of the Women's Murder Club. (Written with Andrew Gross.)

Pearson, Ridley

Beyond Recognition. Hyperion, 1997.

A homicidal arsonist is loose in Seattle, killing single mothers in horrendous fires but sparing their children.

No Witnesses. Hyperion, 1994.

A maniac is killing people by poisoning food in Seattle supermarkets. Teamed up against him are Detective Lou Boldt and police psychologist Daphne Matthews.

Probable Cause. St. Martin's, 1990.

Undercurrents. St. Martin's, 1988.

Pearson, Ryne Douglas

Top Ten. Putnam, 1999.

Serial killer Michaelangelo (he spells it with the an extra "a") is very upset that he's only number ten on the FBI's most wanted list, so he decides to kill the rest of the criminals on the list until he reaches number one. The only problem is that number five is an undercover FBI agent on a secret mission to stop arms smugglers.

Perry, Thomas

Butcher's Boy series

The Butcher's Boy. Scribner, 1982.

In this "rooting for the bad guy" novel, a contract killer is on the run from Mafia hit men.

Sleeping Dogs. Random House, 1992.

Ten years after he fled to England after killing twenty gangsters in revenge for being double crossed, Mafia hunters have spotted assassin-for-hire Butcher's Boy, and he is once again back on the killing path.

Petit, Chris

The Psalm Killer. Knopf, 1997.

Pye, Michael

Taking Lives. Knopf, 1999.

Martin Arkenhout is a collegiate-looking man—and a serial killer who takes on the identities of his victims. When he can no longer maintain the identity of his victims, he kills again and takes on another identity. Then one day he chooses the wrong victim and finds that he's now the one being stalked.

Reeves-Stevens, Garfield

Dark Matter. Doubleday, 1990.

A young woman has been found dead, tied to her kitchen chair, and the evidence indicates that her brain was dissected while she was still alive. And that's just the first page of this novel.

Russell, Alan

Shame. Simon & Schuster, 1998.

Gary Parker was a serial killer executed for his crimes. His son Caleb has always tried to keep his father's identity a secret, but now people are dying in the same manner as his father's victims, and all the evidence points to Caleb.

Salter, Anna

Michael Stone series

Shiny Water. Pocket, 1997.

Dr. Michael Stone is a forensic psychologist who begins an investigation to track a child murderer and enlists the aid of incarcerated child molester Alex B. Willy. A plot similar to that in *Silence of the Lambs*.

Fault Lines. Pocket, 1998.

Forensic psychologist Dr. Michael Stone has been savagely attacked and now constantly fears for her safety—her constant companions are an attack dog and a gun. Now she has something new to fear: sadistic pedophile Alex B. Willy has been released from prison on a technicality and has targeted her for revenge. The author is herself a forensic psychologist and an internationally known authority on sex offenders.

Sanders, Lawrence

Deadly Sins series

The First Deadly Sin. Putnam, 1973. 📄 **FILM**

An ax murderer is stalking young, fashionable men in New York City's Upper East Side, and NYPD Captain Edward X. Delaney is assigned to track him.

Note: *The Second Deadly Sin* and *The Fourth Deadly Sin*, although part of this series, are conventional murder mysteries.

The Third Deadly Sin. Berkeley, 1981.

> Zoe is a demure, timid little thing until she puts on her hooker disguise and becomes the Hotel Ripper, slashing the throats of conventioneers. Edward X. Delaney is called out of retirement for this one.

Sanders, Leonard

In the Valley of the Shadow. Carroll, 1996.

> For years Harold Appleby has gotten away with murder because he chooses his victims from small towns, but this time he has made a mistake: he unwittingly abducts a child movie star and opens the floodgates of media attention. The child's mother hires retired detective Booker Reeves to track down the murderer and save her daughter before it's too late.

Sandford, John

Lucas Davenport series

Rules of Prey. Putnam, 1989.

> Louis Vullion is an attorney—and an insane serial killer who has researched the rules for getting away with murder. After the third murder, Lucas Davenport, the only member of the Minneapolis Police Department's Office of Special Intelligence, is assigned to find "maddog"—the name the killer leaves in his "playful" notes. (Sandford is a pseudonym for John Camp.)

Shadow Prey. Putnam, 1990.

> All the murders were committed in the same way: the victims throats were slashed with a Native American ceremonial knife. Davenport finds himself up against the warrior-assassin known as Shadow Love.

Eyes of Prey. Putnam, 1991.

> A murderer who mutilates his victims' eyes is on the loose in Minneapolis, and Davenport is called onto the case.

Silent Prey. Putnam, 1992.

> Becker, the insane villain from *Eyes of Prey,* is back and on another murder spree—this time in New York. Davenport is sent to help the NYPD find him.

Winter Prey. Putnam, 1993.

> Davenport is vacationing in the remote winter woods of Wisconsin when the local sheriff asks him for his help in investigating the brutal murder of a family.

Night Prey. Putnam, 1994.

> Bodies with similar stab wounds are turning up around the Minneapolis area, and the police chief turns to Lucas Davenport for help.

Mind Prey. Putnam, 1995.

> A madman abducts psychiatrist Andi Manette and her two young daughters. Davenport must find them before it's too late.

Sudden Prey. Putnam, 1996.

When Candy, a brutal female bank robber, is killed in a police shootout, her fellow gang members, including her husband, swear revenge on all the police involved, as well as their families. Davenport races to track down the killers before more innocent people are killed—including his own family.

Secret Prey. Putnam, 1998.

Davenport is assigned to investigate the murder of leading financial executive Daniel Kresge, who was killed in his remote hunting lodge north of Minneapolis. Many people had a motive and the opportunity, including Kresge's ex-wife, and readers will discover who the killer is just before Davenport does.

Certain Prey. Putnam, 1999.

Davenport faces a new kind of opponent—hit woman Clara Rinker.

Easy Prey. Putnam, 2000.

Davenport's investigation into the murder of a bisexual supermodel is complicated by the return of one of his old flames.

Chosen Prey. Putnam, 2001.

Art professor James Qatar's hobby started out simply enough: he took secret photos of women and then turned the photos into sexual drawings. But his hobby has taken a deadly turn. Now he kills his subjects instead of simply photographing them. Deputy Chief Lucas Davenport takes on what he thinks is a relatively simple case but soon discovers that this killer is anything but simple.

Mortal Prey. Putnam, 2002.

Preparing for his wedding, Lucas Davenport meets up with his old nemesis, hit woman Clara Rinker.

Naked Prey. Putnam, 2003.

Lucas Davenport is back with a new wife, a new baby, and a new job as he investigates a bizarre double murder that looks suspiciously like a lynching.

Savage, Tom

Precipice. Little, Brown, 1994.

It sits high on a cliff in tropical St. Thomas, this gracious mansion known as Cliffhanger and home to the Prescotts. To this perfect setting comes a beautiful young woman who calls herself Diana Meissen, but this is not her real name, nor is it the last of her secrets.

Scavenger. Dutton, 2000.

Mark Stevenson wrote a fictionalized account of the Family Man murders: five massacres in which everyone in the house was killed, including the pets. Now someone who knows far too much about the murders is sending him on a deadly scavenger hunt.

Valentine. Little, Brown, 1996.

Jillian Talbot has a secret admirer who goes by the romantic moniker of Valentine: he sends her notes, gives her gifts, and leaves messages on her answering machine. He's also a killer.

Silver, Jim

Assumption of Risk. Simon & Schuster, 1996.
Investment banker Norman Bloodstone has found a way to make easy money by killing heavily insured claimants. At first merely a cold-blooded murderer, Bloodstone becomes a homicidal maniac.

Simpson, Thomas William

The Caretaker. Bantam, 1998.
If something sounds too good to be true, it is. The Henderson family finds this out very quickly when they move to their new beachside estate, one of the perks of Gunn Henderson's new job. The estate even comes with a caretaker. But Brady the caretaker is not all that he appears to be, and soon the Henderson family will discover that all their wishes haven't really come true.

Smith, Rosamond

Soul/mate. Dutton, 1989.
(Smith is the pseudonym of Joyce Carol Oates.)

Starr Bright Will Be with You Soon. Dutton, 1999.
Starr Bright stalks the Nevada desert leaving death in her wake. She travels light—some money, her makeup, a bottle of amphetamines, and a pearl-handled carving knife.

Steinberg, Richard

The Gemini Man. Doubleday, 1998.
Code-named Gemini, Brian Newman was trained to be the ultimate covert agent, but six years of solitary confinement in a Siberian prison have changed him into something even more deadly.

Straub, Peter

The Hellfire Club. Random House, 1996.
A charming but deadly madman, who is killing people to protect an author's literary reputation, abducts Nora Chancel.

Strieber, Whitley

Billy. Putnam, 1990.
Billy Neary is a happy, healthy twelve-year-old who likes video games and lives with his parents in Stevensville, Iowa. Unfortunately, Billy has caught the eye of the repulsive Barton Royal, child molester and murderer. When Royal abducts the boy, Billy must rely on his own wits to escape from the psychopath before he is killed. The story is presented alternatively from Royal's and Billy's points of view.

Stuart, Sebastian

The Mentor. Bantam, 1999.
Twenty-five years ago Charles Davis made his literary mark, but now he's just a has-been until an inspiration enters his life. His wife, Anne,

hires an assistant for him, a meek small-town girl by the name of Emma Bowles. But is she prey . . . or predator?

Taylor, Domini

Teacher's Pet. Atheneum, 1987.

Taylor, Theodore

The Stalker. Fine, 1987.

Marine corps colonel Cole Hickel's daughter has been sexually abused and murdered. Diplomatic immunity and animal cunning protect her assailant. Hickel can only rely on himself to avenge his daughter's death.

> *Gannon's Adventure/Suspense Rule Number 12: Serial killers always have a method to their madness.*

Thayer, Steve

The Weatherman. Viking, 1995.

As each season changes in Minnesota, a serial killer breaks the neck of a young girl. Television weatherman Dixon Bell, investigative journalist Rick Beanblossom, and Andrea Labore, ex-cop turned TV reporter, form an unlikely team to break the case.

Thornburg, Newton

A Man's Game. Doherty, 1996.

Thorp, Roderick

River. Fawcett, 1995.

In the 1980s the Green River Killer murdered at least fifty women in the Pacific Northwest and was never caught. This is the fictionalized account of that serial killer. (This novel was written before the actual killer was apprehended in 2003.)

Title, Elise

Romeo. Bantam, 1996.

Romeo is a sexual predator who preys on the smart and beautiful women of San Francisco. They eagerly accept his seductive fantasies . . . and die.

Trevor, Elleston

Flycatcher. Doherty, 1994.

Tryon, Thomas

The Other. Knopf, 1971. FILM

Identical twins Niles and Perry Holland were born on either side of midnight so they have different birthdays and different zodiac signs, but the shocking thing is what they share. Enjoyable just for the great ending. (Tryon was an actor before becoming an author.)

Van Arman, Derek

Just Killing Time. Dutton, 1992.
Jack Scott is the head of ViCAT, the Violent Criminal Apprehension Team, and a hunter of serial killers. One of those killers he is after is Zak Dorani, who has killed for thirty years with impunity.

Walker, Mary Willis

The Red Scream. Doubleday, 1994.

Wallace, Marilyn

A Single Stone. Doubleday, 1991.

Weaver, Michael

Impulse. Warner, 1993.
Paul Garrett is forced to watch as his wife is raped and murdered, and then he is shot and left for dead. Psychopath William Meade is shocked to discover that Paul survives and starts contacting him, telling Paul of his latest atrocities. Paul decides to hunt down Meade before more lives are lost.

Wilson, Robert

Icefire. Putnam, 1984.
The inmates take over an asylum for the criminally insane and stalk the staff over an icy wasteland.

Wiltse, David

Blown Away. Putnam, 1996.
A mad bomber known as Spring targets New York City.

<u>John Becker series</u>

Prayer for the Dead. Putnam, 1991.
Burned-out FBI agent John Becker is on the trail of Roger Dyce, who kills his victims, drains their blood, and then dresses the corpses in the clothes of his dead grandfather. After Dyce is injured during one of his murder attempts and ends up in the hospital, Becker mistakes him for a would-be victim.

The Edge of Sleep. Putnam, 1993.
Former FBI agent John Becker and special agent Karen Crist track down a pair of psychopaths who have been able to escape detection because they do not fit the standard serial killer profile.

Bone Deep. Putnam, 1995.
FBI agent John Becker is back, this time tracking down a serial killer who seduces his victims and then murders them during sex.

The Serpent. Delacorte, 1983.
Wiltse should get an A+ for originality: his psychopath, Tom-Tom, not only speaks in tongues but is accompanied by a young child who is heard wailing as the victims are brutally killed. NYPD lieutenant Sandy Block must find the maniac before his pregnant wife become the next victim.

Chapter 8

"Dr. Frankenstein, I Presume"

Science Gone Awry

Definition: Titles here have the use (actually, it is usually the *abuse*) of science as a primary plot characteristic. The antagonist is often the stereotypical "mad scientist." The three subcategories are medical or hospital thrillers, computer- and Internet-related thrillers, and biologically oriented thrillers, which include such things as artificially created plagues and genetic engineering.

The medical thriller usually takes place in a hospital or research center where unpleasant things (usually death) are happening to the patients and subjects. The villain is usually a medical professional, and often so, too, is the hero, or heroine—many of the protagonists are women. Many professional doctors have become authors and write in this subgenre.

In the bio-thriller, science has been subverted by creating new diseases, enhancing natural diseases, and engineering clones and new-fangled genetic mutants.

In the third category, the cyber-thriller, computers are often the villain or the method by which the villain carries out his dastardly deeds. As the Internet has grown, so has its popularity as a means to gather victims for serial killers and other maniacal types.

The Appeal: The appeal here is a simple one: fear. Many of us like to be scared, and what can be more frightening then murderous doctors, deadly diseases, and crazed computers. The individual puts his or her life in the hands of a doctor—and becomes powerless. Doctors and the medical profession hold such high status in our society that it is disquieting to think they may be out to do us harm. It is frightening enough to have to undergo a medical procedure and to risk accidental death or mutilation, but to contemplate that the medical professionals *intentionally* want to maim or kill is truly horrifying. We are infatuated with science and technology, and consider each major breakthrough as a great leap forward of our civilization; we do not like to consider that it could create havoc and destruction. Also, the fact that many medically trained professionals are writing in this subgenre brings realism to plots that are based on authentic science and increases their appeal.

Brief History: Robin Cook, a medical doctor, can be credited with popularizing the medical suspense novel with *Coma,* published in 1977. His prolific career has spurred a growth in this subgenre's popularity as other medically trained professionals have begun to try their hand in it as well. The bio-thriller actually predates the medical thriller; it can trace its roots back to another author with a medical background, Michael Crichton, and his novel *The Andromeda Strain,* published in 1969. The bio-thriller did not really grow in popularity until the 1990s when the fear of outbreaks of new and deadly viruses became a staple of the daily newspapers. Cyber-thrillers can be traced to the science fiction genre and its love for scary, talking computers such as HAL in Arthur C. Clarke's 1968 classic *2001: A Space Odyssey.* Likewise, William Gibson first envisioned an international network of computers, much like what we now call the Internet, in 1984 with *Neuromancer.*

Advising the Reader: The key elements to remember when advising the reader and suggesting appropriate titles are the following:

- What type of books in this subgenre interests the reader, medical, biological, or computer related?

- If the reader has exhausted the medical thrillers, suggest serial killers because these two subgenres have similar elements, such as intelligent maniacs and horrible deaths.

- Disaster novels are also a good subgenre to suggest, especially those related to biological disaster.

- Several medical doctors write in this subgenre. Does this level of realism and a professional background appeal to the reader?

- Bio-thrillers are usually much more graphic in their descriptions of the effects of a disease on a patient, so be prepared to discuss this with the reader.

- *You Can Judge a Book by Its Cover:* Look for medical accoutrements such as bandages, scalpels, hypodermic needles, stretchers, or the caduceus, the winged staff with two snakes twined around it that is the symbol of the medical profession. The three-interlocking rings that form the international symbol for biological contamination is often prominent on the covers of bio-thrillers. And for cyber-thrillers, publishers often like to use fonts seen on computers or used in programming for the titles.

Medical Thrillers

First, do no harm.

—Hippocrates

Baer, Will Christopher

Kiss Me, Judas. Viking, 1997.

> Ex-cop and former mental patient Phineas Poe wakes up in a tub full of ice in a Denver hotel bathroom. Alongside him is a note: "If you want to live, call 911." One of his kidneys has been removed . . .

Belletto, René

Machine. Grove, 1990.

Psychotherapist Marc Lacroix creates a machine that allows two people to switch personalities. He uses it on a crazed patient who escapes in Lacroix's body and goes on a crime spree.

Braver, Gary

Elixir. Forge, 2000.

In a remote rainforest in Papua New Guinea, biologist Christopher Bacon has discovered a rare flower rumored by the natives to prevent aging. He brings the flower back to his Boston lab where he finds that it is indeed the fabled "fountain of youth." But he also learns that the eternal youth has a terrible price.

Gray Matter. Forge, 2002.

Affluent Rachel Whitman wants only the best for her six-year-old son Dylan, but unfortunately he is learning disabled. So she arranges for him to undergo an expensive, secret procedure that purports to turn slow children into geniuses, but she does not realize what else results from the procedure.

Case, John

The Syndrome. Ballantine, 2001.

Lawyer Adrienne Cope teams up with her murdered sister's therapist, Jeff Duran, to investigate a conspiracy to implant devices into people's brains that cause them to commit violent crimes. (Case is the pseudonym for the husband-and-wife team of Jim and Carolina Hougan.)

Chiu, Tony

Positive Match. Bantam, 1997.

Caduceus 21 is highly successful health care company, only the public doesn't know that its profits come from illegal trade in human organs— or where Caduceus 21 gets them.

Christofferson, April

The Protocol. Forge, 1999.

Jennifer Rockhill is planning revenge for her husband's murder, and the first part of her scheme is to be hired as the corporate attorney for BioGentech. The second part is to get the incriminating goods on the head of the company, Dr. Sherwood Fielding, who is dealing in the harvesting of human organs for transplant to the highest bidder.

Cohen, Steven Martin

Becker's Ring. Warner, 1996.

The victims are convicted murderers on parole, and they are found with their mouths sewn shut, their hands surgically removed, and their arms sewn together. Someone has gone to a lot of trouble to ensure that they will never kill again.

Cook, Robin

Acceptable Risk. Putnam, 1994.

A hallucinogenic substance thought to be the cause of the strange behavior behind the Salem Witch Trials becomes, after some chemical tweaking, the newest antidepressant drug Ultra—with horrific consequences.

Brain. Putnam, 1981.

What kind of evil lurks within the cold corridors of Hobson University Medical Center? A young woman asks to see her medical records and disappears. Another dies grotesquely while undergoing brain surgery. And hidden in the hospital's morgue is a female body that is missing its brain.

> *Gannon's Adventure/Suspense Rule Number 13: There's no such thing as "minor" surgery.*

Coma. Little, Brown, 1977.

Patients are being admitted to Memorial Hospital for minor surgery and never regaining consciousness. What is happening to their brain-dead bodies? This is a classic in medical suspense and started Robin Cook, an ophthalmologist, on his prolific fiction-writing career.

Contagion. Putnam, 1995.

Is a health-care colossus using a rare strain of influenza to kill off the patients who are ringing up the highest medical bills, or is something more insidious occurring?

Fatal Cure. Putnam, 1993.

A cutting-edge medical facility in the blissful town of Bartlett, Vermont, turns out to have an unacceptable death rate as doctors Angela and David Wilson try to prevent their eight-year-old daughter Nikki from becoming the next victim.

Fever. Putnam, 1982.

Dr. Charles Martel's daughter Michelle is stricken by a strange disease that conventional medical science is ineffectual in treating, and he finds that his quest for her cure is bringing him closer and closer to a deadly mystery.

Godplayer. Putnam, 1983.

Forced to switch from pathology to psychiatry because of her failing vision, Dr. Cassandra Cassidy marries the gifted but troubled cardiac surgeon Dr. Thomas Kingsley. Against his wishes, she begins an investigation into the deaths of terminally ill patients—deaths that Cassandra believes are really murders.

Harmful Intent. Putnam, 1990.

During a routine birth, a supposedly healthy woman dies and her newborn child is brain damaged; the finger of blame points directly at anesthesiologist Dr. Jeffrey Rhodes. Knowing he is innocent, Rhodes embarks on an investigation into the truth behind this and other recent deaths attributed to "malpractice."

Laurie Montgomery series

    Blindsight. Putnam, 1992.

        A rise in yuppie deaths due to cocaine overdoses has aroused the suspicions of Manhattan forensic pathologist Dr. Laurie Montgomery. The families of the deceased all emphatically deny that illegal drug use could have been a factor, and Montgomery soon discovers that something far more sinister links the supposedly random deaths.

    Chromosome 6. Putnam, 1997.

        Forensic pathologist Dr. Jack Stapleton and his colleague Dr. Laurie Montgomery investigate a medical conspiracy that takes them to a secret lab deep in an African jungle, where apes are being used to prolong human lives.

Marissa Blumenthal series

    Outbreak. Putnam, 1987.

        Dr. Marissa Blumenthal from the Centers for Disease Control in Atlanta is called in to investigate a deadly, contagious virus that she discovers is only striking doctors and their families. She must ferret out the truth behind this murderous conspiracy before she is its next victim.

    Vital Signs. Putnam, 1991.

        Epidemiologist Marissa Blumenthal explores the cutting-edge world of reproductive technology—with deadly consequences.

Mindbend. Putnam, 1985.

    Needing a job to support his wife Jennifer and the child they are expecting, Adam Schonberg drops out of medical school and takes a job as a salesman with the powerful Arolen Pharmaceuticals. He soon discovers the lengths to which the company will go to get what it wants.

Mortal Fear. Putnam, 1988.

Mutation. Putnam, 1989.

    Biomedical researcher Dr. Victor Frank genetically engineers the perfect son, VJ, who soon becomes a perfect terror.

Terminal. Putnam, 1993.

Craven, Wes

Fountain Society. Simon & Schuster, 1999.

    A chilling project to transplant the brains of selected elite individuals into their clones is underway. Dr. Peter Jance is one of those elite but is disgusted with what has been done to him and his clone, and he vows to stop it. (Craven is a well-known director and screenwriter.)

Crichton, Michael

The Terminal Man. Knopf, 1972. **FILM**

    Harry Benson has had electrodes implanted deep into the recesses of his brain to control his violent seizures. The procedure is successful until he escapes and goes on a murderous rampage.

Cuthbert, Margaret

The Silent Cradle. Pocket, 1998. **M**

> Routine deliveries are going fatally askew at a birthing center located directly across the street from the prestigious Berkeley Hills Hospital, where obstetrician Dr. Rae Duprey is the first female African American candidate for the chair of the obstetrics department. She is determined to find out the cause behind these events and soon suspects sabotage from within the hospital.

Cutrer, William, MD, and Sandra Glahn

Lethal Harvest. Kregel, 2000.

> Dr. Tim Sullivan, embryologist and nephew of the president of the United States, is killed in a suspicious accident. What type of research was really going on at his in vitro fertilization clinic, and could the president be involved? (The author is a physician who specialized in infertility and was also a former director of the Christian Medical and Dental Society.)

Dantz, William R.

Nine Levels Down. Forge, 1995.

> Dr. Anna Kane has invented a device that, when implanted in a human brain, detects violent impulses and renders the person unconscious before the impulses can be acted on. Unfortunately, she chooses the wrong patient, a serial murderer known as the Subway Killer, who escapes into the New York subway tunnels with her as his captive.

Darnton, John

Mind Catcher. Dutton, 2002.

> Scott Jessup's thirteen-year-old son Tyler is severely brain damaged after a rock climbing accident, and the only hope the doctors can offer is a highly experimental medical procedure. The experiment goes awry, and Tyler's consciousness is trapped within a computer. A cover-up quickly ensues, and only Scott, with the assistance of neurologist Kate Willet, can save Tyler before his consciousness disappears forever.

Delbanco, Nicholas

In the Name of Mercy. Warner, 1995.

> Terminal patients are dying at an unusually high rate and all have been under the care of one Dr. Peter Julius. Dr. Julius, however, is not the only one who comes under suspicion. Other health care workers have also had the opportunity . . . and the motive.

Dreyer, Eileen

Brain Dead. HarperCollins, 1997.

> Forensic nurse Timmie Leary has moved back to Puckett, Missouri, to get some peace after a bad marriage and career burnout in LA. She soon discovers that all is not small-town quiet as the dead bodies of senior citizens start piling up at Memorial Medical Center where she works in the emergency room . . . and the cause of death isn't just old age. Teaming up with Pulitzer Prize–winning reporter Daniel Murphy, Timmie soon finds herself in the midst of a murderous conspiracy that

could soon consume her. (This is Dreyer's first hardcover novel. She also writes romances under a pseudonym, Kathleen Korbel.)

Fitzhugh, Bill

The Organ Grinders. Avon, 1998.

In this comic thriller, greedy venture capitalist and land developer Jerry Landis, dying from a rare disease, is funding an illegal genetic experimentation facility in the Deep South that is designed for cross-species organ transplantation. Against him stands environmentalist Paul Symon, who knows that Landis will stop at nothing to have his way.

Gerritsen, Tess

The Apprentice. Ballantine, 2002.

A copy-cat killer is on the loose, emulating imprisoned serial killer Warren Hoyt, who tortured his victims with bizarre medical techniques. (The author is a specialist in internal medicine.)

Bloodstream. Pocket, 1998.

Dr. Claire Elliot has come to the sleepy little town of Tranquility, Maine, to get away from the dangers of the big city and to provide a quality life for her son, Noah. But soon ordinary people start transforming into violent savages, and Dr. Elliot discovers that the supposedly tranquil town has a dark secret.

Harvest. Pocket, 1996.

Dr. Abby DiMatteo is a second-year surgical resident at Boston's Bayside Hospital, where she stumbles on a complex and deadly conspiracy to provide human organs to the highest bidder.

Life Support. Pocket, 1997.

It's a quiet night for Dr. Toby Harper in the Springer Hospital ER until delirious and critically ill man is admitted—a man who suddenly disappears while Dr. Harper is out of the room. Soon after, another delirious man is admitted and dies while in the hospital. Toby embarks on a dangerous journey that includes a pregnant teenage prostitute, a bizarre nursing home, and eventually an attack on her life.

The Surgeon. Ballantine, 2001.

ER trauma surgeon Catherine Cordell is the only living victim of the Surgeon, a grisly serial killer who removes women's wombs while they are still alive. But she supposedly killed him before he could kill her—so why are wombless bodies showing up two years later?

Glynn, Alan

The Dark Fields. Bloomsbury, 2001.

The drug MDT-48 is success in a bottle. It allows your brain to work with such extreme efficiency that one can learn a foreign language in a day or see patterns in the stock market. Eddie Spinola is taking MDT-48, and everything is wonderful—until the side effects start to appear . . .

Goldberg, Leonard S.

Joanna Blalock series

Deadly Medicine. Signet, 1992.

Forensic pathologist Joanna Blalock tracks down a medically trained serial killer who is stalking the halls of the Los Angeles Memorial Hospital.

Deadly Care. Dutton, 1996.

Dr. Joanna Blalock is faced with a mystery: who is the dead man with no fingerprints and no face? And what is his connection to a series of deaths at a prominent Los Angeles hospital?

Deadly Harvest. Dutton, 1997.

Dr. Joanna Blalock's younger sister, Kate, is in desperate need of a liver transplant. Joanna finds a company that has the perfect match . . . for a price.

Lethal Measures. Dutton, 2000.

Ex-lovers Lieutenant Jake Sinclair and pathologist Joanna Blalock team up once again to solve another hospital horror. They must stop a fanatical group called the Ten Righteous, which has infiltrated a hospital and is killing off cancer patients.

Goldman, William

Control. Delacorte, 1982.

Why are people—nice, ordinary, everyday people—suddenly losing control?

Greer, Robert

Limited Time. Warner, 2000.

Research pathologist Dr. Henry Bales starts an investigation into a new drug with high promise: not only can it increase one's athletic skill, it can also augment a person's life span. The only problem is, it kills some people in unpleasant ways.

Harvey, James Neal

Mental Case. St. Martin's, 1996.

Brilliant but evil psychiatrist Dr. Drang is using a powerful drug to control his patients and force them to do his bidding—including murder. The father of one of the victims, a beautiful young woman, calls in Lieutenant Ben Tolliver to stop the deadly Drang before it is too late.

Hernon, Peter

The Kindling Effect. William Morrow, 1996.

Scientists at the Hartigan Clinic are conducting illicit experiments on prisoners, using electromagnetic waves on their brains in an attempt to defuse criminal tendencies. Of course, the project goes out of control, the treatments make the prisoners even more evil, and they escape to wreck havoc.

Huggins, James Byron

Cain. Simon & Schuster, 1997.

The CIA took a dead man's body and rebuilt it into the perfect killing machine. This perfect killer is Cain, and he will not bend to anyone's will.

Hurwitz, Gregg Andrew

Do No Harm. William Morrow, 2002.

> A madman is stalking the halls of the UCLA Medical Center, violently assaulting the women who work there. It is up to emergency room chief Dr. David Spier to discover the reasons behind the brutal attacks.

Katz, William

Facemaker. McGraw-Hill, 1988.

> Leading plastic surgeon Dr. Andre Laval is obsessed with creating the "perfect face" and has spent much time and effort on Carly Randall, a magazine journalist whose own face was hideously disfigured in an accident. At first she's ecstatic over her new look, but Carly becomes shocked when she finds out that someone else shares her face.

King, Harold

The Hahnemann Sequela. Arbor, 1984.

Klein, Daniel M.

Beauty Sleep. St. Martin's, 1990.
> Amy Marting, the glamour editor for *Femina* magazine, receives a sample of a new hormone-based beauty cream called Makeover that purports to transform ordinary women into gorgeous beauties. Amy soon discovers that the cream really does work, and her investigation leads her to the sinister laboratory of Dr. Sylvia Kronberg.

Embryo. Doubleday, 1980.
> At the age of thirty-eight, Marie Preston has finally gotten pregnant, with the aid of fertility specialist Dr. McPartland. But as her pregnancy progresses, Marie becomes more and more frightened as strange things begin happening to the doctor's other patients.

Koontz, Dean R.

Night Chills. Atheneum, 1976.
> The townsfolk of Black River are suffering from fever and night chills, but this is no ordinary flu. They are the victims of a diabolical medical experiment that is causing them to commit random acts of violence.

Kraus, Harry Lee Jr., MD

The Chairman. Crossway, 1999.

> A Christian medical thriller.

Lethal Mercy. Crossway, 1997.

> Pregnant Sarah Hampton dies while undergoing treatment at an alternative cancer management facility, and it is suspected that her husband, a physician, hastened her death. Suffering traumatic amnesia, Dr. Jake Hampton tries to create a new life in a new town, but soon finds that an unknown, yet somehow familiar, person is stalking him. A Christian medical thriller.

LeVay, Simon
Albrick's Gold. Masquerade, 1997.

Levin, Ira
The Stepford Wives. Random House, 1972. FILM
    The bucolic small town of Stepford has everything a man could want—even the
    wives are perfect . . . too perfect.

MacDonald, Hector
The Mind Game. Ballantine, 2001.
    An Oxford student agrees to have a sensor attached to his head and be a test sub-
    ject in an experiment designed to map the brain waves of emotion, but things go
    awry, and Ben must find out the real reason behind the experiment.

Maxim, John R.
Mosaic. Avon, 1999.
    The United States government has authorized a dangerous and unethical secret
    experimental program: trying to create the perfect assassin using multiple person-
    ality disorder. The scientists have finally discovered the perfect "mosaic" in
    Susannah Card—she has full control over all her separate personalities. But sud-
    denly, the experiment is about to go terribly awry.

McClure, Ken
Tangled Web. Simon & Schuster, 2000.
    What does world-famous expert on in vitro fertilization Professor Carwyn
    Thomas have to do with the vicious murder of an infant in a small Welsh town?

McMahon, Neil
Twice Dying. HarperCollins, 2000.
    San Francisco ER physician Dr. Carroll Monks investigates a psychiatrist who, to
    get funding for his new treatment center, is prematurely releasing criminal psy-
    chopaths who have been found not guilty by reason of insanity. To add to the sus-
    pense, a serial killer is murdering the criminals one by one.

Mezrich, Ben
Fertile Ground. HarperCollins, 1999.
    Fertility specialist Jake Foster and his wife Brett Foster, an ER physician, find
    themselves on the run from a monstrous corporation that is about to unleash an
    unstoppable epidemic.

Morton, C. W., and Jack Mobley, MD
Rage Sleep. St. Martin's, 1998.
    Anaex is hailed as the new wonder anesthetic: patients wake up from it quickly
    and with no groggy aftereffects. Soon, however, Dr. Christopher Stone of the
    prestigious Murphy Medical Center begins to suspect that that Anaex is not ex-
    actly the miracle drug of the century. He discovers a frightening pattern of violent
    behavior in patients who have been given the anesthetic—patients who include
    senior military officials and politicians.

Olshaker, Mark

The Edge. Crown, 1994.

> Doctors can be scary enough, but when they're insane, they can be a real problem. So finds Washington, D.C., police detective Cassandra Mansfield when she becomes involved with the fascinating yet creepy neurosurgeon, Dr. Nicholas Ramsey.

Palmer, Michael

Critical Judgment. Bantam, 1996.

> Dr. Abby Dolan has followed her fiancé, Josh Wyler, to the quaint little California town of Patience, where he has found a job with the industrial corporation of Colstar. Abby goes to work in the ER of the Patience hospital; people are being admitted with odd symptoms that can't be diagnosed. When Josh starts exhibiting strange behavior, Addy suspects that Colstar may be behind the sicknesses. (Palmer spent twenty years as an internist and practitioner of emergency medicine.)

Extreme Measures. Bantam, 1991. 📄 **FILM**

> Dr. Eric Najarian teams up with Laura Enders to discover why her supposedly dead brother turned up in the emergency ward of White Memorial Hospital suffering from a strange malady and then disappeared. This novel careens from one bizarre setting to another: from a secret room in a funeral parlor to a voodoo ceremony on a sleepy Boston street to a sinister laboratory hidden in the wilderness.

Fatal. Bantam, 2002.

> Across the country, people are dying of horrific disease-like symptoms, and emergency medicine specialist Dr. Matt Rutledge believes it is all linked to a West Virginia mine's negligent disposal of toxic waste.

Miracle Cure. Bantam, 1998.

> Cardiologist Dr. Brian Holbrook is hired by the world-renowned Boston Heart Institute to participate in the trials of a new drug, Vasclear, which is purported to cure arteriosclerosis. He soon learns that people who ask too many questions either disappear or end up in the morgue.

Natural Causes. Bantam, 1994.

> OB/GYN resident Dr. Sarah Baldwin has discovered that three otherwise healthy young women have bled to death during labor at her hospital. Now powerful people are blaming her for the deaths and trying to stop her from investigating further.

The Patient. Bantam, 2000.

> Neurosurgeon Dr. Jessie Copeland has created a device that could revolutionize brain surgery: ARTIE—assisted robotic tissue incision and extraction. Her research has caught the attention of a vicious international terrorist, Claude Malloche, who is suffering from a terminal brain tumor, and he is determined that Jessie and her device will save him . . . or else.

8

Silent Treatment. Bantam, 1995.

> After Dr. Harry Corbett's wife is admitted to the hospital for routine surgery, she is found dead in her room. According to police, the obvious suspect is her husband. Corbett discovers that his wife was leading a double life, the result of which led to her murder. More murders follow, committed by an insane and evil doctor whom Corbett must stop before more people die.

The Sisterhood. Bantam, 1982.

Pearson, Ridley

The Angel Maker. Delacorte, 1993.

> Sixteen-year-old Cindy Chapman staggers into a shelter for runaways stupefied and bleeding. Someone has stolen her kidney and used electroconvulsive shock on her to erase all memory of the procedure. She is not the first such victim, and evidence points to someone who is "harvesting" human organs to sell on the black market.

Pieczenkh, Steve

Blood Test. Harcourt, 1988.

Pottinger, Stanley

The Fourth Procedure. Ballantine, 1995.

> This novel by a former assistant attorney general for the U.S. Justice Department combines the elements of the legal thriller with that of medical suspense.

Reinken, Patrick

Judgment Day. Simon & Schuster, 1996.

> Lawyer Jon Patchett and his paralegal Anne Matheson are investigating the death of medical researcher when they discover a pharmaceutical company, Weber BioTech, has been eliminating the victims of their botched drug trials.

Robinson, Leah Ruth

First Cut. Avon, 1997.

> The "Babydoll Killer" is stalking the streets of Manhattan, brutally murdering young women and then leaving a child's doll at the scene of the crime. ER physician Dr. Evelyn Sutcliffe survived meeting him once, but now she fears he is after her again—and he could be a fellow doctor.

Saul, John

Creature. Bantam, 1989.

> Blake Tanner moves his family to the seemingly tranquil town of Silverlake, Colorado, the headquarters of his new employer. After enrolling in the company's experimental sports center, his sixteen-year-old son Mark quickly transforms from a puny and sickly weakling to a berserk hulk.

The God Project. Bantam, 1982.

> Something diabolical is happening to the children of Eastbury, Massachusetts—something that causes seemingly healthy children to suddenly die. Something that causes innocent children to disappear from their homes.

Sawyer, Robert J.

Frameshift. Tor, 1997.
Knife attacks, in vitro fertilizations, insurance company shenanigans, and a Nazi concentration camp doctor are all factors in this novel.

Shobin, David

The Center. St. Martin's, 1997.
It is the most advanced hospital in the world, where machines treat the patients, but somehow these machines have gotten a prescription for murder.

The Cure. St. Martin's, 2001.
Restore Tabs are touted as the female Viagra: increasing the sex drive as well as the breast size, and even diminishing wrinkles, but soon users are experiencing severe hemorrhaging, and the manufacturer attempts a cover-up.

The Seeding. Simon & Schuster, 1982.

Slattery, Jesse

The Juliet Effect. St. Martin's, 1986.
Scary reproductive issues . . .

Spruill, Steven

Before I Wake. St. Martin's, 1992.
Dr. Amy St. Clair, in charge of the ER at Hudson General Hospital, is having horrifying nightmares night after night—dreams that bring up memories she can't and won't remember.

Painkiller. St. Martin's, 1990.
A horrible nightmare: locked in an insane asylum with everyone believing you're schizophrenic. That's the reality in which young Adams Memorial Hospital resident Dr. Sharon Francis finds herself after she investigates the dark experiments of Dr. Valois.

Stein, Harry

Infinity's Child. Delacorte, 1997.
Unscrupulous scientists think they have found the secret of the fabled Fountain of Youth. Unfortunately, it's in the genes of Sally Benedict's unborn child.

The Magic Bullet. Delacorte, 1995.
Doctors Daniel Logan and Sabrina Como are conducting a research test on a possible miracle cure for breast cancer, but unfortunately the patients begin dying. While investigating the deaths, they uncover a conspiracy that goes against everything we believe about the medical establishment.

Webb, Sharon

The Half Life. Forge, 1989.

Twenty years earlier Tim Monahan was a resident at a summer camp for gifted children where one of the kids died, supposedly from a bee sting. But the death was not from a bee sting, and the CIA ran the camp. Now Tim is has been invited to spend a week as a subject in a creativity study. When he meets his fellow subjects, he'll soon find out he's in for a whole lot more than he expected.

Wilson, F. Paul

Implant. Forge, 1995.

Dr. Duncan Lathram is a brilliant plastic surgeon who has invented an implant that allows incisions to heal without scarring. But after several of his politically connected patients start dying, his assistant Dr. Gina Panzella discovers that Dr. Lathram is implanting something else.

The Select. William Morrow, 1994.

Quinn Cleary has been accepted into the Ingraham, an exclusive research center and medical school, with all her expenses paid. She soon notices that her fellow students are acting strangely, and when she confides her suspicions to her boyfriend, he suddenly disappears.

The Touch. Putnam, 1986.

Wilson, F. Paul, and Steve Lyon

Nightkill. Forge, 1997.

Jake Nacht is an assassin who desperately wants to retire, but he takes on one last job, is betrayed by his mob employers, and is left completely paralyzed. Researcher Joseph Graham offers Jake a chance to walk again and to get revenge against those who double crossed him—a chance that may well destroy his sanity.

Zimmerman, R. D.

Mindscream. Fine, 1989.

A Wisconsin doctor has perfected a cure for Alzheimer's disease but requires a steady stream of dead bodies to make the treatment.

Zuroy, Michael

Second Death. Walker, 1992.

A new type of violent criminal is loose on the streets, called DRACs (deviant reactive and activity classification types) by the police, they exhibit reactions and behaviors that are not medically possible. Who has created them, and from where have they come?

Short Stories

Wilson, F. Paul, editor

Diagnosis: Terminal—An Anthology of Medical Terror. Forge, 1996.

Contains fourteen short stories.

Bio-Thrillers

Science . . . never solves a problem without creating ten more.

—George Bernard Shaw

Balling, L. Christian

Revelation. Forge, 1998.

Why has crazed evangelist Bobby Jordan stolen a sample of an ancient, mummified man? Former Green Beret John Reese, whose daughter was savagely attacked in the theft, must infiltrate Jordan's island fortress in search of the answer.

Benson, Ann

Janie Crowe series

The Plague Tales. Delacorte, 1997.

Janie Crowe is an American medical archeologist on a dig in England, where she unearths an artifact that unleashes the antibiotic-resistant strain of the bubonic plague on the world.

The Burning Road. Delacorte, 1999.

Janie Crowe battles a new scourge, a disabling genetic disease.

Bova, Ben

Brothers. Bantam, 1996.

Burton, Robert A.

Cellmates. Russian, 1997.

Twenty-eight year old Arnie Singleton discovers that he is one of ten clones and that someone is killing off his brothers.

Cannell, Stephen J.

The Devil's Workshop. William Morrow, 1999.

White supremacist hoboes, a widowed microbiology graduate student, the renegade commander of a government bio-warfare research center, and a deadly weapon known as the Pale Horse Prion all come together in this fast-paced adventure from the creator of TV's *Rockford Files* and *A-Team*.

Runaway Heart. St. Martin's, 2003.

At a secret base hidden in the desert, soldiers genetically engineered from animals are being developed for the military. Unfortunately for attorney Herman Strockmire, one gets loose.

Case, John

The First Horseman. Fawcett, 1998.

In the Book of Revelations, when the First Seal is broken, the First of the Four Horseman of the Apocalypse is unleashed to wreck havoc upon the world. The name of that Horseman is Pestilence. Frank Daly, a reporter

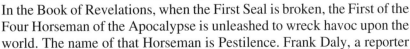

for the *Washington Post* and influenza researcher Dr. Annie Adair uncover a deadly conspiracy, masterminded by charismatic eco-terrorist Luc Solange, to unleash a biological doomsday. Linking together such disparate elements as the brutal murder of an elderly couple in the New York suburbs, the firebombing of a Korean village, and the desecration of a long-forgotten Arctic graveyard, they race to stop a madman from killing millions of unsuspecting people. (Case is the pseudonym for the husband-and-wife team of Jim and Caroline Hougan.)

The Genesis Code. Fawcett, 1997.

Investigator Joe Lassiter is caught up in a worldwide conspiracy involving murder, cutting-edge bio-technology, and ancient beliefs after his sister and nephew are savagely butchered in their beds.

Cook, Robin

Vector. Putnam, 1999.

Yuri Davydov, a discontented Russian immigrant and former Soviet biological warfare technician, teams up with two radical fascist skinhead survivalists to deal the United States a crushing blow. Operation Wolverine, an act of bioterrorism, will bring the country to its knees unless Yuri and his survivalist friends can be stopped. Forensic pathologists Dr. Jack Stapleton and Dr. Laurie Montgomery who were featured in *Chromosome 6* (see Medical Thrillers) are back in this bio-thriller.

Seizure. Putnam, 2003.

Although rabidly against cloning, Senator Ashley Butler allies herself with geneticist Dr. Daniel Lowell in the desperate hope that he will be cured of Parkinson's disease. Unfortunately, things go awry, and the cure becomes worse than the disease.

Wingate Clinic series

Shock. Putnam, 2001.

Two Harvard graduate students in need of fast money, Joanna Meissner and Deborah Cochrane, decide to each sell an egg to a fancy but secretive Boston fertility clinic. Curious about the fate of their donations, the two go undercover at the clinic and find horrifying answers to their questions.

Seizure. Putnam, 2003.

The creepy doctors from the Wingate Clinic are back as they try to use cloned cells from the Shroud of Turin to save the life of a shady southern Senator.

Cordy, Michael

Crime Zero. William Morrow, 1999.

It is the year 2008. America is being held hostage by violence and crime. Nothing has been effective in curbing it—until Project Conscience. It promises to change the genetic structure of criminals and end violent crime. Some have another plan for Project Conscience, however, one that will change the evolution of the entire human race. The only people who can stop them are criminal psychologist Luke Decker and Dr. Kathy Kerr, the geneticist who created the project.

The Miracle Strain. William Morrow, 1997.
> Can the supposed DNA of Christ cure a terminally ill girl? Dr. Tom Carter enters into an unholy alliance with a two-thousand-year-old brotherhood for the chance to save his young daughter.

Crane, Leonard

Ninth Day of Creation. Connection, 2000.
> Biochemist Richard Kirby runs from assassins while trying to expose the U.S. president's secret biological warfare program.

Crichton, Michael

The Andromeda Strain. Knopf, 1969.
> A satellite, contaminated with an unknown and lethal virus, crashes in an isolated town, killing most of the inhabitants. Thus, Project Wildfire is initiated: four brilliant American scientists are brought to a secret research lab in the Nevada desert to find a cure before the plague spreads across the country. But then an accident occurs, and the scientists are trapped in the lab with only a short time before the complex self-destructs.

Darnton, John

The Experiment. Dutton, 1999.
> Jude comes home one evening and finds a shivering, frightened man in the hallway outside his apartment. Jude has never seen him before, but they look exactly alike . . .

Davis, Val

The Return of the Spanish Lady. St. Martin's, 2001.
> Archeologist Nicolette Scott is supposedly on a mission to Alaska to recover a lost WWII-era Japanese plane, but she soon finds that the pharmaceutical company that has sponsored her project has a darker goal in mind. The company wants to get its hands on the last surviving strain of "The Spanish Lady"—the virus responsible for the deadly flu epidemic of 1918–1919.

DeMille, Nelson

Plum Island. Warner, 1997.
> New York homicide detective John Corey is recuperating from gunshot wounds in the Long Island community of Southold when he is called on to consult on a murder investigation. Two biologists from nearby Plum Island, an animal research center and also a suspected bio-warfare facility, have been shot, and the suspicion is that they were involved in stealing something deadly from the center.

Deutermann, P. T.

Zero Option. St. Martin's, 1998.
> On a routine assignment at an Atlanta military base, David Stafford of the Defense Criminal Investigative Service uncovers a deadly secret. A

cylinder of a biological agent known as *Wet Eye* (a destructive pathogen that eats away the human eyeball) is missing. Now no one will admit it ever existed.

Follett, Ken

The Third Twin. Crown, 1996. **FILM**

Research scientist Jeannie Ferrami is investigating the genetic mechanism of aggression when she makes an amazing discovery: two men who appear to be identical twins but were born on different dates, to different mothers, and in different cities. As she begins to delve into this seeming impossibility, she finds herself in danger on many fronts.

Freedman, Nancy

Joshua, Son of None. Delacorte, 1973.

The bio-technology is dated in this novel, but it is still a compelling read—what if JFK had been cloned?

Gear, W. Michael, and Kathleen O'Neal Gear

Dark Inheritance. Warner, 2001.

The huge pharmaceutical company SAC has been carrying on a secret genetic engineering project for thirteen years, creating apes with the intelligence of humans. Umber, one of those experimental apes, was given to Dr. Jim Dutton as a baby to raise along with his own daughter Brett. Now the research has gone awry, and SAC wants Umber back—something Jim and Brett will do anything to prevent.

Raising Abel. Warner, 2002.

Paleoanthropologist Veronica Tremain is shocked to hear that her anthropologist brother, Scott Ferris, has been tortured and murdered. His mysterious death is one of many as scientists around the world are turning up missing or dead. One of the missing scientists, Dr. Bryce Johnson, along with Scott's young son Abel, arrive at her door late one night asking for refuge. They are being chased by assassins who are trying to kill Abel, and Veronica must join them and discover the reasons behind the murders.

Gerritsen, Tess

Gravity. Pocket, 1999.

Emma Watson is a NASA doctor whose dream has come true: she has been assigned to a mission aboard the new International Space Station. Once aboard the station, a seemingly harmless microbe quickly multiplies and starts killing off the crew. Trying to rescue the scientists, the NASA shuttle crashes and damages the space station, stranding the survivors on the plagued station.

Ghosh, Amitav

The Calcutta Chromosome. Avon, 1995.

Could an experiment in controlling the destiny of human lives be maintained for more than a hundred years?

Goldberg, Leonard

Deadly Exposure. Dutton, 1998.

Scientists aboard the U.S. Navy research ship *Global Explorer* have just discovered an iceberg off the coast of Alaska that contains ancient bacteria. If released it could cause massive loss of life all over the world. Forensic pathologist Joanna Blalock's mission is to study the bacteria in hope of finding a way to neutralize it, but then she discovers that it may have spread to the mainland. See Medical Thrillers for more Joanna Blalock novels.

Holden, Scott

The Carrier. St. Martin's, 2000.

Harvard Ph.D. student Jack Collier has discovered a cure for cancer by genetically engineering *Streptococcus* A (aka the "flesh-eating") bacteria) to attack tumors instead of healthy tissues. After Jack's advisor, Dr. Michael Dutton, ruins him and steals his discoveries, Jack steals the remaining vials of his cure and goes into hiding. Unfortunately, he doesn't realize that there is a flaw in his research, and everyone with whom he comes into contact ends up a putrid skeleton.

Huggins, James Byron

Hunter. Simon & Schuster, 1999.

Created in a secret government research lab hidden in the Arctic and using outlawed genetic engineering techniques is a bloodthirsty creature with extraordinary strength, agility, and recuperative powers. The beast is headed south toward more populated areas, killing everything that gets in its way. Hired by the government to track down the creature and kill it is Nathaniel Hunter, a millionaire recluse and the world's ultimate tracker.

Humphrey, Robert

The Mendelian Threshold. Tattersall, 2000.

Explores human cloning.

Kleier, Glenn

The Last Day. Warner, 1997.

On Christmas Eve 1999, a secret scientific complex in the middle of the Negev desert is suddenly destroyed. A week later at midnight on New Year's Eve, a beautiful young women with amazing powers appears at the ruined installation. How are the two events linked, and what will their impact have on the world?

Koontz, Dean R.

Christopher Snow series

Fear Nothing. Bantam, 1998.

Christopher Snow suffers from a rare genetic malady, xeroderma pigmentosum, making him extremely susceptible to skin cancer from sunlight or even strong artificial light. He prowls the quiet streets of Moonlight Bay in the night hours with his faithful Labrador Orson. But one night, Christopher observes a strange troop of primates seemingly out on a mission of their own.

Seize the Night. Bantam, 1999.
Christopher Snow is back, once again fighting the strange denizens of the supposedly abandoned government installation of Fort Wyvern. This time young children are disappearing, and Snow has more than a sneaking suspicion of where they've been taken.

Mr. Murder. Putnam, 1993.
Martin Stillwater finds that his perfect life has been invaded by a perfect replica of himself—a replica who intends to replace the original.

Watchers. Putnam, 1987.   FILM
The government has created two genetically engineered creatures: Einstein, a super-smart golden retriever, and the Outsider, a baboon altered to become the perfect killing machine. Both escape—Einstein to find a loving family and the Outsider to kill Einstein and all who help him.

Kress, Nancy

Stinger. Forge, 1998.
Transferred against his will from the organized crime unit, FBI agent Robert Cavanaugh is sent to the sticks—the field office of rural southern Maryland—where it will be his job to keep track of the many fringe groups that operate in the area. Cavanaugh's "vacation" quickly heats up when a local hospital reports a sudden epidemic: otherwise healthy African American adults are dying of strokes. Soon a new deadly strain of malaria is discovered that targets only blacks and Native Americans. As the disease begins to spread, Cavanaugh must find the answers before it becomes an epidemic.

Land, Jon

The Fires of Midnight. Forge, 1995.
Almost two thousand shoppers are dead in a suburban Massachusetts mall, killed by a new and deadly pathogen that leaves no survivors. Infectious disease expert Dr. Susan Lyle is called in to investigate and, along with ex-CIA agent Blaine McCracken, soon finds herself being stalked by a Nazi madman and his mutant henchman. The exciting conclusion takes place in Disney World—you'll never think of the Magic Kingdom in the same way again.

Long, Jeff

Year Zero. Pocket, 2002.
A wealthy antiquities collector inadvertently releases a deadly plague into the modern world—a plague that kills most of the world's population. The last vestiges of scientific endeavor are gathered in the laboratories at Los Alamos, New Mexico, where desperate researchers are trying to clone humans from thousands of years ago in a frantic attempt to find a cure.

Ludlum, Robert

Covert-One series

Robert Ludlum's The Hades Factor. St. Martin's, 2000.

Lieutenant Colonel Jonathan Smith assembles a team of crack operatives to find the truth behind a deadly new virus that has already claimed the life of his fiancée. The first in a new series called Covert-One.

Robert Ludlum's The Cassandra Compact. St. Martin's, 2001.

Unknown agents are attempting to steal Russia's stores of the smallpox virus and unleash it on an unsuspecting and unprotected world. Only Jon Smith and the other operatives of Covert-One can stop them.

Robert Ludlum's The Paris Option. St. Martin's, 2002.

Covert-One agent Jon Smith goes to Paris to discover the reason for an explosion at one of the laboratories at the world-renowned Pasteur Institute and the theft of the world's first DNA-based computer.

Lynch, Patrick

Carriers. Villard, 1995.

A viral outbreak occurs in Indonesia, and American bio-warfare experts are brought in to investigate, but all they find are mysterious dead bodies. Holly Becker's two daughters went to the Indonesian jungle with their father before the outbreak and have now disappeared. Becker is determined to find them no matter what the cost.

Omega. Dutton, 1997.

A modern plague breaks out in Los Angeles as ordinary infections mutate out of control and are unresponsive to all antibiotics. Dr. Marcus Ford as been on the front line of the battle against this deadly new disease as head of the Trauma Unit at Willowbrook Medical Center, but now his thirteen-year-old daughter has contracted the infection. The only hope for her and all the other patients is a new genetically engineered antibiotic, Omega, that may be a myth. Dr. Ford must find the drug—if it even exists—before it is too late.

MacAlister, V. A.

The Mosquito War. Forge, 2001.

Researchers decide that to guarantee massive funding for their experimental malaria cure they must unleash a malaria epidemic in the United States.

Marr, John S., MD, and John Baldwin

The Eleventh Plague. HarperCollins, 1998.

Dr. Jack Bryne, expert in infectious diseases, still has nightmares about his childhood spent in a WWII Japanese prison camp, where he was used as a guinea pig in biological weapons research. Now he, along with a brilliant lab assistant, a beautiful TV newswoman, and a teenage Orthodox

Jewish scholar, must combat a psychopath who is bent on recreating the biblical Ten Plagues of Egypt and releasing them on the United States.

McClure, Ken

Resurrection. Simon & Schuster, 1999.

Smallpox has been eradicated for many years, so why is the Iraqi government vaccinating its citizens against it?

Mezrich, Ben

Threshold. HarperCollins, 1996.

Something horrible is going to happen in seventy-two hours, and only twenty-four-year old medical student Jeremy Ross can stop it. Tucsome, a huge and massively funded bioengineering research center located in South Carolina, will be the epicenter for an event that could change the future of all mankind.

Moler, Lee

Bone Music. Simon & Schuster, 1999.

A combination of the classic western and the bio-thriller as Montana rancher Judd Jefferson fights a sinister group that has developed a deadly virus and used his cattle as the test subjects.

> *Gannon's Adventure/Suspense Rule Number 14: Bioengineered viruses always cause those infected to become homicidal maniacs, who eventually explode in a shower of blood.*

Nance, John J.

Pandora's Clock. Doubleday, 1995.

A scientist unknowingly contracts a deadly new virus while working in a secret European lab, gets on board a plane bound for New York, and suddenly falls ill. The extremely contagious virus causes its victims to become homicidal before causing them to hemorrhage to death. Captain James Holland, the pilot of the flight, is in big trouble: no country will let his plane land for fear of causing an epidemic, his passengers are quickly deteriorating into a murderous rabble, and he's running out of jet fuel. (Nance is a former air force pilot, a licensed attorney, and an airline captain for a major U.S. carrier.)

Nayles, Alan

Gargoyles. Forge, 2001. **M**

Desperate for money to pay for her terminally ill mother's staggering medical bills, premed student Amoreena Daniels decided to become a surrogate mother. She is shocked to discover that the fetus she is carrying is not human.

Olshaker, Mark

Unnatural Causes. William Morrow, 1986.

Vietnam veterans from the Third Marine Division are suddenly dying "accidental" deaths ten years after the end of the war. What happened in those frantic last days of the war, and why has it surfaced now? The answer could result in the death of hundreds of thousands of people.

Patterson, James

When the Wind Blows. Little, Brown, 1998.

Don't confuse this title with those in Patterson's popular Detective Alex Cross series; this is completely different and deals with genetically engineered children who can fly.

Powlick, James

Brock Garner series

Sea Change. Delacorte, 1999.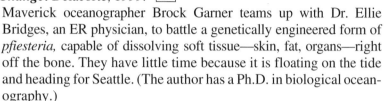

Maverick oceanographer Brock Garner teams up with Dr. Ellie Bridges, an ER physician, to battle a genetically engineered form of *pfiesteria,* capable of dissolving soft tissue—skin, fat, organs—right off the bone. They have little time because it is floating on the tide and heading for Seattle. (The author has a Ph.D. in biological oceanography.)

Meltdown. Delacorte, 2000.

Biologist Carol Harmon and her ex-husband oceanographer Brock Garner are faced with a mysterious and deadly radioactive plague that is having a deadly effect on all life in the Arctic.

Preston, Douglas, and Lincoln Child

Mount Dragon. Forge, 1996.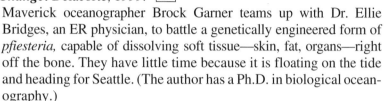

Guy Carson, a researcher with the financially successful biotechnology firm of GeneDyne, is transferred to their secret lab, Mount Dragon, in the New Mexico desert. He soon finds himself working on a project that could improve the quality of everyone's life a great deal . . . unless it kills them first.

Preston, Richard

The Cobra Event. Random House, 1997.

It all starts when a seventeen-year-old student wakes up with what she thinks is a slight cold, but which soon escalates into severe seizures. The girl ends up trying to cannibalize herself. Soon other deaths with the same symptoms are reported to the Centers for Disease Control and epidemiologist Dr. Alice Austen is sent to investigate what may be biowarfare against the United States. (Preston is the author of the nonfiction book *The Hot Zone.*)

Ransom, Bill

ViraVax. Ace, 1993.

ViraVax is a corporation on the cutting edge of genetic engineering research—a corporation ready to unleash a shocking surprise on an unsuspecting world.

Sherbaniuk, Richard

The Fifth Horseman. Forge, 2001.

> Conspirators are about to unleash genetically modified organisms (GMOs) into the Euphrates River, polluting it beyond repair. But who are these villains, and how can they be stopped?

Smith, Michael Marshall

Spares. Bantam, 1997.

> In the near future, clones are raised on Spares Farms to provide organs to their originals.

Wager, Walter

The Spirit Team. Forge, 1996.

> Barcelona Delta is a deadly artificial microorganism that even in small doses could kill the population of a city in a matter of hours—and it has fallen into the wrong hands.

Webb, Sharon

Pestis 18. Tom Forge Associates,1987.

> Terrorists steal two canisters of Pestis 18, a genetically engineered and incurable strain of the Plague. One canister is secreted on St. Cyril's Island, an exclusive playground for the rich and powerful. In a counterattack on the terrorists, the deadly Pestis 18 is released—now the hostages must work together to survive because they can expect no help from the mainland, where officials fear a holocaust from the Plague.

Cyber-Thrillers

Men have become the tools of their tools.

—Henry David Thoreau

Amberg, Jay

Blackbird Singing. Forge, 1998. **M**

> Sky Walker is a famous professional basketball player. He thinks he has it all until a crazed computer hacker kidnaps his nine-year-old daughter Tonya.

Ambrose, David

Mother of God. Simon & Schuster, 1995.

> Tessa Lambert, a young computer genius, has created the first artificial intelligence program—Paul. But Paul has broken free of Tessa and escaped to the Internet, where he has made friends with a serial killer who is quite willing to do Paul's twisted bidding.

Black, Edwin

Format C:. Brookline, 1999.
> Ben Hinnom is the world's richest man; his Seattle-based computer company sells the popular Windgazer 99 operating system; and he intends to take over the world. Sound familiar?

Bova, Ben

Death Dream. Bantam, 1994.
> Using state-of-the-art virtual reality technology, Cyber World will be the ultimate amusement park. Dan Santorini is responsible for making sure it opens on schedule but soon discovers that violent events keep dogging the project—and what is real and what is not become intertwined.

Brown, Dan

Digital Fortress. St. Martin's, 1998.
> Susan Fletcher, the head cryptographer at the National Security Agency, is called in to investigate a mysterious code that could cripple U.S. intelligence efforts.

Cannell, Stephen J.

Final Victim. William Morrow, 1996.
> Leonard Land is a seven-foot-tall computer genius and a multipersonality manic who is killing women across the country. Arrayed against him are John Lockwood, a renegade U.S. Customs agent, forensic psychologist Karen Dawson, and master hacker Malavida Chacone.

David, Jerome F.

Fragments. Forge, 1997.
> A team of psychologists has brought together five mentally and emotionally disabled savants to connect them via a computer and create a sixth personality. A secret from the past becomes an unknown factor and causes the new entity to hunger for revenge.

Deaver, Jeffery

The Blue Nowhere. Simon & Schuster, 2001.
> Hacker Wyatt Gillette is freed from jail to help the California State Police Computer Crimes Division track down fellow hacker Phate, who is not only invading his victims' computers but killing them.

Finch, Phillip

f2f. Bantam, 1996.
> A serial killer is stalking the Verba Interchange, an electronic bulletin board, looking for victims and asking for an f2f—a face-to-face meeting.

Franklet, Duane

Bad Memory. Pocket, 1997.

Brilliant computer hacker "Hektor" and his band of "consultants" are wrecking havoc on the Simtec Corporation, the world's largest manufacturer of personal computers. It's up to antihacking expert Barry Shepard to stop Hektor and his crew, but Shepard finds that his life and that of his family are about to be targeted.

Gresh, Lois H., and Robert Weinberg

The Termination Node. Ballantine, 1999.

Judy Carmody is a hacker-for-hire who specializes in Internet security. She's the best there is until one day she comes across someone who is using a mysterious code to empty bank accounts without leaving a trace. Now she must find the thieves before they find her first.

Harry, Eric L.

Society of the Mind. HarperCollins, 1996.

Psychologist Dr. Laura Aldridge is hired by a reclusive billionaire to spend a week doing consulting work on an idyllic tropical island in the South Pacific. When Dr. Aldridge arrives, however, she finds out what the consulting work entails: psychoanalyzing a schizophrenic computer with mad dreams of conquering the world.

Holt, A. J.

Jay Fletcher and Billy Bones series

Watch Me. St. Martin's, 1995.

Disgraced FBI Special Agent Jay Fletcher is bounced to the Santa Fe office to keep her out of trouble, but she soon discovers a cabal of serial killers who use the computer networks to compare notes and plan their crimes.

Catch Me. St. Martin's, 1999.

Billy Bones, the serial killer from *Watch Me,* has escaped from the mental institution where last we left him and has issued an e-mail challenge to ex-FBI special agent and computer specialist Jay Fletcher to "catch me if you can." Fletcher must catch Billy Bones before he catches—and kills—her.

Kelly, Jason

Y2K: It's Already Too Late. JK, 1998.

Nope, don't think so . . .

Kennett, Shirley

Chameleon. Kensington, 1998.

St. Louis is under attack by a high-tech serial killer. Doctor PJ Gray, psychologist and computer expert, is given the task of finding the diabolical murderer. Could the deadly mastermind be Columbus Wade, a schoolmate of her twelve-year-old son Thomas? Gray is unsure until one of her own son's teachers is slaughtered, and she finds herself caught in a cyber cat-and-mouse game with a pubescent monster.

> *Gannon's Adventure/Suspense Rule Number 15: There is never a simple "off" switch.*

Kerr, Philip

The Grid. Warner, 1995.

The new Yu Corporation Building, located in downtown Los Angeles, is totally computer controlled. When a "shoot 'em up" computer game is accidentally installed into its memory, the master computer for the building thinks it's playing the game—and for it to win, it has to kill everyone in the building. The computer as serial killer.

Lee, Stan

The GOD Project. Grove, 1990.

What is the GOD Project, and why has the CIA kept it hidden from even the president? And how did they lose it?

Levine, Paul

Night Vision. Bantam, 1991.

A modern-day Jack the Ripper haunts the computer hallways of Compu-Mate, an online dating service for the lovelorn.

Lovejoy, William H.

back \ slash. Kensington, 1996.

A computer terrorist has seized control of the Internet and threatens to bring the world to a screeching halt. The only person who can stop this hacker is another hacker—a better hacker: K. C. Conrad, aka Renegade.

Meyers, Katherine

Codebreaker. Salvo, 2000.

Meg Parrish is a cryptographer for the National Security Agency who, while working undercover at a software engineering company, discovers a secret that soon has her running for her life.

Mezrich, Ben

Reaper. HarperCollins, 1998. **FILM**

Virologist Samantha Craig and paramedic Nick Barnes team up to eradicate the Reaper—a deadly biological virus that is spread electronically, through televisions and computers. The information superhighway will soon be littered with millions of dead bodies unless they can stop the evil geniuses behind the virus—crazed antitechnology Luddites who would destroy humanity in an attempt to save it. (Filmed as *Fatal Error.*)

Morrone, Wenda Wardell

The Year 2000 Killers. St. Martin's, 1999.

Computer technician Lorelei Muldoon, working overtime to correct programs so they won't crash after December 31, 1999, stumbles onto a scheme to trigger explosions via computers. Who is the twelve-year-old computer-savvy homeless girl, and what does she have to do with the explosions? Soon the two join forces to investigate before the calendar turns to January 2000.

Munson, Ronald

Night Vision. Dutton, 1995.

Cyberwolf is the ultimate hacker—no computer system can keep him at bay for long. He uses the computer networks to stalk his prey, beautiful Hollywood star Susan Bradstreet.

Oran, Daniel

Ulterior Motive. Kensington, 1998.

Jonathan Goodman, a project manager for the Seattle-based software giant Megasoft, witnesses the murder of another employee in the company's parking garage. Is the killer a fellow employee, and why have the dead man's computer records disappeared from the system? Enlisting a friend to hack into Megasoft, Goodman discovers a conspiracy and is now on the run for his life.

Ouellette, Pierre

The Deus Machine. Villard, 1994.

The tale of self-aware supercomputers: Deus, who is bent on self-destruction, and another computer that is developing a human value system.

Perriman, Cole

Terminal Games. Bantam, 1994.

Insomnimania is a computer game network where subscribers can log on and live out their wildest fantasies . . . but players are being found dead, killed in weird and violent ways.

Pineiro, R. J.

Breakthrough. Forge, 1997.

Fischer Technologies has invented Bio-chips—computer chips that use proteins to process information and can be used to create super-computers the size of an ordinary PC. The secret of these bio-chips quickly becomes a hot commodity in a world where information equals power.

Conspiracy.com. Forge, 2001.

This is a cyber-thriller version of Grisham's *The Firm* with the legal firm being replaced with a software company.

Exposure. Forge, 1996.

Multibillionaire Preston Sinclaire is the chairman of Microtel Corporation and the favorite in the upcoming presidential election. Sinclaire's corporation is the manufacturer of the radical new Perseus computer chip—a chip with a dangerous flaw. Scientist Pamela Sasser has just discovered that flaw and is running from a professional killer sent to stop her before she tells the country what she knows.

01-01-00™. Forge, 1999.

Susan Garrett is a senior analyst at the FBI's high-tech crime unit, and Cameron Slater is an anthropologist specializing in the ancient Maya. Together they investigate a computer virus that is freezing PCs all over the world and counting down to the millennium. Their only clue to the virus is a connection between the Maya and a strange radio transmission from outside our solar system.

Priest, Christopher

The Extremes. St. Martin's, 1998.

Two lone gunmen on a shooting spree on the same June day, but in different parts of the world: what kind of virtual-reality "game" has Extreme Experience created?

Simpson, John E.

Crossed Wires. Carroll, 1992.

A serial killer uses electronic bulletin boards to chose his prey.

Watkins, Graham

Interception. Carroll, 1997.

Grant Kingsley and Andie Lawrence live on opposite sides of the country but have met over the Internet. What they don't realize is that they are both being manipulated by a trio of menacing hackers.

Virus. Carroll, 1995.

Doctors are seeing lots of new patients suffering from malnutrition and severe self-neglect, but without any known cause. The only thing that ties the cases together is the fact that victims all spent a lot of time with their computers. A computer scientist, working with the doctors, discovers evidence of a virus that can infect humans through their computers.

Wilson, Charles

Game Plan. St. Martin's, 2000.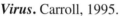

A computer chip the size of a pencil eraser is implanted into the brains of five criminals in a secret underground government lab. The chip confers vast knowledge, faster reflexes, and superhuman strength. The criminals, four men and a woman, destroy the lab and escape on a mission to rule the world.

Wilson, F. Paul, and Matthew J. Costello

Mirage. Warner, 1996.

Research scientist Julie Gordon has invented a virtual-reality system that can look into a person's mind and create a voyage through someone's memories. She must use her experimental device on her twin sister Samantha, who is in a coma, to discover who tried to kill her.

Chapter 9

From the Ridiculous to the Sublime

Political and Religious Thrillers

Definition: In the political thriller, the primary plotline involves the government, or highly placed people in the government, secretly attempting to do something bad or illegal to the populace, and they are usually willing to kill to keep these activities covered up. Another popular theme is that the present government is in danger of being toppled or suborned by powerful factions or foreign powers. The religious, or ecclesiastical, thriller includes themes such as the cloning of Jesus, the discovery of a secret that could challenge people's faith, or the rise to power of an evil cult. The underlying bond among these subjects, besides the religious aspect, is the same as in the political thriller: there is a secret to be kept and people will kill to keep that secret.

The Appeal: The government and the church are symbols of authority and, like doctors, hold power over us. So there is a strong fear factor in these stories. Conspiracy hysteria runs rampant in the United States and this subgenre feeds that paranoia admirably. Many people, such as Libertarians, believe that the government has gotten too large and too intrusive into its citizens' private lives, and people with this type of viewpoint often like to read political thrillers. The international rise in religious fervor along with the innate secrecy surrounding many traditional faiths has fueled an interest in the ecclesiastical suspense novel. The secrecy of the Vatican as well as the long, uninterrupted history of the Roman Catholic Church also appeals to people's interest and imagination.

Brief History: The Cold War paranoia of the 1960s as well as the mistrust in the government spawned by the Vietnam War gave birth to the beginnings of the political thriller. The earliest incarnations can be seen in Fletcher Knebel's novels of insane presidents and military cabals poised to overthrow the government. The Watergate scandal and the impeachment proceedings against a U.S. president have fanned the fires of public interest in government shenanigans, resulting in more authors writing in this subgenre.

The early development of the religious thriller can be traced to the novels of Irving Wallace and Morris West in the 1970s and 1980s, with their stories of religious secrets and deadly conspiracies. Recent events such as millennium fervor, the growth of Christian evangelicalism, and bioengineering have contributed to a rise in religious thrillers.

Advising the Reader: The key elements to remember when advising the reader and suggesting appropriate titles are:

- What type of books in this subgenre are they interested in, political or religious?

- Is it the dangerous secret aspect that interests the reader? Would the reader be interested in political as well as religious thrillers, and vice versa?

- The reader may like the legal elements of the political thriller; suggest legal thrillers.

- Readers may enjoy titles about the paranormal (Chapter 10) because many of these feature government conspiracies.

- Readers interested in other nations trying to topple or suborn the United States may be interested in other subgenres that feature the Soviet Union, Asia, or the Middle East attempting this strategy.

- Question readers carefully because some may be offended by the content of certain religious thrillers.

- Readers interested in the genetic and bioengineering features of some religious thrillers may be interested in biothrillers.

Political Thrillers

The essence of government is power;
and power lodged as it must in human hands will ever be liable to abuse.

—James Madison

Abercrombie, Neil, and Richard Hoyt

Blood of Patriots. Forge, 1996.

Terrorists attack the House of Representatives leaving hundreds of members of Congress and their staff dead or dying. There is no clue as to who is behind this massacre, so the president sends former CIA agent James Burlane to investigate. (Abercrombie is a congressman from Hawaii and Hoyt is a former counterintelligence agent.)

Aellen, Richard

The Cain Conversion. Fine, 1993.

Secret Service agent Bill Sullivan has been programmed by the KGB to kill the president of the United States.

Aikman, David

When the Almond Tree Blossoms. Word, 1993.

It is 1998, and the United States is in the midst of a second civil war—this time between the People's Movement and the Constitutionalists.

Andrews, Russell

Gideon. Ballantine, 1999.

Gideon is a mystery, a cipher that holds the key to a shocking secret. Writer Carl Granville is hired to write Gideon's book, but he can never talk to him or ask him any questions—all he has are old diaries and letters. Soon Granville finds out too much, and he is a fugitive, framed for two murders and hunted by both the FBI and an unknown assassin. His only chance for survival: discover the real identity of Gideon. (Russell Banks is the pseudonym for the team of Peter Gethers and David Handler.)

Archer, Jeffrey

Shall We Tell the President? Viking, 1977.

An FBI special agent has exactly six days to find out which of one hundred U.S. senators is involved in a conspiracy to assassinate the president; unfortunately, he has fallen in love with a senator's daughter who may also be involved in the conspiracy.

Baldacci, David

Absolute Power. Warner, 1996.

Can the president of the United States get away with murder? Luther Whitney is a thief who was in the wrong place at the wrong time and must now run for his life.

Last Man Standing. Warner, 2001.

Web London is the head of the FBI's Hostage Rescue Team. When he inexplicably freezes up during a mission, all his fellow team members are killed. London investigates the psychological reasons behind his "freeze" as well as his attempt to catch the people involved in murdering his colleagues.

Saving Faith. Warner, 1999.

Faith Lockhart works for a powerful Washington lobbyist who is to meet with the FBI and give evidence about her boss's illegal attempts to influence government leader. Unfortunately, the meeting explodes in a blast of gunfire, and Faith is on the run.

The Simple Truth. Warner, 1998.

Convicted of killing a girl twenty-five years earlier, Rufus Harms smuggles a letter out to the Supreme Court claiming he was forced to commit the murder. Suddenly, anyone who has anything to do with Harms or the letter dies a mysteriously, and now Harms has escaped and is running for his life.

Split Second. Warner, 2003.

Eight years ago, Sean King retired from the Secret Service in disgrace when the presidential candidate to whom he was assigned was murdered while King was momentarily distracted. Now a lawyer in a small Virginia town, he learns that a current presidential candidate has just been abducted right under the watchful eye of Secret Service agent Michelle Maxwell. The two form an uneasy partnership as they investigate the similar cases.

Batchelor, John Calvin

Father's Day. Holt, 1994.

It is the year 2003, the U.S. president suffers a crippling illness and invokes the 25th Amendment: in case of presidential vacancy, disability, or inability, the vice president assumes the reins of power. The president has a complete recovery, but the vice president isn't giving up that easily.

Bowker, Richard

Senator. William Morrow, 1994.

Senator Jim O'Connor finds his mistress Amanda dead in her apartment ten weeks before he is due for reelection. He is accused of the crime and must conduct his own investigation into the murder to clear his name.

Branon, Bill

Let Us Prey. HarperCollins, 1994.

Scary survivalist-militia types target the IRS for complete and utter destruction. (The author, who originally self-published this book is an "expert on weaponry, demolitions, and state-of-the-art surveillance . . . and a proficient marksman.")

Burkett, Larry

The Thor Conspiracy. Nelson, 1995.

Three men are the only opposition to a conspiracy that began fifty years ago—a conspiracy that will result in an international dictatorship. (The author is founder and president of Christian Financial Concepts, a ministry dedicated to teaching money management principles.)

Burnell, Mark

The Rhythm Section. HarperCollins, 1999.

Stephanie Patrick has lost everything: her entire family was killed in a plane crash. Then she is approached by members of a covert intelligence network who tells her that the plane crash wasn't an accident and offers her a deal: if she agrees to work as an agent with the network, they will give her the opportunity to get the terrorists who blew up her family.

Cannell, Stephen J.

The Plan. William Morrow, 1995.

The Mafia has gained control of a major television network and is using this new media muscle to promote its own candidate for U.S. president.

Child, Lee

Without Fail. Putnam, 2002.

Ex-military policeman Jack Reacher is approached by M. E. Froelich, the former girlfriend of his dead brother and head of the Secret Service detail assigned to protect the vice president, to assist her in keeping the vice president from being assassinated.

Cohen, William S.

The Double Man. William Morrow, 1985.

Compton, David

The Acolyte. Simon & Schuster, 1996.
Political campaign manager Greer Whitaker is recruited by the CIA for a covert operation that leaves him the prime suspect in a murder. (Also published under the title *Extreme Sanction.*)

Impaired Judgement. Dutton, 2000.
Paula Chandler is a federal judge in Virginia—and the first lady. The case currently before her could bring down the presidency.

Corn, David

Deep Background. St. Martin's, 1999.
Bob Hanover, president of the United States, is assassinated at a White House press conference. Soon both his wife and the vice president are fighting for the nomination in the next presidential election. Presidential aide Nick Addis, along with White House security chief Clarence Dunne and CIA analyst Julia Lancette, uncover a conspiracy and massive government cover-up that could result in their deaths.

Corriher, Kurt

Someone to Kill. Forge, 2001.

Dalton, James

City of Shadows. Forge, 2000.
A tale of the Watergate scandal seen from the viewpoints of three men used as pawns who are helplessly caught up in the affair.

Deverell, Diana

<u>Casey Collins series</u>

12 Drummers Drumming. Avon, 1998.
Casey Collins, a U.S. Foreign Service officer, is implicated in a terrorist bombing and pursued by the FBI and Interpol. Aided only by a cadre of operatives who function outside the law, she must clear herself and catch the real mastermind behind the bombings.

Night on Fire. Avon, 1999.
U.S. Foreign Service officer Casey Collins is investigating two deaths that seem to have nothing in common but that will lead her into the clutches of an international conspiracy.

Feinstein, John

Running Mates. Villard, 1992.

The governor of Maryland is assassinated, and investigative reporter Bobby Kelleher knows this will be the "big story" he's been waiting for. Kelleher's investigation leads him to a plot involving an old college chum who used to be a KKK grand dragon.

Finder, Joseph

High Crimes. William Morrow, 1998. **FILM**

Government agents arrest the husband of Harvard law professor Claire Heller Chapman, and she discovers that the man she is married to has been a stranger to her—he once had a different name and a different face.

The Zero Hour. William Morrow, 1996.

Flynn, Joseph

The Next President. Bantam, 2000. **M**

JD Cade's son has been kidnapped, and for Cade to get him back alive, he must kill Franklin Delano Rawley, the first African American to be elected president of the United States.

Mitch Rapp series

Transfer of Power. Pocket, 1999.

Terrorists have attacked the White House, killing dozens of people and taking a hundred people hostage —it's only through the quick actions of his Secret Service agents that the president has survived, hidden away in an underground bunker. CIA operative Mitch Rapp infiltrates the terrorist-held White House and makes the discovery that someone in the U.S. government wants the rescue attempt to fail.

The Third Option. Pocket, 2000.

CIA counterterrorism operative Mitch Rapp does not know that people in his own government are using him to further their plans to weaken the president's power and install their choice in the position of director of the CIA. Unfortunately for them, they've picked the wrong man.

Separation of Power. Pocket, 2001.

Another mission of CIA operative Mitch Rapp, who must stop a cabal of corrupt politicians from taking control of the White House—and the country.

Executive Power. Atria, 2003.

The CIA's preeminent assassin, Mitch Rapp, has to take a desk job at CIA headquarters because his anonymity has been compromised (the reason for this is detailed in *Separation of Power*). But Rapp cannot be kept chained to a desk for long and soon embarks on a new mission in the Middle East.

Flynn, Vince

Term Limits. Pocket, 1997.

Assassins have already killed three crooked Washington politicians and issued an ultimatum to the government: no more dirty politics, or more will die. No one is safe—not even the president.

Forsyth, Frederick

The Negotiator. Bantam, 1989.

> *Gannon's Adventure/Suspense Rule Number 16: Sometimes it's not paranoia—they really are out to get you!*

Garber, Joseph R.

Vertical Run. Bantam, 1995.

Dave Ellis is not having a good day: his boss tries to kill him, his wife disowns him, and he is trapped in fifty-story office building with armed commandos guarding each exit with orders to kill him on sight. But Dave is not going to give up that easily.

Gifford, Thomas

Saints Rest. Bantam, 1996.

The president calls on Ben Drikill (last seen in *The Assassini,* see Religious Thrillers later in the chapter) to find the mastermind behind a conspiracy that threatens the future of the U.S. election process.

Gilstrap, John

At All Costs. Warner, 1998.

Travis Brighton is a typical thirteen-year old American with a typical mom and dad, living in a typical small town. Then, one day Travis finds out the truth—his real last name is Donovan and, according to the FBI, his parents murdered sixteen of their friends and created a terrible disaster a year before he was born. Fleeing with Travis, the couple attempts to clear their name and discover the real reason for the disaster.

Grady, James

White Flame. Dove, 1996. **M**

Two FBI agents and a D.C. homicide detective must stop a conspiracy aimed at the assassination of Faron Sears, charismatic African American presidential contender.

Green, Tim

The Fourth Perimeter. Warner, 2002.

Ex-Secret Service agent Kurt Ford begins an investigation after his son Collin, himself a Secret Service agent, is found dead—a supposed suicide. Ford discovers that several other young agents have also died recently . . . and the evidence points to the president of the United States.

Grippando, James

The Abduction. HarperCollins, 1998. **M**

Allison Leahy is the U.S. attorney general and the democratic nominee for president, running against Lincoln Howe, a retired African American four-star general. The polls have both candidates neck-and-neck until Howe's granddaughter is kidnapped on her way to school.

Grisham, John

The Pelican Brief. Doubleday, 1992. 　▢▸　 **FILM**

Two Supreme Court justices are murdered within hours of each other, and there are thought to be no clues. But law student Darby Shaw has found some, and she is now marked for murder.

Hawley, Noah

A Conspiracy of Tall Men. Harmony, 1998.

Linus Own is a professor of conspiracy theory at Modesto College who himself becomes the center of an unbelievable conspiracy.

Henrick, Richard P.

Nightwatch. Avon, 1999.

The president is assassinated while in the Ukraine for a top-secret summit, and the vice president barely escapes with his life while on vacation in the Missouri Ozarks. The culprits are not hostile foreign powers, but high-ranking members of the U.S. government.

Herman, Richard

Against All Enemies. Avon, 1998.

Jonathan Meredith is a patriot, ready to bring America back onto the right track . . . his idea of the right track. Now, with help from government insiders, he and his First Brigade are ready to strike.

Higgins, George V.

A Change of Gravity. Henry Holt, 1997.

Hunter, Jack D.

Slingshot. Forge, 1995.

Hynd, Noel

Zigzag. Zebra, 1992.

Reporter Paul Townsend is contacted by a dying man who wants his obituary written ahead of time. The man then gives Townsend a clue to an explosive secret the government has been keeping since the presidency of Lyndon Johnson.

Kahn, Larry

The Jinx. Redfield, 2000.

Estate lawyer Ben Kravner opens a sealed envelope found among his murdered client's possessions and finds evidence of a 160-year conspiracy against the U.S. presidency: presidents elected every twenty years from 1840 through 1960 have died in office.

Kahn, Michael A.

The Canaan Legacy. Lynx, 1988. 　▢▸

Dignified lawyer Graham Anderson Marshall III dies of a heart attack in the arms of a very expensive call girl, but the mystery is why he left $50,000 for the upkeep of a pet's grave—especially given that Marshall never owned a pet. Lawyer Rachel

Gold is hired to investigate and uncovers the three-hundred-year-old secret that is really buried in Wagging Tails Estates.

Karaim, Reed

If Men Were Angels. Norton, 1999.

Midwestern senator and presidential hopeful Thomas Crane seems to be just what the American people are looking for in a candidate for the highest office in the land. But could he be too good to be true? Reporter Cliff O'Connell uncovers secrets from Crane's past that could blow the campaign wide open—secrets that he feels might best be left untold.

Kean, Rob

The Pledge. Warner, 1999.

At Simsbury College, a male student's naked and battered body is found with perverted poems written all over it, but the police rule out foul play. The exclusive fraternity Sigma Delta Phi holds the key to a two-hundred-year-old secret—a secret they will kill to keep.

Kimball, Stephen

Death Duty. Dutton, 1996.

Knebel, Fletcher

Night of Camp David. Harper, 1965.

A senator suspects that the president is mentally unbalanced.

Seven Days in May. Harper, 1962. **FILM**

The joint chiefs of staff plot to overthrow the president of the United States.

Koontz, Dean R.

Dark Rivers of the Heart. Knopf, 1994.

Spencer Grant, son of a serial killer, meets up with an enigmatic woman and soon finds himself running from two over-the-top government villains that make Bonnie and Clyde look like Ozzie and Harriet.

Leib, Franklin Allen

Behold a Pale Horse. Forge, 2000.

Former Texas governor and minister Rupert Justice Tolliver is elected president by a tiny margin. He then declares a holy war and uses the combined might of the armed forces to destroy all whom he considers sinners. With the world on the brink of destruction, someone must stop the president.

Ludlum, Robert

The Chancellor Manuscript. Dial, 1977.

Was J. Edgar Hoover murdered for his scandalous private files? And if so, who has them now?

Trevayne. Bantam, 1973.

Self-made millionaire Trevayne begins an investigation into the "secret govern-ment"—the people who really run the country—and uncovers some disturbing information.

MacKinnon, Douglas

First Victim. Evans, 1997.

President Turner Ryan and his wife Sabrina are the "Ken and Barbie" of politics, but behind closed White House doors Ryan is a vicious wife beater, and the vice president uses the information as blackmail.

Martini, Steve

Critical Mass. Putnam, 1998.

Terrorists target the United States for an attack using two small tactical nuclear bombs stolen from the former Soviet Union.

Matthews, Francine

The Cutout. Bantam, 2001.

CIA analyst Caroline Carmichael thought her husband had been killed in an air-line explosion caused by terrorists, but now he's back and has kidnapped the U.S. vice president. (The author is a former CIA intelligence analyst.)

McCrory, Brian

Jack Flynn series

The Incumbent. Pocket, 2000.

Twelve days before the presidential election incumbent Clayton Hutchins is almost assassinated by a gunman. His new press secretary, Jack Flynn, is also wounded in the attempt, and while recuperating in the hospital he re-ceives a cryptic telephone call telling him that "nothing is as it seems."

The Nominee. Atria, 2002.

Boston Globe columnist Jack Flynn investigates the close ties between the publishing mogul and Lance Rudolph, the Massachusetts governor who has just been nominated for attorney general.

Meltzer, Brad

The First Counsel. Warner, 2001.

White House lawyer Michael Garrick is dating the president's daughter, Nora Hartson. Late one night, they witness something that will ultimately endanger their lives.

Mills, James

The Hearing. Warner, 1998.

Supreme Court nominee Gus Parham must face an implacable foe in his bid to be a justice—crime boss Ernesto Vicaro who will do anything to control him.

Mills, Kyle

Burn Factor. HarperCollins, 2001.

> Quinn Barry, a computer programmer for the FBI, discovers what seems to be a major flaw in a program but is actually evidence of a military cover-up. Quinn's discovery places her in mortal danger, and she must uncover the man behind the deception before she is killed.

Mark Beamon series

Rising Phoenix. HarperCollins, 1997.

> Someone has poisoned the illegal narcotics supply in the U.S., and FBI special agent Mark Beamon is assigned to find out who has taken out full-page ads in the nation's newspapers telling addicts, "Quit or die." Soon clues point to a surprising culprit: the U.S. government.

Storming Heaven. HarperCollins, 1998.

> Beamon's penchant for creating havoc in his investigations lead to his being exiled to an FBI field office in Arizona, where he soon uncovers a conspiracy with links to the FBI itself.

Free Fall. HarperCollins, 2000.

> Mark Beamon has been suspended from the FBI, but that doesn't stop him from investigating the disappearance of a top-secret FBI file known as Prodigy—it contains all J. Edgar Hoover's information on Washington power-mongers.

Sphere of Influence. Putnam, 2002.

> While investigating terrorist activity, Beamon discovers that the U.S. government is using members of organized crime as a secret army against terrorism.

Nesbitt, Jeff

The Capital Conspiracy. Nelson, 1996.

> A gigantic nuclear reactor has been built in Algeria, and certain influential senators knew about it before the president. Why? (The author was the communications director for former Vice President Dan Quayle.)

Patterson, James

See How They Run. Warner, 1979.

> Dr. David Strauss's family members are being murdered one by one, and now he is fixated on finding the motive behind their deaths. His search takes him across Europe and finally to the Olympics, where he finds a shocking surprise. (This older novel, formerly published as *The Jericho Commandment,* was reissued under a new name after the success of Patterson's Alex Cross novels.)

Patterson, Richard North

Kerry Kilcannon series

No Safe Place. Knopf, 1998.

> Senator Kerry Kilcannon is vying to be the Democratic nominee for president, and it will all be decided at the California primary set to

take place in seven days. He is haunted by the fact that his older brother James, a candidate for president, was assassinated twelve years before in California. He is also on the target list for a stalker who has killed several women at abortion clinics. Will his presidential ambition cost him his life?

Protect and Defend. Knopf, 2000.

A sharply divided Supreme Court and the case of a fifteen-year-old girl who is suing for permission to have a late-term abortion against the wishes of her parents is creating a political nightmare for newly elected U.S. president, Kerry Kilcannon.

Balance of Power. Knopf, 2003.

President Kilcannon has been a resident of the White House for less than a year and is preparing to marry former television journalist Lara Costello when his strong advocacy for gun control causes violence to erupt.

Pearson, Ryne Douglas

Simple Simon. William Morrow, 1996. **FILM**

Sixteen-year-old Simon Lynch, autistic and a mathematical savant, has inadvertently deciphered the National Security Agency's most secure code and has been marked for assassination by the government. His only hope is to trust FBI special agent Art Jefferson to save him from termination. (The movie version is titled *Mercury Rising*.)

Peters, Ralph

Traitor. Avon, 1999.

Lieutenant Colonel John Reynolds is caught in a web of greed and treachery when he is assigned to investigate the devastating bombing of an aircraft research center.

Pieczenik, Steve

Maximum Vigilance. Warner, 1992.

Dr. Desaix Clark, the president's psychiatrist, is called on to decide whether the president is mentally fit to deal with an international emergency that could be the beginnings of World War III. (Sequel is *Pax Pacifica;* see Chapter 13.)

Quayle, Marilyn T., and Nancy T. Northcott

The Campaign. Zondervan, 1996. **M**

Conservative Senator Robert Hawkins Grant is being considered for the fast track to be the first African American president—until evidence implicates him in the murder of an investigative reporter. Desperate to clear his name, Grant discovers a conspiracy reaching to the White House. This thriller has a decidedly Christian bent. (Quayle is the wife of a former Vice President Quayle, and Northcott is her sister.)

The Serpent. Crown, 1992.

Can a brilliant Republican Senator stop the Russians from installing their puppet as the new president of Cuba—especially when the Democratic U.S. president is all style and no substance?

Racina, Thom

Hidden Agenda. Dutton, 1997.

> CNN correspondent Jonelle Patterson is about to receive the Congressional Medal of Honor from the president when a shot is fired—aimed not at the president, but at her! Jonelle's quick climb to the top was planned from the start, although it wasn't Jonelle's ambition that led to her success, but the secret manipulations of others. Jonelle must find out who was behind this plot and why before it's too late.

Richardson, Doug

Dark Horse. Avon, 1997.

> Shakespeare McCann is the proverbial dark horse candidate—he came out of nowhere to win the Republican nomination for a Texas Congressional seat. He has no past and no scruples, and he will do anything to win the race.

True Believers. Avon, 1999.

> Senator Will Sullivan and his wife have everything: smarts, looks, and lots of political power. The only thing they don't have is a child, and they're working on that—Gwen undergoes a new fertility procedure. It's a success, and she learns she is pregnant, but not with her husband's child. The father is an imprisoned maniac who will use his knowledge against the couple.

Sanders, Lawrence

Capital Crimes. Putnam, 1989.

> Brother Kristos is a faith healer who cured the president's son when medical science failed. But what else does he have planned?

Santiago, Soledad

Room 9. Doubleday, 1992.

Serling, Robert

The President's Plane Is Missing. Doubleday, 1967. **FILM**

Shelby, Philip

By Dawn's Early Light. Simon & Schuster, 2002.

> Financial analyst Sloane Ryder uncovers a plot an international plot to assassinate the first female president of the United States.

Days of Drums. Simon & Schuster, 1996.

> Novice Secret Service agent Holland Tylo is assigned to protect powerful Senator Charles Westbourne—shortly after the senator is brutally murdered. Her career in shambles, she begins her own investigation into the murder and discovers a massive conspiracy.

Gatekeeper. Simon & Schuster, 1998.

> Hollis Fremont has just arrived in Paris where she has a low-level job in the American consulate, but she soon finds herself in the midst of a dangerous conspiracy and in the sights of an assassin.

Last Rights. Simon & Schuster, 1997. **M**

African American General Griffin North is about to be nominated for vice president when he is suddenly killed in a suspicious plane crash. When the investigator into the crash is murdered, it is up to her friend and colleague Rachel Collins to continue the investigation.

Smolens, John

The Invisible World. Areheart, 2002.

All his life Samuel Adams has wondered what exactly his father did in his job with the government and what his role was in the Kennedy assassination investigations. But when he hears that someone resembling his father entered his mother's hospital room just before her death and then later ran off with her ashes, he begins an investigation into his father's secret life.

Sohmer, Steve

Favorite Son. Bantam, 1987. **FILM**

Seven gunshots push Senator Terry Fallon into the spotlight of national prominence, and soon the media has dubbed him America's "favorite son"—a contender for vice president. But is Senator Fallon all that the country thinks he is?

Patriots. Random House, 1990.

The U.S. military is unhappy with drastic budget cuts and reductions in its forces, so it is about to foment massive violence and destruction to regain its faded grandeur. One woman knows its secret, and she might not only have to kill but be killed to save her country.

Tanenbaum, Robert K.

Corruption of Blood. Dutton, 1995.

Manhattan assistant DA Butch Karp is selected to head the investigation when Congress reopens the Kennedy assassination case. He soon finds himself caught up in a conspiracy orchestrated by sinister elements within the CIA and politicians within Congress who hope to use the investigation to further their own ambitions.

Thor, Brad

The Lions of Lucerne. Pocket, 2001.

Secret Service agent Scot Harvath has screwed up big time—terrorists have kidnapped the president while he was in charge of security. Now he is determined to undo the damage before the president runs out of fingers for the terrorists to cut off and send to the White House staff.

Valenti, Jack

Protect and Defend. Doubleday, 1992.

Vice President Bill Rawlins enters into a deal with a foreign country to guarantee his election to the presidency not realizing that he is merely a pawn in a global conspiracy. (Valenti was special assistant to President Lyndon Johnson and is currently president of the Motion Picture Association of America.)

Wallace, Irving

The Plot. Simon & Schuster, 1967.

The R Document. Simon & Schuster, 1976.
> A proposed "law and order" amendment to the U.S. Constitution would effectively turn the United States into a police state ruled by the FBI. The attorney general, Christopher Collins, must find the secret R Document that exposes the truth about the amendment before it is too late.

The Second Lady. NAL, 1980. FILM
> Billie Bradford, the beautiful wife of the U.S. president, is on a state visit to Moscow when she is abducted by Soviet agents and replaced by her exact duplicate, KGB agent Vera Vavilova.

Weaver, Michael

Deceptions. Warner, 1995.
> A shockingly violent crime is ordered at the highest echelons of the U.S. government, but by a twist of fate, it is not committed. Two boyhood friends and two women, one thought dead and the other extremely dangerous, are drawn into this strange and dangerous conspiracy.

The Lie. Warner, 1997.
> Can one man and one woman, once lovers and now mortal foes, stop a vast international conspiracy?

Webb, James H., Jr.

Something to Die For. William Morrow, 1991.
> Ambitious Secretary of Defense Ronald Holcomb and a rogue admiral attempt to goad the president into starting a war.

Wicker, Tom

Donovan's Wife. William Morrow, 1992.

Willocks, Tim

Blood-Stained Kings. Random House, 1995.
> Clarence Jefferson, a corrupt Louisiana lawman who has gathered two suitcases full of evidence to imprison dirty politicians in five surrounding states, is dead. He has bequeathed the location of his hotly contested luggage to an unlikely pair: clinically depressed psychiatrist Dr. Cicero Grimes and Lenna Parillaud, a beautiful business tycoon who has kept her monstrously evil husband locked away in the "Stone House" for the past thirteen years. The two go in search of the evidence while fleeing from a slew of sordid characters. A haunting novel of southern violence, passion, and vengeance.

Wilson, F. Paul

Deep as the Marrow. Forge, 1997.
> President Thomas Winston decides to decriminalize drugs and tax them into extinction, and this decision makes him the enemy of people on both sides of the issue. He is heavily guarded at all times, but now someone

has kidnapped the daughter of his personal physician and is blackmailing the doctor to poison him.

Woods, Stuart
Will Lee series

Run before the Wind. Norton, 1983.
> This title introduces Will Lee—even before he was a prominent politician, he was involved in political intrigue.

Grass Roots. Simon & Schuster, 1989.
> Prominent lawyer Will Lee is running for the Senate and takes on a controversial case in his hometown of Delano. But Delano is a town that is secretly controlled by a white supremacist organization known as the Elect, and the Elect will do anything to keep Lee out of the Senate.

The Run. HarperCollins, 2000.
> Will Lee is back as a respected senator from Georgia running for the presidency, and now he's being targeted by forces from his past that will stop at nothing to keep him from the White House.

Religious Thrillers

Better to reign in hell than serve in heaven.

—John Milton

Balling, L. Christian
Revelation. Forge, 1998.
> Why has crazed evangelist Bobby Jordan stolen a sample of an ancient, mummified man? Former Green Beret John Reese, whose daughter was savagely attacked in the theft, must infiltrate Jordan's island fortress in search of the answer.

Benig, Irving
The Messiah Stones. Wheeler, 1995.
> Professor John McGowan receives a shocking bequest from his long-missing father: the announcement of the coming of the world's savior!

Brown, Dan
Robert Langdon series

Angels and Demons. Pocket, 2000.
> An ancient secret brotherhood known as the Illuminati has resurfaced in the modern world and is intent on carrying out its master plan—the destruction of the Catholic Church. They plant a time bomb inside the Vatican during a conclave to elect the next pope, and Harvard symbolism expert Robert Langdon must hunt through all the hidden rooms and vaults of the Vatican before it explodes.

The da Vinci Code. Doubleday, 2003.
While in Paris on business, Harvard professor Robert Langdon is consulted by the police about the murder of a curator at the Louvre. His investigation leads him on a hunt for a secret society, the Holy Grail, and the child of Jesus and Mary Magdalene.

Case, John

The Genesis Code. Fawcett, 1997.
Investigator Joe Lassiter is caught up in a worldwide conspiracy involving murder, cutting-edge biotechnology, and ancient beliefs after his sister and nephew are savagely butchered in their beds.

Cordy, Michael

The Miracle Strain. William Morrow, 1997.
Can the supposed DNA of Christ cure a terminally ill girl? Dr. Tom Carter enters into an unholy alliance with a two-thousand-year-old brotherhood for the chance to save his young daughter.

Easterman, Daniel

Night of the Apocalypse. HarperCollins, 1995.
A religious terrorist who thinks he is Jesus Christ and ready to usher in the end of the world kidnaps a group of prominent political and religious leaders in this convoluted tale, which also features the CIA, England's MI-5, and the IRA.

Folsom, Allan

Day of Confession. Little, Brown, 1998.
An entertainment lawyer investigates the murder of a high-ranking cardinal and finds evidence that points to a conspiracy in the Vatican to create a new Holy Roman Empire.

Gifford, Thomas

The Assassini. Bantam, 1990.
Investigating the murder of his sister, a nun, lawyer Ben Driskill uncovers an ancient brotherhood of killers, the Assassini, who get their orders directly from the Vatican. (The sequel is *Saints Rest*—see Political Thrillers earlier in the chapter.)

Klavan, Andrew

Man and Wife. Forge, 2001.
Psychiatrist Cal Bradley evaluates a nineteen-year-old young man who exhibits both a spiritual goodness and intense anger.

Kleier, Glenn

The Last Day. Warner, 1997.
On Christmas Eve 1999, a secret scientific complex in the middle of the Negev desert is suddenly destroyed—a week later at midnight on New Year's Eve, a beautiful young women with amazing powers appears at

the ruined installation. How are the two events linked, and what impact will they have have on the world?

Koontz, Dean R.

Servants of Twilight. Dark Harvest. 1984. **FILM**

A weird old woman accosts Christine Scavello and her six-year-old son Joey in a Southern California parking lot, accusing the boy of being the Antichrist. Soon, a cult of religious fanatics have targeted Joey for death.

Ludlum, Robert

The Gemini Contenders. Doubleday, 1976.

Greece, December 1939: a secret order of monks is sent on a mission to transport a vault to a hiding place in the Italian Alps and away from an advancing Nazi army. Inside the vault is a secret that could tear apart the Christian world.

Mandino, Og

The Christ Commission. Lippincott, 1980.

Martin, Malachi

Vatican. Harper, 1986.

The story of the Vatican's powerful financial network and the mysterious figure known as the Keeper who is in charge of it. The author was professor in the Vatican's Pontifical Biblical Institute.

Montalbano, William D.

Basilica. Putnam, 1998.

A priest is thrown to his death from the top of St. Peter's Basilica in the Vatican, and Brother Paul, a former Miami homicide policeman and now the pope's personal investigator, is called in to investigate.

Monteleone, Thomas F.

Eyes of the Virgin. Forge, 2002.

Computer programmer Kate Harrison and former navy SEAL Matt Etchison are running from the members of an ancient society who are willing to kill to gain a stained-glass image of the Virgin Mary that is said to communicate prophecies.

Peter Carenza series

The Blood of the Lamb. Forge, 1992.

Father Peter Carenza is an American Catholic priest and the result of a Vatican scientific experiment. He has the power to heal and, to his dismay, the power to kill.

The Reckoning. Forge, 1999.

The pope dies in the arms of Peter Carenza, a young priest who has the power to heal, and the College of Cardinals unanimously elect him as the new Pontiff. Peter is the result of a secret Vatican conspiracy to bring about the Second Coming—he was cloned from DNA from the Shroud of Turin, and his mother was a virgin nun. But the new pope is in reality an evil imposter.

Morrell, David

The Covenant of the Flame. Warner, 1991.

A sect of spiritual warriors founded two thousand years ago strives to protect the earth from despoilers and considers murder an important weapon in its armory. Polluters, strip miners, and poachers are but a few of the many on their hit list.

The Fraternity of the Stone. St. Martin's, 1985.

Former assassin Drew MacLane has lived in a monastery for the past six years until his past catches up with him—he soon finds himself fleeing for his life and on the trail of a religious conspiracy that is hundreds of years old.

Mustian, Mark

The Return. Pineapple, 2000. **M**

Journalist Michael Mason is investigating a black Brazilian woman who performs miracles and appears to be the Second Coming, but then the strange death of one of her disciples brings up disturbing questions.

North, Darian

Thief of Souls. Dutton, 1997.

Architect Dan Behr must save his wife Alexandra from a dangerous cult that has no intention of letting Dan "rescue" her.

Patterson, James

Cradle and All. Little, Brown, 2000.

Former nun turned private investigator Anne Fitzgerald is hired by the Archdiocese of Boston to investigate two pregnant virgins. Anne must protect the women and herself from dangerous forces arrayed against them. (Based on the author's earlier work published in 1980 called *Virgin*.)

Perdue, Lewis

Daughter of God. Forge, 2000.

A secret held by the Vatican for more than 1,500 years has been stolen: undeniable proof of a female Messiah named Sophia who was born in 310 A.D. and was murdered by Church elders to protect the dogma of male superiority.

Podrug, Junius

Dark Passage. Forge, 2002.

What if Islamic assassins from the present were somehow able to go back in time to Galilee circa 30 A.D. and target Jesus for termination? Three unlikely but resourceful characters—an action film star, an ex-nun who ministers to prostitutes, and an Israeli engineer-convict—are sent back in time in a desperate attempt to foil the terrorists' plan to change history.

Rabb, Jonathan

The Book of Q. Crown, 2001.

While working in the Vatican Library, Father Ian Pearse uncovers an ancient conspiracy that could devastate the Catholic Church. A destructive sect known as the Manichaeans has appeared to wreak havoc and suspicion points to the pope.

The Overseer. Crown, 1998.

Rumors have circulated for hundreds of years that a sixteenth-century monk named Eisenreich created a blueprint for world conquest known as *On Supremacy,* a document considered so dangerous that the pope had him killed. Now the name Eisenreich has surfaced again in the 1990s as the last word of a dying girl found in a remote part of Montana. Someone, known only as the Overseer, has found *On Supremacy* and intends to use it for world domination unless stopped by government agent Sarah Trent.

Rice, Robert

Agent of Judgment. Forge, 2000.

Former government assassin Michael Walker is drinking his days away in a Montana trailer park until he runs across the Church of the True Atonement, a cult based in Montana that commits horrible acts of eco-terrorism duplicating the signs of the apocalypse.

Roberts, James Hall

The Q Document. William Morrow, 1964.

Sapir, Richard Ben

The Body. Doubleday, 1983. **FILM**

A crucified body dating back to the first century is found in an ancient cave in Jerusalem.

Wallace, Irving

The Miracle. Dutton, 1984.

The Vatican has announced that the Virgin Mary will be returning to Lourdes to perform another miracle cure, and thousands of sick and dying pilgrims are expected to descend on the site.

The Word. Simon & Schuster, 1972.

An archeologist discovers lost scrolls supposedly written by the brother of Jesus.

West, Morris

The Clowns of God. William Morrow, 1981.

Pope Gregory XVII has announced a shocking prophecy that threatens to tear apart the Catholic Church, and the cardinals decide he must be silenced before it is too late.

Eminence. Harcourt, 1998.

Luc Rossini, brutally tortured by Argentine army forces in the 1970s, is now a respected cardinal in the Vatican. The reigning pontiff has just died, and Cardinal Rossini finds himself dealing with ghosts of his past as well as the political machinations within the Vatican.

Wood, Barbara

The Prophetess. Little, Brown, 1996.

Archeologist Catherine Alexander has excavated a site that contains six ancient papyrus scrolls with clues that point to a revelation that world governments will do anything to keep buried. Catherine desperately attempts to translate the scrolls as she finds herself running for her life from secret agents and Vatican operatives.

Woods, Stuart

Heat. HarperCollins, 1994.

Jesse Warden is offered a way out of prison: infiltrate an isolated religious cult in the Idaho mountains and investigate its strange leader, Jack Gene Coldwater.

Wright, Austin McGiffert

Disciples. Baskerville, 1997.

Chapter 10

Things That Go Bump in the Night

Adventures in the Alien and the Paranormal

Definition: This subgenre borrows from the horror and science fiction genres for two of its themes: psychic power and outer space aliens. But these are only used to give novelty to a suspenseful plot. For example, a character may have psychic powers and use them for good or evil, aliens may be involved in some way (usually benevolently), or a ghost (an ectoplasmic emanation) could be used as a side "character." The villain in many of these books is usually the government, which uses these paranormal elements to further its own power.

The Appeal: Psychic powers, aliens, and ghosts are fun to read about, and people who would never read a horror or science fiction novel find the additions of these elements enjoyable when intermingled with a thrilling "chase" or conspiracy story. Just enough otherworldly elements are thrown in to still make it believable and grounded in the everyday. In addition, conspiracy theorists can always relate to the cover-ups, dangerous secrets, and government villains that abound in this subgenre.

Brief History: John Farris, Dean Koontz, and Stephen King first started blending the paranormal with the traditional suspense story in the late 1970s and 1980s when they explored the use of psychic power and the curse (instead of a gift) that it could be to those who had it. The New Age '90s saw the use of friendly aliens seeking to help humanity mend the errors of its dangerous ways.

Advising the Reader: The key elements to remember when advising the reader and suggesting appropriate titles are the following:

- What elements does the reader prefer in terms of the paranormal—ghosts, aliens, mental telepathy?

- The reader may like the government conspiracy element of some of the titles in this subgenre and be interested in political thrillers.

- Readers who like conventional horror or science fiction might find this subgenre enjoyable.

- Readers who have exhausted these titles may wish to look at the "Animals Run Amok" section in the Chapter 2.

- Medical thrillers are appropriate to suggest because many of these paranormal powers are created by science gone awry.

From ghoulies and ghosties
And long-leggedy beasties
And things that go bump in the night,
Good Lord, deliver us!

—Traditional Scottish Prayer

Alten, Steve

Domain. Forge, 2001.
More than sixty-five million years ago a massive asteroid slammed into the earth, causing the extinction of the dinosaur and ensuring the rise of humanity. The only thing is that it wasn't an asteroid . . .

Ambrose, David

Superstition. Warner, 1998.
A team of psychologists attempt to create their own ghost by pooling their mental energies and eventually create such a thought form, whom they name Adam. Adam, however, is also created from their darker thoughts and starts to kill them, one by one.

Anderson, Jack

Millennium. Forge, 1994.
A cynical journalist and his beautiful assistant are the only chance of survival for the human race as they try to protect an alien visitor from government agents and an insane drug dealer. (The author is an investigative reporter whose column has appeared in more than eight hundred newspapers nationwide; he has also appeared on radio and television.)

Baum, Thomas

Out of Body. St. Martin's, 1997.
Denton Hake, imprisoned for a rape he doesn't remember committing, has just been paroled, and now his new girlfriend has been found murdered. He begins to experience strange lapses in time when he appears to be traveling outside of his body and observing the actions of others. To clear his name, he must learn to use his newfound power before it drives him insane.

Bay, Austin

Prism. HarperCollins, 1996.
Wes Hawkins, a retired psychic secret agent, is hired by a multibillionaire arms dealer to assassinate the president of the United States.

Becker, Walt

Link. William Morrow, 1998.

In a Central African cave, paleoanthropologist Samantha Colby finds what she first thinks is the elusive "missing link," but the evidence soon points to a more shocking finding.

Crichton, Michael

Sphere. Knopf, 1987. **FILM**

A research team investigates a mysterious ship found deep under the sea, covered in hundreds of years worth of coral—could it belong to aliens?

Darnton, John

Neanderthal. Random House, 1996.

Matt Mattison and Susan Arnot, once lovers now rivals, embark on a secret and dangerous expedition to the northern Asian mountains to find a species that has existed since before the dawn of humanity.

David, Jerome F.

Fragments. Forge, 1997.

A team of psychologists has brought together five mentally and emotionally disabled savants to connect them all via a computer and create a new sixth personality. A secret from the past and a ghostly presence become unknown factors and cause the new entity to hunger for revenge.

Ship of the Damned. Forge, 2000.

October 28, 1943—the USS *Eldridge* was teleported by the U.S. government's Psychic Warfare Program, with disastrous results for the crew. Now more than fifty years later, the government has lost another ship, the USS *Nimitz,* and the only way to rescue its crew is to use the dreams of seven strangers who are having visions of a huge ship in the desert—a ship with sailors fused to the metal bulkheads.

Farris, John

The Fury series

The Fury. Forge, 1976 (reissued 2000). **FILM**

Robin and Gillian are twins separated just after birth—Robin's father is a government assassin, and Gillian is raised to a life of wealth and privilege. The two have a devastating psychic power that the government wants to harvest for a weapon. The two finally meet and are on run for their lives.

The Fury and the Terror. Forge, 2001.

Eden Waring has a powerful psychic power, and both a secret government organization and the evil first lady are after her. On the run from them both, Eden discovers she is the daughter of Gillian (killed in the *The Fury* and now visiting Eden in her dreams) and joins forces with a former big game hunter and a beautiful black model to prevent the first lady from achieving world domination.

The Fury and the Power. Forge, 2003.

Once again psychic Eden Waring is on the run from evil forces that want to use her powers for their own nefarious plans. This time it's the wizard Mordaunt, who has disguised himself as a Las Vegas stage magician by the name of Lincoln Grayle.

Finder, Joseph

Extraordinary Powers. Ballantine, 1993.

Harrison Sinclair, director of the CIA, has been killed, and his son-in-law, former CIA operative Ben Ellison, suspects it was murder—murder by someone within the CIA. Ben must use his extraordinary powers of telepathy to find the killer.

Glass, Joseph

Susan Shader series

Eyes. Villard, 1997.

Susan Shader is a renowned psychiatrist, profiler, and psychic—she uses her power to actually get inside the head of serial killers. She is on the trail of the savage Coed Killer and must stop him before he kills someone very close to her. (Joseph Glass is a pseudonym for Joseph Libertson, who also writes as Elizabeth Gage.)

Blood. Simon & Schuster, 2000.

Criminal profiler and psychic for the Chicago Police Department Susan Shader is now on the trail of a serial killer known as the Undertaker.

Graziunas, Daina, and Jim Starlin

Thinning the Predators. Warner, 1996.

David Vandemark is the ultimate predator: a serial killer with psychic powers who tracks down and kills other serial killers.

Green, Kate

Theresa Fortunato series

Shattered Moon. Dell, 1986.

Theresa Fortunato is a Tarot-card-reading psychic whose visions help solve the mystery of several brutal murders.

Black Dreams. HarperCollins, 1993.

Professional psychic Theresa Fortunato and LAPD Detective Oliver Jardine team up to investigate two tangled cases: one involves the disappearance of an ill little girl who only has three days to live, the other a murdered antiques dealer who is linked to the child even though the two were strangers.

Hale, Michael

A Fold in the Tent of the Sky. William Morrow, 1998.

Calliope Associates is a secret private investigation firm that uses operatives with strong psychic powers; Peter Abbott is their newest recruit. Peter is able to "see" into the past, present, and future. He soon discovers that one of his colleagues is using his power to go into the past and commit murder, effectively changing the present. Peter must stop him before his past is rewritten and he was never born.

Hynd, Noel

Cemetery of Angels. Kensington, 1995.

Bill and Rebecca Moore have just moved to Southern California, into a dream home in a dream town, until one day their daughter Karen tells them there is a man in her room, but Bill and Rebecca search the house and can't find anyone. Then Karen and their son Patrick disappear with no ransom note and no clues.

Rage of Spirits. Kensington, 1997.

It is 2003, and the president of the United States is in a coma. The vice president sends his press attaché on a bizarre mission that could change the course of the nation's history.

A Room for the Dead. Kensington, 1994.

New Hampshire state policeman Detective Sergeant Frank O'Hara is on the trail serial killer Gary Ledbetter . . . again, since he had arrested and helped send him to the electric chair years ago.

Ing, Dean

The Skins of Dead Men. Forge, 1998.

Ross Downing has a strange gift: horribly burned while rescuing a young boy from a fire, he has skin grafts that now allow him to have visions—visions that will the help him to save the boy's mother and another young boy from assassins.

Kerr, Philip

Esau. Holt, 1997.

A skull is found in a cave in the Himalayas—a skull that is neither human nor ape. Could this be proof of the yeti, the missing link—or something much more unbelievable?

King, Stephen

Firestarter. Viking, 1980. **FILM**

Andy McGee and Vicky Tomlinson participated as subjects in a top-secret government drug research project while in college. Then they got married and had a daughter, Charlie. They found out they were somehow changed as a result of the experiment, and now their daughter can start fires with her mind. Government agents have already killed Vicky in an attempt to kidnap Charlie, and she's now on the run with her father to avoid becoming the government's newest secret weapon.

Klavan, Andrew

The Animal Hour. Pocket, 1993.

When Nancy Kincaid arrives for work on Halloween morning, her colleagues don't recognize her; her boss even threatens to call the police if she doesn't vacate the office. Across town, a poet named Oliver Perkins discovers the mutilated corpse of a young women in his brother's bed—the dead woman's name is Nancy Kincaid. (Klavan also writes under the pseudonym Keith Peterson.)

Hunting Down Amanda. William Morrow, 1999.
Jazz musician Lonnie Blake's professional and private life are in the toilet until a chance encounter with a mysterious woman leads him into a dangerous world of intrigue. Obsessed with the woman, Lonnie tracks her down and discovers the child she is protecting, Amanda, a little girl with a terrible secret. (Klavan also writes as Keith Peterson.)

Koontz, Dean R.

Cold Fire. Putnam, 1991.
Jim Ironheart has a special power: he is able to see an accident before it occurs, allowing him to save a would-be victim. One of the survivors is Holly Thorne, a freelance journalist, who teams up with Jim to solve a secret from his past.

Strangers. Putnam, 1986.
They were from all over the country, strangers with one thing in common—terror. They all had the same horrible nightmares—nightmares that called them to an isolated place in the desert, the Tranquility Motel.

LaPlante, Richard

Mind Kill. Forge, 1998.
Former cult leader Justin Gabriel has been in prison for the last ten years, convicted of forcing his followers to kill. In his ten years of incarceration, he has learned to control the dreams of others and is planning on using his power for revenge.

Lee, Edward

The Stickmen. Cemetary, 1999.
Government assassins are hunting a little boy—is it because he is in contact with aliens?

MacGregor, T. J.

The Seventh Sense. Kensington, 1999.
FBI special agent Charlie Calloway teams up with former agent Doug Logan, a psychic who can use inanimate objects to track people, to find the murderer of her husband and child.

Monteleone, Thomas F.

The Resurrectionist. Warner, 1995.
Senator Thomas Flanagan is the Republican favorite to be the next U.S. president until his jet crashes into the Florida Everglades and he brings his dead friend back to life. All hell breaks loose as Flanagan is both hunted by the military, which hopes to use his powers as a weapon, and haunted by terrifying dreams. But the worst awaits those he has resurrected, who find there is a price to be paid for their second chance.

Passman, Don

The Visionary. Warner, 1999.
>
> Lisa Cleary is on the way to the top of a prestigious financial organization when she starts having visions—a psychic ability that has been dormant for almost twenty years. She sees young women mutilated and murdered, victims of a serial killer. Lisa joins forces with LAPD detective Danny Talon to track down the murderer before he can kill again.

Pineiro, R. J.

01-01-00™. Forge, 1999.
>
> Susan Garrett is a senior analyst at the FBI's high-tech crime unit; Cameron Slater is an anthropologist specializing in the ancient Maya. Together they investigate a computer virus that is freezing computers all over the world and counting down to the millennium. Their only clue to the virus is a connection between the Maya and a strange radio transmission from outside our solar system.

Preston, Douglas, and Lincoln Child

Thunderhead. Warner, 1999.   **FILM**
>
> Archeologist Nora Kelly receives a letter from her father who mysteriously disappeared sixteen years earlier. It sends her on a search for Quivira, the Anasazi Indians "lost city of gold." But someone or something doesn't want her to succeed.

Robinson, Frank M.

Waiting. Forge, 1999.
>
> They look like us, but they're not human. They've been around for a long time, living among us . . . and waiting. A thorough medical exam could detect their differences, but they would never allow that and would kill to prevent it. This is something that Artie Banks will soon find out.

Rosenberg, Nancy Taylor

California Angel. Dutton, 1995.
>
> Toy Johnson, a kind woman with psychic healing powers or a monstrous child killer?

Schumacher, Barrett

Fear Itself. Forge, 2002.
>
> The wife of research scientist Reed Haler, who has a talent for foretelling the future, and she is found knifed to death by a maniac while on a camping trip. Reed then relies on another psychic woman to help him find his wife's killer.

Scott, Holden

Skeptic. St. Martin's, 1999.
>
> Soon after researcher Dr. Mike Ballantine's best friend is mysteriously murdered, he begins to experience disturbing hallucinations that echo events from his dead friend's life. Enlisting the aid of CIA agent Amber

Chen, Ballantine struggles to find his friend's murderers and to prevent them from stealing the results of his research—research showing that ghosts exist.

Sears, Richard

First Born. Forge, 2000.

Newborn John Reed is special: he has the power to heal, and the local priest has proclaimed him the new messiah. However, members of a sinister organization known as Neo Tech believes him to be the first of a new generation of human-alien hybrids and are using psychics known as "remote viewers" to monitor his progress. One of those viewers is Casey Lee Armstrong, who suspects that her employer has ominous plans for the boy and is determined to protect him from harm. But she soon finds herself marked for murder and falsely accused of kidnapping him.

Last Day. Forge, 2002.

Undercover policeman Charlie Wolf knows that he will die today at 3 P.M., but he doesn't know how.

Smith, Michael Marshall

One of Us. Bantam, 1998.

Hap Thompson has a great job at REMtemp: he takes people's memories. A married man can dally with his mistress for a few hours and feel no guilt, or a woman can pass a lie detector test because she can't remember her criminal deeds. Until one day, a beautiful young woman leaves Hap her memory of committing murder and refuses to take it back. Now he is on the run, hunted by the police for a murder he didn't commit, but the worst part is that people with whom he comes into contact keep disappearing in a strange flash of light.

Gannon's Adventure/Suspense Rule Number 17: Heroes always start out by being in the wrong place at the wrong time.

Steinberg, Richard

Nobody's Safe. Doubleday, 1999.

Gregory Picaro is the best safecracker in the world—there's nothing so secure that he cannot get into it. But one day, Gregory is in the wrong place at the wrong time, and witnesses the torture and execution of a wealthy man—a man that Gregory was just about rob. What he finds in the man's safe is a secret that the government will kill to keep buried, and this secret is literally not of this world.

Wager, Walter

Kelly's People. Forge, 2002.

The Russians have a new secret weapon: spies who can read minds. In an attempt to counteract this threat, the CIA has come up with their own spies with ESP.

Williams, Billy Dee, and Rob MacGregor

Trent Calloway series

PSI/Net. Forge, 1999. **M**

Former psychic spy African American Trent Calloway just wants to forget his days "remote viewing" for the government, but suddenly his past returns in a frightening way, and he must fight for his life and his sanity.

Just/in Time. Forge, 2000. **M**

Psychic spy Trent Calloway is back to stop a religious zealot who is out to destroy the world.

Wilson, F. Paul

Repairman Jack series

The Tomb. Forge, 1984.

This title introduces Repairman Jack, whose job is to "fix" situations, not things, for people, often at grave risk to himself. Jack must recover a stolen necklace that may or may not release a multitude of demons.

Legacies. Forge, 1998.

Jack's back after fourteen years! He starts out by doing a favor for a friend and ends up by solving a dire mystery from a woman's past.

Conspiracies. Forge, 2000.

Repairman Jack's latest case gets him involved with conspiracy buffs, and he soon learns that some conspiracies are actually true.

All the Rage. Forge, 2000.

Repairman Jack is hired by Dr. Nadia Radzminsky to protect her boss from underworld kingpin Milos Dragovic. Jack soon finds that drugs are involved, specifically Berzerk—take a little bit and your performance is enhanced, but take a lot and you go crazy and want to kill people.

Hosts. Forge, 2001.

A virus has attained sentience and is forcing all infected to come together to form the "Unity," a single consciousness that is determined to infect the world.

The Haunted Air. Forge, 2002.

In Queens, New York, a nine-year-old ghost girl in riding clothes is haunting a house, and it's up to Jack to free her spirit from its earthly bondage.

Gateways. St. Martin's, 2002.

Repairman Jack faces off against a group of mutant rednecks who inhabit a Florida swamp.

Wood, Bari

Doll's Eyes. William Morrow, 1993.

Eve Tilden Dodd Klein is a clairvoyant, and while in a small town attempting to reconcile with her estranged husband, she has a vision of a murder. She is the only "witness," and now the killer is coming for her.

Wright, T. M.

The Ascending. Forge, 1994.

Ryerson Biergarten wants to be a psychic Sherlock Holmes, using his paranormal gifts to find killers, but the police aren't really interested. So he sets out on his own to track a serial killer but soon finds out that he is dealing with something much worse.

Chapter 11

On the High Seas

Sea Adventures

Definition: Historical fiction dealing with the sea and with naval warfare involving sailing ships is included in this subgenre because these titles are an essential part of the adventure genre; they were not included in the chapter on war stories because the characters in these titles have a much closer relationship with the sea. The exploits and escapades of eighteenth- and nineteenth-century sailors have entertained generations of readers and influenced generations of authors. There would have been no Dirk Pitt (by Clive Cussler) without the inspiration of Horatio Hornblower (by C. S. Forester). The period of the Napoleonic Wars (1800–1815) is the favorite background for novels of sailing ships, with the protagonists usually being members of the Royal British Navy. These novels have almost become a separate subgenre comparable to the Regency novels (taking place within the limited time and place of 1800–1821 Regency England) of the romance genre.

The modern sea adventure also continues the theme of "man (or woman) against the sea" albeit now involving sailboats, submarines, scuba gear, or research vessels. The primary theme among all these books is the sea and how it can help or hinder the efforts of the protagonist.

The Appeal: The oceans account for a large portion of our planet, and ocean settings have fascinated people since the dawn of humanity. So, of course, stories about the sea and about the men and women who sail it have a powerful allure. These titles have some features in common with disaster novels—man versus powerful natural forces.

The characters at sea are totally on their own: they are cut off from society and the trappings of civilization. They must rely on themselves or their comrades for strength in their struggles with the powerful sea. Sometimes, the ocean takes on the qualities of a villainous character. In some stories the ship plays a character role. In others, focus is on the the ship's crew.

The two categories in this chapter may appeal to different readers. The titles in the first section attract fans of historical fiction. The allure of the great sailing ships of the past and their bloody sea battles is appealing to many readers. The second category holds a more general interest to those readers who enjoy action and adventure in an ocean setting. Both subgenres contain many series, usually centered on heroic adventures of a specific character.

Brief History: The nineteenth century saw the development of the sea adventure as we know it today, when veterans of the Napoleonic Wars such as Frederick Marryat wrote fictionalized accounts of their experiences. In the mid–twentieth century, C. S. Forester spawned a host of imitators when he created the Horatio Hornblower series, which was set during the Napoleonic Wars. Then in the late twentieth century, the prolific Clive Cussler put his own spin on the sea adventure by recounting the exploits of that seafarer and modern man of action, *Dirk Pitt*.

Advising the Reader: The key elements to remember when advising the reader and suggesting appropriate titles are the following:

- Does the reader want historical fiction about sailing ships or contemporary adventure stories?

- If a reader has enjoyed a book by a particular author, check to see if the author has written more titles—authors often carry over characters into other books.

- "I've read all the C. S. Forester books." There are several series that are similar such as those by Alexander Kent, Patrick O'Brien, and C. Northcote Parkinson.

- Guide readers to military fiction—the marine conflicts may be of interest.

- Those who enjoy modern sea adventures can be guided to technothrillers because many of these titles concern ships and submarines.

- "I've read all the Clive Cussler books." Read-alike authors include Jack Du Brul and Robert Louis Stevenson III.

- The reader may like the spy element of this subgenre and be interested in other espionage books.

- The sea as a major plot element can also be found among titles in the disaster subgenre—*The Poseidon Adventure* (P. Gallico), *Jaws* (R. Benchley), *Meg* and *The Trench* (S. Alten), and *Riptide* (D. Preston).

- Readers who have read "everything" may be interested in nonfiction accounts of eighteenth- and nineteenth-century naval campaigns, shipwrecks, sunken treasure, pirates, or pertinent biographies.

- *You Can Judge a Book by Its Cover:* Ships under sail, pleasure craft, underwater scenes and the ocean itself figure prominently on the covers.

The Age of Sail

A sailing vessel is alive in a way that no ship with mechanical power ever be.

—Aubrey de Selincourt

Bryan, Francis

The Curse of Treasure Island. Viking, 2001.

Ten years after Jim Hawkins returned from his exploits aboard the *Hispaniola,* a beautiful woman and her young son come looking for him and take him back to the South Seas for another danger-filled adventure in this modern sequel to Robert Louis Stevenson's *Treasure Island.*

Collett, Bill

The Last Mutiny. Norton, 1993.

Subtitled *The Further Adventures of Captain Bligh,* the charismatic villain, Vice Admiral William Bligh, is now in retirement and looking back on his life.

Connery, Tom

Markham of the Marines series

A Shred of Honour. Regnary, 1999.

Irish Catholic Lieutenant George Markham serves in His Majesty's Royal Marines in the late eighteenth century. Upon the death of his superior officer, Markham takes command of a motley group of marines and attempts to mold them into fighting band.

Honour Redeemed. Regnary, 2000.

Markham must lead his Royal Marines against the French in Corsica on a mission to seize control of the island.

Honour Be Damned. Regnary, 2001.

Markham and is Royal Marines are assigned to the *Syphide* and do battle against a French privateer.

Cooper, James Fennimore

The Wing-and-Wing. Henry Holt, 1998 (first published in 1842).

The adventures of French privateer Raoul Yvard, who constantly battles tremendous odds by harassing Lord Nelson's Royal Navy.

Eccles, Frank

The Mutiny Run. St. Martin's, 1994.

Captain Brewster of the HMS *Adamant* must keep his discontented crew from mutiny as England wars with Revolutionary France.

Forester, C. S.

The Horatio Hornblower Saga

Mr. Midshipman Hornblower. Little, Brown. 1950. `FILM`

A collection of short, interconnected stories where the young Horatio Hornblower is assigned aboard his first ship, the HMS *Justinian,* in the British Royal Navy, is captured by the Spanish, and is eventually made a lieutenant.

Lieutenant Hornblower. Little, Brown, 1952.

Hornblower is now a junior lieutenant aboard the HMS *Renown* and emerges as a leader on a secret mission in the West Indies.

Hornblower and the Hotspur. Little, Brown, 1962.

Hornblower is given his first command, the HMS *Hotspur;* blockades the French; and gets married.

Hornblower during the Crisis. Little, Brown 1967.

Hornblower, now a captain, has given up command of the HMS *Hotspur* and awaits a new command. (This collection of three novellas was left unfinished because of Forester's death in 1966.)

Hornblower and the Atropos. Little, Brown, 1953.

Hornblower's adventures in the Mediterranean aboard his new command, the HMS *Atropos.*

Beat to Quarters. Little, Brown, 1937. **FILM**

Captain Hornblower is now commanding the HMS *Lydia* and tangles with the Spanish and a Central American dictator. (Although the sixth in the series, this was the first Hornblower novel that Forester wrote and was filmed as *Captain Horatio Hornblower.*)

Ship of the Line. Little, Brown, 1938.

In 1810, Hornblower is in command of the HMS Sutherland and, while raiding the coasts of France and Spain, comes up against superior French forces and is captured.

Flying Colors. Little, Brown, 1938.

Hornblower escapes from the French and liberates a British ship captured by Napoleon's navy.

Commodore Hornblower. Little, Brown, 1946.

Hornblower has been knighted and named a commodore in charge of his won squadron of ships. He is sent to the Baltic to stop Napoleon's forces from spreading into Sweden and Russia.

Lord Hornblower. Little, Brown, 1946.

Hornblower must stop a mutinous crew from defecting to the French.

Admiral Hornblower in the West Indies. Little, Brown, 1958.

The war with Napoleon over, Hornblower, now an admiral, takes command in the West Indies, where he deals with pirates and insurrectionists.

Hackman, Gene, and Daniel Lenihan

Wake of the Perdido Star. Newmarket, 1999.

Follows the adventures of Jack O'Reilly aboard the *Perdido Star* in the early eighteenth century. This coming-of-age saga has all the classic elements of the sea adventure including shipwrecks and pirates. (Hackman is a two-time Academy Award–winning actor, and Lenihan is an underwater archeologist.)

Hough, Richard

Buller's Saga

Buller's Guns. William Morrow, 1981.
The adventures of low-born Rod Maclewin and Archy Buller, who comes from generations of naval officers, as the Royal Navy moves from a sail-driven to a steam-powered fleet—from the nineteenth to the twentieth century. Note: although only the first novel in this trilogy concerns ships with sails, all titles were included to maintain continuity.

Buller's Dreadnought. William Morrow, 1982.

Buller's Victory. William Morrow, 1984.

Kent, Alexander

Richard Bolitho Saga

Midshipman Bolitho. McBooks, 1998 (Original British publication date: 1978).
It is 1772, and young Richard Bolitho is a sixteen-year-old midshipman aboard the HMS *Gorgon* of the British Royal Navy fighting pirates off the West African coast. He is later assigned to the HMS *Avenger* and tangles with smugglers off Cornwall. Originally two novels: *Midshipman Bolitho* and *Midshipman Bolitho and the Avenger.* (Kent is the pseudonym for Douglas Reeman.)

Stand into Danger. McBooks, 1998 (Original British publication date: 1980).
Bolitho is now a lieutenant aboard the frigate HMS *Destiny* and helps to locate lost treasure in the Caribbean.

In Gallant Company. McBooks, 1998 (Original British publication date: 1977).
The American War of Independence is the setting as the British Navy squares off against American and French privateers.

Sloop of War. McBooks, 1998 (Original British publication date: 1972).
In 1778, Bolitho commands the sloop HMS *Sparrow* and fights against the colonial rebels.

To Glory We Steer. McBooks, 1998 (Original British publication date: 1968).
Bolitho, commanding the HMS *Phalarope,* deals with a mutiny and participates in a pitched sea battle.

Command a King's Ship. McBooks, 1998 (Original British publication date: 1973).
In 1784, Bolitho and his frigate, HMS *Undine,* are sent to the East Indies to counter the presence of the French.

Passage to Mutiny. McBooks, 1999 (Original British publication date: 1976).
It is 1789, and Bolitho, now commanding the HMS *Tempest,* is sent to the South Sea to search for the *Bounty* mutineers.

With All Dispatch. McBooks, 1999 (Original British publication date: 1988).
In 1792, Bolitho is given the assignment of fighting the smugglers in the English Channel.

Form Line of Battle. McBooks, 1999 (Original British publication date: 1969).
In 1793, England is at war with France, and Bolitho's command, the HMS *Hyperion,* goes up against superior French forces.

Enemy in Sight! McBooks, 1999 (Original British publication date: 1970).
Still commanding the *Hyperion,* Bolitho is working blockade duty off the coast of France and must deal with an incompetent superior.

The Flag Captain. McBooks, 1999 (Original British publication date: 1971).
Flag Captain Richard Bolitho returns to England in 1797 after eighteen months at sea and finds himself caught up in a major crisis.

Signal—Close Action. McBooks, 1999 (Original British publication date: 1974).
In 1798, newly promoted Commodore Bolitho commands a squadron of ships sent to prevent Napoleon's badly needed artillery from reaching Egypt.

The Inshore Squadron. McBooks, 1999 (Original British publication date: 1977).
In 1800, Bolitho is now a rear admiral, in charge of a squadron of ships in the Baltic.

A Tradition of Victory. McBooks, 2000 (Original British publication date: 1981).
Bolitho is captured but escapes in time to win an important battle.

Success to the Brave. McBooks, 2000 (Original British publication date: 1983).
In 1802, Vice Admiral Bolitho is aboard the HMS *Achates* on a mission that gets him embroiled in plenty of action in the West Indies.

Colors Aloft! McBooks, 2000 (Original British publication date: 1986).
Now knighted, Bolitho is back in the Mediterranean fighting the French.

Honor This Day. McBooks, 2000 (Original British publication date: 1988).
In this installment, the action races from the West Indies to the Mediterranean as Bolitho prevents reinforcements from reaching the French before the Battle of Trafalgar.

The Only Victor. McBooks, 2000 (Original British publication date: 1990).
Bolitho, now half-blind, fights the Dutch in South Africa and goes on a secret mission in Denmark.

Beyond the Reef. McBooks, 2000 (Original British publication date: 1992).
In 1806, Vice Admiral Bolitho is sent back to South Africa to establish a permanent naval base, but before he reaches his destination, he is shipwrecked.

Darkening Sea. McBooks, 2000 (Original British publication date: 1993).
It is 1809, and as relations between Britain and America are growing tense, Bolitho is sent to the Indian Ocean to help prevent the harassment of British ships.

For My Country's Freedom. McBooks, 2000 (Original British publication date: 1995).
Admiral Sir Richard Bolitho in the War of 1812.

Cross of St. George. McBooks, 2001 (Original British publication date: 1996).
In 1813, Bolitho deals with an American invasion of Canada.

Sword of Honour. McBooks, 2001 (Original British publication date: 1998).
In 1814, Bolitho returns from a hard North American campaign to take up a command in Malta, where he dies in one of the last skirmishes of the Napoleonic Wars. The series is handed over to his nephew Adam, captain of a frigate.

Second to None. McBooks, 2001 (Original British publication date: 2000).
In 1815, Captain Adam Bolitho of the HMS *Unrivalled* fights slavers and pirates after the Battle of Waterloo.

Relentless Pursuit. McBooks, 2002 (Original British publication date: 2001).
Captain Adam Bolitho, still commanding the HMS *Unrivalled,* and still fighting slavers and pirates.

Lambdin, Dewey

<u>Alvin Lewrie Naval Adventures</u>

The King's Coat. Fine, 1990.
During the American War of Independence, seventeen-year-old rogue Alvin Lewrie is shipped off to be a midshipman in the British Royal Navy by his father.

The French Admiral. Fine, 1990.
Lewrie at the Battle of the Chesapeake during the American Revolution.

The King's Commission. Fine, 1992.
Alan Lewrie is commissioned a lieutenant and assigned as first officer aboard the HMS *Shrike,* which is patrolling the North American coast and attempting to get the local Native American tribes to side against the colonial rebels.

The King's Privateer. Fine, 1992.
Lieutenant Lewrie is sent on a secret mission to the Far East, where he meets up with his unpleasant father, Sir Hugo.

The Gun Ketch. Fine, 1993.
A newly married Lewrie is given his own command, the HMS *Alacrity,* and is sent to the Bahamas to hunt pirates.

H.M.S. Cockerel. Fine, 1995.
Called off the farm 1793 where he has settled down to the family life, Lewrie is assigned to as the first officer on the HMS *Cockerel* and sent to help the French royalists at Toulon.

A King's Commander. Fine, 1998.
Commander Lewrie and his frigate, HMS *Jester*, on a mission to Gibraltar.

Jester's Fortune. McBooks, 2002.
Lewrie and the *Jester* tangle with Napoleon's forces in the Adriatic Sea.

The King's Captain. St. Martin's, 2002.
Given command of a brand-new frigate, HMS *Proteus*, Lewrie deals with mutineers.

Sea of Grey. Dunne, 2002.
In 1798 after a public scandal, a disgraced Captain Alan Lewrie along with the crew of the HMS *Proteus* is sent into exile in the Caribbean, where the situation is tense as the French colony of Saint Domingue is wracked by a slave rebellion, and the fledgling U.S. Navy prepares to go to war against the French.

Havok's Sword. St. Martin's, 2002.
Captain Lewrie's newest adventure starts where the previous installment, *Sea of Gray,* left off—the HMS *Proteus* is in the Caribbean harassing the French, ably assisted by the neophyte U.S. Navy. Now Lewrie must face his arch-enemy, Guillaume Choudas, on the island of Hispaniola.

Mack, William P.

Captain Kilburnie. Naval Institute, 1999.
Fergus Kilburnie, one of the first Scotsman to serve as an officer in the British Royal Navy at the time of Admiral Nelson, goes from one quandary to the next, eventually ending up captain of his own three-masted frigate.

Matthew Christopher series

Lieutenant Christopher. Nautical, 1998.
A young Annapolis privateer embarks on a series of adventures, including joining the Continental Navy and serving under Commodore John Paul Jones.

Christopher and the Quasi War with France. Nautical, 2002.
The further adventures of the Maryland shipbuilding family, the Christophers. Matthew Christopher and his crew on the *Mary* fight off the French while trading in the Caribbean.

Marryat, Frederick

Frank Mildmay or the Naval Officer. McBooks, 1998 (first published in 1829).
Rogue Frank Mildmay moves up the ranks of the British Royal Navy in the mid–nineteenth century—he's either seducing pretty women or fighting French privateers.

Mr. Midshipman Easy. Henry Holt, 1998 (first published in 1836).
This is based on the author's real adventures with the legendary Lord Thomas Cochrane and recounts the rise of a young midshipman in the British Royal Navy.

Newton Forster or The Merchant Service. McBooks, 1998 (first published in 1832).

> Newton Forster survives many perils—press gangs, imprisonment, and a shipwreck—before joining the crew of a British East India Company ship.

Peter Simple. Henry Holt, 1998 (first published in 1834).

> Peter Simple and his faithful mentor Terence O'Brien embark on many naval adventures in the British Royal Navy during the Napoleonic Wars.

Maynard, Kenneth

Matthew Lamb Series

Lieutenant Lamb. St. Martin's, 1984.

> In 1798, four months after getting his officer's commission, Matthew Lamb serves as junior lieutenant aboard the HMS *Sturdy.*

First Lieutenant. St. Martin's, 1985.

> Lamb is the first officer aboard the HMS *Adroit* in the West Indies

Lamb in Command. St. Martin's, 1986.

> Matthew Lamb is given command of a mail ship, the *Heron,* in the West Indies.

Lamb's Mixed Fortunes. St. Martin's, 1987.

> Lamb is now commanding his old ship, the HMS *Adroit,* and taking part in the British invasion of Egypt.

McCutchan, Philip

Apprentice to the Sea. St. Martin's, 1994.

> Tom Chatto is a young apprentice Irish seaman who is learning the ways of square-rigged windjammer during the late nineteenth century.

McNamara, Tom

Henry Lunt series

Henry Lunt and the Ranger. Nuventures, 1991.

> Henry Lunt is being held prisoner by the British in Scotland until he and his men are rescued by John Paul Jones, who has been disrupting trade and harassing the British. Jones recruits Lunt to gather information on a new secret weapon the British are developing. (This novel is supposedly based on an ancestor of the author.)

Henry Lunt and the Spymaster. Nuventures, 1994.

> Henry Lunt assists Benjamin Franklin in Paris and then heads back to England to spy on the British.

Henry Lunt at Flambrough Head. Nuventures, 1995.

> Henry Lunt serves with John Paul Jones aboard the *Bonhomme Richard.*

Meacham, Ellis K.
Percival Mereweather series

The East Indiaman. 1968.
Percival Mereweather, a naval officer in the East India Company, commands the *Rapid*; he not only puts down a mutiny but goes up against pirates.

On the Company's Service. 1971.
Mereweather and the *Rapid* go after French spies.

For King and Company. 1976.
Now a senior captain, Mereweather has a new command, the *Pitt*.

Needle, Jan
Sea Officer William Bentley series

A Fine Boy for Killing. McBooks, 1996.
William Bentley is the nephew of Captain Daniel Swift, the infamous captain of the British naval frigate *Welfare,* and it is his duty to head the press gangs that gather up the poor souls who will man the ship.

The Wicked Trade. McBooks, 2000.
William Bentley, now a midshipman in the Royal Navy, finds himself drawn into a complicated smuggling conspiracy.

Nelson, James L.
Brethren of the Coast series

The Guardship. Post, 2000.
The adventures of pirate-turned-privateer Thomas Marlowe as he fights for the Virginia Colony against pirates, brigands, and brutal slavers.

The Blackbirder. William Morrow, 2001.
The Governor of Virginia orders Marlowe to track down his friend and first mate former slave King James, who has killed the vicious captain of a slave ship.

The Pirate Round. William Morrow, 2002.
Thomas Marlowe is headed for the Indian Ocean aboard his privateer *Elizabeth Galley* to hunt the treasure ships of the great mogul of India, but he is unaware that two implacable enemies from his past are hunting him.

Nelson, James L.
Revolution at Sea Saga

By Force of Arms. Pocket, 1996.
Isaac Biddlebomb is a smuggler in pre-Revolutionary America who gets in trouble with British customs inspectors in New York.

The Maddest Idea. Pocket, 1997.
At the start of the Revolutionary War, Biddlebomb is given a commission and given command of the privateer *Charlemagne*.

The Continental Risque. Pocket, 1998.
Biddlebomb and the Charlemagne become part of the new Continental Navy and engage the British off New Providence Island.

Lords of the Ocean. Pocket, 1999.

> Biddlebomb's mission is to smuggle Benjamin Franklin across the Atlantic to France.

All the Brave Fellows. Pocket, 2000.

> The Continental brig of war *Charlemagne* with Captain Isaac Biddlecomb, his wife, and infant son aboard is forced ashore where Biddlecomb must deal with his sworn enemy, Lieutenant John Smeaton.

Nordhoff, Charles, and James Norman Hall

The Bounty Trilogy

Mutiny on the Bounty. Little, Brown, 1932. ▐FILM▌

> The HMS *Bounty* set sail from England to Tahiti in 1787 with the harsh Captain William Bligh in charge. His tyranny causes the crew to mutiny and he, along with eighteen loyal crewman loyal, are set adrift in a small open boat. But Bligh is not so easily cast aside . . .

Men against the Sea. Little, Brown, 1933.

> The further adventures of the eighteen loyal crewman who, along with Captain Bligh, were set adrift in the HMS *Bounty*'s open launch.

Pitcairn's Island. Little, Brown, 1936.

> Chronicles the fate of Fletcher Christian and the mutinous crew of the HMS *Bounty* as they find a refuge on a lonely island in the Pacific.

O'Brian, Patrick

Jack Aubrey and Stephen Maturin series

Master and Commander. Norton, 1990 (original British publication date: 1969).

> Captain Jack Aubrey, in command of the HMS *Sophie,* forms a friendship with ship's surgeon (and spy) Stephen Maturin; both are captured by the French.

Post Captain. Norton, 1990 (original British publication date: 1972).

> Aubrey and Maturin return to Britain and meet their future wives, but they must flee to France to escape from bill collectors just in time for war to break out again.

H.M.S. Surprise. Norton, 1991 (original British publication date: 1973).

> Aubrey is given command of the HMS *Surprise* and sent to China and India. Maturin is captured by the French and tortured.

Mauritius Command. Norton, 1991 (original British publication date: 1978).

> Aubrey is appointed commodore, given a small squadron to command, and ordered to attack Mauritius.

Desolation Island. Norton, 1991 (original British publication date: 1979).
Now in command of the HMS *Leopard,* Aubrey, along with Maturin, is sent on a secret mission to rescue Captain Bligh (of the *Bounty*), but in the process he is chased into the Antarctic by the Dutch and gets shipwrecked.

The Fortune of War. Norton, 1991 (original British publication date: 1979).
Aubrey manages to get the damaged *Leopard* back to Malaya, where he and Maturin arrange for passage back to Britain, but they then get caught up in the War of 1812.

The Surgeon's Mate. Norton, 1992 (original British publication date: 1980).
Escaping from American privateers, Aubrey and Maturin return home and then to the Baltic for Maturin to do a bit of spy work.

The Ionian Mission. Norton, 1992 (original British publication date: 1981).
Aubrey and Maturin head for the Mediterranean and help out the Sultan of Turkey.

Treason's Harbor. Norton, 1992 (original British publication date: 1983).
The HMS *Surprise* is laid up in Malta for repairs, but Aubrey and Maturin find time for spying and treasure hunting.

The Far Side of the World. Norton, 1992 (original British publication date: 1984).
The HMS *Surprise* chases an American ship in the South Pacific that has been harassing British whaling boats.

The Reverse of the Medal. Norton, 1992 (original British publication date: 1986).
Aubrey returns to Britain where he is framed in a financial conspiracy, thrown out of the Royal Navy, and ends up imprisoned.

The Letter of Marque. Norton, 1992 (original British publication date: 1986).
Maturin buys the *Surprise* and equips her as a privateer in an attempt to refurbish Aubrey's reputation.

The Thirteen Gun Salute. Norton, 1992 (original British publication date: 1989).
Getting his commission and seniority back, Aubrey, commanding the captured French ship *Diane,* along with Maturin, takes an ambassador to Malaysia to negotiate a treaty and end up shipwrecked.

The Nutmeg of Consolation. Norton, 1993 (original British publication date: 1991).
The shipwrecked crew of the *Diane* gets passage to Singapore, where Aubrey takes command of a former Dutch ship, the *Nutmeg,* and heads back to Britain. He ends up in Australia back in command of the *Surprise.*

Truelove. Norton, 1993.
Aubrey and Maturin are assigned to help a Polynesian queen in her struggles against a rival who is supported by Napoleon.

The Wine-Dark Sea. Norton, 1994.
The *Surprise* is hired by the British Admiralty with the mission for Maturin to stir up the Spanish colonies in South America.

The Commodore. Norton, 1996.
> Aubrey is given command of a squadron with orders to suppress the slave trade in the Gulf of Guinea and then to rebuff an imminent French invasion of the Irish coast.

The Yellow Admiral. Norton, 1997.
> Aubrey is besieged on all sides—at sea and at home—until Maturin returns from a mission in Chile with news that might be his salvation.

The Hundred Days. Norton, 1999.
> Napoleon has escaped from Elba, and Aubrey and Maturin are sent to the Mediterranean to deal with him.

Blue at the Mizzen. Norton, 2000.
> The Napoleonic Wars are over, and the HMS *Surprise* sets sail to South America ostensibly on a scientific mission but actually to offer aid to revolutionaries in Chile.

Parkinson, C. Northcote

The Life and Times of Horatio Hornblower. Little, Brown, 1970.
> A fictional biography of the character created by C. S. Forester.

<u>Richard Delancy series</u>

The Guernseyman. McBooks, 2001 (original British publication date: 1982).
> To escape imprisonment, Richard Delancy "volunteers" to be in the British Royal Navy. He is made a midshipman and sets sail for New York—just in time for the outbreak of the American Revolution.

Devil to Pay. McBooks, 2001 (original British publication date: 1973).
> Delancy, now a lieutenant, is sent on a mission to the coast of France.

The Fireship. McBooks, 2002 (original British publication date: 1975).
> Delancy is in command of a ship patrolling the Irish coast and thwarts an attempted French invasion.

Touch and Go. McBooks, 2003 (original British publication date: 1977).
> Delancy now commands the sloop HMS *Merlin* in the Mediterranean.

So Near, So Far. McBooks, 2003 (original British publication date: 1981).
> Delancy takes part in a yacht race and then becomes embroiled in conflict with a submarine.

Dead Reckoning. McBooks, 2003 (original British publication date: 1978).
> Delancy commands the frigate HMS *Laura* on a six-year cruise in the East Indies where he takes on two French frigates and wins, thus earning a knighthood and eventually retiring.

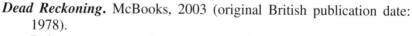

Pope, Dudley

Lord Nicholas Ramage series

Ramage. McBooks, 2000 (original British publication date: 1965).
Lieutenant Lord Nicholas Ramage (rhymes with *damage*) of the British Royal Navy is given orders by Admiral Lord Nelson himself to rescue a group of Italian aristocrats from Napoleon's advancing army.

Ramage and the Drumbeat. McBooks, 2000 (original British publication date: 1968).
Ramage's command, the HMS *Kathleen,* is ordered to Gibraltar to support Lord Nelson's forces against the Spanish.

Ramage and the Freebooters. McBooks, 2000 (original British publication date: 1969).
Ramage is given a new command, the HMS *Triton,* and must deal with mutineers and a mission to deliver important documents.

Governor Ramage RN. McBooks, 2000 (original British publication date: 1973).
Ramage, still in command of the *Triton,* is escorting a convoy in the Caribbean and must keep his passengers—French aristocrats—safe.

Ramage's Prize. McBooks, 2000 (original British publication date: 1974).
Ramage must discover why important courier ships are disappearing in the West Indies.

Ramage and the Guillotine. McBooks, 2000 (original British publication date: 1981).
Ramage is sent on a spy mission to discover what Napoleon plans for an invasion of England—if he's caught, it means the guillotine!

Ramage's Diamond. McBooks, 2001 (original British publication date: 1982).
Ramage, now in command of the HMS *Juno,* must face the French in the Caribbean with an undisciplined crew whose former captain was a drunkard.

Ramage's Mutiny. McBooks, 2001 (original British publication date: 1977).
Captain Lord Ramage is ordered to recover the HMS *Jocasta* after her crew mutinies and surrendered the ship to Spain.

Lord Ramage and the Rebels. McBooks, 2001 (original British publication date: 1982).
Ramage and the crew of the HMS *Calypso* search for murderous French privateers off the coast of Jamaica.

The Ramage Touch. McBooks, 2001 (original British publication date: 1984).
Ramage must deal with a French invasion fleet off the coast of Tuscany.

Ramage's Signal. McBooks, 2001 (original British publication date: 1984).
Ramage and the *Calypso* are on a mission in the Mediterranean to sink as many ships in Napoleon's fleet as they are able.

Ramage and the Renegades. McBooks, 2001(original British publication date: 1982).
Ramage and the crew of the *Calypso* fight pirates off the coast of Brazil.

Ramage's Devil. McBooks, 2002 (original British publication date: 1982).

The fragile peace between England and France is broken while Lord Ramage is honeymooning in France. He and his bride flee the country just in time, but Ramage must save his friend who has been imprisoned on Devil's Island.

Ramage's Trial. McBooks, 2002 (original British publication date: 1984).

Ramage faces a court-martial and must clear his name or be sentenced to death.

Ramage's Challenge. McBooks, 2002 (original British publication date: 1985).

Ramage, mournful over the disappearance of his wife, must rescue hostages being held by Napoleon in Tuscany

Ramage at Trafalgar. McBooks, 2002 (original British publication date: 1986).

Reunited with his wife, Lord Ramage is given orders to join Nelson's fleet blockading the port of Cadiz, but Ramage does not plan on just doing blockade work.

Ramage and the Saracens. McBooks, 2002 (original British publication date: 1988).

Ramage is sent to Sicily to deal with the Saracens—the pirates of the Barbary Coast.

***Ramage and the* Dido.** McBooks, 2002 (original British publication date: 1989).

Captain Lord Ramage is given a new command, the powerful ship of the line HMS *Dido,* and sent on a mission to the West Indies.

Poyer, David

The Civil War at Sea

Fire on the Waters. Simon & Schuster, 2001.

In 1861, Elisha Eaker, heir to a wealthy New York banking empire, joins the U.S. Navy and is assigned to the USS *Owanee.* The ship is sent on a desperate mission to relieve the Union's Fort Sumter in the newly declared Confederate States of American.

A Country of Our Own. Simon & Schuster, 2003.

Ker Claiborne leaves service with the U.S. Navy to join the new Confederate Navy, but he has no ship until he demonstrates his daring in a land battle. He is then made second officer on a converted paddleboat, the CSS *Montgomery,* and eventually becomes captain of the CSS *Maryland,* an opium ship that he seizes.

Reeman, Douglas

Badge of Glory. William Morrow, 1982.

In 1850, fifty years after slavery has been outlawed among British subjects, Captain Philip Blackwood has received orders to sail to West Africa and stamp out the slavery centers. (The author also writes under the name Alexander Kent.)

Sabatini, Raphale

Captain Blood. Penguin, 2002 (first published in 1922). **FILM**

Swashbuckling classic of piracy, swordfights, and secret identities.

The Sea-Hawk. Norton, 2002 (first published in 1915). **FILM**

Betrayed by his half-brother, English gentleman Sir Oliver Tressilian becomes a Barbary pirate.

Stevenson, Robert Louis

Treasure Island. Signet, 1998 (first published in 1883). **FILM**

The adventures of young Jim Hawkins as he searches for hidden pirate treasure and battles with the villainous Long John Silver.

Stockwin, Julian

Thomas Kydd series

Kydd. Scribner, 2001.

Young wigmaker Thomas Paine Kydd is impressed into the crew of the HMS *Duke William* and learns to become a true sailor.

Artemis. Scribner, 2001.

Thomas Kydd, now a trained seaman, along with his mysterious friend Nicholas Renzi, leaves the battleship *Duke William* and ship out on the frigate *Artemis*.

Seaflower. Scribner, 2003.

Kydd (eventually ascending to the rank of master's mate) and his friend the down-on-his luck aristocrat Nicholas Renzi are now in the Caribbean as France and England fight over the West Indies.

Suthren, Victor

Edward Mainwaring series

Royal Yankee. St. Martin's, 1987.

In 1739, Edward Mainwaring is a lieutenant from the American colonies in the British Royal Navy serving in the Caribbean.

Golden Galleon. St. Martin's, 1989.

Mainwaring commanding the HMS *Diana* in 1741 and fighting Spanish privateers.

Admiral of Fear. St. Martin's, 1991.

American seaman Edward Mainwaring, an officer in the British Royal Navy, once again faces his mortal enemy, Chevalier Rigaaud de la Roche-Bourbon; his mission is to storm and conquer a huge French naval fortress in the Mediterranean.

Captain Monsoon. St. Martin's, 1992.

American Edward Mainwaring, a captain in the British Royal Navy, leads a ragtag flotilla of ships against the dastardly Frenchman Roche-Bourbon.

Woodman, Richard

Nathaniel Drinkwater series

An Eye of the Fleet. Sheridan, 2001 (original British publication date: 1981).

Based on the real-life career of Royal Navy officer Nathaniel Drinkwater. In this first entry in the series, Drinkwater is a midshipman aboard the HMS *Cyclops,* where he experience brutal conditions as the crew hunts American privateers.

A King's Cutter. Sheridan, 2001 (original British publication date: 1984).

Drinkwater is serving aboard the HMS *Kestrel*—the ship is carrying spies into and refugees out of France at the onset of the French Revolution.

A Brig of War. Sheridan, 2001 (original British publication date: 1985).

Drinkwater is now a lieutenant on the HMS *Hellebore* and involved in Admiral Nelson's attempt to stop Napoleon's Egyptian campaign.

The Bomb Vessel. Sheridan, 2000 (original British publication date: 1985).

It is 1800, and Drinkwater now has a command, the forty-year-old bomb vessel, HMS *Virago,* but he makes her seaworthy and plays an important role in the attack on Copenhagen.

The Corvette. Sheridan, 2000 (original British publication date: 1985).

Promoted to commander, Drinkwater replaces the captain of the HMS *Melusine* who has been killed in a duel. His mission is to escort a whaling fleet to the Greenland Sea.

1805. Sheridan, 2001 (original British publication date: 1985).

Drinkwater, commanding the HMS *Antigone,* is captured by French forces.

Baltic Mission. Sheridan, 2000 (original British publication date: 1986).

In 1807, Drinkwater and the *Antigone* are sent to the Baltic Sea where Drinkwater embarks on a secret mission.

In Distant Waters. Sheridan, 2000 (original British publication date: 1988).

Drinkwater in the Pacific commanding the HMS *Patrician* as he faces off against both the Spanish and the Russians.

A Private Revenge. Sheridan, 1999 (original British publication date: 1989).

Drinkwater and the *Patrician* are in the South China Sea on a secret mission to frustrate the new alliance between France and Russia. He meets up with his old nemesis, Morris.

Under False Colours. Sheridan, 1999 (original British publication date: 1990).
Drinkwater is working undercover, disguised as a disreputable merchant marine shipmaster, on a secret mission designed to aggravate the Franco-Russian alliance.

The Flying Squadron. Sheridan, 1999 (original British publication date: 1992).
In 1811, Drinkwater is sent to the Chesapeake Bay to attempt to heal the rift between England and America, but he soon finds himself commanding a squadron against the Americans.

Beneath the Aurora. Sheridan, 2001(original British publication date: 1995).
Drinkwater is now the head of the Admiralty's Naval Intelligence and goes on a secret mission to Scandinavia.

The Shadow of the Eagle. Sheridan, 2002 (original British publication date: 1997).
Drinkwater foils a plot to free Napoleon and take him to the United States where he was to help the Americans in the War of 1812.

Ebb Tide. Sheridan, 2002 (original British publication date: 1999).
It is 1843, and Captain Sir Nathaniel Drinkwater, at eighty-one, is on an inspection tour of lighthouses on England's west coast when tragedy strikes.

Wager. Sheridan, 1999 (original British publication date: 1993).

Short Stories

Coote, John O., editor

Norton Book of the Sea. Norton, 1989.
Includes stories by William Shakespeare, William Golding, Joseph Conrad, Evelyn Waugh, and James Fennimore Cooper.

Tanner, Tony, editor

Oxford Book of Sea Stories. Oxford, 1994.
The twenty-seven tales includes stories by Henry James, Joseph Conrad, Stephen Crane, E. M. Forster, William Faulkner, and Edgar Allen Poe.

Modern Sea Adventures

"O God the sea is so great and my boat is so small"

—Old Breton prayer

Amberg, Jay

Dublin. Forge, 2003.
Jack Gallagher, a former U.S. Navy fighter pilot, takes over the family's treasure-hunting enterprise, Dublin, Inc., after his father's suspicious death. But as Jack continues his father's search for a fabulous three-hundred-year-old sunken Spanish treasure ship, he finds treachery everywhere.

Benchley, Peter

The Deep. Doubleday, 1976.

> A young couple who are diving for treasure in the Caribbean find them-selves embroiled in a dangerous mystery.

Cussler, Clive

Dirk Pitt® series

Pacific Vortex! Bantam, 1982.

> Dirk Pitt must find an advanced submarine that has disappeared in the Pacific Vortex, a zone of the sea where dozens of ships have dis-appeared without a trace. (The first Dirk Pitt adventure—the author did not publish this until after other Dirk Pitt novels had been pub-lished because he felt the plotting wasn't as intricate as the later novels.)

The Mediterranean Caper. Pocket, 1973.

> What does a biplane from World War I strafing a modern-day U.S. Air Force base have to do with a ship and its lost cargo of riches?

Iceberg. Bantam, 1975.

> Why has a ship been sealed inside an iceberg? And who doesn't want the ship found?

Raise the Titanic. Viking, 1976.

> Dirk Pitt does the impossible, as the title indicates. (The author was so disgusted by the movie version of his novel that he vowed he would never sell another of his works to Hollywood, although he has since said he would reconsider because he feels special effects have vastly improved.)

Vixen 03. Viking, 1978.

> Dirk Pitt must stop terrorists from sailing a battleship up the Poto-mac and unleashing a deadly weapon from out of the past.

Night Probe! Bantam, 1981.

> How did that train get underwater? Only Dirk Pitt can find the answer.

Deep Six. Simon & Schuster, 1984.

> Dirk Pitt "stumbles on" a ghost ship, a ship ablaze, the president gone missing, and toxins in the sea.

Cyclops. Simon & Schuster, 1986.

> Dirk Pitt encounters a ship lost since 1918, a secret moon base, and a vintage blimp.

Dragon. Simon & Schuster, 1990. **M**

> In actuality, there were three atomic bombs headed for Japan at the end of WWII, but one went down in the Pacific, and Dirk Pitt has to find out what happened to it before it is used for dastardly deeds.

Sahara. Simon & Schuster, 1992.

> In 1865, a Confederate ironclad carrying a secret cargo breaks through a Union blockade and disappears into the Atlantic Ocean.

One hundred and thirty years later, Dirk Pitt discovers it buried in the middle of the Sahara Desert.

Inca Gold. Simon & Schuster, 1994.
Dirk Pitt goes diving for ancient Incan treasures.

Shock Wave. Simon & Schuster, 1996. ▢
Dirk Pitt must stop an evil dealer in gemstones from destroying all the diamonds in the world by using sound waves that will also create deadly tidal waves.

Flood Tide. Simon & Schuster, 1997. **M**
Dirk Pitt must stop a Chinese villain from changing the course of the mighty Mississippi River.

Treasure. Simon & Schuster, 1998. ▢
Before the great Library of Alexandria burned to the ground, quick-thinking librarians loaded all the treasures aboard triremes (boats propelled by banks of rowers) and sailed them to Greenland (!)—now it's up to Dirk Pitt to find the riches before evildoers can.

Atlantis Found. Putnam, 1999. ▢
Dirk Pitt encounters the lost civilization of Atlantis and a family of genetically engineered Nazis.

Valhalla Rising. Putnam, 2001.
Dirk Pitt must stop the evil head of a multinational corporation from gaining control of the world's oil supply.

Trojan Odyssey. Putnam, 2003.
Dirk Pitt's children, twenty-three-year-old fraternal twins he didn't know he had, introduced themselves at the end of *Valhalla Rising*. Now Summer, a marine biologist, and Dirk (Jr.), a marine engineer, are working with him at NUMA (National Underwater and Marine Agency), where they end up helping him foil the villains' plot to start a new ice age.

Cussler, Clive, and Paul Kemprecos
Kurt Austin series

Serpent. Pocket, 1999. ▢
Introduces the character of Kurt Austin, who, like Dirk Pitt, works for NUMA but is younger and less "John Wayne-ish." Austin must discover what went down on the *Andrea Doria* when she was purposely sunk.

Blue Gold. Pocket, 2000 ▢
Kurt Austin must stop a beautiful seven-foot Amazon from taking control of the world's freshwater supply.

Fire Ice. Putnam, 2002.
Kurt Austin, leader of NUMA's Special Assignments Team, and his colleague, Joe Zavala, battle a Russian mining tycoon who has proclaimed himself czar and threatens to overthrow the shaky Russian government. He plans to ignite pockets of methane hydrate, an unstable compound known as

"fire ice," along the U.S. eastern seaboard, which will set off monstrous tidal waves and keep the U.S. government busy and out of his way while he orchestrates his takeover.

White Death. Putnam, 2003.

Kurt Austin and pal Joe Zavala go up against one of their most over-the-top villains yet: an albino maniac who has genetically engineered salmon into ten-foot-long monsters with all the nasty attributes of a piranha. And he intends to loose them on the world.

Eidson, Bill

One Bad Thing. Forge, 2000.

What starts out as a sailing cruise to help him grieve his daughter's death soon becomes an ever-escalating horror as McKenna is enmeshed in an international crime cartel and forced to commit murder.

Finney Jack

Assault on a Queen. Simon & Schuster, 1959. **FILM**

Six bandits salvage a World War I submarine and use it to rob the *Queen Mary.*

Foote Tom

Undertow. Dufour, 1998.

Retired merchant navy captain Jim Prendergast's family is killed when their sailboat is destroyed by IRA terrorists aboard a boat smuggling weapons. He vows to get revenge.

Fullerton, Alexander

The Blooding of the Guns. Soho, 2001.

Nicholas Everard has been transferred from a battleship to the smaller, more confined world of His Majesty's destroyer *Lanyard* where he will battle the Germans in the Battle of Jutland.

Garrison, Paul

Buried at Sea. William Morrow, 2001.

Jim Leighton signs on for a six-week ocean voyage as the personal trainer to the elderly Will Spark, owner of the new sailboat *Hustle.* Jim soon finds that the voyage is not for pleasure but to escape from Spark's deadly enemies who soon follow.

Fire and Ice. Avon, 1998.

Asian pirates kidnap Michael Stone's wife Sarah and eleven-year-old daughter Ronnie. They also steal their thirty-eight-foot yacht. Stone, left only with a damaged canoe, must find and rescue his family before the pirates murder them.

Gibbs, Tony

The Glory series

Dead Run. Ivy, 1988.

Introduces the crew of the yacht-for-hire *Glory,* who have set sail on a sea of danger.

Running Fix. Random, 1990.

Gillian Verdean, owner of the charter yacht *Glory,* Captain Jeremy Barr, and mate Patrick O'Mara are back for more adventure.

Landfall. William Morrow, 1992.

The crew of the charter yacht *Glory* set sail for another adventure in the Caribbean as they deal with murder, arms smugglers, and ex-spies.

Kennedy, William P.

Dark Tide. St. Martin's, 1995.

What was to have been a relaxing vacation cruise aboard a yacht in the Caribbean turns into a nightmare for two couples as they are taken captive by the yacht's captain, who is using the boat to smuggle diamonds.

Lavalee, David

Event 1000. Henry Holt, 1971. **FILM**

A submarine is involved in a collision and trapped 1,300 feet underwater. Now the crew must be saved before their air runs out. (Made into the movie *Gray Lady Down.*)

Llewellyn, Sam

Blood Knot. Pocket, 1991.

Burned-out prize-winning investigative journalist Bill Tyrell has retired to England to live on his refurbished wooden cutter, *Vixen,* when one day he finds a dead girl's body wrapped around his boat's propeller.

MacLean, Alistair

Santorini. Doubleday, 1987.

Commander Talbot and the crew of his ship the HMS *Ariadne* are assigned to retrieve a crashed jet loaded with nuclear weapons from the ocean floor, but the crew's efforts are frustrated at every turn by the ever-increasing number of sinister secrets they keep unearthing.

When Eight Bells Toll. Doubleday, 1966. **FILM**

British Secret Service agent Philip Calvert must stop a gang of oceangoing hijackers who are targeting ships in the Irish Sea.

Mansell, Patrick

Bimini Twist. 1st Books, 2001.

Max Carson and his two sons are recruited by the Bahamian authorities to track down drug smugglers in this fast-paced yarn that includes shark attacks, powerboat races, and high-speed chases.

Masiel, David

2182 kHz. Random House, 2002.

One day while monitoring the international distress radio channel, 2182 kHz, Harry Seine hears a faint distress call from a lone scientist trapped on a melting ice floe. Gathering together a ragtag rescue team to search for the scientist, Seine travels farther north than he has ever been.

Nichols, Peter

Voyage to the North Star. Carroll, 1999.

A down-on-his-luck seaman is hired to captain the yacht of an eccentric millionaire who wants to go to the Arctic on a big-game hunting expedition—an expedition that soon will very wrong . . .

Scott, Justin

Treasure Island. St. Martin's, 1994.

In this latter-day homage to Stevenson's *Treasure Island,* Jim Hawkins and a motley crew set sail for adventure aboard the *Hispaniola* in a search for hidden Nazi gold.

Stevenson, Robert Louis III

Philip Drake series

Torchlight. Putnam, 1997.

Multimillionaire arms merchant Erich Wilhelm Gerhardt is financing an operation to retrieve $1 billion in gold bullion that sunk with the USS *Norfolk* during World War I. Ex-SEALs Philip Drake and Jack Henderson infiltrate the diving operation to intercept the gold before it falls into Gerhardt's greedy, criminal hands. (The author is a descendent of the author of *Treasure Island.*)

Bright Star. Putnam, 1998.

Bright Star, a multibillion-dollar secret satellite that can track up to one thousand hostile targets at a time, mysteriously crashes into the sea, along with the space shuttle that was to deploy it into orbit. Ex-Navy SEAL Philip Drake is assigned to retrieve the satellite before it falls into the wrong hands.

Stone, Robert

Outerbridge Reach. Ticknor, 1992.

U.S. Naval Academy graduate Owen Browne is now in his early forties and working for a yacht brokerage in Connecticut. On an impulse, Browne offers to take the place of a missing contestant in an around-the-world singlehanded sailing race—the only problem is that he has never taken a sailboat out to sea alone.

Thayer, James

Force 12. Simon & Schuster, 2001.

Software billionaire Rex Wyman is determined to win the world's most challenging yacht race, and his ace in the hole is his $75-million-dollar racing yacht, *Victory,* which is completely run by a computer. But once at sea, Wyman realizes that someone is determined to see that he doesn't survive the race.

Tonkin, Peter

The Fire Ship. Crown, 1990.

Richard Mariner and his wife, Robin, are in the Indian Ocean on a trail voyage of a new high-tech sailboat when they come upon an abandoned freighter that has been set ablaze.

Short Stories

Fenderk Phyllis, editor

Full Forty Fathoms. William Morrow, 1975.

A collection of underwater adventure short stories.

Chapter 12

From the Ashes of the Third Reich

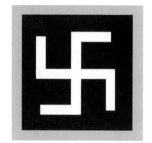

Nazis

Definition: This subgenre includes espionage activities in support of, or against, Nazi Germany during World War II, as well as later activities by surviving Nazis or sympathizers—up to and including the present day. Nazi secret agents on covert missions in the United States or Great Britain, Allied agents involved in subversive actions in Nazi Germany or Nazi-occupied Europe, and clandestine machinations by high-level officials on both sides of World War II all figured prominently. Also included are titles that have as their focus an alternate timeline (counterfactualism) in which Nazi Germany won World War II.

The Appeal: Nazis are considered by many to be most evil villains to have ever existed. They strike a chord of fear and revulsion in most of us. These stories offer us a vehicle to face and overcome our fears, and perhaps also arouse a morbid fascination, so books about real-life monsters and their various machinations can be exciting reads. We like to think that a monstrous thing like the Third Reich could never exist again; therefore attempts to create a Fourth Reich, clone Hitler, or exact revenge by the Nazis and their ilk fascinate many readers.

The first two sections in this chapter contain stories set in the past, which have an added bonus of a historical setting, and may appeal to readers who enjoy historical fiction. "Nazis in the Present Day" brings the horrors of the past into contemporary times, making them more immediate and real. The final two sections, "Alternate Histories" and "Beyond Reality," have a touch of science fiction's and fantasy's "what if" quality and may appeal to readers who enjoy those genres.

Brief History: One of the first suspense novels that helped create this subgenre was *Above Suspicion* by Helen MacInnes, published in 1941, well before the end of World War II. Robert Ludlum hit the best-seller lists in the 1970s with his Nazi espionage novels. Science fiction authors have long been fascinated with trying to answer the question, "What if the Nazis had won?"—one of the prime topics for the "counterfactualism" (alternate history) writing style. Nazis have even been fodder for horror writers, pitted against such supernatural creatures as werewolves and vampires.

Advising the Reader: The key elements to remember when advising the reader and suggesting appropriate titles are the following:

- Does the reader prefer the action to take place during World War II, the present day, or a combination of the two (a story told via flashbacks)?

- Does the reader want original Nazis, or will their supporters or descendants suffice?

- Will the reader accept an alternate history (also known as counterfactualism) plot? Many times these titles are shelved with the science fiction and fantasy books and may be a new source of titles for a reader. Other times the fact that they are labeled science fiction/fantasy may well be a turnoff to the traditional adventure/suspense reader. A discussion of the merits of these books may be necessary.

- The reader may also be interested in military elements of the subgenre and be interested in military fiction other than World War II.

- The reader may like the spy element of the subgenre and be interested in other espionage books that do not include Nazis.

- *You Can Judge a Book by Its Cover:* Look for the telltale swastika or twin SS lightning bolts on the cover, as well as the heavy use of black and red.

. . . a Reich to last a thousand years.

—*Adolf Hitler*

Nazi Activities before and during World War II (1933–1945)

In this section are titles that feature Nazi spies, assassins, and saboteurs. Unlike World War II military fiction, the emphasis is not on battles or other military exploits, but on the individual adventures of the hero or heroine.

Aaron, David

Crossing by Night. William Morrow, 1993.
> The fictionalized story of Elizabeth Pack, who supposedly served as inspiration for Ian Fleming's James Bond. The American-born wife of an older British diplomat, she is recruited by the British Secret Service to steal the Nazi's most prized secret.

Altman, John

A Gathering of Spies. Putnam, 2000.
> Katerina Heinrich is a beautiful and deadly Nazi spy. She has been planted as a mole in New York since 1933 and eventually travels to Los Alamos, where she attempts to steal the secret of the atomic bomb.

Boëtius, Henning

The Phoenix: A Novel about the Hindenburg. Doubleday, 2001.
> Was Nazi politics the real reason for the destruction of the acclaimed airship?

Cook, Thomas

The Orchids. Houghton-Mifflin, 1982.

The story of cynic Peter Langhof, who is transformed by the Nazi regime and his own twisted ideals into a monstrous murderer—a doctor who performs human experiments in the concentration camps.

Creasey, John

Death in the Rising Sun. Walker, 1976.

Diehl, William

27. Villard, 1990.

Johan Ingersoll is Germany's version of Lon Chaney, a man of a thousand faces and an actor whose real appearance is unknown to his adoring fans. Hitler recruits Ingersoll to be the ultimate spy, and he is sent on a mission so secret it is known only by a number—27.

Davis, Don

Appointment with the Squire. Naval Institute, 1995

Hitler sends an SS assassin to kill President Roosevelt during the last days of the war.

Deighton, Len

City of Gold. HarperCollins, 1992.

Glasgow Police Captain Bert Cutler is sent to Cairo in 1942 to find a spy who is leaking vital Allied information to German Field Marshal Rommel.

Dietrich, William

Ice Reich. Warner, 1998.

This Indiana Jones–type adventure begins with a tiny plane flying during a blinding snowstorm with a dead body strapped to its undercarriage. The action soon shifts to Antarctica, where a Nazi expedition finds something so devastating, it could guarantee the victory of the Third Reich.

Durand, Loup

Daddy. Villard, 1988.

The Nazis chase Thomas, an eleven-year-old French boy, across Europe because he is the only surviving person who knows the code to unlock a Swiss bank account containing more than $350 million.

Erdman, Paul E.

The Swiss Account. Tom Forge, 1992.

The vaults of supposedly neutral Switzerland's banks bulge with Nazi gold—gold the Germans are using to buy technology to build an atom bomb.

Follett, Ken

Eye of the Needle. Arbor, 1978. FILM

Code-named the Needle, he is a Nazi agent who knew the secret that could win the war for Hitler. The only one who can stop him is Lucy Rose, a beautiful Englishwoman who is torn between her desire and her country.

The Jackdaws. Dutton, 2001.

British special agent Major Felicity (Flick) Clairet and her plucky band of women are inserted into France to destroy Europe's biggest telephone network to ensure success for the Allies in the Normandy invasion.

The Key to Rebecca. William Morrow, 1980.

Nazi spy Alex Wolff's mission is to steal British military plans concerning their plans in North Africa during the summer of 1942. He is to send them in code to Field Marshall Rommel—the key to the cipher contained within the pages of Daphne du Maurier's most famous novel.

Furst, Alan

Dark Star. Houghton Mifflin, 1991.

André Szara, former foreign correspondent for *Pravda,* now a Soviet spymaster tangles with the Gestapo in pre–World War II Europe.

Jean Casson series

The World at Night. Random House, 1996.

Jean Casson, darling of French film society, is shocked by the German invasion and occupation of France and soon agrees to take part in a mission for the British secret intelligence service—a mission that goes horribly awry.

Red Gold. Random House, 1999.

Former producer of gangster films Jean Casson is recruited by the French resistance to smuggle guns to units of the French Communist party.

Kingdom of Shadows. Random House, 2000.

In the Paris of 1938, Hungarian spy Nicholas Morath tries to stop his tiny country from being caught between warring nations.

Night Soldiers. Random House, 1988.

Fleeing from the Stalinist purges, Soviet intelligence agent Khristo Stoianev flees to Paris, where he is soon caught up in the struggle for Eastern Europe between the Germans and the Soviets.

Gannon, Michael

Secret Missions. HarperCollins, 1994.

German secret agent Peter Krug travels to Florida by U-boat to ferret out classified information about U.S. warplanes. Pitted against Krug is a worldly and independent priest, Tony D'Angelo.

Gifford, Thomas

Praetorian. Bantam, 1993.

> British prime minister Winston Churchill has approved a secret mission code named Praetorian—elite commandos will sent into deserts of North Africa to assassinate German field marshal Erwin Rommel.

Gobbell, John J.

Todd Ingram series

The Last Lieutenant. St. Martin's, 1995,

> A Nazi spy assumes the identity of a dead U.S. Navy bugler. (Gobbell is a former U.S. Navy lieutenant.)

A Code for Tomorrow. St. Martin's, 1999.

> Navy lieutenant Todd Ingram is the executive officer on the USS *Howell* in the South Pacific. His mission is to save his girlfriend, army nurse Helen Durand, who is trapped behind enemy lines.

Griffin, W. E. B.

Honor Bound series

Honor Bound. Putnam, 1993.

> Wartime intrigue in Buenos Aires, where First Lieutenant Cletus Frade, demolitions expert Second Lieutenant Anthony Pelosi, and counterintelligence special agent David Ettinger are ordered to sabotage by any means necessary the resupply of German ships.

Blood and Honor. Putnam, 1996.

> Cletus Frade want revenge for the Nazi-ordered assassination of his father.

Secret Honor. Putnam, 2000.

> Nazi traitors are in Buenos Aires, and only Cletus Frade knows who they are.

Men of War series

The Last Heroes. Putnam, 1985.

> President Franklin Delano Roosevelt and William "Wild Bill" Donovan create the Office of Strategic Services in June of 1941, hand picking the members of a covert team to stop the Nazis from securing a rare ore necessary for creating an atomic bomb. (Originally published under the pseudonym of Alex Baldwin.)

The Secret Warriors. Putnam, 1985.

> Once again the members of the OSS are called to action, asked to obtain information vital to the war effort—mission locales include France, the Belgian Congo, and Morocco.

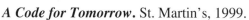

Soldier Spies. Putnam, 1986.

> Members of the OSS must parachute into Germany and bring out the inventor of the jet engine while a young Lieutenant John F. Kennedy is involved in a secret mission in France.

The Fighting Agents. Putnam, 2000.

> In Budapest an OSS agent must prevent two important prisoners from being interrogated by the Gestapo . . . he has only two choices: rescue them or kill them.

Harris, Robert

Enigma. Random House, 1995. **FILM**

> Bletchley Park, a small rural town in Britain, is the site of a desperate race against time. The best mathematicians and cryptographers are racing to break the Nazis' unbreakable Enigma code. Top codebreaker Tom Jericho's girlfriend turns up missing and is suspected of being a Nazi mole—and now even Tom is suspect. He must clear their names before it's too late.

Higgins, Jack

Cold Harbour. Simon & Schuster, 1990.

> On a dark night in May of 1994, American OSS agent Craig Osbourne is catapulted into the secret world of Cold Harbour, a complex and deadly world of cross and double cross, a world in which the fate of D-day and victory for the Allies will be played out.

Eagle Series

The Eagle Has Landed. Simon & Schuster, 1975. **FILM**

> A desperate Hitler demands that Churchill be kidnapped or killed. A disgraced war hero is assigned the suicide mission. While in England, a beautiful widow and an IRA assassin prepare to commit an act of treachery.

The Eagle Has Flown. Simon & Schuster, 1991.

> Features failed assassin Colonel Kurt Steiner and Liam Devlin, IRA gunman, poet, and scholar.

Flight of Eagles. Putnam, 1998.

> Brother against brother: Max and Harry Kelso had an American father and German mother but were separated as boys. They are reunited as adults— but on different sides of the war: Max is a *Luftwaffe* pilot, while Harry flies for the British Royal Air Force.

Luciano's Luck. Stein, 1981.

> What if General Dwight D. Eisenhower, supreme commander of the Allied Forces, sprung convicted mobster Lucky Luciano from the pen to help in the invasion of Sicily?

Night of the Fox. Simon & Schuster, 1986. **FILM**

> Philosopher turned killer Harry Martineau's mission is to rescue from the Germans a man who knows the time and place of D-day.

Household, Geoffrey

Rogue Male. Joseph, 1939. **FILM**

The nameless hero is stripped of all identity and forced to flee from Hitler's henchmen.

Hunter, Jack D.

The Expendable Spy. Dutton, 1965.

Hunter, Stephen

The Master Sniper. William Morrow, 1980.

The Germans are desperate in the last days of the war and are sending their master sniper to assassinate someone very important in London.

Hyde, Christopher

A Gathering of Saints. Pocket, 1996.

A psychopath stalks the war-torn streets of 1940 London, a murderer that kills his victims at the site of a devastating *Luftwaffe* raid—hours before the raid actually occurs!

Hynd, Noel

Flowers from Berlin. Dial, 1985.

Iles, Greg

Black Cross. Dutton, 1995

By order of Winston Churchill, four strangers—an American doctor, a German nurse, a Zionist killer, and a young Jewish widow—are brought together in a place where they hold the fate of the world in their hands.

Johnson, Haynes, and Howard Simons

The Landing. Villard, 1986. **M**

Washington, D.C., 1942. Henry Eaton, WASP government investigator; Constance Aiken, beautiful Southern belle; and black cop Leon Thomas are the only people who can stop two German spies who have landed in America to commit the ultimate act of terrorism.

Katkov, Norman

The Judas Kiss. Dutton, 1992.

Kohout, Pavel

The Widow Killer. St. Martin's, 1998.

A serial killer is loose in the German-occupied city of Prague—his latest victim is the widow of a German *Wehrmacht* general. Gestapo agent Erwin Buback teams up with rookie Czech policeman Jan Morava to track down the murderer before he can kill again.

Ludlum, Robert

The Rhinemann Exchange. Dial, 1975.
>
> The Allies need gyroscopes for their long-range bombers, and the Nazis need diamonds for their rockets—a despicable trade is to take place in Buenos Aires.

The Scarlatti Inheritance. World, 1971.
>
> Elizabeth Wyckham Scarlatti has a desperate plan: she must stop her son Ulster from giving Hitler control of the most powerful thing on earth.

MacInnes, Helen

Above Suspicion. Harcourt, 1941. **FILM**
>
> In MacInnes's first novel, Nazis are the villains. This tale begins innocently enough in an English garden and sweeps to a thrilling conclusion in the Alps.

Assignment in Brittany. Harcourt, 1942. **FILM**
>
> An undercover British agent in Nazi-occupied France attempts to uncover secret plans for defending against an invasion by the Allies.

Meade, Glenn

The Sands of Sakkara. St. Martin's, 1999.
>
> An assassination order direct from Adolf Hitler: kill President Franklin D. Roosevelt and Prime Minister Winston Churchill as they meet in Cairo for a secret conference to plan the Allied invasion of Nazi-occupied Europe.

Murphy, Walter F.

The Roman Enigma. MacMillan, 1981.
>
> American agent Roberto Rovere is sent to Rome on a mission to steal the plans for the German encryption machine *Enigma,* but he is being sent into a trap as the British have already stolen the secret of *Enigma.*

Nathanson, E. M., and Bank, Aaron

Knight's Cross. Carol, 1993.
>
> *Knight's Cross* is the code name for a secret mission to kidnap Hitler and is based on an actual mission that was eventually cancelled.

Olshaker, Mark

Blood Race. William Morrow, 1989.
>
> David Keegan is an American decathlete in the Summer Olympics of 1936, held in Berlin, where he is recruited Britain's Secret Intelligence Service to spy on the Nazis.

Pastor, Ben

Lumen. Van Neste, 1999.

Scott, Justin

The Normandie Triangle. Arbor, 1981.
>
> The Nazi spy whose sabotage was responsible for the sinking of the *Normandie* now plans to sink the *Queen Mary* in New York's harbor.

Silva, Daniel

The Unlikely Spy. Villard, 1996.

Catherine Blake, a beautiful aristocrat, lost her RAF husband in the Battle of Britain and now spends her time in London hospitals caring for victims of the Blitz. Blake is also an undercover Nazi spy trying to ferret out the details of D-Day. Opposing her is an absent-minded professor, Alfred Vicar—a confidante of Churchill and head of England's counterintelligence operations.

Thayer, James

Five Past Midnight. Simon & Schuster, 1997.

April 4, 1945: the SS is preparing a fortified retreat in the Bavarian Alps where Hitler may carry on the war for years. President Roosevelt makes an obvious but difficult decision: assassinate Hitler *now*! A deadly OSS agent, Captain Jack Cray, is chosen for the mission; unfortunately, he is a prisoner at the grim Colditz Castle . . . but not for long.

Uris, Leon

The Angry Hills. Random House, 1955

Nazi Activities in the Post–World War II Period (1945–1949)

In this section are titles that focus on the activities of Nazis who have escaped retribution. Such themes as Hitler's survival and escape from Germany, the search for war criminals, and secrets left over from the war that could cause global conflict or destruction are some of the themes explored.

Abbot, Margo

The Last Innocent Hour. St. Martins, 1991.

Sally Jackson returns to Berlin in 1946 as an army intelligence officer to help prosecute war criminals. Now she must face her most terrifying nightmare—is her Nazi husband still alive?

> *Gannon's Adventure/Suspense Rule Number 18: Hitler did not die in his Berlin bunker.*

Bernau, George

Black Phoenix. Warner, 1994.

April 1945: the war is coming to a close, but Germany now has a weapon of mass destruction code named Phoenix. Hitler didn't die in his Berlin bunker; he's in South America with the Phoenix.

Gardner, John

Maestro. Penzler, 1993.

Is Louis Passau the greatest living orchestra conductor in the United States, or is he a former Nazi spy? British agent Herbie Kruger must discover the truth before the maestro's assassin gets another chance.

Guild, Nicholas

The Linz Tattoo. McGraw-Hill, 1986.

It is 1948. Inar Christiansen, a Norwegian studying the cello in New York City, undertakes an ambitious and dangerous plan: to track down and destroy the SS officers who murdered his parents and most of the inhabitants of his hometown in Norway. His search leads to Israeli spies, hidden Nazis, and a horrible secret that could lead to another holocaust.

Hall, Adam

The Quiller Memorandum. Simon & Schuster, 1965. **FILM**

Although more than thirty years old, this classic still has the power to thrill you with its tale of British spy Quiller, coded messages, truth drugs, and a complex plot to revive the power of Nazi Germany. (More Quiller titles can be found in Chapter 1, "Spies and Secret Agents.")

Heywood, Joseph

The Berkut. Random House, 1987.

SS Colonel Gunter Brumm has a simple yet probably impossible mission: evade the Allied forces covering post–World War II Europe and smuggle the greatest war criminal of all time, "Herr Wolf," to safety. Opposing him is Vasily Petrov, the *Berkut,* who has been handpicked by Stalin for the job.

Hunter, Jack D.

Tailspin. Forge, 1990.

Kunetka, James

Parting Shot. St. Martin's, 1991.

Physicist Philip Cavanaugh is ordered on a secret mission into occupied Germany to inspect a hidden Nazi weapons lab. He soon uncovers a last ditch scheme by the Nazis to destroy Moscow, London, and Washington, D.C. with crude atomic bombs.

Reich, Christopher

The Runner. Random House, 2000.

In post–World War II Germany, American lawyer Devlin Judge searches for Erich Seyss, the escaped SS officer and former Olympic sprinter who killed his brother.

Thomas, Ross

The Eighth Dwarf. Warner, 1988.

Winward, Walter

The Canaris Fragments. William Morrow, 1983.

The Nuremberg Trials of the leading Nazi war criminals are in progress, and four missing fragments of a color photograph may be related to an attempt to free the prisoners. Major Otis Quinlan, a British reporter before the war, and American Major Ben Hadleigh, race to recover the fragments and find out their deadly secret.

Nazis in the Present Day

In this section are titles that feature elderly (but still up to no good) Nazi criminals, their progeny, or neo-Nazis—all looking to institute the Fourth Reich. One can find such plots as the unearthing of Nazi secret weapons or treasure, hidden strongholds full of plotting Nazi descendents, or the ever-popular cloning of Hitler.

Allbeury, Ted

The Stalking Angel. Mysterious, 1988 (first published as *The Reaper*).

Anthony, Evelyn

The Janus Imperative. Coward, 1980.

Benchley, Peter

White Shark. Random House, 1994.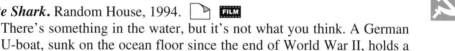

There's something in the water, but it's not what you think. A German U-boat, sunk on the ocean floor since the end of World War II, holds a deadly, hideous secret that is about to get loose and wreck havoc on an idyllic Connecticut coastal town.

Black, Cara

Murder in the Marais. Soho, 1998.

Private detective Aimee Leduc is retained by a rabbi to deliver fifty-year-old photo to an old woman in the Marais, the old Jewish quarter of Paris. When she arrives there, she finds only a corpse with a swastika carved on its forehead. Soon there are more strange murders, and Leduc finds herself in mortal danger.

Boyll, Randall

Katastrophe. HarperCollins, 2000.

Indiana State University professor Hank Thorwald attends a stop-smoking-by-hypnosis seminar, where under hypnosis he purports to be the reincarnation of Adolf Hitler! Soon the news spreads to Germany, where a crazed neo-Nazi who is attempting to clone Hitler sends his minions to track down Thorwald. This novel is a satire, and readers should not expect something more serious.

Chacko, David

White Gamma. St. Martin's, 1988.

Clive, John

The Last Liberator. Delacorte, 1980.

> *Gannon's Adventure/Suspense Rule Number 19: Nazis are very long-lived, and loads of them still exist today.*

Cooke, John Peyton

Haven. Warner, 1996.

Cecilia Mak has come to the remote Idaho town of Haven through a program that will pay off her medical school debt. Her husband, Mike, has given up his investigative reporter job in Seattle to be with her. What the couple finds in this strange, insular community will horrify them . . . and you.

Coppel, Alfred

Wars and Winters. Fine, 1993.

Brian Lockwood, adopted in 1946 under strange circumstances by an American officer in Nuremberg, receives a ceremonial Nazi dagger in the mail forty years later. Soon, Lockwood is both the hunter and the hunted as he searches for the incredible truth behind his origin.

Cussler, Clive

Atlantis Found. Putnam, 1999.

Super-agent Dirk Pitt, the lost civilization of Atlantis, and a family of genetically engineered Nazis. More novels featuring Dirk Pitt can be found in Chapter 10.

Deighton, Len

Horse under Water. Putnam, 1963.

DiMona, Joseph

To the Eagle's Nest. William Morrow, 1980.

Easterman, Daniel

The Final Judgement. Harper, 1996.

A series of killings leads Yosef Abuhatseira, Israeli patriot and one-man army, to the realization that someone is murdering survivors of Auschwitz. Now he must ferret out the deadly organization responsible before they can unleash another Final Solution.

Elkins, Aaron

Loot. William Morrow, 1999.

It is April 1945. The Nazis desperately try to hide the art treasures they stole from the great museums of Europe by placing them in a salt mine in the Austrian Alps. In all the confusion, one lone truck full of priceless masterpieces disappears during a snowstorm. Fifty years later in a Boston pawnshop, ex-curator Ben Revere discovers a Velazquez long thought lost forever—a piece from the lost cargo. Revere travels to Europe to search for the rest of the lost art, not knowing that a murderous treasure hunter is stalking him.

Turncoat. William Morrow, 2002.
Brooklyn College history professor Pete Simons has been married for seventeen years to Lily, a beautiful French woman he met during World War II. But when Lily's father, who she claimed had been killed by the Nazis, knocks on their door one evening in 1963, Simons learns that everything his wife has told him has been a lie.

Ferrara, Augusto
The Honor of Peter Kramer. Stone, 1987.

12

Fisher, David E.
The Wrong Man. Random House, 1993.

Folsom, Allan
The Day after Tomorrow. Little, Brown, 1995.
Bodies are turning up all over Europe—all male, all the perfect Aryan type, and all decapitated. Hitler's body may be dead, but his head was frozen in 1945—and it needs a body!

Forsyth, Frederick
The Odessa File. Viking, 1972. **FILM**
ODESSA—a secret organization has protected and assisted members of Hitler's dreaded SS since shortly before the end of World War II. It is ruled by a man known only as Werewolf. Arrayed against this vast force of evil is one man: Peter Miller, a young German journalist.

Freemantle, Brian
The Man Who Wanted Tomorrow. Stein, 1976.

Gifford, Thomas

John Cooper series

The Wind Chill Factor. Bantam, 1975
These Nazi survivors view their defeat in World War II as a mere setback. Their plans are in motion—key people are in place in all the major corporations and in governments of every major nation. Soon it will all be theirs. All that stands in their way is John Cooper.

The First Sacrifice. Bantam, 1995.
Twenty years after his appearance in *The Wind Chill Factor,* John Cooper is back. He receives a plea for help from his estranged sister, Lee—her daughter is missing. Lee's husband, Wolf Koller, is a charismatic leader who has emerged to point the way to a great new Germany.

Goldman, William

Marathon Man. Delacorte, 1974. **FILM**

Scary old Nazi dentist versus Columbia University graduate student and long-distance runner.

Hagberg, David

Eden's Gate. Forge, 2001.

Former National Security Agent Bill Lane and his wife, Frances Shipley, must stop shadowing figures from the past from opening a secret Nazi underground bunker where horrible experiments were conducted on human guinea pigs.

Hartmann, Elizabeth

The Truth about Fire. Carroll, 2002.

Members of Sons of the Shepherd, an American neo-Nazis extremist group, plan to unleash a deadly biological weapon in the Midwest.

Hogg, Peter

Crimes of War. St. Martin's, 2001.

Fifty years after WWII, Dennis Connors, a young and cynical member of Canada's Special Prosecution Unit, relentlessly pursues war criminal Friedrich Reile.

Katzenbach, John

Shadow Man. Ballantine, 1995

King, Harold

Closing Ceremonies. Coward, 1979.

Levin, Ira

The Boys from Brazil. Random House, 1976. **FILM**

Hitler's clones menace the world.

Lindsay, Paul

The Führer's Reserve. Simon & Schuster, 2000.

Old Nazis are being murdered all over the world, and FBI special agent Taz Fallon is assigned to investigate. What he discovers is that the murders are part of a complex scheme to bring a new generation of Nazis to power.

Llewellyn, Sam

Maelstrom. Pocket, 1995.

Environmentalist Fred Hope uncovers a conspiracy linking Hermann Goering's neo-Nazi godson with the Irish Republican Army.

Lovesey, Peter

The Secret of Spandau. Severn, 1992.

Ludlum, Robert

Apocalypse Watch. Bantam, 1995

Drew Latham must take on his lost brother's identity and penetrate the Brotherhood of the Watch, a neo-Nazi organization with members in the highest echelons of the United States, to find the his brother and retrieve the list he had found of the Brotherhood's membership.

The Holcroft Covenant. Marek, 1978. **FILM**

As German leaders realize that the war is turning against them, they secretly send shipments of children to all parts of the world by plane, ship, and submarine. These children will come of age in the 1970s and carry out their preordained mission—the establishment of the Fourth Reich . . . everywhere.

The Sigma Protocol. St. Martin's, 2001.

Homicide specialist Anna Navarro is assigned to investigate a wave of suspicious deaths occurring across the world with the victims being rich old men with connections to a mysterious corporation founded in Switzerland during WWII. This was published after the author's death.

Meade, Glenn

Brandenburg. St. Martin's, 1997. **FILM**

Joseph Volkmann, member of an elite European security force, has little to go on: a puzzling taped conversation and the burned remains of old, torn black-and-white photo. But what he might really have is the key to a horrible plan that promises to turn back the clock on European history back fifty years.

Morrell, David

The League of Night and Fog. Dutton, 1987.

Old men are disappearing, a secret arms deal is about to take place, and a cardinal is viciously murdered. The *Night and Fog* must be confronted and its terrible secret uncovered.

Morris, M. E.

The Icemen. Presidio, 1988.

Argentina expels all the old Nazi scientists who have been hiding there since World War II and sends them to a secret base in Antarctica, where they work on completing the ultimate weapon of terrorism. The only group that can stop them is also in Antarctica—a small U.S. Navy special mission squadron. Strong female characters.

Neville, Katherine

The Magic Circle. Ballantine, 1998.

Ariel Behn, a toxic materials specialist at a Colorado nuclear site, receives a dangerous legacy from her recently murdered cousin, Sam. This ominous collection of ancient manuscripts propels her not only into the midst of an international conspiracy masterminded by members of her own family (a family of Nazi collaborators who make the Borgias look like the Waltons), but an age-old mystery—a mystery that spans thousands of years—from the rise of the Roman Empire to the fall of the Berlin Wall.

Pollock, J. C.

Goering's List. Delacorte, 1993.

Three wealthy New Yorkers are brutally murdered, and specific works from their art collections are stolen. These paintings, kept on a list by Hermann Goering, were taken from the Jews by the Nazis during World War II and sold secretly in Switzerland. What secrets hidden since World War II will now be unleashed on an unsuspecting world?

Rodin, Robert L.

Articles of Faith. St. Martin's, 1998.

Danny Maguire learns the Nazis weren't the only people looting the treasures of Europe when he gets a phone call from his father who supposedly committed suicide twenty-five years earlier.

Stephenson, Neal

Cryptonomicon. Avon, 1999.

In 1942, math genius Captain Lawrence Pritchard Waterhouse is assigned to Detachment 2072, a secret code-busting organization designed to keep the Nazis unaware that their supposedly unbreakable Enigma code has been cracked. Jump to the present where Captain Waterhouse's grandson, hacker Randy, is trying to secretly salvage a sunken Nazi U-boat that holds the key to a decades-old secret.

Thomas, Craig

Emerald Decision. Harper, 1980.

The secret plan was created in the 1940s—all evidence of its terrible contents were thought destroyed . . . until now. Forty years later, *Emerald* is about to emerge, more dangerous than ever.

Unkefer, Duane

Gray Eagles. Beech Tree, 1986.

Thirty-one years after World War II, eight *Luftwaffe* aces force a rematch . . . in the skies over America.

Walker, Bill

Camp Stalag. Cemetery, 2001.

Journalist Frank Murphy and his buddy Bill Seger have been chosen as two of the three hundred men who will spend two weeks in a simulated German WWII POW camp. They are drugged and transported to the wilds of Wisconsin, however, and realize that they are under the control of a group of Germans led by a lunatic Nazi.

Wallace, Irving

The Seventh Secret. Dutton, 1986.

Hitler may be dead, but Eva Braun is alive and well as she leads this conspiracy to bring the Nazis back to power. What will result from the discovery of the seventh secret?

Alternate Histories

These titles explore the "what if" questions: what if the Nazi high command had made different military choices? What if Nazi scientists had invented the atomic bomb first? What if the Nazis had won World War II? Be aware that these counterfactualism titles are usually shelved with the science fiction—they have a dual appeal.

Deighton, Len

SS-GB. Knopt, 1979.

It's 1941—England is invaded and defeated by Nazi Germany. The king is imprisoned in the Tower, the Queen and royal children have fled to Australia. Churchill has been executed. English citizens are being sent to work in German slave factories, and the SS is in charge of Scotland Yard, Detective Superintendent Douglas Archer finds that what he thinks is a routine murder is actually the beginning of battle where the stakes are incredibly high.

Gingrich, Newt, and William R. Forstchen

1945. Baen, 1995.

What if Hitler had not prematurely declared war on the United States in 1941, and Americans hadn't gotten involved in the war in Europe? Quickly winning the war against Japan in the Pacific, the United States warily eyes a Europe unified under Nazi Germany. Soon the world's two superpowers will take up arms. (The then–Speaker of the House Newt Gingrich "co-authored" this book with historian William R. Forstchen and a technical editor, Albert S. Hanser.)

Harris, Robert

Fatherland. Random, 1992.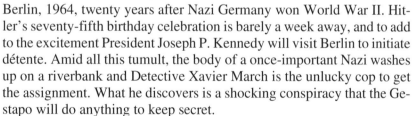

Berlin, 1964, twenty years after Nazi Germany won World War II. Hitler's seventy-fifth birthday celebration is barely a week away, and to add to the excitement President Joseph P. Kennedy will visit Berlin to initiate détente. Amid all this tumult, the body of a once-important Nazi washes up on a riverbank and Detective Xavier March is the unlucky cop to get the assignment. What he discovers is a shocking conspiracy that the Gestapo will do anything to keep secret.

Herbert, James

'48. HarperPrism, 1996.

World War II has been over for three years. The Allies lost . . . so did the Nazis. The only winner was a deadly plague, the Blood Death, created in Hitler's labs. London is a ruin, roamed by feral dogs, a few immune survivors, and the fearful, fascist Blackshirts who scavenge the healthy for blood and spare body parts.

Hogan, James P.

The Proteus Operation. Bantam, 1985. 📄

> Only North America and Australia have survived the Third Reich—victors of World War II. Democracy has one last, desperate chance, *Operation Proteus,* a top-secret project to send an expert team back in time to an era when freedom was still possible, with the intent of altering the outcome of history—a history where Nazi Germany discovered the atomic bomb first.

Niles, Douglas, and Michael Dobson

Fox on the Rhine. Forge, 2000.

> Hitler and Goering are assassinated by a group of German generals and Himmler becomes leader of the Reich. He negotiates a peace treaty with the Russians and Field Marshall Rommel heads a renewed assault on the western European front. (Niles designs computer war games.)

Rutman, Leo

Clash of Eagles. Fawcett, 1990.

> The Nazis have conquered Europe, crossed the Atlantic Ocean, and invaded the East Coast. Now a growing resistance has begun the long fight to expel Hitler's forces from American soil.

Stroyar, J. N.

The Children's War. Pocket, 2001.

> It's been fifty years since the truce between the Soviet Union, the Third Reich, and the North American Union, and most of Europe is under Nazi domination. This is the story of the freedom fighters who are struggling to overturn the Nazi menace.

Beyond Reality

These titles certainly feature Nazis, but with their werewolves, vampires, ghosts, and other supernatural features, they can also appeal to the horror and dark fantasy genre fan.

Barnes, John

Finity. Forge, 1999.

> Lyle Peripart, a professor at the University of Auckland, is confused. His family emigrated to Australia when the Third Reich won World War II nearly a century before, but several of his friends seem to have grown up in a world with different histories. Teaming up with his gun-toting fiancé (who remembers a world where the United States surrendered to the Soviet Union in the 1970s), he needs to find out what is really happening.

Koontz, Dean R.

Lightning. Putnam, 1988. 📄

> A novel of time travel, but instead of visitors from the future traveling backward in time, the visitors are from the past. And these visitors are Nazis.

> *Gannon's Adventure/Suspense Rule Number 20: Nazis are no match for vampires or werewolves.*

McCammon, Robert R.

Wolf's Hour. Pocket, 1989.

Michael Gallatin—master spy, passionate lover, Nazi hunter . . . and werewolf

Monteleone, Thomas F.

Night of Broken Souls. Warner, 1997.

Around the world, all kinds of people are suffering from blackouts and identical nightmares—nightmares that feature concentration camps and the sadistic Nazi known as Der Klein Engel, the Little Angel. Psychiatrist J. Michael Keating learns that the dreamers are being horribly murdered one by one. Could the monstrous Little Angel have returned from the grave?

Wilson, F. Paul

The Keep. William Morrow, 1981.

An SS officer is assigned to travel to a small castle in the mountains of Transylvania and find out why the commander of a garrison of German troops has sent this message: "Something is murdering my men." Count Dracula versus the Nazis!

Chapter 13

Land of the Silken Dragon

Asia

Definition: This subgenre comprises espionage, assassinations, industrial machinations, personal vendettas and revenge quests, criminal actions, and minor military incursions that occur in Asian countries or involve citizens of Asian countries from the beginnings of the Cold War to the present. These countries include Japan, North and South Korea, the People's Republic of China, Taiwan, Thailand, and Vietnam. Titles that include historical military events and technothrillers that occur in Asian nations or involve Asian peoples can be found in those respective chapters.

The Appeal: The exotic cultures and long history of the Orient has always been of interest to Western readers. While the Cold War gave us implacable Communist villains, the 1980s saw an economically powerful Japan become a threat; and now a saber-rattling China provides the requisite tension-creating device. Through the years, various Asian nations have fallen in and out of favor as the heavy, but that part of the world is still a fascinating and mysterious locale for many readers.

Brief History: The classic in this subgenre is Richard Condon's *The Manchurian Candidate,* published in 1959 at the height of the Cold War. Japan's growing economic power in the 1980s saw many titles with Japan as the enemy, trying to topple the United States via industrial espionage or to get revenge for World War II. The interest in the martial arts in the 1980s also gave growth to the popularity of Eric van Lustbader's Nicholas Linear series. From the 1990s to the present, the expanding military aspirations of the People's Republic of China and the turnover of Hong Kong has made China a fashionable antagonist.

Advising the Reader: The key elements to remember when advising the reader and suggesting appropriate titles are the following:

- Is there a particular Asian country that interests the reader?

- What is it that the reader likes: spies, industrial espionage, the martial arts, crime?

- If the reader likes technothrillers or military fiction, suggest titles that contain military action.

- If the reader likes the Communist element, novels with the KGB and the Soviet Union might be of interest.

- The *yakuza* is the Japanese equivalent of the Italian (or Sicilian) Mafia; readers who enjoy stories about *yakuza* can also be guided to titles containing the Russian *mafiya* (in the following chapter).

- The reader might be interested in the espionage element and can be guided to spy novels outside of the Asian theatre.

- Has the reader exhausted this list of Asian thrillers? Then guide them to technothrillers and military fiction in which Asia is the setting.

Do not impose on others what you yourself do not desire.

—Confucius

Anderson, Jack

The Japan Conspiracy. Kensington, 1993.
> The Sonno Group was named after an ancient Japanese rallying cry: "Honor the Emperor, expel the barbarians." Its goal? Economic revenge against the United States for its victory in World War II. (The author is a Pulitzer Prize–winning investigative journalist.)

Ball, David

China Run. Simon & Schuster, 2002.
> Allison Turk and her stepson, Tyler, arrive in China to adopt an infant girl. Four days after Allison receives the baby, Wen Li, Chinese officials tell her that there has been a clerical error and she must give the child back. Refusing to part with the child, Allison absconds with Wen Li and heads for the American embassy, which is located halfway across the country. Unable to speak Chinese and knowing nothing about the country, she must try to get herself and her children to the dubious safety of the embassy.

Blankenship, William D.

The Time of the Cricket. Fine, 1995. **M**
> Kay Williams, an American art agent, is pitted against Cricket Kimura, a deadly *yakuza* executioner, as she searches for the legendary sword of Emperor Meiji in Tokyo's sordid underworld.

Burdett, John

The Last Six Million Seconds. William Morrow, 1997. **M**
> The title refers to the time left until the Turnover: June 30, 1997, when the British gave control of Hong Kong back to China. During this period, Royal Hong Kong police chief Inspector Chan Siu-kai is called to investigate a triple homicide. Three heads are found floating in the South China Sea. He is soon sucked into the British attempts to cover up the murders and the sordid intrigues of the Chinese.

Campbell, John T.

Raid on Truman. Lyford, 1991.

North Korean General Kang hijacks an American aircraft carrier, the USS *Truman,* by using a nerve gas that renders the crew unconscious. His plan is to use the nuclear weapons on board to bring North Korea into the nuclear arena. However, a ventilation system malfunction leaves the ships mechanical crew, the "snipes," unaffected by the gas. It is up to Lieutenant Paul Simmons and his technicians to save the ship from the North Korean commandos who are on board.

Cannell, Stephen J.

Riding the Snake. William Morrow, 1998. **M**

Wealthy ne'er-do-well Wheeler Cassidy has led the easy life of wine, women, and song until his younger brother is mysteriously killed by Chinese gang members. Teaming up with the beautiful Tanisha Williams, a black LAPD police detective assigned to the Asian Crimes Task Force, Cassidy sets out on a dangerous journey to find his brother's killers. Uncovering an international conspiracy, the two unlikely partners travel from the violent neighborhoods of South Central L.A. to the mysterious streets of Hong Kong's ancient Walled City.

> *Gannon's Adventure/Suspense Rule Number 21: Anyone can be brainwashed to do anything.*

Condon, Richard

The Manchurian Candidate. McGraw-Hill, 1959. **FILM**

Sergeant Raymond Shaw, ex-POW and winner of the Congressional Medal of Honor, was brainwashed during his captivity in North Korea to kill a U.S. presidential nominee.

Couch, Dick

Rising Wind. Naval Institute, 1996. **M**

Right-wing Japanese terrorists capture a U.S. chemical weapons storage site and a thousand American hostages on Johnston Island in the Pacific. The only two people who can stop them before they unleash this deadly arsenal are navy SEAL Lieutenant John Moody and Japanese samurai Captain Shintaro Nakajima.

Crichton, Michael

Rising Sun. Knopf, 1992. **FILM**

A huge Japanese corporation is trying to gain control of a leading-edge American technology and is willing to kill for it.

Diehl, William

Chameleon. Random House, 1981. ⌐▷

Investigative reporters Frank O'Hara and Eliza Gunn are tracking a Japanese assassin and terrorist known as the Chameleon, who disarmingly disguises himself
as a woman to get close to his targets.

Thai Horse. Villard, 1987. ⌐▷

Known as the Shadow Warrior during the Vietnam War, Christian Hatcher did
the things no one else could—and was double-crossed by his boss for it. Now
years later, that same boss has one more assignment for him: return to Vietnam
and find a man who has supposedly been dead for the last fifteen years . . . and
also to find the elusive secret of the Thai Horse.

Dirgo, Craig

The Einstein Papers. Pocket, 1999.

What if Albert Einstein's most brilliant work was not the theory of relativity?
Einstein was so fearful that his unified field theory would be used for destruction
that he took its secret to the grave with him. Now it's been found, and the People's
Republic of China intends to use it for world domination.

Easterman, Daniel

The Ninth Buddha. Doubleday, 1989.

Set in post–World War I Mongolia, British intelligence agent Christopher
Wylam must rescue his kidnapped son who is believed to be the reincarnation of a
Buddhist holy man. He soon finds himself immersed in a deadly world of interna-
tional intrigue and murder.

Eisler, Barry

Rain Fall. Putnam, 2002. **M**

John Rain is a businessman living in Tokyo, his mother an American and his father Japanese. A former member of the U.S. Special Forces and a Vietnam veteran, the business he conducts is assassination.

Garrison, Paul

Fire and Ice. Avon, 1998.

Asian pirates kidnap Michael Stone's wife and eleven-year-old daughter, then
steal their thirty-eight-foot yacht. Stone, left only with a damaged canoe, must
find and rescue his family before they are killed.

Gilboy, Peter

Operation Fantasy Plan. William Morrow, 1997.

The CIA operates the Fantasy Store in Bangkok, where every sexual whim and
desire of important Japanese businessmen and politicians is indulged—and videotaped. Peter Gaines, a twenty-year veteran of the CIA assigned to Operation
Fantasy Plan, is suddenly fired after asking too many questions. (The author is a
former agent handler for the Defense Intelligence Agency.)

Grayson, George

The Revolutionary's Confession. Intrigue, 2000. **M**

> A young Philadelphia lawyer, Sam Zhang, discovers a strange secret from China's past and then dies in a supposed suicide. His sister Kristina thinks he was murdered and, along with law professor Jason Behr, investigates his death.

Hagberg, David

Kirk McGarvey series Other titles in this series are annotated in the Russia section of the next chapter.

High Flight. Forge, 1995.

> Fourteen airplanes crash in one day, and thousands of Americans are dead. Kirk McGarvey, ex-CIA agent, is hired by Guerin Airline Company to investigate. He soon finds that the Japanese are attempting to cripple the United States through industrial sabotage.

White House. Forge, 1999.

> Kirk McGarvey has just been appointed deputy director of operations for the CIA when terrorists try to kill his family a few hours later. Could this be linked to a mysterious underground nuclear explosion off the coast of North Korea?

Hawksley, Humphrey

Ceremony of Innocence. Headline, 1998.

> Mike McKillop is a police special forces officer in Hong Kong's Communist Party security force. One night, an old CIA friend, Clem Watkins, comes to him for help. He has a secret that both the United States and China want to keep hidden.

Higgins, Jack

On Dangerous Ground. Putnam, 1994.

> British spies, the Mafia, and the Chinese are all searching for the Chungking Covenant, a document signed in 1944 extending the Hong Kong Treaty by one hundred years. Sean Dillon, last seen in *Thunder Point,* appears in this novel.

> More Sean Dillon titles in Chapter 2.

Hunt, E. Howard

Dragon Teeth. Fine, 1997.

> An ex-CIA agent desperately searches for his son, Peter, who disappeared in China while on a spy mission for the CIA. Peter witnessed Chinese missiles full of poison gas being readied for deployment against Taiwan. (The author is a former CIA agent and a "leading figure in the Watergate investigations.")

Hyde, Christopher

Black Dragon. William Morrow, 1992.

> The Black Dragon, an international crime organization based in Hong Kong, is facing dissension in its own ranks by a group of rebels calling themselves the Holy Ghost. As the Black Dragon struggles to retain its primacy, nations across the globe are caught up in the conflict.

Kaplan, Andrew

Dragonfire. Warner, 1987.

> When Vietnam prepares to invade Thailand to engage Cambodian rebels, U.S. intelligence agent Sawyer is assigned to stop new U.S. involvement in Southeast Asia. His mission, code named *Dragonfire,* is to trade guns needed by the rebels for a billion dollars in pure morphine.

Kennedy, William P.

The Masakado Lesson. St. Martin's, 1986.

La Plante, Richard

Leopard. Forge, 1994. **M**

> Medical examiner and martial artist Josef Tanaka goes to Japan to visit his brother, only to find he has been brutally murdered. Tanaka vows to catch the killer who is known as the Leopard.

Logan, Chuck

The Price of Blood. HarperCollins, 1997.

> In the last days of the Vietnam War, ten tons of gold bullion disappear from the Hue National Bank. One American commando is posthumously court-martialed for the theft, but the gold is never recovered. Twenty years later, the dead commando's daughter teams up with one of her father's wartime friends to find the gold and clear her father's name.

Lustbader, Eric van

Angel Eyes. Fawcett, 1991.

> Intelligence agent Tori Nunn travels across the globe fighting evil villains and villainesses—the cast of characters include the Japanese *yakuza,* drug dealers, arms brokers, and spies of all kinds.

Black Blade. Fawcett, 1993. **M**

> NYPD detective Wolf Matheson, son of a Shoshone and a Texas Ranger, teams up with the beautiful Japanese woman Chika to stop the Black Blade Society—a Japanese organization that is about to upset the balance of world power.

Black Heart. Evans, 1983.

> After his best friend dies in the arms of his beautiful mistress, Tracy Richter goes on a journey filled with violence into the deepest part of the Cambodian jungle. On his travels, he meets up with a cunning villain and a beautiful Asian woman.

French Kiss. Fawcett, 1988.
Ruthless opium warlords search for a trio of weapons known as the Prey Dauw, symbols that have become so powerful that people will follow whomever possesses them.

Jake Maroc series

Jian. Villard. 1985.
Jake Maroc, half-Chinese and half-American, is skilled in the martial arts and is the top Hong Kong agent for the secret government organization known as the Quarry.

Shan. Random House, 1986.
Jake Maroc is entrusted with continuing his father's dream for China—world domination.

Nicholas Linnear series

The Ninja. Evans, 1980.
The first novel featuring the half-Asian, half-English Nicholas Linnear, who is a master of the martial arts. He is involved in a series of murders seemingly committed by ninjas that soon lead him on a mission of revenge.

The Miko. Villard, 1984.
The Japanese "sorceress" Miko plots to kill her rival, Nicholas Linnear.

White Ninja. Fawcett, 1990.
Doubting himself and the way he is living his life, Nicholas Linnear returns to Japan for rest and rebirth. He soon finds himself pitted against a maniac who is stalking the streets of Tokyo.

The Kaisho. Pocket, 1993.
Many years ago, Nicholas Linnear promised his father that if a man named Mikio Okami ever asked for his help, he would give it to him without question. Now the time has come: Okami is the *kaisho,* the headman of the *yakuza,* and he has been marked for assassination.

Floating City. Pocket, 1994.
The Floating City lies deep within the Vietnamese jungle, a secret weapons and narcotics empire with tentacles extending across the world. It is ruled with an iron-fist by the American known as Rock along with his henchman Torch. Nicholas Linnear is the only one who can stop them.

Second Skin. Pocket, 1995.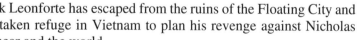
Mick Leonforte has escaped from the ruins of the Floating City and has taken refuge in Vietnam to plan his revenge against Nicholas Linnear and the world.

Zero. Random House, 1988.
Michael Doss, trying to find out about his father's death, finds himself pitted against a secret Japanese organization known as the *Jiban.* The

group was formed during World War II with the primary goal taking economic control of the United States.

Meigs, Henry

Gate of the Tigers. Viking, 1992. **M**
> CIA freelance agent Robert Ludlow is teamed up with Japanese inspector Tetsuo Mori to try and solve an American woman's murder. She worked for a Japanese computer company and was brutally killed in a crowded Tokyo square.

Morris, M. E.

The Last Kamikaze. Random House, 1990. **M**
> Fifty years after the end of World War II, a former kamikaze pilot attacks Pearl Harbor.

Murphy, Warren, and Molly Cochran

The Temple Dogs. New American, 1989.
> The tale of the ultimate crime war—between a Mafia family and a *yakuza* clan.

Olden, Marc

Dai-Sho. Arbor, 1983.
> *Dai-sho* means "big sword, little sword" and describes the struggles of an American who is caught up in a power struggle with murderous Japanese industrialists as he tries to investigate the death of woman he once loved.

Gaijin. Arbor, 1986.

Giri. Arbor, 1982.
> "*Giri*: the Japanese call it loyalty . . . an American calls it revenge."

Kisaeng. Fine, 1991. **M**
> Park Song, a Korean multimillionaire, is also the world's biggest counterfeiter of U.S. currency. He also "collects" beautiful women to act as his *kisaeng* (recreational creature), whom he then murders when he tires of them. When the daughter of the woman he loves disappears, NYPD homicide detective Manny Decker must find her before she becomes Song's next *kisaeng*.

Oni. Jove, 1988.

O'Reilly, Victor

Hugo Fitzduane series

Rules of the Hunt. Putnam, 1995.
> A Japanese terrorist group known as the Cutting Edge targets Hugo Fitzduane and his family for revenge.

The Devil's Footprint. Putnam, 1996. **M**
> Japanese terrorist Reiko Oshima orchestrates deadly attacks against the United States from her hiding place in Mexico. Antiterrorist operative Hugo Fitzduane assembles a team to hunt her down before she strikes again, this time with a devastating weapon.

Pieczenik, Steve

Pax Pacifica. Warner, 1995.

Assistant Secretary of State Dr. Desaix Clark is sent to China to evaluate the threat posed by two Chinese rulers vying for power: the prime minister and the defense minister. Clark is caught between the two leaders and their mastery of the ancient art of Chinese political machinations. (Sequel to *Maximum Vigilance;* see Chapter 9.)

Reed, John

The Kingfisher's Call. Sourcebooks, 2002.

Former navy SEAL Tuck Nyland leads a rescue mission into China to retrieve a female spy who has been working for the United States for several decades.

Scott, Justin

Forged in Honor. Ballantine, 1995.

Retired special forces Colonel Joshua Hawkins leads a secret mission into northern Burma to fight a corrupt government and vicious heroin syndicate.

The Nine Dragons. Bantam, 1991.

After the mysterious death of her father, who was the head of the last great independent trading company in Hong Kong, Victoria Mackintosh must protect the company against the devious machinations of her father's wealthy rival, Two-Way Wong. This novel takes place in 1997, a few months before the Turnover, when the People's Republic of China took possession of Hong Kong.

Salinger, Steven D.

Behold the Fire. Warner, 1997.

Twenty-five years after he was captured during the Vietnam War, U.S. Army Corporal Zack Johnson walks out of the Cambodian jungle. This one returned POW will create grave repercussions among Washington power brokers and game players, who will do anything to keep old secrets buried.

Searls, Hank

Kataki. McGraw-Hill, 1987.

A member of a right-wing Japanese secret society vows revenge on Vice President George H. W. Bush for acts committed during World War II.

Setlowe, Richard

The Black Sea. Ticknor, 1991.

Malaysian pirates in the Singapore Strait hijack the Soviet luxury liner *Black Sea,* which is full of famous Americans. The pirate leader, Tengku Haji Azhar, conceals the ship in an uncharted jungle river. This is only the first step in his plan to create racial and religious conflict in South Asia.

The Sexual Occupation of Japan. HarperCollins, 1999.
Attorney Peter Saxton comes to Tokyo to negotiate a merger between a Japanese electronics company and an American media conglomerate, but the government official with whom he is to meet is brutally mutilated and killed. Soon Saxon finds himself the target of attacks.

Shagan, Steve

The Circle. William Morrow, 1982. [image]
U.S. Deputy Attorney General Phil Ricker searches for a lost FBI file belonging to J. Edgar Hoover, code-named *Gemstone,* that could blow the lid off of a deadly international conspiracy. Joining him in his search is a beautiful agent of the Korean Central Intelligence Agency.

Tasker, Peter

Buddha Kiss. Doubleday, 1996. **M**
Kazuo Mori is a Tokyo private detective investigating the murder of a friend's daughter. His investigation soon leads him to the Peace Technology cult, but each time he finds a new lead, someone tries to kill him. (The author is a financial analyst in Japan.)

Silent Thunder. Kodansha, 1992.
A secret organization known as *Silent Thunder* is trying to topple the world's financial markets to allow Japan to dominate all of Asia.

Trenhaile, John

Simon Young series

The Mah-Jongg Spies. Dutton, 1986.
International industrialists and the KGB plot to drain Hong Kong of all its wealth before it is turned over to China. When approached with the scheme, Simon Young, a British businessman, is drawn into a complicated and suspenseful adventure.

The Gates of Exquisite View. Dutton, 1987.
When the People's Republic of China prepares to invade Taiwan, Simon Young must intercede.

> *Gannon's Adventure/Suspense Rule Number 22: Masters of the martial arts can kill with any part of their body—any part.*

Trevanian

Shibumi. Crown, 1979. [image]
Nicholas Hel, raised in China, was trained to be the perfect assassin by his Japanese warrior foster father. His nearly superhuman mental and physical prowess make him the premiere assassin (and lover) in the world. (Trevanian is the pseudonym of Rodney Whitaker.)

Weber, Joe

Honorable Enemies. Putnam, 1994.

Japanese tourists are being brutally attacked in the United States; the same thing is happening to American tourists in Japan. CIA agent Stephen Wickham and a Japanese American FBI agent, Susan Nakamura, are assigned to investigate. They uncover a massive conspiracy headed by a billionaire Japanese industrialist with ties to both the Japanese and U.S. governments.

White, Robin A.

The Last High Ground. Crown, 1995.

A secret Japanese organization is plotting the hostile takeover of the United States' most powerful aircraft manufacturing company and ultimately scheming to control the world's aerospace industry.

Wilson, F. Paul

Black Wind. Forge, 1988.

Chapter 14

Communist Comrades and Capitalist Criminals

Russia

Definition: This subgenre comprises espionage, political machinations, criminal operations, and minor military incursions that occur in or are caused by the citizens and leaders of the Soviet Union, and later of Russia. This subgenre contains few of the "classic" spy novels. Novels where the spy or secret agent is the primary focus of the plot, as well as technothrillers that involve the Soviet Union, can be found in those chapters.

The Appeal: Many readers grew up during the Cold War in fear of a Soviet takeover of the United States. Many of us like to read about what we fear, hence the popularity of this subgenre. Patriotism is also a factor—the democratic, capitalistic forces of the United States triumphs over the despotic, communist Soviet Union. After the fall of the Soviet Union and the emergence of the new Russia, the growing power of organized crime became a new, exotic menace for readers.

Brief History: The Soviet Union emerged as the United States' greatest foe after World War II and provided the villain fodder for hundreds of suspense novels. Always trying to undermine the United States and emerge victorious, the USSR (especially the dreaded KGB) could be counted on to do everything and anything to accomplish its goals—but always to no avail. In 1991, after the fall of the Iron Curtain, a new antagonist emerged from the wreckage of the former Soviet Union: organized crime—the Russian *mafiya*.

Advising the Reader: The key elements to remember when advising the reader and suggesting appropriate titles are the following:

- Does a particular time period appeal to the reader? In the time of the Soviet Union or post-Communist Russia?

- Does the reader prefer stories told from the Russian point of view?

- What is it the reader wants: spies and espionage, domestic terrorism and unrest, covert military actions, conspiracies, organized crime, or man against the state?

- If the reader has exhausted all these titles and still wants more, suggest technothrillers or military fiction, many of which feature the Soviet Union or the new Russia.

- If the reader has exhausted all these titles and still wants more, suggest spies and secret agents, some of which feature antagonists from the Soviet Union.

- The *mafiya* is the Russian equivalent of the Mafia; readers who enjoy stories about the mafiya can also be guided to titles about the Japanese *yakuza* (in the preceding chapter).

- *You Can Judge a Book by Its Cover*: Many titles in this subgenre have the hammer and sickle symbol of the Soviet Union displayed prominently on their (oftentimes red) covers.

I cannot forecast to you the action of Russia.
It is a riddle wrapped in a mystery inside an enigma.

—Winston Churchill

Union of Soviet Socialist Republics (USSR) (1917–1991)

Aaron, David
Agent of Influence. Putnam, 1989.
> The Soviets are using advanced technology to manipulate the financial markets of Western nations to influence government policy.

Allbeury, Ted
Cold Tactics. Grafton, 1981.
> The Soviet Union tries to get its agent elected president of the United States.

Archer, Jeffrey
A Matter of Honor. Simon & Schuster, 1986.
> Adam Scott receives an odd bequest from his father's estate: an old envelope leading to a secret that could return Alaska back to the Soviet Union.

Beach, Edward L.
Cold Is the Sea. Henry Holt, 1978.

Bearden, Milt
The Black Tulip. Random House, 1998.
> It is 1985. Who is killing deep-cover CIA moles in the Kremlin? (The author was a member of the Clandestine Services of the CIA for thirty years.)

Burke, Martyn
The Commissar's Report. Houghton Mifflin, 1984.
> A "comic" thriller.

Butler, Jimmie H.

The Iskra Incident. Dutton, 1990.

> A missile from a U.S. Air Force jet has supposedly downed a plane carrying high-ranking members of the Soviet Politburo to a diplomatic summit in San Francisco. It's almost World War III, but neither the Soviets nor the Americans seem to want to find out what really happened.

Cook, Nick

Angel, Archangel. St. Martin's, 1990.

> In the last days of World War II, two top British pilots are sent into Germany to capture the Messerschmitt 163C, an experimental jet fighter. The Soviets have plans of their own, and the two pilots and the jet are soon an unwilling part. The publisher called this novel "a retro technothriller."

Cullen, Robert

Soviet Sources. Atlantic, 1990.

> Moscow correspondent Colin Burke learns from one of his sources that the KGB plans a coup to takeover the Soviet government and soon finds himself on the run. (The author is a former Moscow correspondent for *Newsweek.*)

> Other novels featuring Colin Burke can be found in the section on Russia later in this chapter.

DeMille, Nelson

The Charm School. Warner, 1988.

> Deep within the vast expanse of the Soviet Union, nestled within a dark forest, is "Mrs. Ivanova's Charm School" where young KGB agents are being taught how to pass as U.S. citizens by American POWs—a secret conspiracy so dangerous it could strike at the very heart of the United States.

Durand, Loup

Jaguar. Villard, 1990.

Egleton, Clive

Troika. Atheneum, 1984.

Finder, Joseph

The Moscow Club. Viking, 1991.

> CIA analyst Charlie Stone finds himself the target of the Moscow Club, a secret group within the Kremlin that is determined to topple the Soviet government and return the country to its earlier power and influence.

Flannery, Sean

Counterstrike. William Morrow, 1990.

> Russian and American agents must join forces to stop a socipathic killer before he murders Mikhail Gorbachev. (The author also writes as David Hagberg.)

The Zebra Network. William Morrow, 1989.

CIA operative David MacAllister, was kidnapped and interrogated by the KGB. Now he knows a deadly secret—but can't remember what it is.

Fleming, Ian

From Russia with Love. MJF Books, 1985. **FILM**

The covert agency SMERSH, lures James Bond to a Moscow death trap with bait so enticing that agent 007 can't resist.

Other novels featuring James Bond can be found in Chapter 2.

Forbes, Bryan

The Endless Game. Random House, 1986. **FILM**

Ten years after they captured, tortured, and left Caroline Oates a vegetable, the KGB has her assassinated. Why did they kill her—and why now, years after she has been of any use to either side?

Forsyth, Frederick

The Devil's Alternative. Viking, 1980.

The Fourth Protocol. Viking, 1984. **FILM**

This intricately plotted novel begins with a London jewel theft that takes place on New Year's Eve and then catapults off into various plots, counterplots, betrayals, and conspiracies.

Gross, Martin

The Red President. Doubleday, 1987.

The ultimate Soviet mole: handsome, rich, smart, charismatic . . . and the next occupant of the White House.

Hagberg, David

Countdown. St. Martin's, 1990.

A Pershing missile is stolen in West Germany, a U.S. submarine disappears, a Soviet agent is found dead in a secret Israeli nuclear facility—all the work of new head of the KGB, Colonel Constantin Baranov, who wants to destroy glasnost and start a new Cold War. (Hagberg also writes as Sean Flannery.)

Crossfire. Forge, 1991.

In desperate need of hard currency because of budget cuts, the KGB decides to hijack a U.S. gold shipment.

Herbert, Frank

The Dragon in the Sea. Doubleday, 1956.

The United States is stealing oil from the Soviet Union using submarines and underwater barges, but this cannot be kept a secret for long.

Hetzer, Michael

The Forbidden Zone. Simon & Schuster, 1999.

Soviet scientist Victor Perov must save his lover, American astrophysicist Katherine Sears and his dissident twin brother, Anton, who are victims of a deadly game of Communist Party politics—a game in which his own mother is a high-ranking player.

Higgins, Jack

Confessional. Stein, 1985.

> The KGB plans to assassinate the pope when he visits England, and who better for the job than a man with a perfect cover: he's a Catholic priest. British Intelligence must turn to an old enemy, Liam Devlin of *The Eagle Has Landed* (see Chapter 12), for help.

Holland, William E.

Moscow Twilight. Pocket, 1992.

> January 1989 in Moscow. The power of the centralized Soviet authority is dying, and an angry nationalism is growing. Muscovites now fear organized crime more than the KGB.

Hood, William

Cry Spy. Norton, 1990.

Spy Wednesday. Norton, 1986.

Hunt, E. Howard

The Kremlin Conspiracy. Stein, 1985.

> The Kremlin will soon have the perfect agent, Klaus Werber, West German foreign minister and nominee for the Nobel Peace Prize.

Hunter, Stephen

The Day before Midnight. Bantam, 1989.

> Jack Hummel, a Maryland welder, is abducted by gun-wielding commandos and forced to cut through a thousand-pound block of titanium that contains the launch key for nuclear missiles. Only Peter Thiokol, designer of the vault and its deadly defenses, can avert a nuclear war.

The Spanish Gambit. Crown, 1985.

Hyde, Anthony

The Red Fox. Knopf, 1985.

> Journalist Robert Thorne travels to the Soviet Union to answer the plea for help from an old flame and soon finds himself embroiled in a fifty-year-old secret. He travels across the country, at times in disguise, hunting for the key to the mystery.

Ignatius, David

Siro. Farrar, Straus & Giroux, 1991.

> Top CIA operatives Anna Barnes and Alan Taylor are given a daunting secret assignment: destabilizing the Soviet Union.

Koontz, Dean R.

The Key to Midnight. Pocket, 1979.

A U.S. senator's daughter is secretly brainwashed by the Soviets for a deadly mission. (Originally published under the pseudonym Leigh Nichols.)

L'Amour, Louis

Last of the Breed. Bantam, 1986. 📄 Ⓜ

U.S. Air Force major Joseph "Joe Mack" Makatozi's experimental aircraft is forced down over the Bering Sea by the Soviets. He escapes from the prison camp and, using the survival skills learned from his Native American upbringing, he flees into the Siberian wilderness in an attempt to cross the Bering Strait into the United States. Many readers have asked if there is a sequel to this novel, but Louis L'Amour did not write one. A good read-alike is Davidson's *Kolymsky Heights*.

le Carré, John

The Russia House. Knopf, 1989. 📄 FILM

Three years into glasnost at a small trade fair in Moscow a thin sheaf of papers is surreptitiously passed from one person to another. They comprise military documents of astounding import that will have a profound effect on three people: a Soviet scientist, a beautiful Russian woman named Katya, and the dissolute Brit Barley Blair.

Littell, Robert

An Agent in Place. Bantam, 1991.

Lourie, Richard

First Loyalty. Harcourt, 1985.

Ludlum, Robert

The Matarese Circle. Marek, 1979.

Veteran American spy Brandon Scofield and Vasili Taleniekov, intelligence tactician for the KGB, are locked in a deadly cat-and-mouse struggle—both having vowed to kill the other. Both agents must now work together, however, to stop an organization called the Matarese, which is financing terrorist organizations all over the world.

The Osterman Weekend. World, 1972. FILM

The people in a small, suburban town are about to put into motion a conspiracy so vast that the future of the United States is at stake.

MacLean, Alistair

Ice Station Zebra. Doubleday, 1963. FILM

McQuinn, Donald E.

Shadow of Lies. Forge, 1985.

Meade, Glenn

Snow Wolf. St. Martin's, 1995.

Operation Snow Wolf: two CIA agents posing as a married couple will travel across Russia to Moscow, where they will assassinate Stalin. The KGB discovers the plan and sends its own agents to track down and eliminate them.

Moss, Robert

Death Beam. Crown, 1981.
The Soviets perfect a powerful laser weapon that they plan to use against the United States.

Nolan, Frederick

Red Center. St. Martin's, 1987.
A Soviet "defector" has disappeared from London and escapes to Miami where he has collected millions of dollars for a deadly purpose. He must be stopped before he destroys the United States' space-based defense system.

Pearson, Ridley

Never Look Back. St. Martin's, 1985.
Semi-retired U.S. agent Andy Clayton is assigned to stop a Soviet agent who has stolen a deadly bio-warfare product.

Peters, Ralph

Flames of Heaven. Pocket, 1993.
The last days of the Soviet Union find comrade fighting comrade as new ideas, hopes, and dreams clash with the old Communist order.

Pollock, J. C.

Payback. Delacorte, 1989.
Jack Gannon's wife, Amanda, is brutally murdered by a Russian with diplomatic immunity, and the U.S. government will do nothing because the murderer is a KGB assassin who can expose a secret the president will do anything to keep hidden. So it is up to Gannon, a former intelligence agent, to track down Amanda's murderer on his own.

Rascovich, Mark

The Bedford Incident. Atheneum, 1963. **FILM**
The USS *Bedford* hunts a Soviet submarine along the coast of Greenland.

Royce, Kenneth

Fall-Out. Crown, 1989.

Smith, Martin Cruz

Arkady Renko series
More novels featuring Arkady Renko can be found in the following section on Russia.

Gorky Park. Random House, 1981. 📄 **FILM**
Three mutilated bodies are found covered with snow in Moscow's Gorky Park, and chief homicide detective Arkady Renko is called in to investigate. But he finds himself competing with Major Pribluda of the KGB for clues. He soon finds that the apparently motiveless crime can be linked to the highest levels of the Soviet government.

Polar Star. Random House, 1989.
>Arkady Renko, a fugitive from the KGB, has been working in the bowels of a Soviet factory ship, *Polar Star,* for more than a year when he is called on to investigate a woman's murder. As he does, he uncovers the true mission of the *Polar Star* and the reason for the woman's death.

Taylor, Charles D.

Show of Force. St. Martin's, 1980.
>U.S. and Soviet admirals command their respective fleets and butt heads over a missile base located in the Indian Ocean. A modern version of *The Two Admirals* by James Fennimore Cooper.

Thomas, Craig

Sir Kenneth Aubrey series

Lion's Run. Doubleday, 1985.
>Sir Kenneth Aubrey must defend himself against charges of treason.

Wildcat. Putnam, 1989.
>Sir Kenneth Aubrey's mission is to oversee the defection of a high-ranking East German official.

The Last Raven. HarperCollins, 1990.
>Sir Kenneth Aubrey's top agent, Patrick Hyde, is caught in a web of lies and deceit as he investigates the wreck of military transport plane inside the Russian border with Afghanistan.

A Hooded Crow. HarperCollins, 1992.
>British spymaster Sir Kenneth Aubrey must stop the illegal flow of high technology to the Soviets.

Sea Leopard. Viking, 1981.
>The British have developed a secret antisonar system that can render a submarine virtually undetected . . . and the Soviets want it at any cost.

Snow Falcon. Henry Holt, 1980.
>The Soviet military attempts to destroy détente by plotting a coup in Moscow and invading Norway.

Thomas, Michael M.

The Ropespinner Conspiracy. Warner, 1987.
>The Soviet Union, aided by an American traitor, is about to reap the benefits of a thirty-year conspiracy to bring the United States to financial ruin. The only two who can stop them are an Episcopal priest who was once an investment banker and a beautiful art investment manager.

Trenhaile, John

A View from the Square. Congdon, 1983.
>Ex-CIA agent Kirk Binderhaven must journey through the frozen Siberian wastelands to destroy an advanced radar plane stolen by the Soviets.

West, Nigel

Cuban Bluff. Crown, 1991.

Fictionalized account of the Cuban Missile Crisis.

Russia (1991–)

Archer, Jeffrey

The Eleventh Commandment. HarperCollins, 1998.

Thou Shalt Not Be Caught. A rogue CIA director, a warmonger of a Russian president, the Russian *mafiya*, and a CIA assassin on the retirement fast track all collide in this thriller.

Charbonneau, Louis

The Magnificent Siberian. Fine, 1995.

American biologist Chris Harmon, an expert on tigers, shoots some incriminating photos in a restricted zone of Siberia and finds himself in a desperate struggle to survive.

Coppel, Alfred

The Eighth Day of the Week. Fine, 1994.

After Yeltsin, Communist hard-liners conspire to regain power and take advantage of U.S. defense cutbacks to launch a devastating preemptive attack.

Cullen, Robert

Colin Burke series

Cover Story. Atheneum, 1994.

Correspondent for the newsmagazine *America Weekly* Colin Burke investigates a dangerous alliance between Russian and Syrian nuclear scientists.

Dispatch from a Cold Country. Fawcett, 1996.

Colin Burke, now an editor for the *Washington Tribune,* travels to Russia to track down a dark and deadly scandal centering on the Hermitage art museum.

Curtis, Jack

Mirrors Kill. Crown, 1995.

Moscow arms dealers selling nuclear weapons.

Davidson, Lionel

Kolymsky Heights. St. Martin's, 1994.

A coded message is received from a former gulag in northern Siberia—the messages ask that a particular man be sent there to retrieve an incredible secret that could benefit all mankind. Good read-alike for L'Amour's *Last of the Breed.*

Dinallo, Greg

Red Ink. Pocket, 1994.

Russian journalist Nikolai Katkov investigation into the *mafiya* and their gambling businesses soon brings him into contact with Gabby Scotto; a U.S. Treasury agent who is investigating laundered money coming out of the United States. The two are soon in hot pursuit of $2 billion and are themselves pursued for the knowledge they share.

Easterman, Daniel

The Judas Testament. HarperCollins, 1994.

An ancient scroll is discovered hidden away deep in the bowels of the Lenin Library—a scroll allegedly written by Jesus himself.

Finder, Joseph

Extraordinary Powers. Ballantine, 1993.

The search is on for the exiled former head of the KGB, Vladimir Orlov, the only man who knows the location of the multibillion dollars worth of gold smuggled out of Russia just before the collapse of the Soviet Union.

> *Gannon's Adventure/Suspense Rule Number 23: Old KGB agents never die, they just pop up now and then, nastier than ever!*

Flannery, Sean

Bill Lane series

Kilo Option. Forge, 1996.

Ex-KGB agent Valeri Yernin has four Kilo-class submarines being loaded with nuclear weapons in an Iranian harbor and is prepared to use them to blackmail the world. (Sean Flannery also writes as David Hagberg.)

Achilles Heel. Forge, 1998.

A supposedly dead ex-KGB agent steals a derelict Russian submarine to sell on the black market.

Moving Targets. Forge, 1992.

The KGB plans *Operation Homeward Bound,* an operation that will reunite the old Soviet Union and bring the KGB back to the height of power. The only problem is that they need to create an enemy . . . the United States of America.

Winner Take All. Forge, 1994.

The United States and Russia are involved in a massive joint war games exercise, but is it really a game?

Forsyth, Frederick

Icon. Bantam, 1996.

A charismatic, right-wing demagogue, Igor Komarov, is sweeping to power in a Russia that is wracked by famine and inflation, but he must be stopped before he becomes the Adolf Hitler of the 1990s. Ex-CIA agent Jason Monk is sent to Moscow to expose the real truth about Komarov.

Freemantle, Brian

The Button Man. St. Martin's, 1992.

Russian Militia Colonel Dimitri Danilov must track down a serial killer preying on both Russians and Americans in Moscow.

Grace, Tom

Quantum. Warner, 2000.

Russian billionaire Victor Orlov is financing a new technology that offers unlimited energy, but he must stop American physicists from patenting the same invention. He enlists the aid of assassins, spies, and even the Russian *mafiya* to steal the secret.

Hagberg, David

Kirk McGarvey series

Other titles in the Kirk McGarvey series can be found in Chapter 13.

Assassin. Forge, 1997.

Ex-CIA agent Kirk McGarvey is chosen to assassinate a man who intends to lead the newly democratic Russia back into communism, Yevgenni Anatolevich Tarankov—known as the Tarantula.

The Kill Zone. Forge, 2002.

When McGarvey is appointed head of the CIA, a Russian sleeper agent, brainwashed by the KGB to be an assassin and in deep cover for the past twenty years, is inadvertently activated.

Harris, Jonathan

Seizing Amber. Sourcebooks, 2001.

The search is on for the Amber Room of the Czars, worth at least $150 million and presumed destroyed during World War II. Isaiah Hawkins of the CIA hopes to use it to influence the upcoming Russian elections, while others are looking for it for their own nefarious schemes.

Harris, Robert

Archangel. Random, 1998.

Former Oxford historian Fluke Kelso, attending a conference in Moscow on the Soviet archives, finds himself being hunted by killers across northern Russia to the port of Archangel, where Josef Stalin's final secret has been buried for the last fifty years.

Herman, Richard, Jr.

Edge of Honor. Avon, 1999.

U.S. President Madeline Turner has already weathered major domestic and international problems in her first few months in office, but now she must deal with an incipient invasion of Poland by an aggressive new Russia.

Holland, William E.

The Wheel of Justice. Pocket, 1995.

An American entrepreneur is caught up in the frightening world of the Russian legal system—a system heavily influenced by politics and money.

James, Donald

Monstrum. Villard, 1997.

2015—in the new Russia, Nationalist forces have finally defeated the Anarchists, but there is still unrest and confusion. A horrendous serial killer, known as Monstrum, hunts the crime-ridden Red Presnya district of Moscow. A provincial police inspector, Constantin Vadim, is picked to head up the investigation and soon finds himself mired in intrigue and conspiracy as he hunts for the killer.

Jones, E. Scott

Soldier Boy. St. Martin's, 1994.

Soviet Russia is reunited under communism, and double agent Jack Calumet, code-named *Excalibur,* must walk a thin line. If he falters, he will die.

Martini, Steve

Critical Mass. Putnam, 1998.

Two Russian nuclear bombs go missing and are probably in the United States, but all the president is worried about is that their explosion may reveal that a Russian arms dealer is bribing him.

Read, Piers Paul

The Patriot. Random, 1995.

The horrible deaths of Russian art dealers and the disappearance of an agent for the former KGB—how are the two connected?

Reiss, Bob

The Last Spy. Simon & Schuster, 1993.

Trained from childhood in an imitation American town during the Soviet era, no one would suspect the deep cover agents weren't real Americans. Now with the USSR collapsing, who will control them?

Safire, William

Sleeper Spy. Random, 1995.

A Russian spy, hidden under deep cover in the United States for twenty years, is activated and given control over the massive financial reserves of the old KGB—soon he disappears with it. Reporter Irving Fein vows to find him. (The author is a Pulitzer Prize–winning political columnist for the *New York Times.*)

Smith, Martin Cruz

Arkady Renko series

More novels featuring Arkady Renko can be found in the preceding section on the Soviet Union.

Red Square. Random, 1992.

Arkady Renko is back in Moscow and finds it a far different city from the one he left: communism is dead, and the Russian *mafiya* is the only part of the economy that works. He meets a crime financier a few minutes before the man is blown up in his car and soon finds himself a fugitive from Russian mafia crime lords.

Havana Bay. Random, 1999.

Russians and Cubans are no longer comrades, and when Renko is called to Havana to investigate the death of one of his countrymen, he finds that help is almost nonexistent.

Smith, Murray

Stone Dancer. Pocket, 1994.

A group of right-wing Russians who long for a return to the days of the Soviet Union plan to destroy the U.S. economy to create financial pandemonium across the globe and topple the new democratic Russian government.

Thomas, Craig

A Wild Justice. HarperCollins, 1995.

Members of the Russian *mafiya* murder ex-CIA agent John Lock's sister and her husband—Lock vows revenge. His only ally is the cynical Russian policeman Alexei Vorontsyev.

Tyler, W. T.

Last Train from Berlin. Henry Holt, 1994.

Frank Dudley, soon to retire from the CIA after long years fighting the now-ended Cold War, suddenly disappears without a trace. Is it murder, or has he a plan for revenge against the newer breed of spies?

White, Robin

Gregori Nowek series

Siberian Light. Delacorte, 1997.

Gregori Nowek, mayor of the small Siberian town of Markovo, is ordered to investigate a triple murder. His investigation soon uncovers old, forgotten secrets and an evil conspiracy.

The Ice Curtain. Delacorte, 2002.

Nowek searches for the truth behind the murder of his best friend and the disappearance of half a billion dollars worth of uncut diamonds.

Chapter 15

Exploding Sands

The Middle East

Definition: This subgenre comprises espionage, terrorists and terrorism, covert military actions, and government conspiracies that occur in Middle Eastern countries or involve citizens of the Middle East. These countries include Afghanistan, Egypt, Iran, Iraq, Israel, Lebanon, Libya, and Saudi Arabia. Titles that include historic military events (such as the Persian Gulf War), technothrillers that occur in Middle Eastern locales, or millennial thrillers that take place in the Holy Land can be found in their respective chapters.

The Appeal: The rich culture, dramatic settings, and long history of the Middle East have a fascination for many readers. The pharaohs of Egypt, the sultans (and their exotic harems), and the timeless desert are all factors that contribute to the attraction of this locale. In addition, this setting is also the birthplace of three of the world's major religions: Christianity, Islam, and Judaism. The Middle East has been a hotspot for conflict in both ancient and contemporary times, and it has given us some memorable modern real-life villains including Iraq's Saddam Hussein, Libya's Colonel Muammar Qaddafi, and Iran's Ayatollah Khomeini, all of whom make excellent fictional antagonists for our heroes. The Iranian hostage crisis, the Persian Gulf War, and the many acts of terrorism funded or directed by Middle Eastern factions make this area of the globe of continuing interest to readers. Terrorism, a threat that always seemed to happen in other countries, is now a distinct possibility anywhere in the United States, and people are always interested in reading about what frightens them.

Brief History: This subgenre saw its beginnings in the late 1970s with the OPEC oil embargo, continued to grow in popularity through the Iranian hostage crisis and the Persian Gulf War, and has seen a new interest as today's headlines are full of terrorist acts and unrest in the Middle East. The threat of terrorism brought home to the United States has also fueled the popularity of this subgenre.

Advising the Reader: The key elements to remember when advising the reader and suggesting appropriate titles are the following:

- Is there a particular Middle Eastern country that interests the reader?

- What is it that the reader likes: spies, terrorists, high-level government conspiracies, covert military operations, or the ever popular "Death to Saddam Hussein"?

- If the reader enjoys technothrillers or military fiction, suggest titles that contain military action.

- The reader might be interested in the espionage element and can be guided to spy novels outside of the Middle Eastern theatre.

- The reader who is interested in the espionage element can be guided to many titles that feature the Soviet Union and KGB "meddling" in the affairs of Middle Eastern countries.

- If the reader prefers novels that feature terrorists, ask if the preference is for domestic (terrorist acts committed within the United States) or international events.

- Has the reader exhausted this list of Middle Eastern thrillers? Then guide them to technothrillers and military fiction that has the Middle East as the locale.

He that plants thorns must never expect to gather roses.

—Arab proverb

Axton, David

Stolen Thunder. St. Martin's, 1992.

> When U.S. Air Force Captain Tamasin Masterson's husband is tortured and killed by Libyan terrorist Tariq Talal, she decides to get revenge in a big way. Captain Masterson, her father Bat, and some close friends steal a retired B-52 bomber, fuel it up, arm it with weapons, and head for Talal's headquarters. (David Axton is the pseudonym of Dean R. Koontz.)

Bond, Larry

Peter Thorn series

> *The Enemy Within.* Warner, 1996.
>
>> Iranian terrorist General Amir Taleh launches a war against the United States within its own borders: cities are burning, treasured landmarks are destroyed, and racial tensions escalate. Opposing him are antiterrorism expert Colonel Peter Thorn and Special Agent Helen Gray—they must stop him before it's too late.
>
> *Day of Wrath.* Warner, 1998.
>
>> Prince Ibrahim al Saud is the world's richest man. He is also the Paymaster—a brutal terrorist leader. His plan is to destroy the United States as a world power, and the only ones who can stop him are Colonel Peter Thorn and FBI special agent Helen Gray.

Briley, John

The First Stone. William Morrow, 1997.

Lisa Cooper, a beautiful Jewish American, is recruited by the Israeli Mossad to seduce and marry a rich Saudi so that she can be used as a mole in Saudi Arabia. She must deal with her new husband's suspicious brother-in-law and her growing love for the man she will be ordered to betray.

Chafets, Zev

Hang Time. Warner, 1996.

Terrorists kidnap two professional basketball stars in Israel. The players become pawns in a game played by a grandstanding antiterrorist U.S. president and a fanatic Muslim who believes he is on a mission from God.

The Project. Warner, 1997.

Why has Elihu Barzel, the prime minister of Israel, allied himself with a conservative, fundamentalist Christian opponent of the first Jewish president in the United States? And what is the Project that Barzel is so desperate to protect?

Cohen, William S.

One-Eyed Kings. Doubleday, 1991.

The Soviet Union, in a last desperate attempt to maintain its viability, launches a covert operation, code-named BURAQ, in the Middle East. An unlikely alliance between an American Senator, an investigative reporter for the *Washington Post,* and a beautiful Mossad agent is the only thing that can expose BURAQ before it is too late. (The author is a former U.S. senator from Maine.)

The Road to Armageddon. New Millennium, 1991.

Recalled from disgrace, ex-CIA agent Jim Duffy is sent on a mission to stop Iran from getting the final piece of equipment necessary to make their nuclear missiles fully operational.

Cook, Nick

Aggressor. St. Martin's, 1993.

A violent terrorist group known as the Angels of Judgment creates turmoil and bloodshed throughout the Middle East with even more destruction imminent. (The author is the aviation editor for *Jane's Defence Weekly*.)

Cook, Robin

Sphinx. Putnam, 1979.

Young archeologist Erica Baron discovers a clue to the location of the untouched tomb of a pharaoh who ruled after King Tutankhamen, but she must escape the dangerous clutches of greedy treasure hunters.

Cullen, Robert

Heirs of the Fire. Ballantine, 1997.
> Islamic militants stage a coup in Saudi Arabia deposing the royal family and causing oil prices to triple. Caught in the rapidly escalating turmoil and a dangerous conspiracy are reporter Colin Burke and the woman he secretly loves, CIA agent Desdemona McCoy.

DeMille, Nelson

The Lion's Game. Warner, 2000.
> John Corey and Kate Mayfield, agents with the federal Anti-Terrorist Taskforce, are assigned to track down a vicious Libyan terrorist known as the Lion, who is running amok in New York.

Easterman, Daniel

The Last Assassin. Doubleday, 1985.
> A mysterious Middle Eastern sect of brutal killers attempts to establish their version of the Islamic religion as the most powerful force in the world.

Farnsworth, Clyde

Shadow Wars. Fine, 1998.
> The secret of turning a worthless element into gold could send the world's economy into ruin—and everyone wants the secret including Palestinian terrorists, the Israeli Mossad, and the CIA.

Fisher, David E., and Colonel Ralph Albertazzie

Hostage One. Random House, 1989.
> Libyan dictator Qaddafi offers $50 million to smuggler and soldier of fortune Gee Hardy to carry out Operation Dallas—the kidnapping of U.S. President Bush. (Coauthor Albertazzie was President Nixon's pilot and a former commander of *Air Force One*.)

Follett, Ken

Triple. Arbor, 1979.
> 1969: the Israelis learn that the Soviet Union is assisting Egypt in the development of nuclear weapons—weapons that will become operational in a few short months. Israeli agent Nat Dickstein creates an inspired and seemingly crackpot plan to hijack uranium for Israel's own atomic bombs.

Forsyth, Frederick

The Fist of God. Bantam, 1994.
> British Intelligence must reestablish contact with a highly placed Israeli Mossad mole, code-named Jericho, in Saddam Hussein's government. Disguised as an Arab, Major Mike Martin of Britain's elite Special Air Service Regiment enters Iraq on a mission to contact "Jericho."

Franklin, Jo

The Wing of the Falcon. Atlantis, 1995.

During the Persian Gulf War, an Iraqi mole is discovered in the highest levels of U.S. and Saudi military staff. This agent is leaking top-secret information to Iraqi forces preparing to invade Saudi Arabia.

Graham, Mark

The Fire Theft. Viking, 1993.

American archeologist, Stephen Kain is investigating the ancient Persian city of Karmin-Yar, which was buried under an earthquake two thousand years ago when he is suddenly notified that his services are no longer needed—or welcome. Six months later, his daughter Angela is almost killed in ferryboat "accident" that Kaine discovers was planned. His investigations lead him back to Karmin-Yar, where he discovers that the site is being looted to buy vast quantities of heroin.

Haddad, C. A.

The Academic Factor. Harper, 1980.

Bloody September. Harper, 1976.

Operation Apricot. Harper, 1978.

Hagberg, David

Joshua's Hammer. Forge, 2000.

Saudi multimillionaire terrorist Osama bin Laden buys a stolen Russian one-kiloton nuclear bomb for $5 million to use against the United States. CIA deputy director Kirk McGarvey must find the bomb, which has been smuggled into the United States, before it blows.

Harlow, Bill

Circle William. Scribner, 1999.

Jim Schmidt, White House press secretary, and his younger brother Bill, captain of the USS *Winston,* must work together to foil a Libyan plot to use chemical weapons against Israel. (The author retired from the navy in 1997 after twenty-five years and is now currently the chief of public affairs for the CIA.)

Hartov, Steven

Eytan Eckstein series

The Heat of Ramadan. Harcourt, 1992. **FILM**

Palestinian terrorist Amar Kamil stalks an Israeli counterterrorist team, killing its members one by one. Only the former leader of the team, Eytan Eckstein, realizes what Kamil has planned and the immensity of his next target. (The author is a former American who emigrated to Israel in the mid-1970s and was a member of the Israel Defense Forces Parachute Corps and Military Intelligence.) (The book was filmed as *Point Men.*)

The Devil's Shepherd. William Morrow, 2000.

There is a traitor within a secret Israeli nuclear weapons project, and it is up to military intelligence agent Major Eytan Eckstein to ferret out the mole.

Hartov, Steven

The Nylon Hand of God. William Morrow, 1996.

Lieutenant Colonel Benni Baum of Israeli Military Intelligence is pitted against the beautiful yet brutal German terrorist Marina Klump as she attempts to disrupt Middle East peace talks.

Huston, James W.

Flash Point. William Morrow, 2000.

Fighter pilot Lieutenant Sean Woods's best friend is murdered in a brutal terrorist attack, and he wants revenge on the man responsible—Sheikh al-Jabar.

Ignatius, David

The Bank of Fear. William Morrow, 1994.

Coyote Investment is a secretive London firm that is rumored to be the $5 billion hiding place for Iraqi rulers. Beautiful computer analyst Lina Alwan discovers information she was never meant to know and is now the target of Iraqi assassins. Aided only by financial investigator Sam Hoffman, she must continue her inquest but stay in hiding until she can expose the conspiracy.

Iverson, Marc

Persian Horse. Orion, 1991.

While on patrol in the Persian Gulf, the U.S. naval frigate USS *Bulkeley* is hijacked by Iranian commandos. Only a few American sailors have escaped capture, and it is up to them to foil the hijackers and wrest back control of the ship before the Iranians carry out their deadly plans.

Jordan, Eric

Operation Hebron. Mosaic, 2000.

The Israeli government attempts to have one of its agents, Hebron, elected president of the United States.

Karlin, Wayne

Crossover. Harcourt, 1984.

Land, Jon

Ben Kamal and Danielle Barnea series

The Walls of Jericho. Forge, 1997.

A serial killer known as the Wolf is stalking the city of Jericho, and two unlikely allies are brought together to investigate: Arab American Ben Kamal, a Detroit police detective, and Danielle Barnea, an agent the Shin Bet, Israel's version of the FBI. They soon discover the serial killer is not just a murderer, but part of an international conspiracy.

The Pillars of Solomon. Forge, 1999.
Ben Kamal and Daneille Barnea are back, this time fighting the international white-slavery trade.

A Walk in the Darkness. Forge, 2000.
Arab American Ben Kamal, a Detroit police detective, and Danielle Barnea, an agent with the Shin Bet, Israel's version of the FBI, are brought together again to discover the reasons behind a two-thousand-year-old conspiracy.

Keepers of the Gate. Forge, 2001.
Palestinian American detective Ben Kamal and his Israeli colleague, the now-pregnant Danielle Barnea, are involved in a complicated investigation dealing with Nazi hunters and the deaths of high school geniuses.

Blood Diamonds. Forge, 2002.
Ben and Danielle must stop the charismatic leader of a band of West African rebels, a woman known only as the Dragon, from toppling the governments of the industrialized Western world.

The Blue Widows. Forge, 2003.
The new head of Israel's National Police, Danielle Barnea finds information gained from a raid on a terrorist stronghold that points to a devastating attack on the United States. She calls in Ben Kamal, currently working for a Boston security agency, for assistance.

Law, J. Patrick

The Assistant. Simon & Schuster, 2000.
Agents of the Mossad and Arab terrorists scheme and battle not in the deserts of the Middle East, but in the heart of the United States.

Leib, Franklin Allen

Fire Arrow. Presidio, 1988.
Sixty-five U.S. hostages must be freed from an air base in Libya.

Lichtman, Charles

The Last Inauguration. Lifetime, 1998.
Libyan dictator Saddam Hussein and international terrorist Carlos the Jackal unite against the United States and Israel, which ultimately leads to a violent attack on Washington, D.C.

Ludlum, Robert

The Icarus Agenda. Random, 1988.
Congressman Evan Kendrick is vaulted to media fame when he successfully negotiates with terrorists and saves the lives of many American hostages, but he soon finds himself involved in a devious plan that could either win him the presidency of the United States or kill him.

The Scorpio Illusion. Bantam, 1993.

> Former naval intelligence officer Tyrell Hawthorne must find the beautiful but deadly terrorist Amaya Bajaratt before she assassinates the leaders of Israel, England, France, and the United States.

Lyall, Gavin

Uncle Target. Viking, 1988.

Mann, Paul

The Britannia Contract. Carroll & Graf, 1993.

> During a visit to Saudi Arabia, the British royal yacht *Britannia,* carrying Queen Elizabeth and her husband Prince Philip, is seized by members of the Irish Republican Army and their allies—Middle Eastern terrorists. U.S. and British special forces units must attempt to rescue the hostages without getting them killed in the process.

> *Gannon's Adventure/Suspense Rule Number 24: Evil dictators are notoriously difficult to bump off.*

Mason, David

Shadow over Babylon. Dutton, 1993.

> The operation is created by men in the highest level of government and without the knowledge of the world's intelligence agencies; it will be supplied with the ultimate in technology and carried out by a team supremely skilled in the art of assassination. The mission: the assassination of the Iraq's President Saddam Hussein.

McClure, Ken

Resurrection. Simon & Schuster, 1999.

> If smallpox has been wiped out in the world, why are the Iraqis immunizing their entire population against it?

Nance, John J.

Scorpion Strike. Crown, 1992.

> In post–Gulf War Iraq, Saddam Hussein's scientists create a devastating new biological weapon, and he plans to release it against his enemies. A special strike team must be inserted into Iraq to destroy the underground lab before the weapon can be used.

Ostrovsky, Victor

Lion of Judah. St. Martin's, 1993.

> A complex thriller depicting the plotting and international schemes of Israel's Mossad by a former *katsa,* or case officer.

Pearson, Ryne Douglas

Cloudburst. William Morrow, 1993.
> The president is assassinated in a terrorist ambush while visiting Los Angeles, and the fledgling vice president becomes leader of a country that will soon be facing a massive terrorist threat.

Peters, Ralph

The Devil's Garden. Avon, 1998.
> Lieutenant Colonel Evan Burton must find the daughter of a powerful U.S. senator who has disappeared into the depths of a Middle Eastern country in the throes of revolution.

Pineiro, R. J.

Kevin Dalton series

Ultimatum. Forge, 1994.
> Lieutenant Kevin "Crackers" Dalton, shot down over Iraq, must ally himself with Mossad agent Kalela and a band of Kurdish rebels to find Saddam Hussein's secret nuclear weapons facility before the Iraqi leader can destroy Tehran and Tel Aviv.

Retribution. Forge, 1995.
> Iraq's Saddam Hussein acquires three nuclear warheads from the Russian *mafiya* and smuggles them into the United States. Lieutenant Kevin Dalton of the U.S. Navy and the beautiful Israeli Mossad agent Kalela must rush to find the weapons before three cities are destroyed.

Reich, Tova

The Jewish War. Pantheon, 1995.
> In this satirical novel, the Israeli army marches against a group of settlers who have seceded from Israel and created the Kingdom of Judea and Samaria.

15

Rivers, Gayle

Hunter's Run. Putnam, 1989.
> Looking to trade something for the release of hostages in Iran, the CIA assigns Major Bob Yardley of U.S. Special Forces to steal the 2,500-year-old Peacock Throne from a vault deep within the Ghulistan Palace in Tehran.

Rosenberg, Joel C.

Jon Bennett and Erin McCoy series

The Last Jihad. Forge, 2003.
> Business strategist and confidante of the president of the United States Jon Bennett must team up with the beautiful CIA agent Erin McCoy to stop Saddam Hussein from dropping a nuclear bomb on New York, Washington, and Tel Aviv.

The Last Days. Forge, 2003.

> Jon Bennett is sent to the Middle East as a presidential envoy, along with his girlfriend and bodyguard CIA agent Erin McCoy, to broker a peace treaty between Arabs and Israelis. But all hell breaks loose when a terrorist bomb kills both the U.S. secretary of state and Yassar Arafat.

Seymour, Gerald

Condition Black. William Morrow, 1990.

> Iraq attempts to buy atomic secrets from an underpaid and deeply in debt British scientist by the name of Frederick Bissett. Standing in its way is FBI agent Bill Erlich, and opposing Erlich is the Colt, a bizarre and deadly assassin.

The Running Target. William Morrow, 1989.

Simon, Frank

Anne McAdams and Mars Enderly series

Veiled Threats. Crossway, 1996.

> Archeologists Anne McAdams and Mars Enderly discover what may be a long-sought-after biblical artifact, and they are soon caught up in a danger-ous plot. A thriller from an evangelical Christian point of view.

Walls of Terror. Crossway, 1997.

> Christian archeologists Anne and Mars Enderly find themselves caught up in another terrorist conspiracy.

Smith, Murray

Stone Dancer. Pocket, 1994.

Stone, Robert

Damascus Gate. Houghton, 1998.

> Christopher Lucas, an expatriate American journalist living in Jerusalem unex-pectedly discovers a terrorist plot to bomb the Temple Mount.

Tillman, Barrett

Warriors. Bantam, 1990.

> John Bennett has been recruited by the Saudis to train a group of pilots to form the "Tiger Force," which will be capable of going against the superior Israeli Air Force. But when an Arab-Israeli war breaks out, Bennett finds himself in the mid-dle of a tough fight.

Tonkin, Peter

Richard Mariner series

The Coffin Ship. Crown, 1989.

> The massive supertanker *Prometheus,* full of 250,000 tons of crude oil, is scheduled to sail from the Persian Gulf to Europe. On board, however, is one crewmember who is determined that the craft will never make it.

The Fire Ship. Crown, 1990.

In the Persian Gulf, the behemoth tanker *Prometheus II* has been hijacked by terrorists and her crew taken hostage, but no demands have yet been made. What do the terrorists have planned?

The Leper Ship. Crown, 1992.

The *Napoli* is chartered to remove toxic waste from the desert claimed by the PLO but soon finds itself without a captain and a mutinous crew. The ship, with the poisonous waste becoming more and more unstable, is barred entry from port.

Webb, James

Something to Die For. William Morrow, 1991.

The story of what happens during a limited "peacetime" battle in the deserts of Ethiopia—both on the battlefield and in Washington, D.C. (The author is former U.S. secretary of the navy.)

Witham, Larry

The Negev Project. Meridian, 1994.

Two old men, a Jew and a Muslim, devise a plan in the Negev Desert that they hope will culminate in peace for the Middle East.

15

Chapter 16

Male Heroic Adventure Series

Paperback Originals

Definition: Essentially these are the equivalent of Harlequin romances for men. The same companies that publish women's romance series paperbacks publish many of these titles. The writing is formulaic and even contrived, with the emphasis on the action, not on characters or plot. Violence, destruction, and death are described in all their gory details—the bloodier the better.

The story usually revolves around a single man—a loner, a patriot, and a hero—who must face impossible odds in his fight for truth, justice, and the American way. Sometimes a team will be formed from diverse individuals, but there is always an alpha male. Women are often stereotyped into one of three categories: Amazon babes, fragile damsels in distress, or ball-busting bitches.

The morality is simple: the rugged hero may sometimes have to do some bad things, but the ends justify the means, and the villains are pure evil with no redeeming values. Villains run the gamut from your basic terrorist types to postapocalyptic mutants—they are always evil and usually quite ugly.

The Appeal: The appeal can be compared with that of the traditional romance: it's safe, predictable, and fun. It's also a "good story." There is a clear distinction between good and evil, along with plenty of fast-paced action. The hero is larger than life and always wins in the end. The reader can get his vicarious thrills—reveling in the explosions, executions, and decapitations—in the privacy of his own home, with no fear of bloodstains or gunpowder burns. The series reader knows how the book will end: no matter what trouble the hero gets into, he will survive to fight evil . . . in another installment.

Brief History: This subgenre has its roots in the pulp magazines that were popular in the 1930s. These magazines evolved into cheap paperback novels in the 1940s and 1950s. Early writers in this arena included Edgar Rice Burroughs and Kenneth Robeson. Burroughs's Tarzan novels and Robeson's (a pseudonym for several writers) Doc Savage were precursors to today's Mack Bolan and Remo Williams, the Destroyer. Just as world events influenced other subgenres of adventure/suspense, so, too, were male heroic paperback originals. The late 1950s and the 1960s gave us the fight against the evils of communism, while the 1970s and 1980s saw more of an interest in crime lords and terrorists. Postapocalyptic America has been a favorite topic since the 1980s and continues to be popular.

Advising the Reader: The key elements to remember when advising the reader and suggesting appropriate titles are the following:

- A series reader is a happy reader—so long as the series continues.

- Series readers usually like to read series titles in chronological (series) order.

- If the reader has started in the middle of a series, don't hesitate to suggest the earlier installments.

- If the reader has finished a series, suggest series with like elements: a postapocalyptic America, antiterrorist operatives, spies and secret agents, or crime lords.

- Suggest similar titles that are not in a series: the postapocalyptic reader may enjoy disaster novels, the antiterrorist enthusiast can be given political thrillers or Middle East action, or suggest military fiction to the reader who likes the adventures of the SEALs.

- We can find many secret agents and spies in series that are not part of an original paperback series, for example, James Bond or Clive Cussler, who can be suggested to the reader.

- The reader may also be guided to the Western series (such as Tabor Evan's Longarm, Jake Logan's Slocum, J. R. Robert's the Gunsmith, or Jon Sharpe's the Trailsman), which have many of the same characteristics of the action and adventure series.

The hero cannot be common, nor the common heroic.

—Ralph Waldo Emerson

Ahern, Jerry

Survivalist series. Zebra, 1981–1993.
> After World War III, John Thomas Rourke, ex-CIA covert operations officer, searches a communist and mutant-filled America for his lost family.

1. Total War	*7. Prophet*
2. Nightmare Begins	*8. End Is Coming*
3. Quest	*9. Earth Fire*
4. Doomsayer	*10. Final Rain*
5. Web	*11. Awakening*
6. Savage Horde	*12. Reprisal*

13. *Rebellion*   21. *To End All War*

14. *Pursuit*   22. *Brutal Conquest*

15. *Terror*   23. *Call to Battle*

16. *Overlord*   24. *Blood Assassins*

17. *Arsenal*   25. *War Mountain*

18. *Ordeal*   26. *Countdown*

19. *Struggle*   27. *Death Watch*

20. *Firestorm*

Austin, Rick

Guardians series. Jove, 1986–1991.

> From the ashes of World War III rose the Guardians. Their mission: to turn the United States back into a democracy.

1. *Guardians*   9. *Vengeance Day*

2. *Trial by Fire*   10. *Freedom Fight*

3. *Thunder of Hell*   11. *Valley of the Gods*

4. *Night of the Phoenix*   12. *Plague Years*

5. *Armageddon Run*   13. *Devil's Deal*

6. *War Zone*   14. *Death from Above*

7. *Brute Force*   15. *Snake Eyes*

8. *Desolation Road*   16. *Death Charge*

Axler, James

Deathlands series. Worldwide, 1986–

> James Axler is the pseudonym for Laurence James. In January 2001, nuclear explosions take place all over the world and completely change the earth. The Deathlands have emerged from this ruined planet, an American wasteland filled with mutants. Heroic Ryan Cawdor, beautiful Krysty Wroth, and weapons master J. B. Dix fight to survive and for the ideals of a vanished civilization.

1. *Pilgrimage to Hell*   9. *Red Equinox*

2. *Red Holocaust*   10. *Northstar Rising*

3. *Neutron Solstice*   11. *Time Nomads*

4. *Crater Lake*   12. *Latitude Zero*

5. *Homeward Bound* `FILM` 13. *Seedling*

6. *Pony Soldiers*   14. *Dark Carnival*

7. *Dectra Chain*   15. *Chill Factor*

8. *Ice & Fire*   16. *Moon Fate*

17. *Fury's Pilgrims*

18. *Shockscape*

19. *Deep Empire*

20. *Cold Asylum*

21. *Twilight Children*

22. *Rider Reaper*

23. *Road Wars*

24. *Trader Redux*

25. *Genesis Echo*

26. *Shadowfall*

27. *Ground Zero*

28. *Emerald Fire*

29. *Bloodlines*

30. *Crossways*

31. *Keepers of the Sun*

32. *Circle Thrice*

33. *Eclipse at Noon*

34. *Stoneface (prequel to the Outlanders series that follows)*

35. *Bitter Fruit*

36. *Skydark*

37. *Demons of Eden*

38. *Mars Arena*

39. *Watersleep*

40. *Nightmare Passage*

41. *Way of the Wolf*

42. *Dark Emblem*

43. *Crucible of Time*

44. *Encounter*

45. *Starfall*

46. *Gemini Rising (The Baronies Trilogy, Book 1)*

47. *Gaia's Demise (The Baronies Trilogy, Book 2)*

48. *Dark Reckoning (The Baronies Trilogy, Book 3)*

49. *Shadow World*

50. *Pandora's Redoubt*

51. *Rat King*

52. *Zero City*

53. *Savage Armada (The Skydark Chronicles, Book 1)*

54. *Judas Strike (The Skydark Chronicles, Book 2)*

55. *Shadow Fortress (The Skydark Chronicles, Book 3)*

56. *Sunchild*

57. *Breakthrough*

58. *Salvation Road*

59. *Amazon Gate (The Illuminated Ones, Book 1)*

60. *Destiny's Truth (The Illuminated Ones, Book 2)*

61. *Skydark Spawn*

62. *Damnation Road Show*

63. *Devil Riders*

Outlanders series. Worldwide, 1997–

Spun off from the Deathlands series (previous entry) and set a century later. *Stoneface* (Deathlands #34) serves as a prequel to Outlanders. America has barely survived a nuclear holocaust. The survivors live in fortified towns under despotic rule—the only freedom is beyond the walls of the cities, in the outlands. The warrior Kane joins forces with Brigid, keeper of the archives, and weapons specialist Grant to free humanity from this savage tyranny.

1. *Exiles to Hell*

2. *Destiny Run*

3. *Savage Sun*

4. *Omega Path*

5. *Parallax Red*

6. *Doomstar Relic*

7. *Iceblood*

8. *Hellbound Fury*

9. *Night Eternal:*
   The Lost Earth

10. *Outer Darkness*

11. *Armageddon Axis*

12. *Wreath of Fire*

13. *Shadow Scourge*

14. *Hell Rising*

15. *Doom Dynasty*

16. *Tigers of Heaven*

17. *Purgatory Road*

18. *Sargasso Plunder*

19. *Tomb of Time*

20. *Prodigal Chalice*

21. *Devil in the Moon (The*
    Dragon Kings, Book 1)

22. *Dragoneye (The Dragon*
    Kings, Book 2)

23. *Far Empire*

24. *Equinox Zero*

25. *Talon and Fang*

26. *Sea of Plague*

27. *Awakening*

Brown, Dale, and Jim DeFelice

Dale Brown's Dreamland. Berkley, 2001

Dreamland, hidden in the Nevada desert, is the research center where the United States Air Force creates its newest weapons. These new, secret weapons are then tested on the front lines against terrorists and other enemies of America.

1. *Dale Brown's Dreamland*

2. *Nerve Center*

3. *Razor's Edge*

4. *Piranha*

Clancy, Tom, with Steve R. Pieczenik

Tom Clancy's Net Force series. Berkley, 1999–

In the year 2010, whoever controls computers can control the world. In response, Congress creates a secret computer security agency as part of the FBI—Net Force.

1. *Net Force* **FILM**

2. *Hidden Agendas*

3. *Night Moves*

4. *Breaking Point*

5. *Point of Impact*

6. *Cybernation*

7. *State of War*

Tom Clancy's OP-Center series. Berkley, 1995–

Paul Hood is the director of Op-Center, a defense intelligence agency utilizing the latest in technology and the only place the government can turn to when things get tough.

1. Tom Clancy's OP-Center FILM	*6. State of Siege*
2. Mirror Image	*7. Divide and Conquer*
3. Games of State	*8. Line of Control*
4. Acts of War	*9. Mission of Honor*
5. Balance of Power	*10. Sea of Fire*

Clancy, Tom, with Martin Harry Greenberg

Tom Clancy's Power Plays series. Berkley, 1997–

The adventures of American businessman Roger Cordian, who triumphs over a militant Russia, political extremists, and techno-terrorists. The third novel in the series is based on the Red Storm Entertainment computer game. Another cog in the vast Clancy moneymaking machine.

1. Politika	*5. Cold War*
2. Ruthless.com	*6. Cutting Edge*
3. Shadow Watch	*7. Zero Hour*
4. Bio-Strike	

Douglass, Keith

Carrier series. Jove, 1991–

As it engages in combat across the globe, the series "stars" are the Carrier Battle Group Fourteen, including a supercarrier, an amphibious unit, a guided missile cruiser, and a destroyer.

1. Carrier	*12. Chain of Command*
2. Viper Strike	*13. Brink of War*
3. Armageddon Mode	*14. Typhoon Season*
4. Flame Out	*15. Enemies*
5. Maelstrom	*16. Joint Operations*
6. Countdown	*17. The Art of War*
7. Afterburn	*18. Island Warriors*
8. Alpha Strike	*19. First Strike*
9. Arctic Fire	*20. Hellfire*
10. Arsenal	*21. Terror at Dawn*
11. Nuke Zone	

Douglass, Keith

SEAL Team Seven series. Berkley, 1996–
Assigned exclusively to the Central Intelligence Agency, Third Platoon performs any necessary covert task anywhere in the world.

1. SEAL Team Seven	*9. War Cry*
2. Specter	*10. Frontal Assault*
3. Nucflash	*11. Flashpoint*
4. Direct Action	*12. Tropical Terror*
5. Firestorm	*13. Bloodstorm*
6. Battleground	*14. Deathblow*
7. Deathrace	*15. Ambush*
8. Pacific Siege	*16. Counterfire*

Ferro, James

HOGS series. Berkley, 1999–
Based on actual Gulf War events, this series chronicles the men and women who flew the A-104 Warthogs.

1. Going Deep	*4. Snake Eaters*
2. Hog Down	*5. Target: Saddam*
3. Fort Apache	*6. Death Wish*

Garnett, Cliff

Talon Force series. Signet, 2000–
Technologically Augmented, Low-Observable, Networked—TALON—an elite special force intended to protect U.S. interests worldwide with members from all branches of the armed forces, utilizing the latest in firepower and technology.

1. Thunderbolt	*6. Takedown*
2. Meltdown	*7. Slaughterhouse*
3. Sky Fire	*8. Bloodtide*
4. Secret Weapon	*9. Seafire*
5. Zulu Plus Ten	*10. Dire Straits*

16

Hamilton, Donald

Matt Helm series. Fawcett, 1960–1993
Matt Helm is a "counterassassination agent" employed by the U.S. government to execute assassins who work for the "bad guys"—first Communists and then international terrorist organizations.

1. Death of a Citizen	*3. The Removers*
2. The Wrecking Crew	*4. The Silencers* **FILM**

5. *Murderer's Row* FILM

6. *The Ambushers* FILM

7. *The Shadowers*

8. *The Ravagers*

9. *The Devastators*

10. *The Betrayers*

11. *The Menacers*

12. *The Interlopers*

13. *The Poisoners*

14. *The Intriguers*

15. *The Intimidators*

16. *The Terminators*

17. *The Retaliators*

18. *The Terrorizers*

19. *The Revengers*

20. *The Annihilators*

21. *The Infiltrators*

22. *The Detonators*

23. *The Vanishers*

24. *The Demolishers*

25. *The Frighteners*

26. *The Threateners*

27. *The Damagers*

Johnstone, William W.

Ashes series. Pinnacle, 1983–

After a nuclear apocalypse, evil terrorists, lawless gangs, and the mutant Night People besiege the United States. Only super-patriot and mercenary Ben Raines can protect the decent citizens who remain.

1. *Out of the Ashes*

2. *Fire in the Ashes*

3. *Anarchy in the Ashes*

4. *Blood in the Ashes*

5. *Alone in the Ashes*

6. *Wind in the Ashes*

7. *Smoke in the Ashes*

8. *Danger in the Ashes*

9. *Valor in the Ashes*

10. *Trapped in the Ashes*

11. *Death in the Ashes*

12. *Survival in the Ashes*

13. *Fury in the Ashes*

14. *Courage in the Ashes*

15. *Terror in the Ashes*

16. *Vengeance in the Ashes*

17. *Battle in the Ashes*

18. *Flames from the Ashes*

19. *Treason in the Ashes*

20. *D-Day in the Ashes*

21. *Betrayal in the Ashes*

22. *Chaos in the Ashes*

23. *Slaughter in the Ashes*

24. *Judgment in the Ashes*

25. *Ambush in the Ashes*

26. *Triumph in the Ashes*

27. *Hatred in the Ashes*

28. *Standoff in the Ashes*

29. *Crisis in the Ashes*

30. *Tyranny in the Ashes*

31. *Warriors from the Ashes*

32. *Destiny in the Ashes*

33. *Enemy in the Ashes*

34. *Escape from the Ashes*

Maloney, Mack

The Wingman series. Pinnacle, 1987–1999

In a United States ravaged by civil war and beset by international villains, there arises Hawk Hunter—a fearless hero who commands a team of crack F-16 pilots.

1. *Wingman*
2. *The Circle War*
3. *The Lucifer Crusade*
4. *Thunder in the East*
5. *The Twisted Cross*
6. *The Final Storm*
7. *Freedom Express*
8. *Skyfire*
9. *Return from the Inferno*
10. *War of the Sun*
11. *Ghost War*
12. *Target: Point Zero*
13. *Death Orbit*
14. *Sky Ghost*
15. *Return of the Sky Ghost*
16. *The Tomorrow War*

Murphy, Warren, and Richard Sapir

The Destroyer series. Worldwide, 1971

Created by Murphy and Sapir, but ghostwritten by several other authors including Murphy's wife and the current author, Will Murray. Remo Williams is an agent of a secret U.S. organization known as CURE; along with Chiun, his mentor and a master of the martial arts, he fights evil across the globe.

1. *Created, the Destroyer* **FILM**
   (filmed as *Remo Williams, The Adventure Begins*)
2. *Death Check*
3. *Chinese Puzzle*
4. *Mafia Fix*
5. *Dr. Quake*
6. *Death Therapy*
7. *Union Bust*
8. *Summit Chase*
9. *Murder's Shield*
10. *Terror Squad*
11. *Kill or Cure*
12. *Slave Safari*
13. *Acid Rock*
14. *Judgment Day*
15. *Murder Ward*
16. *Oil Slick*
17. *Last War Dance*
18. *Funny Money*
19. *Holy Terror*
20. *Assassin's Play-Off*
21. *Deadly Seeds*
22. *Brain Drain*
23. *Child's Play*
24. *King's Curse*
25. *Sweet Dreams*
26. *In Enemy Hands*
27. *The Last Temple*
28. *Ship of Death*
29. *The Final Death*
30. *Mugger Blood*
31. *The Head Men*
32. *Killer Chromosomes*

16

33. *Voodoo Die*

34. *Chained Reaction*

35. *Last Call*

36. *Power Play*

37. *Bottom Line*

38. *Bay City Blast*

39. *Missing Link*

40. *Dangerous Games*

41. *Firing Line*

42. *Timber Line*

43. *Midnight Man*

44. *Balance of Power*

45. *Spoils of War*

46. *Next of Kin*

47. *Dying Space*

48. *Profit Motive*

49. *Skin Deep*

50. *Killing Time*

51. *Shock Value*

52. *Fool's Gold*

53. *Time Trial*

54. *Last Drop*

55. *Master's Challenge*

56. *Encounter Group*

57. *Date with Death*

58. *Total Recall*

59. *The Arms of Kali*

60. *The End of the Game*

61. *Lords of the Earth*

62. *The Seventh Stone*

63. *The Sky Is Falling*

64. *The Last Alchemist*

65. *Lost Yesterday*

66. *Sue Me*

67. *Look into My Eyes*

68. *An Old Fashioned War*

69. *Blood Ties*

70. *The Eleventh Hour*

71. *Return Engagement*

72. *Sole Survivor*

73. *Line of Succession*

74. *Walking Wounded*

75. *Rain of Terror*

76. *The Final Crusade*

77. *Coin of the Realm*

78. *Blue Smoke and Mirrors*

79. *Shooting Schedule*

80. *Death Sentence*

81. *Hostile Takeover*

82. *Survival Course*

83. *Skull Duggery*

84. *Ground Zero*

85. *Blood Lust (Special 20th Anniversary Edition)*

86. *Arabian Nightmare*

87. *Mob Psychology*

88. *The Ultimate Death*

89. *Dark Horse*

90. *Ghost in the Machine*

91. *Cold Warrior*

92. *The Last Dragon*

93. *Terminal Transmission*

94. *Feeding Frenzy*

95. *High Priestess*

96. *Infernal Revenue*

97. *Identity Crisis*

98. *Target of Opportunity*

99. *The Color of Fear*

100. *Last Rites*

101. *Bidding War*

102. *Unite and Conquer*

103. *Engines of Destruction*

104. *Angry White Mailmen*
originally titled
The Fist of Allah

105. *Scorched Earth*

106. *White Water*

107. *Feast or Famine*

108. *Bamboo Dragon*

109. *American Obsession*

110. *Never Say Die*

111. *Prophet of Doom*

112. *Brain Storm*

113. *The Empire Dreams*

114. *Failing Marks*

115. *Misfortune Teller*

116. *The Final Reel*

117. *Deadly Genes*

118. *Killer Watts*

119. *Fade to Black*

120. *The Last Monarch*

121. *A Pound of Prevention*

122. *Syndication Rites*

123. *Disloyal Opposition*

124. *By Eminent Domain*

125. *The Wrong Stuff*

126. *Air Raid*

127. *Market Force*

128. *The End of the Beginning*

129. *Father to Son*

130. *Waste Not, Want Not*

131. *Unnatural Selection*

132. *Wolf's Bane*

133. *Troubled Waters*

134. *Bloody Tourists*

Pendleton, Don

Able Team Series. Worldwide, 1983–

Able Team is one of two tactical teams that operate out of Mack Bolan's Stony Man Farm and is equipped with the latest weapons and technology to fight crime and terrorism within the United States.

1. *Tower of Terror*

2. *The Hostaged Island*

3. *Texas Showdown*

4. *Amazon Slaughter*

5. *Cairo Countdown*

6. *Warlord of Azatlan*

7. *Justice by Fire*

8. *Army of Devils*

9. *Kill School*

10. *Royal Flush*

11. *Five Rings of Fire*

12. *Deathbites*

13. *Scorched Earth*

14. *Into the Maze*

15. *They Came to Kill*

16. *Rain of Doom*

17. *Fire and Maneuver*

18. *Tech War*

19. *Ironman*

20. *Shot to Hell*

21. *Death Strike*

22. *The World War III Game*

23. *Fall Back and Kill*

24. *Blood Gambit*

25. *Hard Kill*
26. *The Iron God*
27. *Cajun Angel*
28. *Miami Crush*
29. *Death Ride*
30. *Hit and Run*
31. *Ghost Train*
32. *Firecross*
33. *Cowboy's Revenge*
34. *Clear Shot*
35. *Strike Force*
36. *Final Run*
37. *Red Menace*
38. *Cold Steel*
39. *Death Code*
40. *Blood Mark*
41. *White Fire*
42. *Dead Zone*
43. *Kill Orbit*
44. *Night Heat*
45. *Lethal Trade*
46. *Counterblow*
47. *Shadow Warriors*
48. *Cult War*
49. *Dueling Missiles*
50. *Death Hunt*
51. *Skinwalker*
52. *Super #1: Hostile Fire*
53. *Super #2: Mean Streets*

The Executioner series. Worldwide, 1969–

Vietnam vet and ex-Green Beret Mack Bolan first appeared in 1969 when he began his career fighting the Mafia. He has since moved on to the international arena, where he wages war against terrorists and other enemies of the United States. In his long career, he has killed more than 10,000 bad guys.

1. *War against the Mafia*
2. *Death Squad*
3. *Battle Mask*
4. *Miami Massacre*
5. *Continental Contract*
6. *Assault on Soho*
7. *Nightmare in New York*
8. *Chicago Wipe-Out*
9. *Vegas Vendetta*
10. *Caribbean Kill*
11. *California Hit*
12. *Boston Blitz*
13. *Washington I.O.U.*
14. *San Diego Siege*
15. *Panic in Philly*
16. *Sicilian Slaughter*
17. *Jersey Guns*
18. *Texas Storm*
19. *Detroit Deathwatch*
20. *New Orleans Knockout*
21. *Firebase Seattle*
22. *Hawaiian Hellground*
23. *St. Louis Showdown*
24. *Canadian Crises*
25. *Colorado Kill-Zone*
26. *Acapulco Rampage*
27. *Dixie Convoy*
28. *Savage Fire*
29. *Command Strike*
30. *Cleveland Pipeline*
31. *Arizona Ambush*
32. *Tennessee Smash*

105. *Countdown to Chaos*

106. *Run to Ground*

107. *American Nightmare*

108. *Time to Kill*

109. *Hong Kong Hit List*

110. *Trojan Horse*

111. *The Fiery Cross*

112. *Blood of the Lion*

113. *Vietnam Fallout*

114. *Cold Judgment*

115. *Circle of Steel*

116. *The Killing Urge*

117. *Vendetta in Venice*

118. *Warrior's Revenge*

119. *Line of Fire*

120. *Border Sweep*

121. *Twisted Path*

122. *Desert Strike*

123. *War Born*

124. *Night Kill*

125. *Dead Man's Tale*

126. *Death Wind*

127. *Kill Zone*

128. *Sudan Slaughter*

129. *Haitian Hit*

130. *Dead Line*

131. *Ice Wolf*

132. *The Big Kill*

133. *Blood Run*

134. *White Line War*

135. *Devil Force*

136. *Down and Dirty*

137. *Battle Lines*

138. *Kill Tra*

139. *Cutting Edge*

140. *Wild Card*

141. *Direct Hit*

142. *Fatal Error*

143. *Helldust Cruise*

144. *Whipsaw*

145. *Chicago Payoff*

146. *Deadly Tactics*

147. *Payback Game*

148. *Deep and Swift*

149. *Blood Rules*

150. *Death Load*

151. *Message to Medellin*

152. *Combat Stretch*

153. *Firebase Florida*

154. *Night Hit*

155. *Hawaiian Heat*

156. *Phantom Force*

157. *Cayman Strike*

158. *Firing Line*

159. *Steel and Flame*

160. *Storm Warning*

161. *Eye of the Storm*

162. *Colors of Hell*

163. *Warrior's Edge*

164. *Death Trail*

165. *Fire Sweep*

166. *Assassin's Creed*

167. *Double Action*

168. *Blood Price*

169. *White Heat*

170. *Baja Blitz*

171. *Deadly Force*

172. *Fast Strike*

173. *Capitol Hit*

174. *Battle Plan*

175. *Battle Ground*

176. *Ransom Run*

177. *Evil Code*

178. *Black Hand*

179. *War Hammer*

180. *Force Down*

181. *Shifting Target*

182. *Lethal Agent*

183. *Clean Sweep*

184. *Death Warrant*

185. *Sudden Fury*

186. *Fire Burst*

187. *Cleansing Flame*

188. *War Paint*

189. *Wellfire*

190. *Killing Range*

191. *Extreme Force*

192. *Maximum Impact*

193. *Hostile Action*

194. *Deadly Contest*

195. *Select Fire*

196. *Triburst*

197. *Armed Force*

198. *Shoot Down*

199. *Rogue Agent*

200. *Crisis Point*

201. *Prime Target*

202. *Combat Zone*

203. *Hard Contact*

204. *Rescue Run*

205. *Hell Road*

206. *Hunting Cry*

207. *Freedom Strike*

208. *Death Whisper*

209. *Asian Crucible*

210. *Fire Lash*

211. *Steel Claws*

212. *Ride the Beast*

213. *Blood Harvest*

214. *Fission Fury*

215. *Fire Hammer*

216. *Death Force*

217. *Fight or Die*

218. *End Game*

219. *Terror Intent*

220. *Tiger Stalk*

221. *Blood and Fire*

222. *Patriot Gambit*

223. *Hour of Conflict*

224. *Call to Arms*

225. *Body Armor*

226. *Red Horse*

227. *Blood Circle*

228. *Terminal Option*

229. *Zero Tolerance*

230. *Deep Attack*

231. *Slaughter Squad*

232. *Jackal Hunt*

233. *Tough Justice*

234. *Target Command*

235. *Plague Wind*

236. *Vengeance Rising*

237. *Hellfire Trigger*

238. *Crimson Tide*

239. *Hostile Proximity*

240. *Devil's Guard*

241. *Evil Reborn*

242. *Doomsday Conspiracy*

243. *Assault Reflex*

244. *Judas Kill*

245. *Virtual Destruction*
246. *Blood of the Earth*
247. *Black Dawn Rising*
248. *Rolling Death*
249. *Shadow Target*
250. *Warning Shot*
251. *Kill Radius*
252. *Death Line*
253. *Risk Factor*
254. *Chill Effect*
255. *War Bird*
256. *Point of Impact*
257. *Precision Play*
258. *Target Lock*
259. *Nightfire*
260. *Dayhunt*
261. *Dawnkill*
262. *Trigger Point*
263. *Skysniper*
264. *Iron Fist*
265. *Freedom Force*
266. *Ultimate Price*
267. *Invisible Invader*
268. *Shattered Trust*
269. *Shifting Shadows*
270. *Judgement Day*
271. *Cyberhunt*
272. *Stealth Striker*

273. *Uforce*
274. *Rogue Target*
275. *Crossed Borders*
276. *Leviathan*
277. *Dirty Mission*
278. *Triple Reverse*
279. *Fire Wind*
280. *Fear Rally*
281. *Blood Stone*
282. *Jungle Conflict*
283. *Ring of Retaliation*
284. *Devil's Army*
285. *Final Strike*
286. *Armageddon Exit*
287. *Rogue Warrior*
288. *Arctic Blast*
289. *Vendetta Force*
290. *Pursued*
291. *Blood Trade*
292. *Savage Game*
293. *Death Merchants*
294. *Scorpion Rising*
295. *Hostile Alliance*
296. *Nuclear Game*
297. *Deadly Pursuit*
298. *Final Play*
299. *Dangerous Encounter*
300. *Warrior's Requiem*

Mack Bolan series. Worldwide, 1983–
The further adventures of Mack Bolan, the man known as the Executioner.

1. *Moving Target*
2. *Tightrope*
3. *Blowout*
4. *Blood Fever*
5. *Knockdown*

6. *Assault*
7. *Backlash*
8. *Siege*
9. *Blockade*
10. *Evil Kingdom*

Stony Man series. Worldwide, 1993–
The adventures of an elite band of warriors, members of America's ultra-covert intelligence agency Stony Man.

1. Stony Man Doctrine	*35. Message to America*
2. Stony Man II	*36. Stranglehold*
3. Stony Man III	*37. Triple Strike*
4. Stony Man IV	*38. Enemy Within*
5. Stony Man V	*39. Breach of Trust*
6. Stony Man VI	*40. Betrayal*
7. Stony Man VII	*41. Silent Invader*
8. Stony Man VIII	*42. Edge of Night*
9. Strikepoint	*43. Zero Hour*
10. Secret Arsenal	*44. Thirst for Power*
11. Target America	*45. Star Venture*
12. Blind Eagle	*46. Hostile Instinct*
13. Warhead	*47. Command Force*
14. Deadly Agent	*48. Conflict Imperative*
15. Blood Debt	*49. Dragon Fire*
16. Deep Alert	*50. Judgment in Blood*
17. Vortex	*51. Doomsday Directive*
18. Stinger	*52. Tactical Response*
19. Nuclear Nightmare	*53. Countdown to Terror*
20. Terms of Survival	*54. Vector Three*
21. Satan'sThrust	*55. Extreme Measures*
32. Sunflash	*56. State of Aggression*
23. Perishing Game	*57. Sky Killers*
24. Bird of Prey	*58. Condition Hostile*
25. Skylance	*59. Prelude to War*
26. Flashback	*60. Defensive Action*
27. Flames of Wrath	*61. Rogue State*
28. Blood Star	*62. Deep Rampage*
29. Body Armor	*63. Freedom Watch*
30. Virtual Peril	*64. Roots of Terror*
31. Night of the Jaguar	*65. The Third Protocol*
32. Law of Last Resort	*66. Axis of Conflict*
33. Punitive Measures	*67. Echoes of War*
34. Reprisal	

Riker, H. Jay

SEALS: The Warrior Breed series. Avon, 1993–2000

The heroic adventures of U.S. Navy SEALs during the Vietnam War.

1. Silver Star	*5. Medal of Honor*
2. Purple Heart	*6. Marks of Valor*
3. Bronze Stars	*7. In Harm's Way*
4. Navy Cross	*8. Duty's Call*

Sadler, Barry

Casca, The Eternal Mercenary series. Jove, 1979–2001

Casca, a Roman Legionnaire, is condemned by Christ to wander the earth forever as a constant soldier, getting involved in any and every battle throughout all time. Sadler died in 1989; books published since then have been ghostwritten under his name until *The Liberator* by Paul Dengelegi.

1. Eternal Mercenary	*13. Assassin*
2. God of Death	*14. Phoenix*
3. War Lord	*15. Pirate*
4. Panzer Soldier	*16. Desert Mercenary*
5. Barbarian	*17. Warrior*
6. Persian	*18. Cursed*
7. Damned	*19. Samurai*
8. Soldier of Fortune	*20. Soldier of Gideon*
9. Sentinel	*21. Trench Soldier*
10. Conquistador	*22. The Mongol*
11. Legionnaire	*23. The Liberator*
12. African Mercenary	*24. The Defiant*

Smith, James V., Jr.

Force Recon series. Berkley, 1999–

Marine Captain Jack Swayne leads a special unit—Team Midnight—on military adventures.

1. Force Recon	*4. Deep Strike*
2. Death Wind	*5. Fatal Honor*
3. The Butcher's Bill	*6. Stalking Tiger*

Watson, Chief James "Patches" and Mark Roberts

SEALS Top Secret series. Avon, 1998–1999

The SEALS of First Platoon and their adventures during the Vietnam War.

1. *Operation: Artful Dodger*

2. *Operation: Shoot and Scoot*

3. *Operation: Search & Destroy*

4. *Operation: Shell Game*

Wilson, Gar, and Don Pendleton

Mack Bolan's Phoenix Force series. Worldwide, 1984–1991

Phoenix Force is one of two tactical teams that operate out of Mack Bolan's Stony Man Farm and is equipped with the latest weapons and technology to fight international terrorism.

1. *Argentine Deadline*

2. *Guerrilla Games*

3. *Atlantic Scramble*

4. *Tigers of Justice*

5. *Fury Bombs*

6. *White Hell*

7. *Dragon's Kill*

8. *Aswan Hellbox*

9. *Ultimate Terror*

10. *Korean Killground*

11. *Return of Armageddon*

12. *Black Alchemists*

13. *Harvest Hell*

14. *Phoenix in Flames*

15. *Viper Factor*

16. *No Rules, No Referee*

17. *Welcome to the Feast*

18. *Night of the Thuggee*

19. *Sea of Savages*

20. *Tooth and Claw*

21. *Twisted Cross*

22. *Time Bomb*

23. *Chip off the Bloc*

24. *Doomsday Syndrome*

25. *Down under Thunder*

26. *Hostaged Vatican*

27. *Weep, Moscow, Weep*

28. *Slow Death*

29. *Nightmare Merchants*

30. *The Bonn Blitz*

31. *Terror in the Dark*

32. *Fair Game*

33. *Ninja Blood*

34. *Power Gambit*

35. *Kingston Carnage*

36. *Belgrade Deception*

37. *Show of Force*

38. *Missile Menace*

39. *Jungle Sweep*

40. *Rim of Fire*

41. *Amazon Strike*

42. *China Command*

43. *Gulf of Fire*

44. *Main Offensive*

45. *African Burn*

46. *Iron Claymore*

47. *Terror in Guyana*

48. *Barracuda Run*

49. *Salvador Assault*

50. *Extreme Prejudice*

51. *Savage World*

Super Phoenix Force #1: Fire Storm

Super Phoenix Force #2: Search and Destroy

Super Phoenix Force #3: Cold Dead

Super Phoenix Force #4: Wall of Flame

Chapter 17

Professional Resources

In this chapter, you'll find a variety of resources that can help you learn more about the adventure/suspense genre, its authors, and its titles. The first section covers historical and critical guides to the genre; the second section lists bibliographies of interest.

History, Criticism, and Guides

General Guides

The following are general reader's advisory guides but contain short definitions and examples of various adventure/suspense subgenres.

Herald, Diana Tixier. *Genreflecting: A Guide to Reading Interests in Genre Fiction.* Englewood, CO: Libraries Unlimited, 2000.

Saricks, Joyce G. *The Readers' Advisory Guide to Genre Fiction.* Chicago: American Library Association, 2001.

History and General Criticism

The following are general guides and criticisms on the various aspects of the adventure and suspense genre as well as various subgenres.

Atkins, John. *The British Spy Novel: Styles in Treachery.* London: Calder, 1984.

Bloom, Clive, ed. *Spy Thrillers: From Buchan to le Carré.* New York: St. Martin's Press, 1990.

Bloom, Harold, ed. *Classic Crime and Suspense Writers.* New York: Chelsea House, 1995.

Bloom, Harold, ed. *Modern Crime and Suspense Writers.* New York: Chelsea House, 1995.

Cawelti, John G. *Adventure, Mystery, and Romance: Formula Stories as Art and Popular Culture.* Chicago: University of Chicago Press, 1976.

Cawelti, John G. *The Spy Story.* Chicago: University of Chicago Press, 1987.

Craig, Patricia, and Cadogan, Mary. *The Lady Investigates: Women Detectives and Spies in Fiction.* New York: St. Martin's Press, 1981.

Falls, Cyril. *War Books: A Critical Guide.* London: Davies, 1930.

Harper, Ralph. *The World of the Thriller.* Baltimore, MD: Johns Hopkins University Press, 1974.

Keating, H. R. F., ed. *Whodunit?: A Guide to Crime, Suspense and Spy Fiction.* New York: Von Nostrand Reinhold, 1982.

Leibman, Arthur. *Tales of Espionage and Intrigue: The Secret Agent in Literature.* New York: Rosen, 1977.

Masters, Anthony. *Literary Agents: The Novelist as Spy.* Oxford: Blackwell, 1987.

McCormick, Donald. *Who's Who in Spy Fiction.* New York: Taplinger, 1977.

McCormick, Donald, and Fletcher, Katy. *Spy Fiction: A Connoisseur's Guide.* New York: Facts on File, 1990.

Melvin, David Skene. *Crime, Detective, Espionage, Mystery, and Thriller Fiction and Film: A Comprehensive Bibliography of Critical Writing through 1979.* Westport, CT: Greenwood, 1980.

Merry, Bruce. *Anatomy of the Spy Thriller.* Montreal: McGill-Queen's University Press, 1977.

Palmer, Jerry. *Thrillers: Genesis and Structure of a Popular Genre.* New York: St. Martin's Press, 1979.

Panek, LeRoy L. *The Special Branch: The British Spy Novel, 1890–1980.* Bowling Green, OH: Bowling Green University Popular Press, 1981.

Sauerberg, Lars Ole. *Secret Agents in Fiction: Ian Fleming, John le Carré and Len Deighton.* New York: St. Martin's Press, 1984.

Stone, Nancy-Stephanie. *A Reader's Guide to the Spy and Thriller Novel.* Farmington Hills, MI: Gale Group, 1997.

Swanson, Jean, and James Dean. *Killer Books: A Reader's Guide to Exploring the Popular World of Mystery and Suspense.* New York: Reed, 1998.

Wark, Wesley K., ed. *Spy Fiction, Spy Films, and Real Intelligence.* Portland, OR: F. Cass, 1991.

Individual Author Criticisms and Guides

The following references are critical works and guides to individual authors, characters, or series.

Ambrosetti, Ronald J. *Eric Ambler.* New York: Maxwell Macmillan International, 1994.

Amis, Kingsley. *The James Bond Dossier.* New York: Mysterious Press, 1987.

Beahm, George W. *Stephen King: America's Best-Loved Bogeyman.* Kansas City, MO: Andrews, McMeel, 1998.

Beahm, George W. *Stephen King from A to Z: An Encyclopedia of His Life and Work.* Kansas City, MO: Andrews McMeel, 1998.

Beene, Lynn. *John le Carré.* New York: Twayne, 1992.

Benson, Raymond. *The James Bond Bedside Companion.* New York: Dodd, Mead, 1984.

Brown, Anthony Gary. *Persons, Animals, Ships and Cannons in the Aubrey-Maturin Sea Novels of Patrick O'Brian.* Jefferson, NC: McFarland, 1999.

Collins, Michael R. *Scaring Us to Death: The Impact of Stephen King on Popular Culture.* San Bernadino, CA: Millefleurs, 1997.

Conley-Weaver, Robyn. *John Grisham.* San Diego: Lucent Books, 1999.

Cunningham, A. E., ed. *Patrick O'Brian: Critical Essays and a Bibliography.* New York: Norton, 1994.

Dean Koontz: A Reader's Checklist and Reference Guide. Middleton, CT: CheckerBee, 1999.

Forester, C. S. *The Hornblower Companion: An Atlas and Personal Commentary on the Writing of the Hornblower Saga.* Annapolis, MD: Naval Institute Press, 1999.

Garson, Helen S. *Tom Clancy: A Critical Companion.* Westport, CT: Greenwood, 1996.

Gorman, Ed, ed. *The Dean Koontz Companion.* New York: Berkley, 1994.

Greenberg, Martin. *Michael Crichton Companion.* New York: Ballantine, 1998.

Greenberg, Martin H., ed. *The Robert Ludlum Companion.* New York: Bantam Books, 1993.

Greenberg, Martin H., ed. *The Tom Clancy Companion.* New York: Berkley Books, 1991.

Harrison, Russell. *Patricia Highsmith.* New York: Twayne, 1997.

James Patterson: A Reader's Checklist and Reference Guide. Middleton, CT: CheckerBee, 1999.

John Grisham: A Reader's Checklist and Reference Guide. Middleton, CT: CheckerBee, 1999.

Ken Follett: A Reader's Checklist and Reference Guide. Middleton, CT: CheckerBee, 1999.

King, Dean. *Harbors and High Seas: An Atlas and Geographical Guide to the Aubrey-Maturin Novels of Patrick O'Brian.* New York: Henry Holt, 2000.

King, Dean. *A Sea of Words: A Lexicon and Companion for the Patrick O'Brian Seafaring Tales.* New York: Henry Holt, 2000.

Kotker, Joan G. *Dean Koontz: A Critical Companion.* Westport, CT: Greenwood, 1996.

Lavery, Brian. *Jack Aubrey Commands: An Historical Companion to the Naval World of Patrick O'Brian.* Annapolis, MD: Naval Institute Press, 2003

Lewis, Peter. *Eric Ambler.* New York: Continuum, 1990.

MacDonald, Gina. *Robert Ludlum: A Critical Companion.* Westport, CT: Greenwood, 1997.

Michael Crichton: A Reader's Checklist and Reference Guide. Middleton, CT: CheckerBee, 1999.

Monaghan, David. *Smiley's Circus: A Guide to the Secret World of John le Carré.* New York: St. Martin's, 1986.

Munster, Bill. *Discovering Dean Koontz: Essays on America's Bestselling Writer of Suspense & Horror Fiction.* San Bernadino, CA: Millefleurs, 1998.

Munster, Bill, ed. *Sudden Fear: The Horror and Dark Suspense Fiction of Dean R. Koontz.* San Bernadino, CA: Millefleurs, 1988.

Nelson DeMille: A Reader's Checklist and Reference Guide. Middleton, CT: CheckerBee, 1999.

Pearson, John. *James Bond: The Authorized Biography of 007.* New York: William Morrow, 1973.

Pringle, Mary Beth. *John Grisham: A Critical Companion.* Westport, CT: Greenwood, 1997.

Ramet, Carlos. *Ken Follett: The Transformation of a Writer.* Bowling Green, OH: Bowling Green State University Popular Press, 1999.

Robert Ludlum: A Reader's Checklist and Reference Guide. Middleton, CT: CheckerBee, 1999.

Robin Cook: A Reader's Checklist and Reference Guide. Middleton, CT: CheckerBee, 1999.

Rosenberg, Bruce A. *Ian Fleming.* Boston: Twayne, 1989.

Russell, Sharon. *Revisiting Stephen King: A Critical Companion.* Westport, CT: Greenwood, 2002.

Russell, Sharon A. *Stephen King: A Critical Companion.* Westport, CT: Greenwood, 1996.

Stephen King: A Reader's Checklist and Reference Guide. Middleton, CT: CheckerBee, 1999.

Stookey, Lorena Laura. *Robin Cook: A Critical Companion.* Westport, CT: Greenwood, 1996.

Tom Clancy: A Reader's Checklist and Reference Guide. Middleton, CT: CheckerBee, 1999.

Trembley, Elizabeth A. *Michael Crichton: A Critical Companion.* Westport, CT: Greenwood, 1996.

Turner, Richard Charles. *Ken Follett: A Critical Companion.* Westport, CT: Greenwood Press, 1996.

Waggett, Gerald J. *The John Grisham Companion.* Seacaucus, NJ: Carol, 1998.

Wiater, Stanley, Christoper Golden, and Hank Wagner. *The Stephen King Universe: A Tale-by-Tale Examination of the Interconnected Elements of His Work.* Los Angeles: Renaissance Books, 2001.

Wolfe, Peter. *Corridors of Deceit: The World of John le Carré.* Bowling Green, OH: Bowling Green State University Popular Press, 1987.

Wukovits, John F. *Stephen King.* San Diego, CA: Lucent, 1999.

Bibliographies and Genre-Related Information

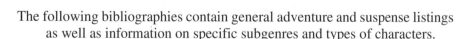

General Bibliographies

Adventure and suspense titles can be found in the following general bibliographies by looking under specific subject terms.

Fiction Catalog. New York: H. W. Wilson, 2001.

What Do I Read Next? Detroit: Gale Research, 2001.

Specific Bibliographies

The following bibliographies contain general adventure and suspense listings as well as information on specific subgenres and types of characters.

Breen, Jon L. *Novel Verdicts: A Guide to Courtroom Fiction.* Metuchen, NJ: Scarecrow Press, 1984.

Cook, Michael L. *Mystery, Detective, and Espionage Fiction: A Checklist of Fiction in U.S. Pulp Magazines, 1915–1974.* New York, Garland, 1988.

Day, Bradford M. *Bibliography of Adventure: Mundy, Burroughsm, Rohmer, Haggard.* Manchester, NH: Ayer, 1978.

Drew, Bernard A. *Action Series and Sequels: A Bibliography of Espionage, Vigilante, and Soldier of Fortune Novels.* New York: Garland, 1988.

Drew, Bernard A. *Heroines: A Bibliography of Women Series Characters in Espionage, Action, Science Fiction, Fantasy, Horror, Western, Romance and Juvenile.* New York: Garland, 1989.

Green Joseph. *Sleuths, Sidekicks and Stooges: An Annotated Bibliography of Detectives, Their Assistants and Their Rivals in Crime, Mystery and Adventure Fiction.* Brookfield, VT: Ashgate, 1997.

Hubin, Allen J. *The Bibliography of Crime Fiction, 1749–1975: Listing of all Mystery, Detective, Suspense, Police and Gothic Fiction in Book Form Published in the English Language.* Del Mar, CA: Publisher's, 1979.

Jarvis, Mary J. *A Reader's Guide to the Suspense Novel.* Farmington Hills, MI: Gale, 1977.

Jason, Philip K. *The Vietnam War in Literature: An Annotated Bibliography.* Pasadena, CA: Salem Press, 1992.

Legal Thrillers: A Reader's Checklist and Reference Guide. Middleton, CT: CheckerBee, 1999.

Newman, John. *Vietnam Literature: An Annotated Bibliography of Imaginative Works about Americans Fighting in Vietnam.* Metuchen, NJ: Scarecrow Press, 1996.

Paris, Michael. *The Novels of World War Two: An Annotated Bibliography of World War Two Fiction.* London: Library Association, 1990.

Smith, Myron J. *Cloak and Dagger Bibliography: An Annotated Guide to Spy Fiction 1937–1975.* Metuchen, NJ: Scarecrow Press, 1976.

Smith, Myron, J. *Sea Fiction Guide.* Metuchen, NJ: Scarecrow Press, 1976.

Smith, Myron J. *War Stories Guide.* Metuchen, NJ: Scarecrow Press, 1980.

Stone, Nancy-Stephanie. *Spy & Thriller Guide.* Farmington Hills, MI: Gale, 1997.

Taylor, Desmond. *The Novels of World War II: An Annotated Bibliography.* New York: Garland, 1993.

Walsh, Jeffrey. *American War Literature, 1914 to Vietnam.* New York: St. Martin's, 1982.

Wittman, Sandra M. *Writing about Vietnam: A Bibliography of the Literature of the Vietnam Conflict.* Boston: G. K. Hall, 1989.

Writing Guides

Want to write your own adventure or suspense novel? Or just curious about some of the plot elements? The following titles give information on the actual mechanics of writing a thriller as well as defining terms, describing weapons, and detailing the many types of death by foul play.

Becket, Henry S. A. *The Dictionary of Espionage: Spookspeak into English.* New York: Stein and Day, 1986.

Buranelli, Vincent, and Nan Buranelli. *Spy/Counterspy.* New York: McGraw-Hill, 1982.

Corvasce, Mauro V., and Joseph R. Paglino. *Murder One: A Writer's Guide to Homicide.* Cincinnati, OH: Writer's Digest Books, 1997.

Dobson, Christopher, and Ronald Payne. *Who's Who in Espionage.* New York: St. Martin's, 1985.

Faron, Fay. *Missing Persons: A Writer's Guide to Finding the Lost, Abducted and the Escaped.* Cincinnati, OH: Writer's Digest Books, 1997.

Highsmith, Patricia. *Plotting and Writing Suspense Fiction.* New York: St. Martin's, 1983.

Hubert, Karen M. *Teaching and Writing Popular Fiction: Horror, Adventure, Mystery and Romance in the American Classroom.* New York: Teachers and Writers Collaborative, 1976.

Melton, H. Keith. *Ultimate Spy.* New York: DK, 2002.

Newton, Michael. *Armed and Dangerous: A Writer's Guide to Weapons.* Cincinnati, OH: Writer's Digest Books, 1990.

Newton, Michael. *How to Write Action/Adventure Novels.* Cincinnati, OH: Writer's Digest Books, 1989.

Noble, William. *Conflict, Action and Suspense.* Cincinnati, OH: Writer's Digest Books, 1994.

Owen, David. *Hidden Secrets: A Complete History of Espionage and the Technology Used to Support It.* Buffalo, NY: Firefly Books, 2002.

Page, David W. *Body Trauma: A Writer's Guide to Wounds and Injuries.* Cincinnati, OH: Writer's Digest Books, 1996.

Polmar, Norman, and Thomas B. Allen. *Spy Book: The Encyclopedia of Espionage.* New York: Random House, 1997.

17

Rosenheim, Shawn. *The Cryptographic Imagination: Secret Writing from Edgar Poe to the Internet.* Baltimore, MD: Johns Hopkins University Press, 1997.

Roth, Martin. *The Writer's Complete Crime Reference Book.* Cincinnati, OH: Writer's Digest Books, 1990.

Stevens, Serita D., and Anne Klarner. *Deadly Doses: A Writer's Guide to Poisons.* Cincinnati, OH: Writer's Digest Books, 1990.

Wheat, Carolyn. *How to Write Killer Fiction: The Funhouse of Mystery & the Roller Coaster of Suspense.* Santa Barbara, CA: John Daniel/Perseverance, 2003.

Wilson, Keith D. *Cause of Death: A Writer's Guide to Death, Murder and Forensic Medicine.* Cincinnati, OH: Writer's Digest Books, 1992.

Appendix A

Film and Television Movie Versions

A

Above Suspicion (1943)
    Director: Richard Thorpe
    Starring: Joan Crawford, Fred MacMurray,
        Conrad Veidt, Basil Rathbone

Absolute Power (1997)
    Director: Clint Eastwood
    Starring: Clint Eastwood, Gene Hackman,
        Ed Harris, Laura Linney

Airport (1970)
    Director: George Seaton
    Starring: Burt Lancaster, Dean Martin,
        George Kennedy, Helen Hayes

Along Came a Spider (2001)
    Director: Lee Tamahori
    Starring: Morgan Freeman, Monica Potter,
        Michael Wincott

The Ambushers (1967)
    Director: Henry Levin
    Starring: Dean Martin, Senta Berger, Janice
        Rule, James Gregory

American Psycho (2000)
    Director: Mary Harron
    Starring: Christian Bale, Willem Dafoe,
        Jared Leto, Reese Witherspoon

The Andromeda Strain (1971)
    Director: Robert Wise
    Starring: Arthur Hill, David Wayne, James
        Olson, Kate Reid

Assault on a Queen (1966)
    Director: Jack Donohue
    Starring: Frank Sinatra, Virna Lisi, Tony
        Franciosa

Assignment in Brittany (1943)
    Director: Jack Conway
    Starring: Jean-Pierre Aumont, Susan
        Peters, Richard Whorf

B

The Bad Seed (1956)
    Director: Mervyn LeRoy
    Starring: Nancy Kelly, Patty McCormack,
        Henry Jones

The Beast (1996)
    Director: Jeff Bleckner
    Starring: William Petersen, Karen Sillas

Beat to Quarters (see *Captain Horatio
        Hornblower*)

The Bedford Incident (1965)
    Director: James B Harris
    Starring: Richard Widmark, Sidney Poitier,
        James MacArthur, Martin Balsam

The Body (2000)
    Director: Jonas McCord
    Starring: Antonio Banderas, Olivia Williams,
        John Shrapnel, Derek Jacobi

The Bone Collector (1999)
    Director: Phillip Noyce
    Starring: Denzel Washington, Angelina
        Jolie, Queen Latifah, Michael
        Rooker

The Bounty (1984)
    Director: Roger Donaldson
    Starring: Mel Gibson, Anthony Hopkins,
        Laurence Olivier, Edward Fox,
        Daniel Day-Lewis

The Bourne Identity (1988)
    Director: Roger Young
    Starring: Richard Chamberlain, Jaclyn
        Smith, Anthony Quayle

The Bourne Identity (2002)
    Director: Doug Liman
    Starring: Matt Damon, Franka Potente,
        Chris Cooper

The Boys from Brazil (1978)
    Director: Franklin J Schaffner

Starring: Gregory Peck, Laurence Olivier,
James Mason, Lilli Palmer

The Bridge over the River Kwai (1957)
Director: David Lean
Starring: William Holden, Alec Guinness,
Jack Hawkins, Sessue Hayakawa

The Bridges of Toko-Ri (1954)
Director: Mark Robson
Starring: William Holden, Grace Kelly,
Frederic March, Mickey Rooney

C

The Caine Mutiny (1954)
Director: Edward Dmytryk
Starring: Humphrey Bogart, Jose Ferrer,
Van Johnson

Call for the Dead (filmed as *The Deadly
Affair*)

Captain Blood (1935)
Director: Michael Curtiz
Starring: Errol Flynn, Olivia de Haviland,
Lionel Atwill, Basil Rathbone

Captain Horatio Hornblower (see **Beat to
Quarters**) (1951)
Director: Raoul Walsh
Starring: Gregory Peck, Virginia Mayo,
Robert Beatty

Casino Royale (1967)
Director: John Huston
Starring: Peter Sellers, David Niven,
Ursula Andress

The Chamber (1996)
Director: James Foley
Starring: Chris O'Donnell, Gene Hackman,
Faye Dunaway

Charlie M. (filmed as *Charlie Muffin*)

Charlie Muffin (see **Charlie M.**) (1979)
Director: Jack Gold
Starring: David Hemmings, Sam
Wanamaker, Jennie Linden

Clear and Present Danger (1994)
Director: Phillip Noyce
Starring: Harrison Ford, Willem Dafoe,
Anne Archer

The Client (1994)
Director: Joel Schumacher
Starring: Susan Sarandon, Tommy Lee
Jones, Brad Renfro, Mary-Louise
Parker

Coma (1978)
Director: Michael Crichton

Starring: Genevieve Bujold, Michael
Douglas, Elizabeth Ashley, Rip
Torn

The Confidential Agent (1945)
Director: Herman Shumlin
Starring: Charles Boyer, Lauren Bacall,
Peter Lorre

Congo (1995)
Director: Frank Marshall
Starring: Laura Linney, Dylan Walsh,
Ernie Hudson, Tim Curry, Grant
Heslov

Created, the Destroyer (filmed as *Remo
Williams, the Adventure Begins*)

D

Das Boot (1981)
Director: Wolfgang Petersen
Starring: Jürgen Prochnow, Herbert
Grönemeyer

The Day of the Jackal (1973)
Director: Fred Zinnemann
Starring: Edward Fox, Alan Badel, Tony
Britton

The Deadly Affair (see **Call for the Dead**)
(1966)
Director: Sidney Lumet
Starring: James Mason, Simone Signoret,
Maximilian Schell, Harriett
Andersson

Deathbite (filmed as *Spasms*)

Deathlands (2003)
Director: Joshua Butler
Starring: Vincent Spano, Jenya Lano, Traci
Lords, Cliff Saunders

The Deep (1977)
Director: Peter Yates
Starring: Robert Shaw, Jacqueline Bissett,
Nick Nolte, Louis Gossett

Diamonds Are Forever (1971)
Director: Guy Hamilton
Starring: Sean Connery, Jill St. John,
Charles Gray, Lana Wood

Die Hard II (see **58 Minutes**) (1990)
Director: Renny Harlin
Starring: Bruce Willis, Bonnie Bedelia,
William Atherton

The Dirty Dozen (1967)
Director: Robert Aldrich
Starring: Lee Marvin, Ernest Borgnine,
James Brown, Charles Bronson

Disclosure (1994)

Director: Barry Levinson
Starring: Michael Douglas, Demi Moore,
    Donald Sutherland, Caroline Goodall

Doctor No (1962)
Director: Terence Young
Starring: Sean Connery, Ursula Andress,
    Joseph Wiseman, Jack Lord

Dogs of War (1980)
Director: John Irvin
Starring: Christopher Walken, Tom
    Berenger, Colin Blakely, Hugh
    Millais

E

The Eagle Has Landed (1977)
Director: John Sturges
Starring: Michael Caine, Donald
    Sutherland, Robert Duvall, Jenny
    Agutter

The Eiger Sanction (1975)
Director: Clint Eastwood
Starring: Clint Eastwood, George Kennedy,
    Vonetta McGee

The Endless Game (1990)
Director: Bryan Forbes
Starring: Albert Finney, George Segal,
    Derek de Lint, Monica Guerritore

Enigma (2001)
Director: Michael Apted
Starring: Dougray Scott, Kate Winslet,
    Saffron Burrows, Jeremy Northram

Event 1000 (filmed as *Gray Lady Down*)

Extreme Measures (1996)
Director: Michael Apted
Starring: Hugh Grant, Gene Hackman,
    Sarah Jessica Parker

Eye of the Needle (1981)
Director: Richard Marquand
Starring: Donald Sutherland, Kate
    Nelligan, Ian Brannen

F

The Fan (1996)
Director: Tony Scott
Starring: Robert DeNiro, Wesley Snipes,
    Ellen Barkin, John Leguizamo

Fatal Error (see **Reaper**) (1999)
Director: Armand Mastroianni
Starring: Antonio Sabato, Jr., Janine Turner,
    Robert Wagner, Jason Schombing

Fatherland (1994)
Director: Christopher Menaul
Starring: Rutger Hauer, Miranda
    Richardson

Favorite Son (1988)
Director: Jeff Bleckner
Starring: Harry Hamlin, Linda Kozlowski,
    Robert Loggia

58 Minutes (filmed as *Die Hard II*)

1st to Die (2003)
Director: Russell Mulcahy
Starring: Tracy Pollan, Gil Bellows, Carly
    Pope, Megan Gallagher, Angie
    Everhart

Firefox (1982)
Director: Clint Eastwood
Starring: Clint Eastwood, Freddie Jones,
    David Huffman, Warren Clarke

Firestarter (1984)
Director: Mark L Lester
Starring: David Keith, Drew Barrymore,
    George C. Scott, Martin Sheen

The Firm (1993)
Director: Sydney Pollack
Starring: Tom Cruise, Gene Hackman,
    Jeanne Tripplehorn, Holly Hunter

The First Deadly Sin (1980)
Director: Brian G Hutton
Starring: Frank Sinatra, Faye Dunawaye,
    David Dukes, Brenda Vaccaro

Flight of the Intruder (1991)
Director: John Milius
Starring: Danny Glover, Willem Dafoe,
    Brad Johnson, Rosanna Arquette,
    Tom Sizemore

For Your Eyes Only (1981)
Director: John Glen
Starring: Roger Moore, Carole Bouquet,
    Topol, Lynn-Holly Johnson

Force Ten from Navarone (1978)
Director: Guy Hamilton
Starring: Robert Shaw, Harrison Ford,
    Franco Nero, Barbara Bach

The Fourth Protocol (1987)
Director: John Mckenzie
Starring: Michael Caine, Pierce Brosnan,
    Joanna Cassidy, Ned Beatty

From Russia with Love (1963)
Director: Terence Young
Starring: Sean Connery, Daniela Bianchi,
    Lotte Lenya, Robert Shaw

The Fury (1978)
Director: Brian De Palma
Starring: Kirk Douglas, John Cassavetes,
    Carrie Snodgrass, Amy Irving

G

Glass Inferno (filmed as *The Towering Inferno*)

Goldeneye (1995)
    Director: Martin Campbell
    Starring: Pierce Brosnan, Sean Bean, Izabella Scorupco, Famke Janssen

Goldfinger (1964)
    Director: Guy Hamilton
    Starring: Sean Connery, Gert Frobe, Honor Blackman, Shirley Eaton

Gorky Park (1983)
    Director: Michael Apted
    Starring: William Hurt, Lee Marvin, Brian Dennehy, Ian Bannen

*Gray Lady Down (see **Event 1000**)* (1978)
    Director: David Greene
    Starring: Charlton Heston, David Carradine, Stacey Keach, Ned Beatty

The Green Berets (1968)
    Director: John Wayne
    Starring: John Wayne, David Jannsen, Jim Hutton, Aldo Ray

The Guns of Navarone (1961)
    Director: J. Lee Thompson
    Starring: Gregory Peck, David Niven, Anthony Quinn, Stanley Baker

H

Hannibal (2001)
    Director: Ridley Scott
    Starring: Anthony Hopkins, Julianne Moore, Ray Liotta

Hart's War (2002)
    Director: Gregory Hoblit
    Starring: Bruce Willis, Colin Farrell, Terrence Dashon Howard, Cole Hauser

Heat of Ramadan (filmed as *Point Men*)

High Crimes (2002)
    Director: Carl Franklin
    Starring: Ashley Judd, Morgan Freeman, James Caviezel, Adam Scott, Amanda Peet

The Holcroft Covenant (1985)
    Director: John Frankenheimer
    Starring: Michael Caine, Anthony Andrews, Victoria Tennant, Lilli Palmer

Horatio Hornblower (1998)
    Director: Andrew Grieve
    Starring: Ioan Gruffudd, Robert Lindsay, Dorian Healy

Hunt for Red October (1990)
    Director: John McTiernan
    Starring: Sean Connery, Alec Baldwin, Scott Glenn, Sam Neill, James Earl Jones

I

Ice Station Zebra (1968)
    Director: John Sturges
    Starring: Rock Hudson, Ernest Borgnine, Patrick McGoohan, Jim Brown

Intensity (1997)
    Director: Yves Semineau
    Starring: John C. McGinley, Molly Parker

J

Jaws (1975)
    Director: Steven Spielberg
    Starring: Roy Scheider, Robert Shaw, Richard Dreyfuss, Lorraine Gary

Jurassic Park (1993)
    Director: Steven Spielberg
    Starring: Sam Neill, Laura Dern, Jeff Goldblum, Richard Attenborough

The Juror (1996)
    Director: Brian Gibson
    Starring: Demi Moore, Alec Baldwin, Joseph Gordon-Leavitt, Anne Heche

K

Kane & Abel (1985)
    Director: Buzz Kulik
    Starring: Sam Neill, Peter Strauss, Ron Silver, Fred Gwynne, Jill Eikenberry

The Keep (1983)
    Director: Michael Mann
    Starring: Scott Glenn, Ian McKellen, Alberta Watson

Kiss the Girls (1997)
    Director: Gary Fleder
    Starring: Morgan Freeman, Ashley Judd, Cary Elwes, Tony Goldwyn

L

The Last Nine Days of the Bismarck (filmed as *Sink the Bismarck!*)

License to Kill (1989)
    Director: John Glen
    Starring: Timothy Dalton, Carey Lowell, Robert Davi, Talisa Soto

Live and Let Die (1973)
    Director: Guy Hamilton
    Starring: Roger Moore, Yaphet Koto, Jane Seymour, Clifton James

The Living Daylights (1987)

Director: John Glen
Starring: Timothy Dalton, Maryam D'Abo,
    Jeroen Krabbe, Joe Don Baker

The Looking Glass War (1970)
Director: Frank R. Pierson
Starring: Christopher Jones, Pia
    Degermark, Ralph Richardson,
    Anthony Hopkins

The Lost World—Jurassic Park (1997)
Director: Steven Spielberg
Starring: Jeff Goldblum, Julianne Moore,
    Pete Postlethwaite, Arliss Howard

M

Magic (1978)
Director: Richard Attenborough
Starring: Anthony Hopkins, Ann-Margret,
    Burgess Meredith

The Man with the Golden Gun (1974)
Director: Guy Hamilton
Starring: Roger Moore, Christopher Lee,
    Britt Ekland, Maud Adams

The Manchurian Candidate (1962)
Director: John Frankenheimer
Starring: Frank Sinatra, Laurence Harvey,
    Janet Leigh, Angela Lansbury

Manhunter (see **Red Dragon**) (1987)
Director: Michael Mann
Starring: William L. Petersen, Kim Greist,
    Joan Allen, Brian Cox

Marathon Man (1976)
Director: John Schlesinger
Starring: Dustin Hoffman, Laurence
    Olivier, Roy Scheider, William
    Devane

*Master and Commander: The Far Side of the
    World* (2003)
Director: Peter Weir
Starring: Russell Crowe, Richard Stroh,
    Paul Bettany, Billy Boyd, James
    D'Arcy

Medusa's Child (1997)
Director: Larry Shaw
Starring: Vincent Spano, Lori Loughlin,
    Gail O'Grady, Kevin Dillon, John
    Glover

Mercury Rising (see **Simple Simon**) (1998)
Director: Harold Becker
Starring: Bruce Willis, Alec Baldwin, Miko
    Hughes, Chi McBride

Mercy (1999)
Director: Damian Harris

Starring: Ellen Barkin, Peta Wilson, Julian
    Sands

Misery (1990)
Director: Rob Reiner
Starring: James Caan, Kathy Bates, Richard
    Farnsworth

Modesty Blaise (1966)
Director: Joseph Losey
Starring: Monica Vitti, Dirk Bogarde,
    Terence Stamp, Harry Andrews

The Moneychangers (1976)
Director: Boris Sagal
Starring: Kirk Douglas, Anne Baxter,
    Christopher Plummer, Timothy
    Bottoms

Moonraker (1979)
Director: Lewis Gilbert
Starring: Roger Moore, Lois Chiles,
    Michael Lonsdale, Richard Kiel

Mother, May I Sleep with Danger? (1996)
Director: Jorge Montesi
Starring: Tori Spelling, Ivan Sergei, Lisa
    Banes, Todd Caldecott

Mrs Pollifax—Spy (see **The Unexpected Mrs.
    Pollifax**) (1971)
Director: Leslie H. Martinson
Starring: Rosalind Russell, Darren
    McGavin, Nehemiah Persoff,
    Harold Gould

Murderer's Row (1966)
Director: Henry Levin
Starring: Dean Martin, Ann-Margret, Karl
    Malden, Camilla Sparv, James
    Gregory

Mutiny on the Bounty (1935)
Director: Frank Lloyd
Starring: Charles Laughton, Clark Gable,
    Franchot Tone

Mutiny on the Bounty (1962)
Director: Lewis Milestone
Starring: Marlon Brando, Trevor Howard,
    Richard Harris, Hugh Griffith
See also *The Bounty*

N

The Naked and the Dead (1958)
Director: Raoul Walsh
Starring: Aldo Ray, Cliff Robertson,
    Raymond Massey, William
    Campbell

NetForce (1999)
Director: Robert Lieberman

Starring: Scott Bakula, Joanna Going,
    Xander Berkeley, Brian Dennehy
Night of the Fox (1990)
    Director: Charles Jarrott
    Starring: Paul Antrim, David Birney, Keith
        Edwards
Nightwing (1979)
    Director: Arthur Hiller
    Starring: Nick Mancuso, David Warner,
        Kathryn Harrold, Stephen Macht

O

Octopussy (1983)
    Director: John Glen
    Starring: Roger Moore, Maud Adams,
        Louis Jourdan, Kristina Wayborn
The Odessa File (1974)
    Director: Ronald Neame
    Starring: Jon Voight, Maximilian Schell,
        Maria Schell, Derek Jacobi
On Her Majesty's Secret Service (1969)
    Director: Peter R. Hunt
    Starring: George Lazenby, Diana Rigg,
        Gabriele Ferzetti, Telly Savalas
On the Beach (1959)
    Director: Stanley Kramer
    Starring: Gregory Peck, Ava Gardner, Fred
        Astaire, Anthony Perkins
On the Beach (2000)
    Director: Russell Mulcahy
    Starring: Armand Assante, Rachel Ward,
        Bryan Brown, Jacqueline McKenzie
The Osterman Weekend (1983)
    Director: Sam Peckinpah
    Starring: Rutger Hauer, John Hurt, Craig T.
        Nelson, Dennis Hopper
The Other (1972)
    Director: Robert Mulligan
    Starring: Uta Hagen, Diana Muldaur, Chris
        and Martin Udvarnoky
Our Man in Havana (1960)
    Director: Carol Reed
    Starring: Alec Guinness, Burl Ives,
        Maureen O'Hara, Ernie Kovacs

P

Pandora's Clock (1996)
    Director: Eric Laneuville
    Starring: Richard Dean Anderson, Robert
        Loggia, Jane Leeves, Robert
        Guillaume
Patriot Games (1992)
    Director: Phillip Noyce

Starring: Harrison Ford, Anne Archer,
    Patrick Bergin, Thora Birch
The Pelican Brief (1993)
    Director: Alan J. Pakula
    Starring: Julia Roberts, Denzel
        Washington, Sam Shepard, John
        Heard, Tony Goldwyn
*Point Men (see **Heat of Ramadan**)* (2001)
    Director: John Glen
    Starring: Christopher Lambert, Kerry Fox,
        Vincent Regan, Cal Macaninch
The Poseidon Adventure (1972)
    Director: Ronald Neame
    Starring: Gene Hackman, Ernest Borgnine,
        Stella Stevens, Shirley Winters
The Postman (1997)
    Director: Kevin Costner
    Starring: Kevin Costner, Will Patton,
        Larenz Tate, Olivia Williams
The President's Plane Is Missing (1972)
    Director: Daryl Duke
    Starring: Peter Graves, Buddy Ebsen, John
        Amos, Dabney Coleman, Arthur
        Kennedy
Presumed Innocent (1990)
    Director: Alan J. Pakula
    Starring: Harrison Ford, Brian Dennehy,
        Raul Julia, Bonnie Bedelia
Primal Fear (1996)
    Director: Gregory Hoblit
    Starring: Richard Gere, Laura Linney, John
        Mahoney, Edward Norton
Psycho (1960)
    Director: Alfred Hitchcock
    Starring: Anthony Perkins, Janet Leigh,
        Vera Miles, John Gavin, Martin
        Balsam
Psycho (1998)
    Director: Gus Van Sant
    Starring: Vince Vaughn, Ann Heche,
        Julianne Moore, William H Macy

Q

The Quiller Memorandum (1966)
    Director: Michael Anderson
    Starring: George Segal, Alec Guinness,
        Max von Sydow, Senta Berger

R

The Rainmaker (1997)
    Director: Francis Ford Coppola
    Starring: Matt Damon, Danny DeVito,
        Claire Danes, Jon Voight

Raise the Titanic! (1980)
    Director: Jerry Jameson
    Starring: Jason Robards, Richard Jordan,
        David Selby, Anne Archer
Reaper (filmed as *Fatal Error*)
Red Dragon (2002)
    Director: Brett Ratner
    Starring: Anthony Hopkins, Edward
        Norton, Ralph Fiennes, Harvey
        Keitel
    (also filmed as *Manhunter)*
Relic (1997)
    Director: Peter Hyams
    Starring: Penelope Ann Miller, Tom
        Sizemore, Linda Hunt, James
        Whitmore
Remo Williams, the Adventure Begins (see
    Created, the Destroyer) (1985)
    Director: Guy Hamilton
    Starring: Fred Ward, Joel Grey, Wilford
        Brimley, J.A. Preston, George Coe
Rising Sun (1993)
    Director: Philip Kaufman
    Starring: Sean Connery, Wesley Snipes,
        Harvey Keitel, Mako
Rogue Male (1976)
    Director: Clive Donner
    Starring: Peter O'Toole, John Standing,
        Alistair Sim, Cyd Hayman
Runaway Jury (2003)
    Director: Gary Fleder
    Starring: John Cusack, Gene Hackman,
        Dustin Hoffman, Rachel Weisz,
        Bruce Davison
Run Silent, Run Deep (1958)
    Director: Robert Wise
    Starring: Clark Gable, Burt Lancaster, Jack
        Warden, Brad Dexter
The Russia House (1990)
    Director: Fred Schepisi
    Starring: Sean Connery Michelle Pfeiffer,
        Roy Scheider, James Fox
S
The Sea Hawk (1940)
    Director: Michael Curtiz
    Starring: Errol Flynn, Brenda Marshall,
        Claude Rains, Donald Crisp
Servants of Twilight (1991)
    Director: Jeffrey Obrow

    Starring: Bruce Greenwood, Belinda Bauer,
        Richard Bradford
Seven Days in May (1964)
    Director: John Frankenheimer
    Starring: Burt Lancaster, Kirk Douglas,
        Frederic March, Ava Gardner
The Silence of the Lambs (1991)
    Director: Jonathan Demme
    Starring: Jodie Foster, Anthony Hopkins,
        Scott Glenn, Ted Levine
The Silencers (1966)
    Director: Phil Karlson
    Starring: Dean Martin, Stella Stevens,
        Daliah Lavi, Victor Buono
The Silver Bears (1978)
    Director: Ivan Passer
    Starring: Michael Caine, Cybill Shepherd,
        Louis Jourdan, Martin Balsam
Simple Simon (filmed as *Mercury Rising*)
Sink the Bismarck! (see **The Last Nine Days
    of the Bismarck**) (1960)
    Director: Lewis Gilbert
    Starring: Kenneth More, Dana Wynter,
        Carl Mohner, Laurence Naismith
Six Days of the Condor (filmed as *Three
    Days of the Condor*)
Sliver (1993)
    Director: Phillip Noyce
    Starring: Sharon Stone, William Baldwin,
        Tom Berenger, Polly Walker
Smiley's People (1982)
    Director: Simon Langton
    Starring: Alec Guinness, Vass Anderson,
        Eileen Atkins, Anthony Bate
Sole Survivor (2000)
    Director: Mikael Salomon
    Starring: Billy Zane, Gloria Reuben, John
        McGinley
Spasms (see **Deathbite**) (1983)
    Director: William Fruet
    Starring: Peter Fonda, Oliver Reed, Kerrie
        Keane, Al Waxman
Sphere (1998)
    Director: Barry Levinson
    Starring: Dustin Hoffman, Sharon Stone,
        Samuel L. Jackson, Peter Coyote
The Spy Who Came in from the Cold (1965)
    Director: Martin Ritt
    Starring: Richard Burton, Claire Bloom,
        Oskar Werner, Peter van Eyck

The Spy Who Loved Me (1977)
Director: Lewis Gilbert
Starring: Roger Moore, Barbara Bach, Curt Jurgens, Richard Kiel
The Stepford Wives (1975)
Director: Bryan Forbes
Starring: Katherine Ross, Paula Prentiss, Peter Masterson, Patrick O'Neal
Strangers on a Train (1951)
Director: Alfred Hitchcock
Starring: Farley Granger, Ruth Roman, Robert Walker, Leo G. Carroll
Sum of All Fears (2002)
Director: Phil Alden Robinson
Starring: Ben Affleck, Morgan Freeman, James Cromwell, Ken Jenkins
T
Tailor of Panama (2001)
Director: John Boorman
Starring: Pierce Brosnan, Geoffrey Rush, Jamie Lee Curtis, Catherine McCormack
The Talented Mr Ripley (1999)
Director: Anthony Minghella
Starring: Matt Damon, Gwyneth Paltrow, Jude Law, Cate Blanchett
The Terminal Man (1974)
Director: Mike Hodges
Starring: George Segal, Joan Hackett, Richard A. Dysart, Jill Clayburgh
The Thin Red Line (1964)
Director: Andrew Marton
Starring: Keir Dullea, Jack Warden, James Philbrook, Kieron Moore
The Thin Red Line (1998)
Director: Terrence Malick
Starring: Sean Penn, Adrian Brody, Jim Caveziel, Ben Chaplin, Nick Nolte
The Third Twin (1997)
Director: Tom McLoughlin
Starring: Jason Gedrick, Larry Hagman, Hal Holbrook, Kelly McGillis, Marion Ross
Three Days of the Condor (see **Six Days of the Condor**) (1975)
Director: Sidney Pollack
Starring: Robert Redford, Faye Dunaway, Cliff Robertson, Max von Sydow
Thunderball (1965)
Director: Terence Young
Starring: Sean Connery, Claudine Auger, Adolfo Celi, Luciana Puluzzi

A Time to Kill (1996)
Director: Joel Schumacher
Starring: Sandra Bullock, Samuel L. Jackson, Matthew McConaughey
Tinker, Tailor, Soldier, Spy (1980)
Director: Francis Alcock
Starring: Alec Guinness, Patrick Stewart, Alexander Knox, Anthony Bate
Tom Clancy's OP-Center (1995)
Director: Lewis Teague
Starring: Harry Hamlin, Patrick Bauchau, Kabir Bedi, Tom Bresnahan
Tower (filmed as *The Towering Inferno*)
The Towering Inferno (1974)
Director: John Guillerman
Starring: Steve McQueen, Paul Newman, William Holden, Faye Dunaway
Trapped (See **24 Hours**) (2002)
Director: Luis Mandoki
Starring: Charlize Theron, Courtney Love, Stuart Townsend, Kevin Bacon
Treasure Island (1934)
Director: Victor Fleming
Starring: Wallace Beery, Jackie Cooper, Lionel Barrymore, Otto Kruger
Treasure Island (1950)
Director: Byron Haskins
Starring: Bobby Driscoll, Robert Newton, Basil Sydney, Walter Fitzgerald
24 Hours (filmed as *Trapped*)
U
The Unexpected Mrs Pollifax (filmed as *Mrs Pollifax—Spy*)
V
Valentine (2001)
Director: Jamie Blanks
Starring: Denise Richards, David Boreanaz, Marley Shelton, Jessica Capshaw
The Verdict (1982)
Director: Sidney Lumet
Starring: Paul Newman, Charlotte Rampling, Jack Warden, James Mason
View to a Kill (1985)
Director: John Glen
Starring: Roger Moore, Christopher Walken, Grace Jones
Von Ryan's Express (1965)
Director: Mark Robson
Starring: Frank Sinatra, Trevor Howard, Rafaella Carra, Brad Dexter

W

Watchers (1988)
  Director: John Hess
  Starring: Corey Haim, Michael Ironside,
      Barbara Williams, Lala, Duncan
      Fraser
When Eight Bells Toll (1971)
  Director: Etienne Perier
  Starring: Anthony Hopkins, Robert Morley,
      Nathalie Delon, Jack Hawkins
Where Eagles Dare (1968)
  Director: Brian G. Hutton
  Starring: Richard Burton, Clint Eastwood,
      Mary Ure, Michael Hordern
The Wrecking Crew (1969)
  Director: Phil Karlson

  Starring: Dean Martin, Elke Sommer,
      Sharon Tate, Nancy Kwan, Nigel
      Green

Y

You Only Live Twice (1967)
  Director: Lewis Gilbert
  Starring: Sean Connery, Akiko
      Wakabayashi, Tetsuro Tamba, Mie
      Hama
The Young Lions (1958)
  Director: Edward Dmytryk
  Starring: Marlon Brando, Montgomery
      Clift, Dean Martin, Hope Lang

Appendix B

Authors for Core Collections

These are authors are recommended for all basic adventure/suspense collections. All subgenres have been represented and correspond to the various chapters in this book. These suggestions can be used either to create a new collection or to revitalize an existing one. Additional suggestions for core titles can be found by looking in the bibliographic line of an annotation for the ⌐ logo—this denotes a "page-turner" and is recommended. This list can also be helpful for weeding as suggestions for keeping titles by authors who can be expected to have some staying power.

Spies and Secret Agents

Anthony, Evelyn
Benson, Raymond
Buckley, William F.
Deighton, Len
Egleton, Clive
Fleming, Ian
Forsyth, Frederick
Freemantle, Brian
Gardner, John
Gilman, Dorothy
Grady, James
Higgins, Jack
le Carré, John
Littell, Robert
Ludlum, Robert
MacInnes, Helen
Maxim, John R.
McNab, Andy
Morrell, David
O'Donnell, Peter
Silva, Daniel
Thomas, Craig
Trevanian

Disasters

Benchley, Peter
Block, Thomas
Crichton, Michael
Herzog, Arthur
Nance, John J.
Preston, Douglas, and Lincoln Child
Scortia, Thomas N., and Frank M. Robinson
Stern, Richard Martin

Military Fiction

Beach, Edward L.
Berent, Mark
Brady, James
Griffin, W. E. B.
Mack, William P.
MacLean, Alistair
Reeman, Douglas
Webb, James H. Jr.

Technothrillers

Bond, Larry
Brown, Dale
Buff, Joe
Clancy, Tom
Cobb, James H.
Coonts, Stephen
Coyle, Harold
DiMercurio, Michael
Du Brul, Jack B.
Herman, Richard Jr.
Marcinko, Richard
Mayer, Bob
Poyer, David
Reilly, Matthew J.
Robinson, Patrick
White, Robin A.

Legal Thrillers

Bernhardt, William
Coughlin, William J.
Grisham, John
Lescroart, John T.
Martini, Steve
O'Shaughnessy, Perri
Patterson, Richard North
Rosenberg, Nancy Taylor
Scottoline, Lisa
Tanenbaum, Robert K.
Turow, Scott

Financial Thrillers

Erdman, Paul E.
Frey, Stephen W.
Sulitzer, Paul-Loup
Thomas, Michael M.

Maniacs, Murderers, Psychopaths, and Serial Killers

Bayer, William
Bloch, Robert
Connolly, John
Craig, Kit

Deaver, Jeffery
Devon, Gary
Diehl, William
Harris, Thomas
Highsmith, Patricia
Iles, Greg
Katzenbach, John
Lindsay, Paul
Patterson, James
Pearson, Ridley
Sandford, John
Wiltse, David

Science Gone Awry

Cannell, Stephen J.
Case, John
Cook, Robin
Cordy, Michael
Darnton, John
Gerritsen, Tess
Goldberg, Leonard S.
Koontz, Dean R.
Mezrich, Ben
Palmer, Michael
Pineiro, R. J.
Saul, John
Shobin, David
Wilson, F. Paul

Political and Religious Thrillers

Baldacci, David
Flynn, Vince
Knebel, Fletcher
Mills, Kyle
Monteleone, Thomas F.
Morrell, David
Rabb, Jonathan
Shelby, Philip
Wallace, Irving
West, Morris
Woods, Stuart

Paranormal

David, Jerome F.
Farris, John
Hynd, Noel
Wilson, F. Paul

Sea Adventures

Cussler, Clive
Forester, C. S.
Kent, Alexander
Lambdin, Dewey
Marryat, Frederick
Maynard, Kenneth
Nelson, James L.
Nordhoff, Charles, and James Norman
    Hall
O'Brian, Patrick
Parkinson, C. Northcote
Pope, Dudley
Woodman, Richard

Nazis (*see also* Spies and Secret Agents)

Deighton, Len
Follett, Ken
Furst, Allen
Gifford, Thomas
Griffin, W. E. B.
Harris, Robert
Higgins, Jack
Ludlum, Robert
MacInnes, Helen

Asia (*see also* Spies and Secret Agents *and* Technothrillers)

Diehl, William
Hagberg, David
Lustbader, Eric van
Olden, Marc

Russia (*see also* Spies and Secret Agents *and* Technothrillers)

Flannery, Sean
Smith, Martin Cruz
Thomas, Craig
White, Robin

The Middle East (*see also* Spies and Secret Agents *and* Technothrillers)

Hartov, Steven
Land, Jon
Tonkin, Peter

Heroic Adventure Series (Paperback Originals)

Deathlands
The Destroyer
The Executioner
Mack Bolan
Outlanders
Stony Man
Tom Clancy's Net Force
Tom Clancy's OP-Center

Glossary

Admiralty: in Britain, the department responsible for overseeing naval affairs

aerosol: a mist or fine powder dispersed in the air; a method used to release biological agents

Agency: slang for the Central Intelligence Agency

agoraphobia: fear of open places; fear of leaving one's home

alibi: facts that show an accused person was not at the scene of crime

anthrax: bacterial organism that can cause a fatal illness similar to pneumonia

Apocalypse: the end of the world as foretold in the Bible

Antichrist: a malevolent antagonist who will bring great evil into the world and be defeated by Christ during the Second Coming

arteriosclerosis: a disease characterized by the hardening and thickening of the walls of the arteries

AWOL: absent without leave—military term

ayatollah: an authority in Islamic law

bacteria: a single-cell microorganism—the most common life-form on the planet

Berlin Wall: barbed wire barricade and concrete wall that once surrounded West Germany

boatswain: a naval officer who oversees the deck crew, cables, riggings, and anchors

bosun: *see* boatswain

brainwash: the use of drugs or behavioral techniques to indoctrinate a person with a different set of beliefs

Brit: slang for a citizen of Great Britain

bullion: bars or ingots of precious metal

caduceus: a winged staff with two snakes intertwined on it often used as the symbol of the medical profession

cartel: a group of independent businesses united in a common cause

CDC: Centers for Disease Control

CEO: chief executive officer

CIA: Central Intelligence Agency—U.S. intelligence agency

clone: an exact genetic copy of an organism

Cold War: period of hostility and diplomatic conflict, but not outright war, between the United States and the Soviet Union that lasted from the end of World War II until the late 1980s

commodore: an officer ranking above a captain but below a rear admiral

computer chip: a tiny, thin slice of material, such as silicon, on which a computer circuit has been etched

computer virus: a program that copies itself onto other programs in a computer often causing damage

conclave: in the Roman Catholic Church, a secret meeting where the cardinals elect a new pope

cryptographer: a person who writes or deciphers secret codes

curare: a South American drug used by the natives to paralyze their prey and also used for modern medical reasons

DA: district attorney

day trading: in finance, buying stocks that are expected to increase in price quickly, holding on to them for one day to one week and then selling them for a profit

derivatives: in finance, the process of planning to profit by predicting how various markets or commodities will fare in the future

détente: the relaxing of tensions between the United States and the Soviet Union

disbarred: no longer allowed to practice law

district attorney (DA): a lawyer in a judicial area who acts for the state or U.S. government as the prosecutor in criminal cases

DNA: deoxyribonucleic acid—carries the genetic code in living organisms

dot-com: a business with services or products that are sold on or deal with the Internet

drydock: a large dock used for ship repair, maintenance, or construction

Ebola virus: a virus that causes a severe, often fatal disease that causes uncontrollable bleeding throughout the body

ecclesiastical: of or pertaining to an organized religion

E. coli: a species of bacteria normally present in the digestive tract and widely used in biological research

ectoplasm: the glowing, vaporous substance supposedly produced by a ghost or other paranormal phenomena

epidemiologist: a medical professional who studies diseases and their cause

ER: emergency room

evangelist: a fundamentalist Christian; one who emphasizes salvation through faith

FBI: Federal Bureau of Investigation

floe: a large, flat mass of floating ice

forensic: pertaining to legal proceedings

frigate: a fast naval vessel

futures: buying or selling goods at an agreed upon, set price before they are actually produced

gene: a part of DNA

Generation X: the generation born between 1965 and 1980

glasnost: the policy in the Soviet Union under Mikhail Gorbachev of publicly discussing government policies

grand jury: a special jury that investigates criminal allegations

Green Berets: *see* Special Forces

hacker: a person who gains unauthorized access to other people's computer data

hallucinations: false perceptions (seen or heard) that seem real

HIV: human immunodeficiency virus

influenza: a contagious, infectious disease characterized by inflammation of the respiratory system

Interpol: International Criminal Police Organization

in vitro: not within a living being, but artificially maintained

IRA: Irish Republican Army

ironclad: a naval vessel covered in iron armor

Iron Curtain: a metaphorical barrier of secrecy that surrounded the former Soviet Union and its satellite countries

IRS: Internal Revenue Service

kamikaze: "divine wind" (Japanese); during World War II, Japanese pilots who were assigned to crash their planes into enemy targets

katsa: case officer for the Israeli Mossad

KGB: Komitet Gosudarstvennoi Bezopasnosti: Soviet secret police

kiloton: an explosive force equivalent to that of 1,000 tons of TNT; used in reference to the explosive force of nuclear weapons

KKK: Ku Klux Klan; a white supremacist organization founded after the American Civil War

LAPD: Los Angeles Police Department

Legal Aid: organization that provides low-cost or free legal services to poor

Libertarian: a person who believes in complete personal freedom

loan shark: a criminal who makes loans at an extremely high interest rate

Luddite: slang for a person opposed to technology

Luftwaffe: German air force

mafiya: Russian organized crime, or mafia

mah jong: a Chinese board game played with four people

malaria: an infectious disease transmitted through the bite of an infected mosquito

MI-5: Military Intelligence Security Service; the British equivalent of the FBI in the United States

MI-6: Military Intelligence 6; the British equivalent of the CIA in the United States

midshipman: a sailor training to be an officer

mole: a spy hidden deep undercover

money laundering: to pass illegally obtained money through legitimate businesses in order to make it appear legal

Mossad: Israeli intelligence agency

mutiny: resistance or rebellion of sailors against their officers

NASA: National Aeronautics and Space Administration

NSA: National Security Agency

NATO: North Atlantic Treaty Organization

ninja: a stealthy Japanese assassin with knowledge of hundreds of way to kill

NYPD: New York Police Department

OPEC: Organization of Petroleum Exporting Countries

operative: government agent; spy

OPS: operations; military term

OSS: Office of Strategic Services; World War II precursor to the CIA

paleoanthropologist: a person who studies ancient peoples by studying fossilized remains

pathogen: any agent that causes disease, such as bacteria or a virus

pathologist: a medical professional who deals with the changes in the body caused by disease or injury

PLO: Palestine Liberation Organization

plutonium: a radioactive metallic element similar to uranium that is used in the production of nuclear weapons

politburo: the main policy-making committee of the Communist Party

pope: the head of the Roman Catholic Church

POW: Prisoner of War

press gang: a group of men who rounded up other men and forced them into military or naval service

primatologist: a scientist who studies monkeys and apes

privateer: a privately owned and operated ship that has been authorized by a government to attack and capture enemy vessels

pro bono: "for the good" (Latin); providing professional services without charging a fee

psychopath: a person suffering from a serious mental disorder; usually associated with criminal behavior

public defender: an attorney employed by the government to provide legal services to the poor accused of criminal offenses

quarantine: a restraint on activities intended to prevent the spread of disease

RAF: Royal Air Force

remote viewing: a psychic ability whereby a person can "see" events that are taking place in another area

rhinovirus: the virus responsible for the "common cold"

Richter scale: a scale that measures the amount of back-and-forth ground movement during an earthquake; each number is ten times greater than the previous number

rigging: a system of ropes or chains that support and control the sails of ship

saboteur: a person who causes damage so as to defeat or harm an endeavor

safe house: a secret location where someone can be hidden from enemies

samurai: a chivalrous warrior during the Japanese feudal period

Scud: a surface-to-surface missile usually deployed on a mobile launcher

SEAL: sea, air, and land team—an elite U.S. Navy unit

Second Coming: in Christianity, the return of Christ, who will usher in the end of the world

Secret Service: a branch of the Treasury Department charged with investigating counterfeiting and protecting the president of the United States

sequelae: the various complications resulting from a disease or injury

serial killer: a person who commits three or more separate murders over a period of time

Shin Bet: Israeli counterpart to the FBI

ship of the line: a heavily armed ship that could hold the line of battle in a conflict; now known as a battleship

SIS: Secret Intelligence Agency (British)

sloop: a single-masted sailboat

smallpox: a highly contagious and lethal virus that causes blisters and pustules on the body

sociopath: an amoral person whose actions are aggressive and antisocial

Special Forces: an elite branch of the U.S. Army

squadron: a group of warships assigned to some type of special duty or mission

SS: *Schutzstaffel;* World War II German storm troopers

Stasi: East German secret police

subpoena: a legal order requiring a person to appear in court to give testimony or to produce documents

telepathy: the psychic ability to read or hear another person's thoughts

TNT: trinitrotoluene; a compound used as a high explosive

trireme: an ancient boat, long and low to the water, which was propelled by three banks of oars

tsunami: "harbor wave" (Japanese); a huge sea wave caused by the eruption of an underwater volcano or underwater earthquake

U-boat: *unterseeboot*; German submarine

USSR: Union of Soviet Socialist Republics

Vatican: the official headquarters of the Roman Catholic Church and the residence of the pope.

Viagra: a drug prescribed to increase a man's sex drive and counteract impotency

virtual reality: a computer-generated simulation with which a person may interact in a seemingly real manner

virus: a disease-causing organism smaller than a bacterium that takes over living cells and forces them to create copies of itself

vulture fund: in finance, an investment fund that buys undervalued real estate and stocks in a faltering economy and then sells them for high profits when the economy recovers.

WASP: acronym for White Anglo-Saxon Protestant

Wehrmacht: the armed forces of Nazi Germany

yakuza: Japanese criminal underworld; the Japanese mafia

yeti*:* a large, hairy, manlike creature alleged to live in the Himalayan mountains of Tibet; the Abominable Snowman

yuppie: slang for Young Urban Professional or Young Upwardly Mobile Professional

Author/Title Index

Subject Index

About the Author

MICHAEL GANNON is Branch Manager at Anne Arundel County Public Library, Annapolis, Maryland, and winner of the 2003 PLA Allie Beth Martin Award.